# Combat Command

# Combat Command

by

DR./COL. PHILIP ('TOM') COBLEY MBE late PARA

ISBN (Hardback): 978-1-905006-77-9
ISBN (Perfect bound): 978-1-905006-90-8


First Published 2015 in the UK by The London Press.

# ABSTRACT

The U.S. Department of Veterans Affairs (2013) official estimates indicated that of the 1.64 million service members who have served in the recent wars in Afghanistan and Iraq, 20%, or 328,000, are experiencing depression, anxiety, stress, or PTSD. However, despite this new research, there still remains no effective pre-combat education programmes or leadership training that addresses the negative effects of combat on infantry soldiers. The purpose of the qualitative case study was to document infantry soldiers' experiences and perceptions of the negative physiological and psychological effects of combat and their recommendations for effective pre-combat education programmes and leadership training to prepare soldiers to counter the negative effects of combat. This qualitative case study was implemented through interviews and the direct observation of 10 infantry veterans who have been involved in combat operations within the last two years. The natural setting for evidence collection was within British Army bases in the U.K. and Western Europe. During the study, four main themes emerged from the data gathered, and these included: (1) infantry soldiers continue to be inadequately prepared for the physiological and psychological effects of combat due to leadership and training programmes protocols that need to be strengthened, (2) the main mental health problems identified were depression, anxiety, adjustment problems, mood swings, personality disorders, and alcohol misuse/dependence, (3) there is a continuing number of infantry soldiers who return home from operational deployments with mental health problems, they remain chronically unwell, and are vulnerable to social exclusion, and (4) soldiers with mental health problems as a result of combat stress continue to leave military service prematurely, either voluntarily or due to being unfit for continuing military service. Recommendations include that a future study be undertaken, utilising the Minnesota Multiphase Personality Inventory (MMPI-2-RF) for recruit training to ascertain if more pre-combat education programmes and leadership training will reduce the incidence of combat stress and PTSD.

# Contents

# List of Tables

# LIST OF FIGURES

# Acknowledgements

*To,*

5 Platoon, B Company
1st Battalion, The Pacific Islands Regiment, 1973-1975

B Company
8/9th Battalion, The Royal Australian Regiment, 1980-1981

A Company
1st Battalion, The Staffordshire Regiment, 1985-1988

C Company
2nd Battalion, The Parachute Regiment, 1989-1990

4th Battalion
The Kings Own Royal Border Regiment, 1994-1997

Chief Operations Officer
United Nations Observer Mission in Georgia (UNOMIG), 1997

NATO Headquarters
Stabilization Force (SFOR) – Bosnian-Herzegovina, 1998

NATO Kosovo Air War Operations Centre
Supreme Headquarters Allied Powers Europe (SHAPE), 1999

Gali Sector Commander
United Nations Observer Mission in Georgia (UNOMIG), 2000-2001

*Acknowledgements*

Chief Plans Officer (Kabul)
International Stabilization and Assistance Force (ISAF), 2003-2004

Chief Operations and Intelligence Officer (Baghdad)
NATO Training Mission – Iraq (NTM-I), 2005

EU Operations Headquarters – Bosnian-Herzegovina
European Force (EUFOR), 2006-2010

It was my honour and privilege to have commanded you all in war, security operations and/or peace, and the narratives of your experiences of infantry combat, along with those of other infantry soldiers, forms the heart and soul of this research study.

# Definition of Key Terms

**Aggression.** In psychology, the term "aggression" refers to a range of behaviours that can result in both physical and psychological harm to oneself or others in the environment. The expression of aggression can occur in a number of ways, including verbally, mentally, physically, and emotionally (American Psychiatric Association, 2000).

**Armed Conflict.** An armed conflict is defined as open and declared conflict between the armed forces of two or more states or nations (American War library, 2008).

**Combat-Fatigue.** Combat-fatigue is defined as post-traumatic stress that is a psychological disorder that develops in individuals that have had a major traumatic experience and, for example, have been in a serious accident or through war. The person is typically numb at first but later symptoms include depression, excessive irritability, guilt (for having survived while others died), recurrent nightmares, flashbacks to the traumatic scene, and overreaction to sudden noise (American Psychiatric Association, 2000).

**Combat-veteran.** A combat veteran is defined as a person who has experienced any level of hostility resulting from offensive, defensive or friendly fire military action involving a real or perceived enemy in any pre- or post-designated theatre of combat (war) operations (American War Library, 2008).

**Disruptive Reactions.** Where the person appears dazed, confused and disorientated while wandering aimlessly and exhibits either a complete or partial memory loss (U.S. Marine Corps, MCRP 6-11C, dated 23 June 2000).

**Leadership.** Leadership in the military is the process by which the military commander influences subordinates by providing the purpose, direction and motivation in order to accomplish the unit's mission (Army Officer's Guide, 2009).

**Loss of Adaptability.** Where the person is subject to uncontrolled emotional outbursts such as crying, yelling, or laughing. However, the person may also become withdrawn, silent, or try to isolate themselves (U.S. Marine Corps, MCRP 6-11C, dated 23 June 2000).

**Physiological Stress.** Physiological stress is defined as the failure of the individual organism to respond adequately to mental, emotional, or physical demands, whether actual or imagined. When the person perceives a threat, their nervous system responds by releasing a flood of stress hormones, including adrenaline (American Psychiatric Association, 2000).

**Post-Traumatic Stress Disorder (PTSD).** Post-Traumatic Stress Disorder (PTSD) is described as a severe anxiety disorder that can develop after exposure to any event that results in psychological trauma. This event may involve the threat of death to oneself or to someone else, or to one's own or someone else's physical, sexual, or psychological integrity, overwhelming the individual's ability to cope (American Psychiatric Association, 2000).

**Psychological Stress.** Psychological stress is defined as an event or situation that precipitates an emotional response, such as anxiety or depression. The events must be appraised as a harmful, threatening, challenging, and relevant to the individual in order to elicit the emotional response (American Psychiatric Association, 2000).

**Service Engagement.** The normal service engagement in the British Army is for 22 years, with the minimum service required before resignation being three years (British Army Terms and Conditions of Service, 2014).

**Shell-Shock.** Shell-shock is defined as psychiatric loss of sight, memory, etc. resulting from psychological strain during prolonged engagement in warfare; also combat neurosis (American Psychiatric Association, 2000).

**Syllabus.** A syllabus is a descriptive outline and summary of the topics to be covered in an education or training course (British Army Officer's Guide, 2009).

**Training.** Training in the military is the military process that has been designed to establish and improve the capabilities of military personnel in their respective tasks, all of which are aimed at achieving the unit's designated mission (Army Officer's Guide, 2009).

# Foreword

by
General Sir Peter Wall GCB CBE DL
Chief of the General Staff (CGS)
2010-2014

Viewed from a strategic perspective warfare is an extension of policy and its outcomes are, in the final analysis, political. Thanks to the analysis and teaching of Carl von Clausewitz this is well understood.

Viewed from the opposite end of the command telescope, the front line, warfare is a tough, frightening, physical and mental grind: a battle of wills that depends upon the fighting soldier, and it is he or she that feels the consequences most deeply. In contrast to the thoughts of Clausewitz, the psychological element of those consequences on soldiers and veterans is much less well understood, even by current military practitioners.

Military forces, whether regular or irregular, depend on the right equipment, the right tactics and techniques, and the right training as a basis for their combat effectiveness. The critical ingredient for success, however, is in the moral domain, rather than the physical. It is the moral commitment to fight and win: the collective determination to prevail in the battle of wills against equally determined and potentially fanatical opponents.

On the battlefield it is that will to fight that we are seeking to erode in our enemies, and which, reciprocally, our enemies are trying to erode in us. Munitions, projectiles and high explosives are designed, and employed, as much to frighten the enemy and sap his will and as they are to injure, maim and kill. Hence the psychological horror of war.

The British Army has an ethos and a variety of characteristics, disciplines, and codes of behaviour it has evolved over generations in order to generate and sustain the will to fight and to win, or succeed. These include the regimental system, the emphasis on transformational leadership and discipline, the imperative for resilient training and a dependency on high quality equipment. Each of these features contributes to the 'esprit de corps' that enables soldiers to suppress their personal fears and instincts in the heat of battle in favour of their loyalty and service to their comrades. Where pride in any of those ingredients is lacking there is a risk of faltering courage and commitment during battle, or soon afterwards. Even when fighting units and their soldiers succeed, the longer-term psychological consequences of combat can be grave and protracted, and they can inflict delayed pain, many years later, on soldiers and their families and friends.

A century ago the inability to carry the fight to the enemy for mental health reasons, such as 'shell shock,' tended to be seen as cowardice, and often carried the death penalty. Since the Great War mental illness has been formally recognized as a consequence of military combat, and we have drawn extensive evidence of the effects of combat stress from successive campaigns.

The body of evidence from the British Army's recent campaigns in Iraq and Afghanistan is still growing, and is not yet conclusive. A number of qualitative considerations suggest that we should be prepared for a greater psychological impact on veteran soldiers over the next few years than the experiences from earlier campaigns might indicate. The reasons for this include the nature of modern society, in comparison with which the battlefield is a more extreme place than ever; the protracted duration of the two campaigns; the prevalence of indirect and intangible threats, for example indirect fire, sniping and IED's; and the unrelenting courage of fundamentalist opponents, operating from within their own cultures and societies.

Tom Cobley's detailed and painstaking research, laid out logically in this very thorough book, seeks to shed light on the nature and the characteristics of the conflict into which our soldiers were thrust in Afghanistan. He examines the way in which the Army set about continuously improving its combat capability for the specific situation in that theatre whilst devising methods to alert soldiers to the threats to their mental health, and containing the psychological impact.

From his analysis and findings he makes tutored recommendations on how the Army might adapt its approach to better prepare soldiers for the extreme mental and physical demands of combat. *Combat Command* should stimulate a very healthy and timely debate on these critical issues.

In future the British Army will surely sustain the courage and moral commitment that have been hallmarks of its will to win and hence its combat effectiveness through history. But that will not be enough. We need to reduce the psychological impact on individuals. The firm hope is that Tom Cobley's important work leads to a lesser toll on the well-being of soldiers and their mental health from their shocking experiences in battle.

*General Sir Peter Wall GCB CBE DL*          *Rickford, Somerset*

*President of Combat Stress,*
*The Military Mental Health Charity*          *26 August 2015*

# Preface

The career of Doctor/Colonel Philip ('Tom') Cobley MBE, late PARA spans 41 years of continuous active service in two armies, initially commencing with 16 years in the Australian Regular Army, and then a further 25 years in the British Army. During this time, he saw service in five infantry regiments (The Pacific Islands Regiment, The Royal Australian Regiment, The Staffordshire Regiment, The King's Own Royal Border Regiment, and The Parachute Regiment), which included a score of operational deployments. Doctor/Colonel Tom Cobley was born in Paignton, Devon in 1950, and his parents immigrated to Australia under the 'Assisted Passage Scheme' in 1958. He then finished his schooling at Sydney Grammar School, where he gained a scholarship to the Royal Military College, Duntroon, as well as receiving a Commonwealth Secondary School Scholarship.

He joined the Royal Military College, Duntroon in January 1969, and as a Fourth Class Cadet he was embroiled in the 'bastardisation scandal' that engulfed the college during that year. In December 1972, after four years, he graduated from the college and volunteered for service in the Pacific Islands Regiment in Papua New Guinea, where he served as a Platoon Commander and Instructor from 1973-75. Upon his return to Australia, he served as a Company Second-in-Command in the 8/9th Battalion, Royal Australian Regiment in Enoggera, Queensland (1976-77), then as the Adjutant of the Officer Cadet School, Portsea, Victoria (1978-79). He then returned to the 8/9th Battalion as a Company Commander (1980-81), and finally served as a Staff Officer in the Office of the Chief of the General Staff (OCGS) in Canberra (1982-84).

It was at this time, by then having completed 16 years in the Australian Regular Army, that he realised that the operational opportunities to serve overseas, due to the political and military climate post-Vietnam, were negligible. As a result, he applied to transfer his regular commission to the British Army, which was at the time fully engaged at the height of the Cold War. After successfully transferring his commission, his initial service was as a Mechanised, then Armoured Infantry Company Commander in the 1ˢᵗ Battalion, The Staffordshire Regiment, which was part of the famous 7ᵗʰ Armoured Brigade (The Desert Rats), based in Fallingbostel, West Germany (1985-88). Upon his return to the U.K. at the end of this posting, he became a Staff Officer at HQ South East District, Aldershot, where the GOC at the time was General Sir Peter de la Billière. The general wholeheartedly supported Doctor/Colonel Cobley in his attempt to pass Parachute Regiment selection, which he did at 39 years and 10 months of age, becoming the oldest man to have ever attempted and passed the course up to that time.

Then followed a posting to the 2ⁿᵈ Battalion, The Parachute Regiment as a Company Commander (1989-90). During this time, the battalion deployed to County Fermanagh in Northern Ireland on anti-terrorist operations, and during this period, he was awarded the MBE. He then served as the Training Major 15ᵗʰ Battalion (SV), The Parachute Regiment in Glasgow (1991-92). Soon after, promotion to Lieutenant Colonel followed and a posting to Air Force Department at the MoD Main Building, Whitehall (1993-94), where he was responsible for all parachuting and parachute trials/development undertaken by U.K. forces worldwide. This included training Special Forces personnel in High Altitude Low Opening (HALO) and High Altitude High Opening (HAHO) skills. He was responsible for the development of the Low Level Parachute (LLP), Low Level Aerial Delivery System (LLADS), and the High Altitude Aerial Delivery System (HAADS) during this time.

Next came selection to become the Commanding Officer of the 4ᵗʰ Battalion, The King's Own Royal Border Regiment based in Cumbria and Northern Lancashire (1994-1997). After completing this command appointment, Doctor/Colonel Cobley was then involved in a prolonged series of operational deployments. Initially this was as the Chief Operations Officer, United Nations Observer Mission in Georgia (UNOMIG), former Soviet Union, in Sukhumi, Abkhazia from February to August 1997. He was then posted to the Supreme Headquarters Allied Powers Europe (SHAPE) in Mons, Belgium, where he deployed to the NATO

Stabilisation Force (SFOR) in Bosnia during 1998 and then to Kosovo Force (KFOR) during the NATO 'Air War' from March to July 1999. Then he became the first British officer ever to return to UNOMIG for a second tour, this time as the Gali Sector Commander in Abkhazia from November 2000 to May 2001.

Upon returning from the Republic of Georgia, he gained another appointment in SHAPE, where he became involved in the 'Global War on Terrorism.' This initially involved deployments to the International Stabilisation and Assistance Force (ISAF) in Afghanistan from 2003-04. As the NATO commitments broadened to Iraq, Doctor/Colonel Cobley volunteered for service there, and as a result, he became the Chief J2/3 (Intelligence and Operations) for the NATO Training Mission in Iraq (NTM-I) from February to November 2005. Because of this deployment, he was promoted to the acting-rank of full Colonel and was awarded the Meritorious Service Medal (MSM), which is NATO's highest decoration for operational service. The final tour for Colonel Cobley was a posting to the European Union Force (EUFOR), becoming the J1/4 (Personnel and Logistics) Staff Officer responsible for the EUFOR mission in Bosnia.

As well as pursuing his 41-year military career, Doctor/Colonel Cobley has made time to undertake a variety of academic studies, gaining a Bachelor of Arts degree in 1983 and then a Bachelor of Educational Studies degree in 1987, both from the University of Queensland. In later years, he went on to study dual master's degrees in Education and Human Relations with the University of Oklahoma and was awarded both these degrees in 2005. After completing these studies he wrote his autobiography *The Final Tally,* which was published in 2009, with the second edition being released in 2011. In 2008, at the same time as he was writing his autobiography, he embarked upon a research study for a doctorate and was awarded his Ph.D. from the Northcentral University, Phoenix, Arizona in 2015. The research from this study forms the basis for *Combat Command,* which graphically illustrates the detrimental physiological and psychological results of combat on infantry soldiers and includes recommendations for combating these effects.

CHAPTER ONE

# *Introduction*

After the terrorist attacks on the Twin Towers in New York on September 11, 2001, U.S. and Coalition Forces became engaged in Operation Enduring Freedom (OEF), commencing in October 2001, and then Operation Iraqi Freedom (OIF), which followed soon after in March 2003.[1] The conflict in Afghanistan has now been ongoing for over a decade and has even surpassed Vietnam as America's longest undeclared war.[2] However, even after all this time in Afghanistan, the conflict remains with no identifiable political or military solution, while casualties continue to increase among U.S. and Coalition forces.[3]

In this regard, there is belief among researchers and analysts that one important factor causing this stalemate is that U.S. and Coalition forces had struggled to design and implement a strategy for the reduction in the negative effects of combat on infantry soldiers.[4] That is, the pre-combat education programmes and leadership training for these forces had been lacking, and as a result, this led to the increase in combat related stress casualties.[5] So, with no end in sight and public support waning, the U.S. and the Coalition governments were forced to declare their withdrawal from the conflict by the end of 2014.

During these conflicts, it is considered that U.S. and Coalition forces were not being provided with appropriate and effective pre-combat education programmes and leadership training that would counter the negative effects combat had on infantry soldiers.[6] During World War I, the psychological and emotional trauma that results from combat was called "shell-shock," in World War II it was renamed "combat stress" or "war neurosis."[7] In later wars, it was defined as "post-traumatic stress disorder" or PTSD by the American Psychiatric Association. However, PTSD was not defined as a health condition before 1980, at which time the American Psychiatric Association officially included PTSD in its diagnostic guidebook and established explicit diagnostic criteria. Although there has been academic and medical acknowledgement that post-combat trauma is a debilitating condition, there has been at best only a grudging acceptance of this by the military authorities.[8]

The fact is that it is only in the last decade that U.S. and Coalition forces have discovered the many physiological and psychological realities of infantry combat, with researchers learning about auditory exclusion, intensified sound, tunnel vision, and post-traumatic responses.[9] There also remains many more physiological and psychological phenomenon that relate directly to infantry combat operations and that are only just being discovered. These include automatic responses, diminished visual clarity, slow motion time, temporary paralysis, memory loss/distortions, and perceptual distortions.[10] However, despite this new research, there are still no effective pre-combat education programmes or leadership training that addresses the negative effects of combat on infantry soldiers.[11] In addition, in 2014, Coalition forces seem likely to become involved in the renewed conflict in Syria and Iraq, which will inevitably see the further deployment of infantry soldiers on combat operations.

## Background

Combat stress is the normal human response to extraordinary challenges faced by infantry soldiers in combat.[12] However, when infantry soldiers are faced with intense life-threatening experiences daily, there are significant physiological and psychological consequences. These responses are immediate and automatic. They are based on the severity of the combat situation and cannot be consciously controlled by the individual soldier.[13] These responses to combat are so powerful they deeply affect the brain and mind of the soldier, often permanently. Therefore, the unfortunate legacy of the wars in Afghanistan and Iraq are to be found in the neurology and orthopaedic wards of our hospitals and not just in our war cemeteries.

Today, soldiers are surviving these wars both physiologically and psychologically in greater numbers than any previous conflict. This is based on the advances in battlefield (trauma) medicine and evacuation procedures that continue to save lives at an amazing rate.[14] To elaborate on this point, there were 38 deaths for every 100 wounded in World War II, and during the Vietnam conflict, this ratio dropped to 28 deaths per 100 wounded.[15] The current ratio is six deaths for every 100 soldiers wounded according to the U.S. Department of Defense study (2013). Therefore, increasingly soldiers survive one battlefield only to face another. A physically injured soldier requires time to heal and return to active duty, if deemed medically fit, or he/she transitions back to civilian life. Equally, soldiers who have combat-related stress injuries face similar challenges in a related healing process. These stress injuries are just as debilitating as any physical injuries, with it often being easier to mend a broken bone than to repair a damaged brain or psyche.

Some stresses, such as PTSD, may have a delayed onset, as the incidence of stress-related illness is on a continual rise as more and more soldiers are repeatedly exposed to combat operations. More than 245,000 soldiers were deployed twice to either Afghanistan or Iraq, with a better than 50% increase in the incidence of combat-related stress as the numbers of deployments increased. In addition, according to the U.S. Department of Veterans Affairs (2013), over 91,000 soldiers were deployed three times and 48,000 were deployed four times to either Afghanistan and/or Iraq. Since 2001, there have been 31,848 service members physically wounded in Afghanistan and Iraq.[16] The Department of Defense and the Office of the Surgeon General report that there have been over 40,000 reported cases of PTSD by service members since 2003. However, the Army reported 38,000 PTSD cases in 2007 alone, an annual increase of over 46% among U.S troops deployed to Afghanistan and Iraq.[17]

The latest U.S. Department of Veterans Affairs (2013) official estimates indicated of the 1.64 million service members with combat experience in Afghanistan and/or Iraq, that 20%, or 328,000, are experiencing depression, anxiety, or stress. The most recent Rand study not only corroborates this estimate but considers that the percentage may be even higher at 26%.[18] Other research studies have shown that more than 50% of soldiers who needed psychological treatment for combat-related stress illnesses are not willing to seek medical assistance. This is due to the fact that disclosing mental health difficulties may result in a medical discharge from military service or a medical downgrade that will preclude further combat deployments, which will in turn limit promotion prospects as well as the possibility for extended military service. So, for these reasons, it is believed that the number of veterans who are actually suffering from combat-related mental stress illnesses is much higher than the current statistics indicate.

In addition, the U.S. military has discharged over 720,000 service members who were in the service on September 11, 2001. More than 200,000 of these ex-service members have applied for disability benefits from Veterans Affairs.[19] Of these, 120,000 veterans from the Afghanistan and Iraq wars have been seen at Veterans Affairs hospitals for mental health issues, and of these, 60,000 have received preliminary diagnosis of PTSD. This will result in a lifetime of disability payments for many of those who have returned from the wars, and as a result, Veterans Affairs currently spends $2.8 billion on mental health care annually.[20]

In the British military, the total number of personnel deployed to the Afghanistan and Iraq wars from October 2001-June 2014 was 219,420 soldiers.[21] Each year, approximately 24,000 personnel leave the U.K. armed forces, but unlike the U.S., where veterans receive medical care through the Veterans Affairs hospitals, the U.K. has no equivalent veteran care. Retiring or discharged British military personnel have to rely on the U.K.'s public National Health Service (NHS). Therefore, after leaving the armed services U.K., veterans join the rest of the population in seeking medical assistance for stress, depression, or PTSD, and so there are no statistics specifically related to veterans. However, statistics from the MoD confirms that there are over 11,000 serving members of the military currently diagnosed with combat stress mental conditions, including PTSD.[22] On top of these figures, "Combat Stress," which is the U.K.'s leading mental health charity for former armed forces personnel, believes that there are at least 10,000 veterans living with mental health conditions related to their service who require urgent medical assistance. This mental health charity currently has a total caseload of more than 5,400 veterans across the U.K. and it received 358 new Afghanistan veteran referrals in 2013, a 57% rise from 228 referrals in 2012.[23] Due to these significant increases, the MoD allocated an additional £7.2 million in 2013 towards improving mental health services for veterans.

## *Statement of the Problem*

The problem addressed in this study was that the minimalist pre-combat education programmes and leadership training given to British Army infantry soldiers to help them cope with the negative physiological and psychological effects of combat were proving to be increasingly inadequate.[24] According to infantry soldiers, throughout the period of the wars in Afghanistan and Iraq, there is no evidence that soldiers have been provided with adequate pre-combat education programmes or leadership training interventions to prepare them for the negative physiological and psychological effects of combat operations. The one common outcome that resonates is that the more intense and prolonged the combat exposure, the more likely it is that soldiers develop the symptoms of combat stress and/or PTSD.

According to the U.S. Department of Veterans Affairs (2013), this phenomenon has resulted in more than 78,000 veterans seeking help for mental health related issues as a result of the recent conflicts in Afghanistan and Iraq. Within the British armed forces, over 11,000 serving members of the military are currently diagnosed with combat-related mental conditions including stress, depression, and PTSD.[25] This problem stems from the lack of pre-combat education programmes and leadership training, as the negative physiological and psychological effects of combat on infantry soldiers were not being addressed prior to infantry soldiers being deployed on combat operations. To this point, in the last decade more than 2,700 U.S. soldiers have committed suicide within two years of leaving the service, and half of these were undergoing treatment for PTSD or other combat-induced mental disorders.[26] The statistics for British military personnel is equally disturbing, as in 2012 a total of 21

serving soldiers and 29 veterans committed suicide. This total of 50 suicides during the year becomes more alarming when it is compared with
the British death toll in Afghanistan in 2012, which was a total of 44
killed, of whom 40 died in combat operations against the Taliban.[27]

## Purpose of the Study

The purpose of the qualitative case study was to investigate serving
British infantry soldiers' experiences and perceptions of the negative
physiological and psychological effects of combat and their recommendations for effective pre-combat education programmes and leadership
training to help prepare soldiers to cope with the effects of combat. This
study used open-ended interviews for data collection and compared the
participants' transcribed answers to training manuals that were used prior
to deployment. The participants were all serving British Army service
men and women who were all be over 18 years of age. The reason for
choosing two years was that greater than two years and the subjects may
lose clarity of their experiences. The size of the sample was estimated at a
minimum of 10 serving Army personnel. The natural setting for evidence
collection was British Army bases in the U.K. and Western Europe where
soldiers had recently (last two years) returned from operational service
in Afghanistan. This study was unique and distinctive, as it addressed a
problem that has not been studied in any depth by the education and
medical communities or the military professions.

## Theoretical Framework

This study used a theoretical framework based upon historical and
contemporary studies in the fields of education and leadership. The
two theories that informed and supported this study are Adult Learning Theory (education) and Transformational Leadership Theory (leadership). Adult Learning Theory is a set of assumptions about how adults
learn that has specific theoretical and practical approaches that are based
upon a humanistic concept of self-directed and autonomous learning,
the teacher simply being the facilitator of that learning. This theory encompasses several assumptions that are related to motivation within the

field of adult learning: Adults need to know the reason for their learning. Experience provides the basis for adult learning activities. Adults need to be involved in the planning and evaluation of their own instruction. Adults want to know the relevance of what they are learning to what they want to achieve in their work and/or personal lives. And, adult learning is problem-centred rather that content-orientated, and finally, adults respond better to internal rather than external motivators. The assumptions made by Knowles (1986) are directly related to the military as its culture is mission-centred and so adult learning is conducted in the military by providing a structured and clear format, specific goals, and with learning activities that are linked to those goals.

Within military decision-making and problem solving are two skill domains that are fundamental to most types of tasks. Also, as many military tasks involve the operation of equipment, the sensory-motor skills in military personnel are well developed. In addition, as a great deal of tactical military knowledge relies on facts leading to the memory skills of recall, recognition, and retention, these competencies are also well developed in military personnel. Therefore, the strategies for military student engagement, retention, and academic success address the unique needs of these adult learners by applying approaches that stress self-direction, motivation, experience, and practical application of knowledge.

Knowles' assumptions dovetailed with the thoughts and theories of Merriam and Caffarella (1999), who noted experience, critical reflection, and development as being the keys to adult learning. Within the military, it remains important to be able to distinguish the unique abilities of adult learners in order to better incorporate the various principles of adult learning into the design of the instruction for pre-combat education programmes. In the military, combat experience provides the basis for soldiers' learning activities, so by interviewing infantry combat veterans, their experiences formed the basis for recommendations for improvements in pre-combat education programmes by assisting the military in planning more effective programmes.

The three main methods to foster learning in the military are first through problem-based learning, which seeks to increase problem solving and critical thinking skills. Then second by cooperative learning, which builds communication and interpersonal skills, and finally through situated learning that targets specific technical skills that are directly applied to military requirements. Each of these methods support Knowles' six assumptions; as military personnel are self-directed, they require their learning to be directly applicable to their field of employment, and they are able to contribute more to collaborative learning through their military experiences.

Transformational Leadership Theory has led to the proposition that the success of any fighting force is dependent on a leadership that maintains a balanced focus between mission accomplishment and troop welfare. Burns (1978) first introduced the concept of "transforming" leadership, which he saw as a process where leaders and followers helped each other to advance to a higher level of morale motivation. Bass (1985) extended the work of Burns and used the term "transformational" instead of "transforming." He also added to the work of Burns by explaining how transformational leadership could be measured and how it impacted on follower motivation and performance. The followers of such a leader would feel trust, admiration, loyalty, and respect for their leader, as they were provided with an inspiring mission and vision that gave them an identity. So the leader transforms and motivates followers through charisma, intellectual stimulation, and individual consideration.

Three decades of research and a number of meta-analyses have shown that transformational leadership positively predicts a wide variety of performance outcomes, including individual, group, and organisational level variables. The study by Bass and Bass (2008) introduced four elements of transformational leadership: (a) "individualised consideration" is the degree to which the leader attends to each followers needs, acts as a mentor to the followers and listens to the followers concerns and needs; (b) "intellectual stimulation" is the degree to which the leader challenges assumptions, takes risks, and solicits followers ideas, thereby stimulating and encouraging creativity in their followers; (c) "inspirational motivation" is the degree to which the leader articulates a vision that is appealing and inspiring to the followers; and (d) "idealised influence", where the leader provides a role model for high ethical behaviour, instils pride, and gains respect and trust from the followers. As a developmental tool, transformational leadership spread to all sectors of western society including most national defence forces.

The transformational leader is seen as being the key to building and maintaining high morale and peak performance, confirming that "the leader matters." This is achieved by the leader knowing his/her soldiers and understanding each of their individual strengths and weaknesses. To maintain this level of morale and efficiency in combat, the leader must first recognise, then attempt to prevent, and finally personally contend with reactions to combat stress when it occurs in the unit. Due to these important factors, the military has adopted transformational leadership as the primary leadership technique being taught in military leadership training. The framework adopted is based on four major components: (a) individualised consideration, (b) intellectual stimulation, (c) inspirational motivation, and (d) idealised influence. These components produce leaders who embrace change and ensure the direction of a military unit in accordance with the vision of the overall commander. The military has also introduced the effective application of counselling, mentorship, training, education, attitude, and a personal leadership development plan as methods of instilling transformational leadership qualities in military leaders. Transformational leadership is now fully integrated within the military, as it provides leaders at all levels of command the ability to guide soldiers within their units by focusing on one clear and directed vision.[28]

The purpose of this study was based upon the current research findings, which indicated that prior to and during the period of the wars in Afghanistan and Iraq, there was no evidence that infantry soldiers were adequately provided with pre-combat education programmes or leadership training in order to prepare them for the negative physiological and psychological effects of combat. This left the unit leader with the task of educating each soldier so that their perception of the danger was balanced by the sense that the unit had the ability to prevail over the enemy in combat situations. As a result, the leader must keep the unit functioning at a level of stress that sustains performance and confidence. If soldiers lose confidence in themselves and their leader, unit cohesion will collapse. Therefore, the leader must be able to recognise this phenomenon as well as any subtle or dramatic alterations in behaviour in each soldier, as persistent and progressive symptoms that deviate from the baseline may demonstrate the early warning signs of combat stress.

## Research Questions

The research questions were designed to identify the status of British Army pre-combat training programmes and leadership training, which were initiated in order to help soldiers cope with the negative effects of combat on infantry soldiers. The open-ended questions asked in the interviews allowed for the participants to fill-in the details and provide a rich narrative of their infantry combat experiences. The researcher asked questions directly to the subjects based on a case study approach, and this allowed for the collecting, analysing, and interpreting of the data. It was this logical model of proof that allowed the researcher to draw inferences concerning causal relations among the variables under investigation. The following questions guided this study:

*Q1.* According to infantry soldiers' combat experiences, what types of pre-combat education programmes and leadership training were provided to soldiers, pre-tour of duty, to help them cope with negative physiological and psychological effects of combat?

*Q2.* According to infantry soldiers' combat experiences, what were the negative physiological and psychological effects that soldiers experienced during and after combat?

*Q3.* According to infantry soldiers' combat experiences, what types of pre-combat education programmes and leadership training interventions could be effective in helping soldiers cope with the negative physiological and psychological effects of combat?

## Nature of the Study

A qualitative case study research method and design was employed, and as a result, there was little control over events, as the focus was on a contemporary phenomenon within a "real-life" context. This case study research design included procedures that protected against threats to validity, maintained a chain of evidence, and investigated and tested rival explanations. The natural setting for this evidence collection was with units at British Army bases in the U.K. and Western Europe. Data came from serving soldiers who had returned from operational service in Afghanistan in the last two years. As already stated, the reason for choosing two years was that greater than two years and the subjects may lose clarity of their experiences.

The size of the sample was estimated at a minimum of 10 serving British Army personnel, or fewer if it is found that saturation has been achieved. The purpose of this qualitative case study was to document infantry soldiers' experiences and perceptions of the negative physiological and psychological effects of combat and their recommendations for effective pre-combat education programmes and leadership training to prepare soldiers to counter the negative effects of combat. The soldier participants in the case study were serving British Army men and women over 18 years of age. The sample population was stratified as the case study research design targeted serving male and female British Army officers, warrant officers, non-commissioned officers, and soldiers. Additionally, because 9.1% of all British Army personnel were females, it ensured that this percentage was represented in the sample. Also within the British Army, there were 5.5% officers, 10.7% warrant officers, 19.3% non-commissioned officers, and 64.5% soldiers, and these percentages were duplicated within the sample.[29]

After Northcentral University IRB and MoDREC approvals, the Chief of the General Staff (CGS) of the British Army, General Sir Peter Wall GCB, CBE and Lieutenant General J.D. Page CB, OBE (Commander Force Development and Training) were contacted in order to gain permission to interview serving British Army infantry soldiers. Once Minisrty of Defence Research Ethics Committee (MODREC) approval was granted, the commanding officers of the relevant British Army infantry bases in the U.K. and Western Europe were approached, provided with a letter or poster providing the information about the study and contact details for the researcher to enable potential participants to contact him directly with expressions of interest. Once the researcher had received the names of the volunteers for the study each was approached individually with an introductory letter that asked them whether they would like to learn more about the study and consider participation in it. Once the researcher had an expression of interest from individuals he mailed them the Participant Information Sheet, Informed Consent Form, and Arrangements for No Fault Compensation. There was a 24-hour consideration period from the provision of the Participant Information Sheet to confirming consent.

Each participant was interviewed at least once for a period of 60-90 minutes. However, there was a caveat that a second or even a third interview would be conducted with an individual if it was warranted, if it was considered positive and appropriate for the integrity, veracity, and reliability of the study. The interviews were conducted at British Army bases, as previously described, over a three- to five-day period depending on the number of soldier study participants at each location.

The research method was qualitative and utilised a case study design with the data being collected in the field by using face-to-face in-depth interviews, which were digitally recorded. This was the primary source of data collection. The information for the research study was gathered by talking directly to soldiers in their military environment, where it was considered that they would feel more at ease. The instrument for this case study was the interview guide/protocol and data were collected through interviewing combat veterans and examining documents, such as education documents from the current pre-combat leadership training programme. The data analysis for this case study consisted of examining, categorising, tabulating, testing, and/or recombining evidence to draw empirical conclusions. The use of multiple sources of evidence in this case study allowed the researcher to develop "converging lines of inquiry" a process of triangulation that allowed the comparison of data from the participant's interview answers to each other and to the training documents. The notes were digitally recorded, transcribed, and placed in password-protected, secure, electronic files. They were stored in the database and organised according to major subjects in such a fashion that they were readily retrievable. This ensured that the case study notes were organised, categorised, complete, and available for later access from the database. All study files will be securely stored for five years and then destroyed.

## *Significance of the Study*

This qualitative research case study was relevant, germane, and timely given the number of infantry soldiers who had been repeatedly exposed to combat operations. This research contributed to the current literature and will contribute to Adult Learning and Transformational Leadership Theory. It has contributed to the body of knowledge by adding to the research on the documentation of the detrimental physiological and psychological effects of combat stress on infantry soldiers. It has also added to the base of information concerning stress caused by prolonged exposure to combat operations and its immediate, mid, and long-term effects on the individual infantry soldier. This is significant as the previous research had centred primarily on surveys that statistically addressed the incidence of stress among soldiers and veterans, thereby only concentrating on the post-combat stress treatment rather than pre-combat stress prevention.

In addition, the study findings have provided further understanding and knowledge about the effects of stress using the words of the study participants to provide the information and context from the soldiers own unique perspectives. As a natural and inevitable inclusion, the study has also provided insights and understanding into the effects of the stress into other areas of the participants' private lives, such as family relationships, productivity, health, and social functioning.

Finally, this qualitative research case study has intentionally concentrated on infantry soldiers who are combat veterans, as studies in this area have historically been under-represented. Instead the focus of the previous research has been upon "a force under stress," referring to the military in general instead of concentrating on certain elements of the military that have borne the brunt of repeated operational deployments and exposure to the stress of ground combat, namely the infantry soldier. Unfortunately, many of these soldiers who are combat veterans are still struggling psychologically with what they have seen, heard, and felt on the battlefield.

## Summary

The conflict in Afghanistan was ongoing for over a decade and surpassed even Vietnam as America's longest undeclared war. However, even after all this time in Afghanistan, the conflict remains with no identifiable political or military solution, while casualties continue to increase among Coalition forces. In this regard, there is a belief among researchers and analysts that one of the most significant factors contributing to the stalemate was that the U.S. and Coalition forces had struggled to design and implement a strategy for the reduction in the negative effects of combat on infantry soldiers.

The problem was that many infantry soldiers experienced physiological and psychological trauma during combat operations, and this resulted in the denigration of the combat effectiveness of U.S. and Coalition forces during the recent conflicts in Afghanistan and Iraq. The research confirmed that higher rates of trauma were associated with increased exposure to intense infantry ground combat. The purpose of the qualitative case study was to investigate serving infantry soldiers' experiences and perceptions of the negative physiological and psychological effects of combat and their recommendations for effective pre-combat education programmes and leadership training to help prepare soldiers to cope with the effects of combat.

This qualitative case study was implemented through interviews and the direct observations of 10 infantry combat veterans who had been involved in combat operations within the last two years. The size of the sample population was estimated at a maximum of 10 serving British Army personnel, as typically this is when saturation is achieved. The sample population was stratified as the case study research design targeted serving male and female British Army officers, warrant officers, non-commissioned officers, and soldiers.

# Chapter Two

## *Stress and the Brain*

The most current military research found that war-related mental health disorders were highly prevalent among veterans returning from Afghanistan and Iraq. According to data from the U.S. Department of Defense Task Force on Mental Health (2013), post-deployment health assessments of the 222,620 military personnel who returned from Afghanistan between May 2010 and April 2013, 42,506 (19%) reported mental health problems and 68,923 (31%) used mental health services during the first year after returning home. The same report found that 151 (17%) of 882 U.S. combat infantry personnel and 127 (16%) of 813 U.S. combat marines met screening criteria for major depression, severe anxiety, or PTSD. For British military personnel, the prevalence of the combat-related symptoms of depression, stress and PTSD has increased from 11.8% to 16.7%, and even more concerning, these rates in reservists have dramatically increased from 12.7% to 24.5%.[1]

The statistics showed that infantry soldiers faced the potential for stress on a daily basis in a combat zone where they are often faced fight-or-flight situations that affected their very survival. In a fight-or-flight situation, the brain directs the body to begin shutting down some systems while increasing activities for other parts of the body. Blood flow and increased heart rate are two prime examples of how the brain tells the body to prepare for the fight-or-flight.

The term "stress" was first introduced by Hans Selye (1936), and it is now widely used to describe a state of tension often seen as being related to modern life, and so psychological stress concerns the state of "normal" tension, pre-occupation, and agitation reported by many people.[2] This is sometimes extreme and is considered a precipitating factor in the development of various physical and mental disorders. However, all too often, researchers and clinicians used clinical psychiatric tools such as Present State Examination, the Brief Symptom Inventory, or the Beck Depression Inventory to assess stress.[3] These were designed for pathological disorders and validated using dysfunctional clinical populations. As a result, their statistical distributions were not normal, and they were not sensitive below the critical diagnostic threshold. In contrast, the concept of stress refers to a set of affective, cognitive, somatic, and behavioural manifestations within the range of functional integrity.

Due to these inconsistencies, Lemyre and Tessier (2013) developed a general theoretical framework based upon a biopsychosocial model of stress that included environmental parameters and individual processes of perception and coping with stressors. Stress was recognised as a target construct in the process of adapting to life events and circumstances. This stress model was developed outside the field of psychopathology, and so it is ideal for assessing psychological stress. Lemyre and Tessier (2013) found that the state of stress depended upon the interaction between an individual's environment and his or her representation of that environment. As importantly, they found that stress disorders occurred only as a result of stress of great intensity or long duration or when pathogenic processes were present. Therefore, psychological stress is a hinge construct associated with both psychological phenomena and factual parameters.

In 2008, Medina conducted a stress assessment of Vietnam veterans that used survey research design, and a total number of 435 veterans were selected for the study using a proportionate purposive sampling technique. Three sets of surveys titled "Stress Assessment Scale," "Psychological Well-Being Scale," and "Behaviour Scale" were used for the data collection. The findings from the study revealed that prolonged exposure to stress or chronic stress increased the risk of cognitive, emotional, or physical illness. The researcher's broad and in-depth research found that effects of combat stress could range from memory problems at the cognitive end to depression on the emotional side, and to obesity and/or heart disease as a physical illness. However, the study was limited in the number of women who were selected, and so the perception of the influence of combat stress on women's physiological and psychological well-being was limited.

Gabriel (2010) measured the effects of stress on cognition of 184 Special Operations soldiers returning from operations in Afghanistan from 2007-2009. These soldiers had been exposed to trauma or stress and had completed pre-stress measures of dissociation. In his study, the 184 soldiers were randomised into one of three assessment groups. The ability of the stress group to copy and recall was significantly impaired in comparison to the pre-stress and control group. Copy performance was piecemeal, and recall ability was impaired for the stressed group. However, one limitation of Gabriel's research design was that it did not enable him to conclude that the stress exposure of these soldiers impaired their visual-spatial ability and working memory.

In the past decade, neuroscientists have conducted critical analysis of several studies that have documented memory discrepancies in patients with stress disorders. Fishback (2008) pointed to the limbic system as being the key to understanding more about stress, memory, and learning. Fishback defined memory as the ability to use or retrieve information that was previously encoded or processed. The validity of her sample selection process was based on the testing of 654 soldiers who were combat veterans. This involved administering a battery of mental tests to the soldiers both before and after deployment to Iraq. Her detailed analysis, which was based on mental tasks, measured both verbal and spatial memory. The relevance of her findings were that the 654 soldiers performed significantly poorer in all the mental tasks when compared to 307 soldiers who were administered the same test but who had not been deployed to Iraq.[4]

Other studies have focused on measuring hippocampal volume with Magnetic Resonance Imaging (MRI) and used control groups to assess various methods of memory, recall, and/or attention. Pavic (2007) measured hippocampal volume in both a control group and a group that tested positive for PTSD. His findings from the evidence revealed that the hippocampus was smaller in both hemispheres for those who had previously screened positive for PTSD. This indicated that chronic stress putatively damages the hippocampus and impairs cognitive functions in humans.[5] Werner (2009) used MRI to measure both hippocampal volume on soldiers who had already screened positive for PTSD, but also measured memory function as part of cognitive attention and recall using standard neuropsychological tests. These results suggested PTSD had a measurable impact on memory-related brain function. However, critically, his evidence was unable to prove that the soldiers suffering from PTSD displayed weaker pre-frontal activation functions in comparison to healthy control group soldier participants.

A further critical comparison conducted by Kitayama (2010) also used MRI as the primary research design but with a larger sample and conducted a meta-analysis of hippocampal volume spread over nine studies. There were 334 soldier participants in his study. The researchers used three groups to conduct the research: subjects with chronic PTSD, healthy controls, and traumatised controls. However, his analysis was unable to find that the hippocampus volume was smaller in both left and right hippocampal in those subjects with chronic PTSD.

The use of fear to understand stress and its application have shown great success in a number of clinical trials. McEwen and Lasley (2008) attempted to learn what it was about emotion/fear that led to the brain's inability to control that fear, which in turn led to mental disorders including anxiety, PTSD, and other irrational fears or phobias. During their broad based research, it was discovered that the stress hormones that interacted within the hippocampus made it possible to etch memorable experiences into our declarative memory. More importantly, this critical analysis discovered that chronically elevated levels of these same hormones could damage the very part of the brain that shuts them off.[6] Therefore, soldiers found that on operational deployments, a sense of fear was part of their environment, which generated stress on a regular basis. These stress-inducing moments created the distinct possibility of creating an overload of hormones in the brain that eventually lead to poor health. Some of the medical conditions caused or exacerbated by stress were atherosclerosis, obesity, heart attack, heart disease, high blood pressure, autoimmune diseases, stroke, and diabetes.

Combat soldiers are faced with the potential for daily stress, as fight-or-flight situations are constantly emerging from the fog of war. In these fight-or-flight situations, the brain automatically directs the body to begin shutting down some systems while increasing activity in other parts of the body. Increased blood flow and heart rate are the two primary examples of how the brain prepares the body for fight-or-flight. In these circumstances, blood flow is increased to the larger muscles so that they can work harder, pupils dilate in order to better focus eyesight, reaction times speed-up, and blood vessels contract to prevent blood loss if there is an injury.[7] Medina (2008) found during his research that this was "good stress," as it was only the body's immediate reaction to the threat of danger. As this reaction is usually temporary, Median found that there were no long-term negative effects from the release of the stress hormones. This biological response by the body was designed to both protect and support the body. However, this reaction by the body is always automatic, as it cannot make the immediate distinction between a physiological and a psychological threat. Also, it is difficult to turn off, as particularly in the modern world, stress can either be self-induced or created by external factors.

The brain is the most complex organ in the human body, and it has evolved over time to ensure survival. This most complex of all organs weighs less than three pounds, is usually less than 2% of total body weight, uses 20% of the body's blood supply, and 20% of the oxygen supply.[8] However, the brain is designed to contend with stress that only lasts for a short time and is not designed to handle stress for prolonged periods. Stress negatively influences or limits the memory and executive functions of the brain, and over time, it can disrupt the immune system and/or the body's motor skills. Medina (2008) found from his research that a brain that was stressed did not react the same way, just as the body does not react the same way under stress, so too the brain reacts to the environmental stress stimuli (signals) that it receives. How the brain receives this information, decodes it, and stores it has an impact on how it later retrieves it from the memory.

In the late 20th century, stress hormones proved their value in the laboratory with neuroscience researchers being able to leverage the imaging technology of MRI to take pictures of a human brain in action.[9] McEwen and Lasley (2008) were among the first researchers to show where emotions could be located within the brain and found that the easiest emotion to work with was fear. The research also began to confirm the important role of adrenaline and cortisol. The findings showed that adrenaline worked in the bloodstream to help the body react and protect itself from stressful situations. That is, it is released in a stressful fight-or-flight situation by carrying blood to the brain. However, neuroscientists are still unsure exactly how adrenaline-enriched blood transmits signals from the blood vessels that traverse the brain to specific parts of the brain.[10] On the other hand, cortisol is a hormone that enters the brain and enhances memory. The brain, and specifically the hippocampus, is dotted with cortisol receptors. The role of cortisol is memory formation while also appearing to be evolutionary or survival based.

When released in small amounts, both adrenaline and cortisol help protect the body by providing a boost when physically it needs a boost from these hormones. The release of these hormones in a fight-or-flight situation is exactly the condition they were designed for, which is to help the body survive. Conversely, when the body is under constant or chronic stress, these hormones can produce a detrimental effect. Medina (2008) found that stress damages every type of cognitions, and adrenaline creates scars in the human blood vessels that can cause a heart attack or stroke, while too much cortisol damages the cells in the hippocampus, thereby crippling the ability to learn and remember. Therefore, the stress response system in the human body is the very system that leaves it vulnerable if it is activated too frequently.

When researching this balance within the body, McEwen (2000) used the term "allostatic load." The medical definition of balance is defined by the term "homeostasis" and as a result, stress is anything that throws a human being out of this homeostatic balance.[11] Allostasis is the response of the body to outside factors as it attempts to maintain a balance or equilibrium within the body. Therefore, "allostatic load" refers to chronic or prolonged exposure to stress, and without timely deactivation of the stress response within the body, it is the physiological impact of chronic stress. McEwen (2000) referred to allostatic load as the cumulative biological wear and tear that can result from an excessive cycle of response (too frequent and/or of inappropriate duration or scope) in these systems as they seek to maintain allostasis in the face of environmental challenges.

The brain is the organ that is the control centre for the challenges associated with both allostasis and allostasis load, as it is both the sender and receiver for all neurological transmissions throughout the body. As a result, it is also a receptor for hormones released during periods of stress, and it is both analyst and a target for the challenges associated with the release of these hormones.[12] The principal hormonal moderators for the stress response within the body have both protecting and damaging effects. The hormones connected with stress protect the body in the short term, but in the long term, allostatic load imbalance can cause detrimental effects in the body that can lead to disease or mental health problems. Chronic stress arises when there are frequent occurrences of allostatic load on the body, which the brain is unable to control in a judicious manner and excess hormones remain in the body without dissipating. Therefore, stress hormones can in the short term assist in memory and help people to think more clearly, but over an extended period of time, the neurons do not work as clearly and so the memory functions begin to fade.

Traumatic Brain Injury (TBI) is the signature combat injury of the wars in Afghanistan and Iraq as the enemy, whether they be the Taliban or Iraqi insurgents, has employed the use of improvised explosive devices (IEDs) as their weapon of choice. As a result, both of these wars have seen widespread use of explosives in the war zone, which has caused a significant increase in the number of soldiers suffering from TBI. The ongoing research finds that 65% of soldiers deployed on operations will have combat experience. In total, 97% of the combat injuries were from explosives, with 61% of these being from IEDs, and 36% from mines.[13] These explosive munitions generate an instantaneous rise in pressure over the atmospheric pressure, thereby causing a blast-induced, over-pressurised wave. The increased survival rate amongst soldiers is due to advanced body-armour and Kevlar helmets. Soldiers who have experienced the effect of such an explosion and over-pressurised wave call this phenomenon "ringing the bell," as they feel their brain being distorted within their helmet.

In addition to the injuries sustained in the primary blast, casualties are often sustained from the secondary blast of projectiles and from soldiers suffering bodily displacement caused by the tertiary blast injury. The soldiers suffered from blast-related neurological injuries characterised by abnormal neurological examination and profiles. The analysis of these injuries identified five TBI-related symptoms, with these being: headaches, dizziness, loss of balance, irritability, and memory impairment/loss. Headache (81%) and dizziness (59%) were identified as being the predominant symptoms immediately after injury. Some symptoms tended to resolve with time (headache, dizziness, and loss of balance), while other symptoms persisted (irritability and memory impairment/loss). In half of these latter cases, the symptoms developed over time.[14] The research has found that one in five soldiers returning from an operational deployment after one year will have suffered a TBI.

Until recently, psychological and biomechanical trauma have been thought to have little in common with the co-occurrence of post-traumatic stress disorder (PTSD) and traumatic brain injury (TBI) being considered a rare clinical event. This inattention to PTSD-TBI comorbidity has been reflected in the fact that PTSD has been the province of mental health professionals, while TBI has been the primary focus of neurologists, neuropsychologists, neurosurgeons, and physical medicine and rehabilitation specialists. This professional separation is reflected in each of the professions use of the word "trauma." Mental health professionals understand trauma to be an event associated with the individual experiencing the threat of harm or loss of life, which causes extreme fear or horror. On the other hand, neurologists understand trauma to be as a result of destructive biomechanical forces acting on the brain or parts of the body.[15]

Many soldiers fighting in the wars in Afghanistan and Iraq have experienced multiple episodes of witnessing the death or injury of their comrades. They have also been exposed to the shockwaves from explosions that have the potential to cause TBI. The research has found that repeated combat deployments add more opportunities for additional trauma and a resulting likely worsening of PTSD and TBI. These wars have also highlighted an additional compounding factor, which is that soldiers often have high exposure rates to psychologically traumatic events at times that are unrelated to the possible exposure to TBI.[16] Additional research is required to understand the extent to which PTSD and TBI comorbidity can be considered to reflect the joint effects of a single exposure, which has both emotional and biomechanical traumatic aspects. As opposed to the cumulative effects of distinct and separate emotional and biochemical trauma exposures.

The condition "mild TBI," which is also known as concussion, is characterised by an alteration in the level of consciousness or a loss of consciousness for up to 30 minutes. The findings from the research by Orb, Eisenhauer, and Wynaden (2012) highlighted the relationship between PTSD and mild TBI in military, with it being found that of the U.S. soldiers returning from the Iraq war, the 44% who reported loss of consciousness also met the criteria for PTSD. They found that combat-incurred mild TBI doubled the risk of PTSD. However, the current clinical presentation of symptoms, using existing nomenclature, has been classifying soldiers with either PTSD or mild TBI. The symptoms are commonly fatigue, indecision, and irritability among others. Therefore, Orb, Eisenhauer, and Wynaden argue that the current (DSM-IV) diagnostic criteria for PTSD and TBI fails to fully capture the range and configuration of the symptoms displayed by soldiers who have experienced the trauma of the new 21$^{st}$ century battlefield.

In fact, the military has increasingly avoided the term PTSD in favour of the term "combat stress reaction" as this has the dual advantage of incorporating the milder TBI symptoms and is less stigmatising. The common fallacy is that PTSD is caused by a psychological injury to the psyche, while mild TBI is caused by a biomechanical injury to the brain. The research shows that either a failure to recover from acute to mild TBI symptoms or PTSD can occur following either emotional or physical trauma, which may or may not involve injury to the brain. However, the research is unclear as to whether the particular characteristics of the traumatic exposure (psychological or physical) and/or of the individual's temperament will determine which set of symptoms will predominate. One fact is clear, and that is that there is an increased rate of psychiatric disorders occurring in soldiers who have sustained TBI.[17] There is such a marked overlap between PTSD and TBI post-concussive symptoms that many soldiers who sustain brain injury will have the symptoms of both.

The recent research by Solomon, Shklar, and Mikulincer (2013) suggests mild TBI may diminish the brain's capacity to employ cognitive resources that would normally be engaged in problem solving and regulating emotions, thus leaving the soldier more susceptible to stress-related problems and PTSD. Their findings show that psychological and biomechanical trauma can result in impaired information processing, with 10-15% of those suffering brain injury having persistent cognitive and behavioural conditions. The main areas of cognitive impairment are the loss of working and short-term memory, reduced attention span, executive functioning, and speed of information processing.

Interestingly, the research also shows that IQ prior to trauma exposure was inversely associated with the risk of psychological health problems. Thompson (2009) identified that soldiers in the highest quartile of cognitive ability had a 46% lower risk than the soldiers in the lowest quartile of suffering from PTSD. He also found that a one-standard-deviation decrease in cognitive ability correlated with a 37% increase in risk of PTSD.[18] These data are consistent with the "cognitive reserve" hypothesis that individual differences in brain structure and function can cushion the effects of neuropathology on a variety of mental disorders. Therefore, the research is leading to the assumption that an individual's lower cognitive reserve, either congenital or acquired (mild TBI), will increase the risk of negative mental health and functional outcomes.

In order to advance the understanding of mild TBI and PTSD and their intersection, it is critical that future research addresses both disorders when designing and conducting research studies. This is as a result of the expertise in these areas being distributed across numerous medical disciplines, these being psychiatry, neurology, neurosurgery, neuropsychology, physical medicine and rehabilitation. The first responsibility for these interdisciplinary teams will be to formalise and ratify a common terminology to be used when examining the overlapping or intersecting symptoms of mild TBI and PTSD. The next task will be to design studies that study brain-injured patients using a longitudinal design that will follow the subjects from time of injury to five to 10 years into the future. The fundamental question, which these new research endeavours must be designed to answer, is whether the PTSD caused by the emotional trauma of a soldier seeing a comrade being killed are the same as the PTSD caused by an improvised explosive device that rendered the soldier unconscious for 15 minutes.

The symptoms of TBI and PTSD include nightmares, intrusive memories, increased vigilance, flashbacks, social impairment, and memory/concentration problems. While these symptoms are regarded as psychological problems, some or all of them may be caused by the physical effects of extreme stress on the brain. In fact, the most current research studies have shown that combat veterans actually experience physical alteration to their hippocampus, which is the part of the brain responsible for learning and memory, as well as the handling of stress. As importantly, the hippocampus also works closely with medial pre-frontal cortex, which is the area in the brain that regulates the emotional response to fear and stress. The research findings have found that TBI and PTSD sufferers frequently have impairments in one or both of these areas of the brain. The studies have also found that impairment in these areas can lead to learning and memory problems.[19]

The other typical symptoms of TBI and PTSD in veterans include intrusive memories, fragmented memory, dissociation (the unconscious separation of some mental processes from others), and pathological emotions, all of which are related to the impairment of the hippocampus. Memory loss plays a large part in TBI and PTSD, as veterans report deficits remembering facts or lists, gaps in memory that last for minutes to days, and fragmentation of memory.[20] The psychiatric symptoms associated with TBI and PTSD can be summarised as follows:

a. Nightmares
b. Flashbacks
c. Avoidance
d. Intrusive memories
e. Abnormal startle responses
f. Hyper arousal
g. Hyper vigilance
h. Memory and concentration problems
i. Amnesia
j. De-realisation
k. Out-of-body experiences
l. Fragmented memory
m. Claustrophobia
n. Panic attacks

Damage to the hippocampus from stress cannot only cause problems in dealing memories and other effects of past stressful experiences; it can also impair new learning. Once again, the most recent research by Watson and Gardiner (2013) has shown that the hippocampus has the capacity to regenerate nerve cells or neurons as part of its normal functioning; however, stress impairs this functioning by stopping or slowing the regeneration. This study also examined whether TBI and PTSD symptoms coincided with a measurable loss of neurons in the hippocampus by testing combat veterans suffering from memory problems caused by TBI or PTSD. By using brain imaging, it was found that these combat veterans had a 9% reduction in the right hippocampal volume of the brain when measured with magnetic resonance imaging (MRI) technology. Significantly, during this study, no other differences in volume were found in the other areas of the brain.[21] The diminished volume in the right hippocampal in the veterans suffering from TBI and PTSD was linked with short-term memory loss.

Other recent studies have shown that hippocampal volume reduction is specific to TBI and PTSD and is not linked to disorders such as anxiety or stress disorders. One fact that is not in dispute is that the hippocampus plays an important role in organising and then connecting the different aspects of a memory by defining the memory of an event in its correct time, place, and location. Besides the hippocampus, abnormalities in the pre-frontal cortex of the brain are also associated with TBI and PTSD. The medial pre-frontal cortex is responsible for the regulation of fear responses, which it has been found is an underlying factor in the evidence of pathological emotional responses seen in veterans. To support these findings, the latest study by Watson and Gardiner (2013) when using a combat simulator, which incorporated images, sights, sounds and smells of a battlefield environment, found that combat veterans with TBI and PTSD had a decreased blood flow in the area of the medial pre-frontal cortex. It was significant that this study did not find the same decreased blood flow in veterans who were not suffering from TBI or PTSD.

As regards the U.K. military forces, the recent research by Mulligan, Jones, and Woodhead (2010) into the mental health of U.K. military personnel while on deployment in Iraq produced a number of key findings. First, the prevalence rates of psychological distress, TBI, and PTSD identified within the study were similar to other recent studies conducted in both Afghanistan and Iraq. Second, the data illustrated that the main risk factors for psychological stress were weak unit cohesion, poor leadership, female gender, and non-receipt of the pre-deployment stress brief. Third, better health was associated with officer rank, strong unit cohesion, and having taken a period of R&R during the deployment. However, it is accepted that deployed military personnel are at an increased risk of mental health and behavioural problems such as depression, anxiety, substance misuse, and aggressive behaviour. As a result, due to the extended nature of the operations in Afghanistan and Iraq, the numbers of casualties, both mental and physical, have proved to be greater than initially anticipated.[22]

Due to these factors, the U.K. military forces have invested considerably in ensuring that soldiers within units deployed on operations are able to support each other after experiencing a traumatic event. This peer support programme aims to identify the psychological risk to soldiers who have been exposed to combat stressors and then engages them with medical professionals and/or social support from comrades within the unit. The aim of the programme is to provide a further pro-resilience factor which assists military personnel who are operating in a highly stressful environment to gain support from each other as the "first-line" of psychological support.[23] The research evidence has shown that U.K. military personnel have largely remained resilient to the psychological stress of the 21st century battlefield despite having suffered a significant number of deaths and injuries in the recent wars in Afghanistan and Iraq. The reason for this resilience may well be as a result of the U.K.'s military forces' considerable efforts that it has made to ensure that soldiers when they are deployed are well trained, well led members of a cohesive unit which has high-quality mental health services readily available.

In conclusion, Grossman (2009) identified that war and the experiences of combat are significant emotional events that can have a transformational effect on a soldier's life. The critical analysis of this research evidence showed that in the case of soldiers returning from combat, it was having an enormous effect on their lives. The Rand Corporation and their Centre for Military Health Policy in their extensive research found that over 273,000 soldiers were suffering from PTSD, or major depression, as a result of their service in Afghanistan and/or Iraq. The Rand Corporation's earlier research, which was conducted in 2007, found that 26% of the 1.64 million service members who had then experienced combat in Afghanistan and/or Iraq were suffering from some form of combat-related stress or PTSD.[24] All these far-reaching research studies have shown that soldiers in combat deal with a daily routine that is often unpredictable, stressful, and out of the ordinary. McEwen and Lasley (2008) identified that these circumstances caused the soldier to lose control and this lack of control was exactly what the APA (1994) examined when they wrote about a sense of helplessness leading to PTSD symptoms in soldiers. In conclusion, many infantry soldiers experience physical and psychological trauma during combat operations, as indicated by these recent studies conducted on stress and the brain. Also, results have shown that higher rates of trauma are associated with increased exposure to intense infantry ground combat.

## CHAPTER THREE

# Stress and Soldiers

Stress has been a known but misunderstood dynamic of infantry combat since men first began fighting other men. From the early Greeks to the present time, whenever men fought, they faced various forms of stress. The first modern war that reported on the combat stresses that faced soldiers in any detail was the American Civil War. These reported but incomplete accounts from the Civil War indicated that combat-stress-induced medical disorders did exist, and during that time, it was known as "soldier's heart" or "soldier's melancholy." These early findings were more observations than research, but they identified that soldiers who suffered from soldier's heart were overwhelmed by fatigue and so became incapable of performing their duties.[1] However, it was not until World War I that military leaders and medical personnel officially recognised the effects of combat stress and named it "shell-shock."[2] During World War II, combat stress was renamed "battle or combat fatigue" in order to describe the psychiatric casualties of combat.

There have been many contradictions and inconsistencies in the research into stress, but it was Grossman (1995), in his pivotal research, who discovered that combat stress was a normal human reaction to the combat experience. However, he more critically also found that the stress caused was unpredictable and invisible. Some of this had to do with soldiers conducting multiple tours and how they were counted, as well as the associated increase in stress from those multiple deployments.[3] In order to highlight these inconsistencies, it is worth critically analysing the current findings. Morgan (2011) placed the incidence of stress at 16-17%, while Kertsh (2010) found it as high as 41%. However, Tanielian

COMBAT COMMAND

(2010) indicated that 26% of returning soldiers were suffering from the consequences of combat-induced stress. Despite these conflicting statistics, the fact is that there is a significant amount of stress induced in soldiers as a result of direct combat with the enemy.

To further this critical analysis of the clinical research findings, the U.S. Army's Mental Health Advisory Team (MHAT, 2008) conducted post-combat surveys and interviews with 652 soldiers and marines returning from Operation Iraqi Freedom (OIF) during 2005-2007. Over 75% reported being in situations where their personal safety was at risk, and where there was a likelihood of personal injury or death. They all indicated in the survey that they experienced intense fear, helplessness, and/or horror (MHAT, 2008). This intense fear or helplessness are the exact terms used by the APA in their determination of the symptoms that must be present for PTSD, or some form of combat-related stress, to be diagnosed by medical professionals (APA, 1994).

The majority of the British research into the physiological and psychological effects of combat on infantry soldiers over the last 15 years has been undertaken at the King's Centre for Military Health Research (KCMHR) at King's College, London. Researchers surveyed a cohort of 4,722 military personnel who deployed during the Coalition forces invasion of Iraq in March 2003. The early research findings indicated a prevalence of the symptoms of PTSD among these soldiers to be 4.8%. As the KCMHR continued to monitor the research outcomes during the period 2005-2007, the war in Iraq intensified, resulting in more British infantry soldiers being involved in direct ground combat. These factors resulted in an increasing number of military personnel being diagnosed with combat-related depression, stress, or PTSD, with the rates rising to 7.4% and then eventually to 11.8% at the time of the Coalition forces final withdrawal from the country in 2011 (KCMHR, 2014). A similar study was conducted by the KCMHR with 5,550 British military personnel who had served in the war in Afghanistan, and the rates of combat-related mental illness rose steadily during 2009 through 2013 to peak at 16.7% (KCMHR, 2014).

Additionally, Stouffer (2010) conducted a research study of 2,863 U.S. soldiers one year after their return from operations in Iraq and found a direct correlation between physical health problems and combat-related PTSD. Stouffer utilised a standardised, self-administered, screening instrument, which provided the basis for the collected data. Of the 2,863 soldiers surveyed, there were 475 soldiers who met the screening criteria for combat-related PTSD, which represented 17% of the soldiers surveyed. This analysis found that these 475 soldiers had significantly higher health risks, more physical ailments, and a higher incidence of somatic symptoms than their non-PTSD peers.[4]

In 2013, Watson and Gardiner conducted a longitudinal study investigating the stress and psychological distress suffered by soldiers during combat operations. This longitudinal study incorporated four different time-waves during the years 2009-2012 and targeted 359 combat veterans returning from operations in Afghanistan after a 12 to 15-month deployment. The results of this research study found that stress levels, psychological distress, and life events were all associated with time and across time. It was identified that the pattern of psychological distress differed between newly recruited soldiers and those soldiers who had experienced combat in previous deployments. Significantly, Watson and Gardiner (2013) found that stress, individual traits, adverse life events, and psychological distress were all interrelated.

The Holmes-Rahe Stress Inventory listed 43 events that are all considered stressful occurrences in daily life. In 1967, Holmes and Rahe surveyed over 5,000 people to determine if they had experienced any of the 43 stressful events in the previous two years.[5] Their findings indicated a correlation between those events and the potential for illness. This inventory is also called the Top Ten Stressful Life Events. Homes and Rahe (1967) evidence supported their argument that people may experience many of these events in their lives, but few experience four or five of these stressful events within the span of one to two years. Watson and Gardiner (2013) through a careful examination of the inventory list, in which they used their knowledge and understanding of a soldier's life while on combat operations, were able to identify that some soldiers experienced four or more of these events within their normal deployment of 12-15 months.

Grossman and Christensen (2008) found that soldiers operated in a stressful environment every day by forcing their bodies to remain in an automatic stress reaction mode. Their research found that it was harder for soldiers to shut off their stress reactions after the stressful situation had passed. So, instead of levelling off after a stressful event, the blood levels and other bodily reactions continued to remain high, thereby exposing the body to increased risks from other medical problems. Grossman (2009) subsequently identified what he believed military battles had in common. This was the human behaviour of men struggling to reconcile their instinct of self-preservation with their sense of honour and the achievement of their mission, over which other men are ready to kill them. In order to support these original research findings, a later critical analysis by Asken, Grossman, and Christensen (2010) found that the study of infantry combat was always a study of fear, courage, faith, and vision. Two of the leading contemporary researchers on the topic of combat are Grossman and Christensen, who during their qualitative research study in 2007-2010 interviewed 246 infantry soldiers who had experienced combat in Afghanistan and Iraq in the previous four years.

As a result of this four-year, in-depth qualitative research study, they introduced the concept of what they called the "Universal Human Phobia."[6] To understand this concept, they critically identified that a phobia is much more than just fear, as it is the irrational and uncontrollable fear of a specific object or event, and they identified the "Universal Human Phobia" as being interpersonal human aggression. They found that when violence is perpetrated on one human being by another, the experience is devastating, as one does not expect another human being would try to kill or severely injure him/her. The most important outcome of this research was that they specifically identified that any time the causal factor of a stressor is human in nature, the degree of trauma and stress is usually more severe and long lasting.[7]

Grossman and Christensen (2010) continued with this research, and they unexpectedly found that PTSD is comparably rare and mild in response to natural disasters and traffic accidents, but when it is another human being who causes fear, pain, and suffering, the results are devastating. The researchers also identified disparities in the present military conflicts in the published percentages of soldiers suffering from combat stress brought about by the "Universal Human Phobia." Northouse (2009) placed the incidence of stress at 16-17%, while Gabriel (2010) placed it as high as 41%. Gray (2008) indicated that 26% of returning soldiers may be suffering from some form of mental disorder. Morgan (2011), from his critical analysis, found that more that 20% of deployed forces were suffering from combat-induced stress. The reality is that although figures vary, research shows that there is a significant amount of stress placed on soldiers when engaged in combat.

Interestingly, it was Grossman (2009) who graphically portrayed that unchecked extreme stress was an emotional and physical carnivore. To reinforce this view, by way of a critical analysis in World War I, World War II, and Korea, the number of soldiers evacuated from the front line, as they had become psychiatric casualties, was greater than the number of those who were killed by the enemy in combat.

Nye (2009), in his quantitative research study, examined this phenomenon in World War II, and his findings were that U.S. military forces lost 504,000 men due to psychiatric illness resulting from combat operations. Furthermore, Grossman (2009) portrayed that in the toxic, corrosive, and destructive domain of the "Universal Human Phobia," soldiers are asked to live, fight, and to ultimately die for the good of their country. The critical finding from this research by Grossman was that if soldiers are asked to intentionally move into the "Universal Human Phobia," where other human beings are trying to kill them, it was vital that they understood that realm if they were going to survive, succeed, and eventually emerge victorious.[8] The findings of Shay (2009), in his research based on interviews with 232 Vietnam veterans, found that while others fled, it was the infantry combat soldier who moved to the sound of the guns in order to close with and either kill or capture the enemy.

The study of the human nervous system has produced as many contradictions and inconsistencies as has the study of stress.[9] However, the research conducted by Shephard (2008) clarified and corrected some long-held misconceptions. The human autonomic nervous system (ANS) consists of the sympathetic nervous system (SNS) and the parasympathetic nervous system (PNS). These most generally work opposite to each other. The SNS directs the body's energy resources for action and stress responses, such as the fight-or-flight response. The PNS is concerned with the activities that increase the body's supply of stored energy, and so at night, when asleep, the PNS process is totally ascendant. Then, upon waking and during a normal day, homeostasis or a balance exists between the sympathetic and parasympathetic.[10]

However, in a qualitative study of 657 soldiers, Shephard (2008) found that if during the course of a normal day somebody tries to kill someone else, then the response is total SNS arousal, and the PNS processes shut down. He found that in combat, salivation shuts down, and this causes what many combat veterans call "dry mouth or cotton mouth." His conclusion was that there is a total mobilisation of all the body's assets toward just one thing, and that is "survival." As critically, he also found that as soon as the danger was over, there was a crash, which is a parasympathetic backlash of enormous magnitude.[11]

As Shephard (2008) broadened his research, he found that life-and-death combat incidents were comparatively rare, but when they did occur, managing the emotional and psychological stress after the event could be even more important, as after a combat situation is when a soldier is at his/her most vulnerable. De Becker (2010) also found that when the body is in a fight-or-flight mode, the brain reacts to that danger by igniting chemical alarms throughout the nervous system. This critical issue of the brain's response to physical danger or fear is complex, and we have yet to define how soldiers, after spending extended periods of time in this biologically alerted state, adjust back to the restoration of peaceful conditions. This adjustment by a soldier back into civilian life, or life in a non-combat environment, and how the soldier transitions, still has to be defined.[12]

Other research pertaining to stress and the soldier was conducted by Kosslyn and Koenig (2009), which involved 152 participants and explored the little-known topic of sleep deprivation. The researchers discovered, surprisingly, that sleep deprivation was the best way to physically predispose a soldier to becoming a stress casualty. Then specifically studying the effects of sleep deprivation on soldiers, Kosslyn and Koenig (2013) found that it impaired their actions, time judgement, vision, information processing, short-term memory, performance motivation, vigilance, and patience. Findings also showed that the human body builds up a sleep deficit, and just as one could catch up on dehydration and malnutrition, so there is a need to catch up on sleep.[13]

Earlier studies also found that throughout history, sleep has always been a soldier's best medicine. During World War I and II, it was identified that when soldiers rotated back from the front line, the first thing they would do was sleep. Unfortunately, the U.S. Department of Defense Task Force on Mental Health (2007) found that in Afghanistan and Iraq, U.S. soldiers coming off combat patrols would often return to their barracks, and instead of sleeping, play video games, watch DVDs and television, and/or use the Internet. The study found that these activities gave the soldiers a sense of control over the situation, but in reality, lack of sleep was a self-inflicted wound that greatly increased their vulnerability to PTSD and also to illness, as the immune system diminishes with sleep deprivation.[14]

As a result of the conclusions and recommendations from this Department of Defense study, the U.S. military conducted a critical analysis of soldiers' sleep habits in order to re-learn the lesson that sleep deprivation could be a major war-winning or war-losing factor.[15] So, now officers and senior NCOs are responsible for monitoring, and if necessary ordering soldiers to get the sleep that they need in order to remain combat effective.

Grossman and Christensen (2008) further studied soldiers and sleep and identified that if soldiers are deprived of sleep for 24 hours, they are virtually the physiological and psychological equivalent of being "legally drunk." The researchers also found that the condition of sleep deprivation was then compounded by the fact that soldiers in combat are already more physically and emotionally fatigued due to the duration of sustained military operations. Therefore, after these research findings, the U.S. Department of Defense accepted that stress was a key disabler of soldiers, and that lack of sleep is a key factor which predisposes soldiers to becoming stress casualties, to physical illness, and to PTSD.[16]

The relationship between heart rate and performance remains much of a mystery, as do the effects of stress, the human nervous system, and sleep deprivation on infantry soldiers engaged in combat operations (Marlowe, 2001). Grossman and Christensen (2008) also discovered in their research that during combat, as the level of fear/arousal in a soldier increased, various conditions were identified that coincided with specific heart rate levels. They found that there is a zone that exists between 85 and 115 beats per minute (bpm) where the soldier is at the optimal survival and combat-effectiveness level, which means that the complex motor skills, visual reaction time, and cognitive reaction times are all at their peak. However, it has been shown that over 115 bpm, fine motor skills begin to deteriorate. This linking of specific heart rates with task performance has resulted in later researchers creating what was termed a "Unified Model of Stress and Performance," which utilises a colour code system of "Conditions White, Yellow, Red, Grey, and Black." These heart rates apply only to survival stress or fear-induced heart rate increases as the effects of normal strenuous exercise heart rate increase would not be the same as when fear or survival stress causes the increase.[17]

In 2010, working together, Grossman and Siddle categorised conditions of heart rates in relationship to combat stress which are: Condition White 60-80 bpm (normal resting heart rate), Condition Yellow 80-115 bpm (optimal combat effectiveness), Condition Red 115-145 bpm (fine and then complex motor skill deterioration), Condition Grey 145-175 bpm (cognitive processing deterioration, auditory exclusion, loss of near vision, and loss of depth perception), and Condition Black above 175 bpm (irrational fight-or-flight reaction, catastrophic breakdown of mental, and physical performance). This research by Grossman and Siddle (2010) concluded that when the average soldier experiences a stress/adrenaline induced heart rate increase of about 145 bpm, there was a significant breakdown in combat effectiveness.

However, this was not true of all soldiers. Grossman and Christensen, earlier in 2008, had found that soldiers who had practised their military skills extensively and who were already combat veterans could continue to perform above 145 bpm, as they had become what were described by the researchers as having undergone "stress inoculation." Their research found that there are two issues associated with fight-or-flight stress: 1) The reaction of the body is always automatic, as it cannot make the immediate distinction between physical and psychological threat, and 2) it is difficult to turn-off. The brain responds to the threats by introducing stress hormones into the body, which makes the pulse quicken, the mouth goes dry, and pupils dilate, while the brain prepares the body for fight-or-flight (Grossman and Christensen, 2008).

Crump (2011), in his longitudinal research study on combat stress, which included 353 Afghanistan and Iraq war veterans, identified that a set of perceptual distortions could occur in combat that alters the way that a soldier views the world and perceives reality. It is only now that this altered state of consciousness is becoming apparent. In his research, Crump considered that even though more research is required, on this topic, the dominant theory today is that these biomechanical changes to the sensory organs are a side effect of vasoconstriction and other stress responses that are induced by combat. He also found that the process of tuning out sensory input happens all the time, and so the brain must constantly tune out sensory data or otherwise run the risk of it being overwhelmed. In the extreme stress of combat, this screening process could be even more intense, as senses tune out unnecessary data except for that needed for survival.[18] However, Dohrenwend (2013) argued that this function has both a mental cognitive and a physical component, as reports from the audiology research community indicate that the ear can physically and mechanically shut out loud sounds, just as the eyelid can shut out bright light.

The U.S. Department of Defense Task Force on Mental Health also reported back in 2007 that a biomechanical shut-down in the ear could occur in a millisecond in response to sudden and loud noises. The report identified that two things happen in combat. There is a form of aural or auditory "tunnel vision" in which specific sounds are tuned out under high stress. Then there is a form of aural or auditory "blink" in which loud noises are physically and mechanically muted or silenced for a brief moment. The report further identified a response that occurs under the extreme stress of combat, when the ears shut out all sounds so that the soldier does not remember hearing anything afterward. It showed that this was associated with exceptional stress, extreme heart rates, and intense physiological arousal, with the greater the stress the more powerful the effect. It further identified that a third response occurs when a soldier shuts out all sounds of gunshots but still hears everything else.

What appears to be a Condition Red response, identified by Grossman (2009), in which the body was capable of biomechanically shutting down the ear in a millisecond in response to the leading edge of the shock-wave of a gunshot, and then reopening immediately to hear everything else. It was Grossman who described "Type-1 Auditory Exclusion" where soldiers firing their weapons report that they did not hear the sound or that the sound was muffled, and that their ears did not ring afterward. However, Grossman identified that "Type-1 Auditory Exclusion" did not happen when a soldier was on the shooting range. It only happened in the actual killing circumstances of deadly inter-personal combat. Then Grossman found that "Type-II Auditory Exclusion" happened when a soldier was completely relaxed and this appeared to be as a result of the body receiving two simultaneous and overwhelming sensory stimuli: the sound of the gun and the feel of the bullet hitting. He found that eight out of 10 soldiers surveyed experienced tunnel vision during combat. He saw that tunnel vision, along with auditory exclusion and a host of other perceptual distortions were commonly associated with high levels of anxiety that were present in all soldiers involved in potentially lethal combat.[19]

The quantitative research study conducted by Artwohl and Christensen (2009), in which 137 Afghanistan and Iraq veterans were participants, found that 74% of the soldiers involved in infantry combat acted automatically and without conscious thought. Unfortunately, in many situations, soldiers were still being trained using blank ammunition and man-shaped silhouettes. According to their research, a far superior training medium was to use a photo-realistic target complete with a face, clothing, and a weapon. They then defined that in biomechanics and kinesiology this was called the "Law of Specificity."[20] Soldiers could be taught how to perform a specific action required for survival without conscious thought. Their research showed that whatever was taught and drilled in training would be reflected in the soldier's actions during combat. Grossman (2009) believed that the findings from all this research was that soldiers do not rise to the occasion in combat; they sink to their level of training. His findings were that any natural resistance to killing, any sense of the sanctity of human life, any human emotions, any remorse or compassion, could be overcome with effective training for combat.

In many combat situations, scientific research and anecdotal evidence indicated that the individual soldier had a sudden visual clarity. Artwohl and Christensen (2009) found that 72% of their survey group reported heightened visual clarity during combat. Then there is slow-motion time, where they found that 65% of soldiers involved in combat experienced this phenomenon. They further identified that the slow-motion time effect was random, unpredictable, and sometimes a useful response in combat. Within their qualitative research study they further found that 7% of soldiers involved in combat experienced temporary paralysis or freezing, this they observed was clearly not a survival mechanism. However, in some cases, they also found that those who thought they were experiencing temporary paralysis were actually experiencing slow-motion time.[21]

As detailed as the study was by Artwohl and Christensen, it is Vore (2010), in his clinical study, who presented a critical analysis of the most compelling evidence of the effects of stress on cognition. In this study, he measured the effects of stress on cognition of 184 Special Forces soldiers attending survival school who were randomised into one of three assessment groups. The ability of the stress group to copy and recall was significantly impaired in comparison to the pre-stress and control group. This clinical study concluded that the stress exposure of these soldiers impaired their visual-spatial ability and working memory.

The early research by Marshal (1947) recorded that nearly half of all soldiers involved in combat experienced memory loss from the event. This statistic was subsequently confirmed by Artwohl and Christensen

(2009), who found that 47% of soldiers involved in combat suffered from memory loss of at least part of their actions. So, memories of life-threatening situations are often vivid, indistinct, or even missing.[22] This is a phenomenon that Siddle (2008) termed "critical incident amnesia." The most recent research by Kertsh (2010) found that it was common that within the first 24 hours to recall roughly 30% of the occurrences, then 50% after 48 hours, and then 75-95% after 72-100 hours. According to the research by Artwohl and Christensen (2009), 21% of soldiers involved in combat experienced memory lose and that in life-and-death combat situations, soldiers often envisioned possibilities, and sometimes these possibilities become reality in their minds.

Despite these impressive findings, it was Fishback (2008) who identified the limbic system as being the key to understanding more about stress, memory, and learning. The areas of the limbic system mentioned in this research were the hippocampus and the amygdala. In this research, the hippocampus was not only extensively involved in the formation of memory and learning, but it was also extremely susceptible to stress. Fishback administered a battery of mental tests to 654 soldiers before and after their deployment to Iraq. These mental tasks measured both verbal and spatial memory. It was found that the soldiers performed significantly poorer in all mental tasks upon their return from combat operations.[23]

Now having examined the research by Artwohl and Christensen (2009), it is appropriate to discuss another major study into sensory distortions in combat. This research was conducted by Klinger (2010), and the study involved a survey and interviews with soldiers who were in combat, shot at, and subsequently killed the enemy. One of the most important new findings of this study, an area that no one had previously explored, are his revelations as to what soldiers thought and felt before, during, and after their combat experience. Klinger noted that "fear-for-self" and "fear-for-others" had occurred in the majority of cases. He discussed how some subjects were "concerned" about others, while having a negative response to the word "fear," claiming that they did not have any "emotional trepidation." It is useful to note that in the prior-to-shooting phase, at least one distortion was experienced by 88% of soldiers. In the shooting phase, the percentage increased to 94%.[24] This implied that when the shooting begins, stress increases, as does the incidents of perceptual distortions regarding the combat experience. Klinger also observed that the rates for auditory distortions changed substantially across the two time frames as the rate of diminished sound increased from 42-70%. The figure for intensified sound was halved from 10-5%.

These findings concurred with many other studies that have noted that diminished sound was most likely to occur when the soldier was shooting (King, 2013). Many combatants reported that their shots were quiet, although they heard the subsequent echo of the shots and/or the rattle of their ejected shell casings hitting the ground. However, Klinger's most valuable contribution to the study of the physical and physiological effects of infantry combat on soldiers was that individual soldiers may not always be aware of the sensory distortions that they experience.[25] Based on the research, Tables 1-4 summarise the significant physical and mental effects of combat on soldiers (Grossman 1995, 2009; Grossman & Christensen, 2008; Siddle, 2009; Grossman & Siddle, 2010; King, 2013).

**Table 1**

*Physical Stressors in Combat*

| Environmental | Physiological |
|---|---|
| Bright light | Dehydration |
| Difficult or arduous terrain | Illness or injury |
| Directed-energy weapons/devices | Impaired immune system |
| Heat, cold, or wet | Malnutrition |
| High altitude | Muscular and aerobic fatigue |
| Hypoxia (insufficient oxygen) | Obesity |
| Infectious agents/diseases | Over or under use of muscles |
| Ionizing radiation | or organ systems |
| Noxious odours (fumes, poisons, or | Poor health |
| chemicals) | Poor hygiene |
| Physical work | Sleep deprivation |
| Poor visibility | Substance abuse |
| Vibration, noise, or blast | |

**Table 2**

*Mental Stressors in Combat*

| Cognitive | Psychological |
| --- | --- |
| Ambiguity, uncertainty, or unpredictability | Bereavement |
| | Boredom or inactivity |
| Communication (too much/too little information) | Conflicting loyalties |
| | Exposure to combat |
| Difficult decisions | Fear and anxiety |
| Hard choices or no choice | Frustration or guilt |
| Organisational dynamics | Home sickness |
| Previous failures | Interpersonal conflict |
| Recognition of impaired functioning | Isolated, or lonely |
| Sensory overload | Resentment, anger, or rage |
| Time pressure or waiting | Victimisation or harassment |
| Working beyond skill level | |

**Table 3**

*Physical Reactions Following Combat*

| Emotional | Physiological |
| --- | --- |
| Anger | Abdominal distress |
| Anxiety | Ailments |
| Apathy | Appetite decrease/increase |
| Concern for family | Back pain |
| Confusion | Chest pains |
| Despair | Disturbed sleep |
| Emotional mood swings | Dizziness |
| Feeling of helplessness | Fatigue |
| Feeling of isolation | Feeling of weakness |
| Feeling of loss | Headaches |
| Feeling of numbness | Heaviness in arms or legs |
| Frustration | Hot or cold spells |
| Guilt | Hyperventilation |
| Inability to relax | Increased allergies |
| | Increased blood pressure |
| | Irregular breathing |

| Emotional | Physiological |
| --- | --- |
| Intrusive memories | Nausea |
| Irritability | Nervousness |
| Loss of sense of control | Numbness and tingling |
| Negativity | Shaking |
| Nightmares | Sore muscles |
| Relief | Sweating |
| Re-living of past trauma | Tightness in throat/stomach |
| Shame | Trembling |
| Vulnerability | Urinary incontinence |

**Table 4**

*Mental Reactions Following Combat*

| Cognitive | Psychological |
| --- | --- |
| Awareness of mortality | Aggressiveness |
| Confusion | Agitated |
| Forgetfulness | Attempted suicide |
| Inability to make decisions | Avoidance |
| Inability to relate | Compulsiveness |
| Intrusive thoughts | Difficulty with normality |
| Lack of concentration | Disruption of social norms |
| Lack of objectivity | Hyperactive |
| Loss of reality | Inability to express self |
| Memory loss | Mistrust of others |
| Obsessive thought | Nervous actions |
| Over-association | Over work |
| Poor judgment | Reckless |
| Pre-occupation | Relationship problems |
| Rigidity | Withdrawal |
| Self-criticism | Increased alcohol, drugs, tobacco, or food intake |

In conclusion, stress has been a known but misunderstood dynamic of infantry combat since men first began fighting other men. There have been many contradictions and inconsistencies in the research into stress and soldiers, but it was Grossman (1995) in his pivotal research that dis-covered that combat stress was a normal human reaction to the combat experience. However, he found more critically that the stress caused was unpredictable and invisible. Now by conducting a critical analysis of the statistics, it could be seen that there is a disparity in the current Afghani-stan and Iraq conflicts among the percentages presented to the public. This fact leads to the contention that the conceptual framework, whilst guiding research, evolves and unfolds both generatively and recursively as the research process progresses. So, the conceptual framework for this study was an essential bridge between paradigms that explained the re-search issues and the actual practice of investigating those issues.

# Chapter Four

## *Combat and Soldiers*

The examination of the effects of combat on infantry soldiers is a field of enquiry that has largely been neglected by empirical research. Most of the historic studies of warfare have focused on those generals and politicians who made the major decisions rather than on the infantry soldiers on the front line who were in close and deadly conflict with the enemy. Also most of the clinical studies have focused on the experiences of those infantry soldiers who were suffering from some form of negative reaction to combat. As a result, there has been very little research analysis into the physiological and psychological effects of combat on war-fighters as a population.[1] Therefore, this study is designed to fill this gap by describing in a systematic way the physical, mental, emotional, social, and spiritual demands placed upon our current generation of infantry soldiers. In this regard, the physical and mental challenges of participating in combat operations vary in their intensity and duration. Some of these being so overwhelming that they could be expected to immediately confuse and devastate a soldier. While others are more subtle and enduring, as they slowly erode the soldiers will to continue killing. However, the most toxic of these stressors are those that have the greatest impact. These typically involve the soldier surviving a near-to-death experience or having witnessed the violent death or injury of their comrades.[2] The less overwhelming combat experiences nevertheless remain as deadly as they persist for hours, days, and months, leading inevitably to the soldier's breaking point being reached.

All the research has shown that the human mind, just as with the human body, has a limited capacity to withstand external forces without suffering either short or long-term damage. Interestingly, the word "trauma" originates for the Greek word for "wound", and there is increasingly the conclusion that overwhelming stress inflicts literal injuries, or wounds, in the brains and minds of soldiers when experiencing combat.[3] However, the term "injury" has gained prominence over "wound" as it has advantages when conveying to soldiers the nature of their reactions to severe stress. That is soldiers understand that stress injuries are part of everyday life and that most of these heal naturally without professional assistance. To reinforce this point, the British military has increasingly employed the term "stress injury" to describe enduring medical conditions related to combat stress, thereby de-stigmatising the ailment. Several approaches have been used in order to separate combat stress injuries into three categories based upon "traumatic stress," caused by the impact of terror, horror, or helplessness; "operational fatigue," resulting from accumulates stress; and "grief" occasioned by the loss of a close comrade.[4]

The core feature of combat-related stress injury is exposure to an event that is so harmful that a complete and adaptive response by the individual is impossible. This traumatic experience causes an impact injury to the brain just as a bullet will cause an impact injury to the soldier's body. The unavoidable conclusion is that combat of any kind is potentially toxic and the findings of Hoge (2004) revealed that there was a strong, positive correlation between the number of combat experiences and the severity of the psychological stress symptoms. Hoge further identified four main peritraumatic processes that happen to the brain at the moment of traumatic impact. These were physiological hyper-arousal, shame and guilt, dissociation, and damage to core beliefs. To examine these in more detail, human beings react to immediate threats to their well-being with an adaptive physiological fight-or-flight hyper-arousal. This arousal in response to a threat is a universal adaptive mechanism. However, if there is excessive physiological arousal in response to the threat, then traumatic stress injuries will occur. The research has shown that arousal is a necessary response to threats, but arousal beyond a certain point will prove toxic. Then intense self-reproach in the form of shame or guilt is a common symptom of traumatic stress injuries in combat. This is caused by the soldiers believing in their own strength and competence until they become completely helpless during a traumatic event and witness the violent death of a comrade.[5] Dissociation describes the short-term and long-term disability that follows a traumatic combat-related stress injury. During combat, this sudden and acute disruption in the capacity of the brain and mind to process information can produce hazards to the soldier as well their comrades. Finally, a continuing theme from the research into traumatic combat stress injuries is that they destroy the soldier's deeply held core beliefs. That is the soldier faces the possibility of their own mortality, and this destroys their belief in social trust as their belief that human beings are basically caring and good is shattered.

Those that have experienced combat can be further subdivided into categories contingent on their combat roles, the reactive role, and the initiative role. That is the infantry soldier is placed upon the battlefield in close contact with the enemy in a reactive fight-or-flight/kill-or-be-killed reactive role. Whereas the attack helicopter pilot is in a position to initiate, control, and more specifically withdraw to safety at any time during the combat. The infantry soldier is placed on the battlefield to fulfil the role "to close with and kill or capture the enemy in any weather, climate, or terrain." This leads the combat to be measured in feet. The helicopter pilot meanwhile fires at the enemy below with rockets and machine guns, with the confrontation between opposing sides being measured in hundreds of feet. The reality is that there is a tremendous difference between viewing the aftermath of a battle from a distance when compared to viewing it from a position where the sight of dismembered bodies, the smell of death and the touching of corpses are routine.[6] The results of this close ground combat on the infantry soldier include feelings of guilt that often turn to self-punishment, feelings that they have been betrayed by their country, rage aimed at discriminate and indiscriminate targets, psychic numbing or emotional shutdown, alienation from themselves and others, and doubt in their own ability to love or trust others.[7]

As if the trauma was not enough, the harsh self-judgment and personal rebuke of the sufferer exacerbates the condition. These dysfunctional moods lead to negative thoughts, which increase the symptoms and initiate the cycle anew. Soldiers can lapse into destructive internal discourse that weighs heavily on their mood. On the other hand, soldiers may avoid their experiences that consciously recall their war experiences and withdraw entirely. The "one-thousand-yard stare" noted in those suffering from combat stress results from both this negativity and evasion. Stressors may be re-experienced through conditioned responses and sometimes as hallucinatory episodes during which a soldier "sees" the enemy upon awakening, "hears" a bomb explode when a door bangs loudly, or "feels" shrapnel entering their body when jostled in a crowd.[8] Similarly, the reactions to stressors can re-emerge in night-time dreams and nightmares, or periods of dissociation in which the stressor seems to recur, braking into the soldier's awareness, behaviour, or self-identity. In these ways, the stressors come to dominate the soldiers waking life, usually unexpectedly, and in ways that are maladaptive and dysfunctional.[9]

A combat environment by its very nature can produce a dramatic range of emotional responses in soldiers where the potential exists for optimal human decision-making and performance of goal-directed activities to be seriously compromised.[10] Many of the stressors found in a combat situation are due to the deliberate enemy actions aimed at killing, wounding or demoralising our soldiers. Other stressors are due to the natural environment, such as intense heat or cold, humidity, harsh mountainous or jungle terrain, or a toxic environment. However, the research findings by Solomon, Shklar, and Mikulincer (2013) indicate that focused stress is vital to survival and mission accomplishment during combat operations.

Gabriel (2010) found in his research that in every war soldiers have fought during the 20th century, the likelihood of becoming a psychiatric casualty due to the stresses of combat were greater than being killed or wounded by enemy fire. This finding was illustrated in the U.S. forces during World War II when over 800,000 service personnel were classified as unfit for military service due to psychiatric causes.[11] In their post-war research study of this phenomenon, Swank and Marchand (1946) concluded that after 60 days of continuous combat, 98% of the surviving soldiers will become psychiatric casualties. A further common finding from these two research studies was that this phenomenon of soldiers spending months on combat operations only occurred on the battlefields of the 20<sup>th</sup> century. More recently this fact has been compounded by the asymmetrical nature of the most recent wars in Afghanistan and Iraq, where the threat of death or injury is present 24 hours a day and can appear from a 360-degree radius. To illustrate this constant stress to soldiers from immediate danger, one only has to look at the incidences of what is now termed "green-on-blue" attacks. That is Afghani soldiers or border guards turning their weapons on Coalition soldiers, in what would be consider a relatively secure barrack environment, and killing those who had fed, paid, clothed, and mentored them when they joined the security forces. As a result of this threat, Coalition soldiers have been ordered to carry a personal protection weapon with them at all times, thus further raising the stress levels in soldiers who are already under enormous mental pressure. The likelihood of being "murdered when asleep in your own bed" is no longer a phantasy but more of a real and constant threat.

As indicated, combat is intrinsically challenging, as there are so many stressors involved, with the research having found that there are three stages of adaption to combat.[12] The first is that of the "novice soldier" who engaged the enemy in combat for the first time. The novice soldier experienced anxiety about the unknown and during combat struggled to perform routine tasks. After the experience, the novice soldier was relieved to have survived. The second stage of the adaptation was the "experienced soldier" who still had some anxiety about the next combat but was more confident after having survived previous similar situations. During combat, the experienced soldier responded calmly and concentrated on effectively carrying out all the assigned tasks/orders. After the combat, the experienced soldier had high levels of stress when remembering the risks undertaken. The final stage was the "overstressed soldier" who prior to combat experienced high anxiety and was apprehensive about the risks involved. During combat, the overstressed soldier had difficulty performing allocated tasks/orders. After the combat, the overstressed soldier felt sustained anxiety and could not keep from thinking about the experiences just endured.

**Figure 1**

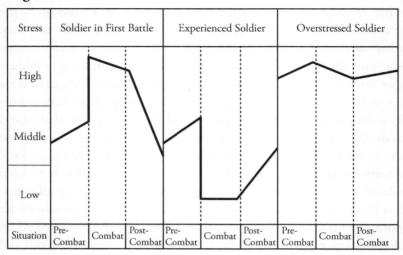

*Figure 1*. Soldiers' combat adaptation stages. Figure 1 was created by the author and it is designed to visually display the combat adaption stages that soldiers experience during combat operations.

All the research findings stressed that combat was the most frightening event soldiers could experience in their lives as they felt an overwhelming sense of fear, anger, and anxiety.[13] However, of all the physiological and psychological effects that soldiers experienced during combat, the single most traumatic event was the act of killing an enemy combatant. Soldiers felt that the act of identifying another human being, making the decision to kill that human being, carrying out the act, and watching that human being die was the most traumatic event they experienced during combat. In this regard, the research by Grossman and Siddle (2010) identified that there were five main stages a soldier experienced in response to killing an enemy combatant.

First the act of killing was identified and the natural instinct not to kill another human being was overridden during the soldier's countless hours of training, which was designed to sanitise the soldier's feelings toward killing the enemy in combat. The training conditioned the soldier to killing instinctively without thinking. However, despite this, the novice soldier continued to be concerned about their ability to carry out this duty during combat. The second stage was the actual killing of the enemy, which was reported to be an instinctive reflex that required no conscious thought. The soldier that killed in combat then entered the third stage of response, which was an increase in adrenaline that produced an increased feeling of euphoria and excitement. Then once the adrenaline rush receded, the fourth stage was a profound remorse for having killed another human being, with nausea and vomiting being common reactions. In this remorse, the soldier contemplated who he may have killed and what the results of that action were. The final stage of the killing response was the process of rationalisation, where the soldier accepted that there was no other choice but to kill the enemy soldier.[14]

Zappf, Dormann, and Frese (2013) defined combat and operational stress behaviour as the generic term for the full spectrum of combat and operational stress behaviours covering a range of reactions from adaptive to maladaptive. Many reactions appear to be the symptoms of mental illness, such as panic anxiety, depression or hallucinations, but these are only transient reactions to the traumatic stress of combat and the cumulative stresses of military operations. Also the distinctions between adaptive stress reactions, misconduct stress behaviours, and combat operational stress reactions are not always apparent. The research by Tanielian (2010) further identified that it was common for these stress reactions to persist or arise long after the exposure to distressing combat experiences. Figure 2 provides a listing of typical adaptive and maladaptive stress behaviours of soldiers in combat.

The process where the human body responds to extended periods of exposure to stress is known as "general adaptive syndrome." This is where after the initial fight-or-flight reaction, the body becomes more resistant to combat stress in an attempt to lessen the sympathetic nervous responses and return to homeostasis.[15] During this period, the physiological and psychological symptoms of combat stress reaction will be drastically reduced as the body attempts to manage the additional stress. Catecholamine hormones, such as adrenaline or noradrenaline, will facilitate

**Figure 2**

| STRESS BEHAVIOURS IN COMBAT | | |
|---|---|---|
| **ADAPTIVE STRESS REACTIONS** | **COMBAT STRESS REACTIONS** | **BEHAVIOURAL STRESS REACTIONS** |
| Courage | Anger/Rage/Irritability | Alcohol/Drug Abuse |
| Esprit de Corps | Anxiety/Hyper-alertness | Combat Refusal |
| Heroism | Apathy/Immobility | Desertion/AWOL |
| Mental Resilience | Carelessness/Inattention | Indiscipline/Recklessness |
| Mission Focus | Delusions/Erratic Outbursts | Killing Non-combatants |
| Morale | Depression/Apathy | Killing Prisoners |
| Physical Endurance | Fear/Terror/Panic | Looting/Pillage/Rape |
| Religious Beliefs | Guilt/Grief/ Self-doubt | Malingering/Negligence |
| Self-Sacrifice | Memory/Skills Loss | Self-inflicted wounds |
| Unit Cohesion | Vision/Hearing Impairment | Torture/Brutality |

| LONG-TERM REACTIONS |
|---|
| Alcohol/Drug Misuse/Indiscipline |
| Depression/Anxiety/Intrusive Memories |
| Difficulty with Social Relationships |
| Guilt/Flashbacks |
| Insomnia/Startled Responses |
| Withdrawal/Alienation/Social Isolation |

*Figure 2*. Stress behaviours in combat. Figure 2 depicts the stress behaviours that soldiers experience in combat. These are divided into the categories of combat, adaptive, and behavioural stress reactions, and the long-term reactions to combat stress are depicted.

immediate physical reactions associated with the preparation for violent muscular action. The problem arises during extended combat operations where the body is kept from homeostasis, thereby depleting its resources and rendering the soldier unable to function normally. This causes the third stage of general adaptive syndrome, which is exhaustion. In this exhaustion phase, the reactions of the sympathetic nervous system to additional stress are markedly sensitised as fight-or-flight symptoms return. Should the body remain in this state of stress for an extended period of time, much more severe combat stress reactions will appear, which will commonly be cardiovascular and digestive degeneration that can permanently damage the body. Although the fight-or-flight response normally ends with the removal of the threat, in the recent wars in Afghanistan and Iraq, soldiers remain in constant mortal danger due to the asymmetric nature of a battlefield where they can never fully relax their guard.

Historically attempts to categorise combat stress reactions in soldiers has laboured under several difficulties. The first is that the medical labelling of combat stress reactions has always carried a burden of stigma, thus discouraging those suffering from this stress to seek medical assistance. The second difficulty is that despite all the physiological and psychological research findings for combat stress reactions, these have failed to fully explain symptoms or predict their outcomes. Finally, current classifications describing combat stress reactions have failed to draw a distinction between normal, reversible, and irreversible repercussions to this stress that has exceeded the adaptive capabilities of human beings.[16] It is hoped that additional research will determine a stress injury concept of combat stress reactions that will reduce the stigma of such injuries and promote a broader understanding of how stress can damage the mind.

As the war in Afghanistan now surpasses even the length of the war in Vietnam, infantry soldiers have been exposed to ever-longer ground combat operations. This fact has been compounded by multiple deployments, with some infantry units deploying three to four times to the wars in Afghanistan and/or Iraq over a five to six-year period. Then the military has lengthened the deployments from 12-15 months in the case of the U.S. Army, and from 8-12 months in the case of U.S. Marines.

The Pentagon then reintroduced their "stop-loss policy," which prevented service personnel who had fully completed their term of military engagement from leaving the service as they are deemed to be filling an essential and/or specialist post that could not be otherwise filled.[17] Finally, after returning from a 15-month operational deployment, the Pentagon stipulated that Army units were only entitled to a three-month period back in the U.S. before they were eligible for redeployment back on operations in either Afghanistan or Iraq for another 15-month tour. This resulted in soldiers being repeatedly exposed to high-intensity combat with insufficient time at home to rest and heal before redeploying.

These factors were further exasperated during the height of the Iraq insurgency from 2004-2007, when Army units who were redeploying from Iraq back to the U.S., having completing their 15 months of combat operations, were stopped mid-stream and re-assigned back to operations as the military commanders deemed that the tactical situation had deteriorated so badly that they could not be sparred. In some cases, this meant that the units' advanced elements had already returned to the U.S. and had been reunited with their families only to be told that they had to immediately return to Iraq to rejoin the remainder of their units. These emergency extensions of infantry units' operational deployments were for a further three months, meaning that the total deployment time for these Army units was 18 months. Therefore, the already extreme combat stress that the infantry soldiers had endured was then combined with an unexpected extension of their combat deployments, thus placing enormous psychological pressure on soldiers and their families.

However, when considering these facts, another essential part of the equation is that even though infantry soldiers were under this constant stress of "combat deployment followed by combat deployment," they were surviving these wars in greater numbers than previous conflicts. The fact is that with the major advances in battlefield (trauma) medicine and evacuation procedures, lives were being saved at an increasing rate. The statistics illustrate this fact, as during World War II, there were 38 deaths for every 100 wounded, and by the time of the war in Vietnam, this ratio had dropped to 28 deaths per 100 wounded.[18] Warfare in the recent wars in Afghanistan and Iraq have produced fundamental changes in how the Coalition forces operate by improving the health care provided on the battlefield, and due to these enhancements, the current ratio in the wars in Afghanistan and Iraq is six deaths for every 100 wounded.[19] Improved evacuation procedures have streamlined the movement of wounded soldiers from the battlefield to medical units in theatre, significantly increasing survival rates. The point is that increasingly, infantry soldiers survive one battlefield only to face another. This is eloquently expressed by King (2013), who identified that the legacy of the wars in Afghanistan and Iraq is not found in the war cemeteries but in the orthopaedic and neurology wards of our hospitals.

Therefore, soldiers are surviving both the physiological and psychological attacks on the bodies and minds in increasing numbers. A physically injured soldier requires time to heal and move on with their lives, whether it is to return to active duty, if deemed medically fit, or to transition back to civilian life. A mentally injured soldier suffering from combat-related stress injuries finds that they are just as real and debilitating as any physical injury. The evidence illustrates that it is easier to fix a broken bone than it is to repair a damaged psyche, and this fact is complicated by some combat-stress disorders, such as PTSD, not manifesting themselves immediately.[20] This incidence of combat-stress-related illness continued to rise as more and more soldiers were exposed to repeated and often extended combat deployments. The research findings announced by the then U.S. Army Chief of Staff General Peter J. Schoomaker in 2007 confirmed that soldiers who had deployed twice to either Afghanistan or Iraq showed a better than 50% increase in the incidence of combat-related stress. However, this statistic did not include the 144,000 soldiers who had deployed three times to Afghanistan or Iraq, or the 73,000 who had deployed four times.[21]

Watson and Gardiner (2013) found that research conducted after other military conflicts indicated that deployment stressors and increased exposure to combat resulted in considerable risks of mental health problems. The post-deployment surveys further support the findings of Watson and Gardiner and indicate that 32% of Navy marines, 39% of Army soldiers, and 51% of Army National Guardsmen suffer from some form of stress-related illness.²² These surveys have found that Army Reserve and Army National Guardsmen suffer a disproportionately higher rate of combat stress and related mental health issues in comparison to active duty soldiers. Other studies have shown that more that 50% of soldiers who needed treatment for combat-related stress issues were not willing, or were afraid, to seek medical treatment as the stigma of mental illness on their medical records would severely handicap, if not terminate, their military career.

As regards U.K. military forces, it has been engaged in a prolonged combat missions in Afghanistan and Iraq, where it has been involved in challenging military operations, while conducting counter-insurgency operations. This has resulted in an extended period of troop deployment and a greater number of casualties than had initially been estimated. During this extended period of deployment, the intensity and scope of the conflicts increased, especially in Helmand province where British soldiers faced a violent and protracted insurgency, which employed the widespread use of improvised explosive devices and other forms of asymmetric threats such as snipers and suicide bombers. However, in comparison with the U.S findings, the prevalence of symptoms of combat-stress-related illnesses and PTSD were slightly lower with the most common mental disorders being depression and anxiety.

Traumatic Brain Injury (TBI) is characterised by short-term loss of consciousness and/or altered mental state as a result of a head injury from a blast explosion. A prevalence of 15% suffering from TBI was found in several research studies that were conducted by the U.S. during the Iraq war. However, other U.S. studies reported an incidence of from 12 to 23% rising to 40% in soldiers who had been wounded by a blast.²³ However, the U.K. research findings found that prevalence of TBI within British soldiers deployed in a combat role was only 9.5%., once again being lower than the U.S. findings. Initially these differences were explained by the fact that the U.S. forces were engaged in more dangerous duties than British forces, and thus had greater combat exposure. Although this may have explained the initial differences in the statistics, since 2006, the U.S.

and U.K. forces have both been engaged in the same intensity and frequency of combat operations. Another potential impediment to assessing the true prevalence of mental disorder symptoms among British soldiers is the continuing unwillingness among military personnel to declare their symptoms for fear of stigmatisation, potential termination of military service and/or curtailment of promotion prospects.

An insight into the factors that may increase the resilience among U.K. forces has been provided by Jones (2012), who carried out a study into possible mitigating effects of cohesion, morale, and leadership on the risk of developing mental health problems. A sample of 1,431 British soldiers serving in Afghanistan in 2010 participated in the study, which showed that combat exposure was associated with both common mental disorders and PTSD. Of the 1,431 participants, 17.1% were found to be suffering from mental disorder and 2.7% were classified as having PTSD. Greater reported levels of unit cohesion, morale, and sound leadership were all associated with lower levels of mental disorder and PTSD. Although Jones (2012) acknowledged the limitations in assessing cause in a cross-sectional study, there was firm evidence to support the theory that these factors did modulate the effects of combat exposure and mental health symptoms among U.K. personnel. This study thereby provided support to the hypothesis that within the military, which relies on team cohesion, resilience to combat stress can be thought of as a social construct between individuals supporting each other in time of trauma.

As an example, in 2013, the British Ministry of Defence (MoD) recorded 11,934 active duty patients who had been diagnosed with either PTSD or depression, which is a significant proportion of the 177,000 serving personnel. According to the Defence Analytical Services, the MoD department that monitors mental health issues since 2003, some 123 British soldiers have died of suspected or confirmed suicide while still serving in the military, compared with 619 recorded as dying in Afghanistan and Iraq from all causes. They further report that the rate of PTSD cases has also "significantly increased' during 2012-13. As disturbingly, more British soldiers and veterans took their own lives in 2012 than died in combat, with a total of 50 (21 serving soldiers and 29 veterans) committing suicide, while only 44 died in Afghanistan, of which 40 were combat related.

Unlike the majority of the U.S. military, the U.K. forces are required to spend 36 hours undergoing "Third Location Decompression (TLD)" before returning home from an operational deployment. This TLD is a supportive, social, and educational intervention following a prolonged operational deployment that aims to smooth the transition between operations and the home environment. The results suggest that the TLD has had a positive impact in decompressing soldiers and thus reducing the incidence of mental health difficulties, including multiple physical symptoms and PTSD. The U.K. military has also invested in ensuring that soldiers within deployed units can support each other after a traumatic combat event. This "Trauma Risk Management" (TriM) programme has been widely used by the U.K. armed forces since 2007.[24] TriM has been the subject of a number of studies which have shown that it is well received by military personnel, that it is capable of detecting alterations in post-incident mental health, promotes social support, and improves organisational support of the soldier at risk.

The relationship between heart rate and performance has been as much of a mystery as the effects of stress, the human nervous system, and sleep deprivation on infantry soldiers engaged in combat operations. In order to clarify these inconsistencies, Grossman and Christensen (2008) in their research discovered that during combat, as the level of fear/arousal in a soldier increases, various conditions were identified that coincide with specific heart rate levels. They found that there is a zone that exists between 85 and 115 beats per minute (bpm), where the soldier is at the optimal survival and combat effectiveness level. That is the complex motor skills, visual reaction time, and cognitive reaction times are all at their peak. However, it has been shown that at 115bpm, the fine motor skills begin to deteriorate. This linking of specific heart rates with task performance was reinforced by Siddle (2009), and these initial findings have continued to be updated and modified as new information becomes available. This has resulted in later researchers creating what is termed a "Unified Model of Stress and Performance," which utilises a colour code system of "Conditions White, Yellow, Red, Grey, and Black."[25] These heart rates apply only to survival stress or fear-induced heart rate increases as the effects of normal strenuous exercise heart rate increase will not be the same as when fear or survival stress causes the increase.

In conclusion, these conditions have been categorised by Grossman and Siddle (2010) as being: Condition White 60-80bpm (normal resting heart rate), Condition Yellow 80-115bpm (optimal combat effectiveness), Condition Red 115-145bpm (fine and then complex motor skill deterioration), Condition Grey 145-175bpm (cognitive processing deterioration, auditory exclusion, loss of near vision, and loss of depth perception), and Condition Black above 175bpm (irrational fight-or-flight" reaction, catastrophic breakdown of mental, and physical performance). This new research by Grossman and Siddle (2010) has concluded that when the average soldier experiences a stress/adrenaline induced heart rate increase of about 145bpm, there is a significant breakdown in combat effectiveness. However, this was not true of all soldiers as those who had practiced their military skills extensively and who were already combat veterans could continue to perform above 145bpm as they had, what were described by Grossman and Christensen, undergone "stress inoculation" in order to create a more robust "state of mind" within in each soldier. Their research found that there are two issues associated with fight-or-flight stress. The reaction of the body is always automatic as it cannot make the immediate distinction between physiological and psychological threat, and secondly, it is difficult to turn-off. The brain responds to the threats by introducing stress hormones into the body, which makes the pulse quicken, the mouth goes dry, and pupils dilate, while the brain prepares the body for fight-or-flight.

# Chapter Five

## *Stress and PTSD*

The stress of combat is an assault on a soldier's mind and body that affects numerous human sub-systems, with these being the physiological, psychological, neurological, and/or social-emotional. This trauma often leads to lasting psychiatric disorders, including anxiety that will not abate, depression that will not fade, and psychosomatic injuries that will not heal.[1] The multiple conditions that populate the broad term "Post-traumatic Stress Disorder" (PTSD) share the distinction of being negative conditions resulting from trauma. The American Psychiatric Associations, Diagnostic and Statistical Manual (4th Edition), 2000 defines PTSD as a condition that results from experiencing or witnessing life-threatening events that are beyond the individual's coping capacity. This official definition stipulates that for an individual to be diagnosed with PTSD they must:

a. Have experienced a traumatic event or series of events.
b. Repeatedly re-live or re-experience the trauma in some form, which includes flashbacks, intrusive memories, and/or nightmares.
c. Experience sleep disturbances rage, irritability, startle responses, lack of concentration and/or hyper-vigilance.
d. Experience a numbing of emotions, a difficultly in remembering the event, and an increasing tendency to avoid people, places, and/or locations that arouse memories of the trauma.

The stress of PTSD describes the remaining strain on the mind and body system caused by the original catastrophic stressor, as the original trauma has not been relegated to the past and so it is still a significant influence on the individual's behaviour. However, the symptoms of PTSD vary from one soldier to another, as the psychological make-up of each person differs.[2] This difference means that one person will be able to manage a catastrophic stressful event while another will develop PTSD. Before a traumatic experience is recognised as a threat, the person must screen it through their cognitive and emotional process within their minds. It is this individual difference in the appraisal process that produces different traumatic thresholds, making some people more susceptible to developing the clinical symptoms of PTSD.

Although post-traumatic symptoms develop as a result of traumatic combat stressors, PTSD is, by definition, a delayed reaction to that combat experience. Symptoms may emerge one, two, or even twenty or more years later. These symptoms of combat tend to emerge after combat duty, as it is only after the soldier returns to the relative safety of home that they have the opportunity to realise the true extent of the horrors they experienced. Among career military personnel, symptoms of combat trauma may not emerge until after retirement or medical discharge, as being in a military environment provides a support network.[3] It is when soldiers leave the military that they lose that structure and sense of belonging, leading to the emergence of the symptoms.

The unique feature of PTSD is the re-experiencing of the traumatic experiences (re-experiencing stage), followed by attempts to bury the memories of the trauma and the feelings associated with the trauma (the numbing stage). This PTSD cycle sets PTSD apart from all other official psychiatric disorders.[4] The cycle is repeated in this sequence over and over with the two parts of the cycle having no particular time frame. Those who are in the re-experiencing stage suffer from nearly constant intrusive thoughts, flashbacks, nightmares, anxiety or panic attacks and usually find it almost impossible to function. The research findings have shown that people may stay in the "numbing stage" for hours, weeks, or even years. In this stage, although the individual is unhappy, it is possible to be emotionally numb and still functioning even at a minimal level. Just as the body can be traumatised, so can the psych. On this psychological level, trauma refers to the wounding of the soldier's emotions, spirit, will to live, dignity, and sense of security. This assault on the soldier's psyche can be so pervasive that the normal ways of handling stress in the past are now inadequate.

As an example, in combat, learning to duck when being fired upon by the enemy is vital for battlefield survival. However, in civilian life, ducking for cover when a car backfires is inappropriate. These behaviours are called contingency and rule-governed behaviours, as they are produced in response to a very specific set of circumstances. Therefore, the essential hallmark of PTSD is the development of these characteristic symptoms following the soldier being exposed to an extreme traumatic stressor involving direct personal experience of an event that threatened death or serious injury. As if this was not enough, the self-rebuke of the sufferer aggravates the condition with dysfunctional moods leading to negative thoughts that increase the symptoms.[5]

The experience of combat shocks the soldier's body, emotions and view of the world, and even more disturbingly, it calls into question the soldier's basic beliefs about themselves, human nature, and the nature of the world. That is soldiers who have endured combat trauma are forced to reconsider three things about themselves and the world: that they are personally invulnerable, that the world is orderly and meaningful, and that they are good and strong people. As a result, some veterans suffer from a profound despair and come to believe that life is meaningless. Therefore, combat duty, whether it involves engaging in ground combat, caring for the wounded, or performing logistic or intelligence assignments, also involves physical stresses that can cause lifelong psychological as well as physiological consequences.

When using strict definitions of PTSD, depression and other mental illnesses, recent research studies have found a significant increase in mental disorders after duty in Afghanistan and Iraq. The recent findings found that 11-17% of returning soldiers were at risk of PTSD or other forms of combat stress, with higher rates being found among those returning from Iraq. Unfortunately today, even though PTSD was officially recognised by the American Psychiatric Association in 1980, not every mental health professional is familiar with it or other combat-related traumas. To compound this fact the diagnosis of combat-related stress reactions can be a demanding task, as it coexists with a range of other psychological problems including paranoia, schizophrenia, and alcoholism. Another reason why we do not accurately know how many soldiers and veterans suffer from PTSD is the fact that many either deny their own symptoms or actively hide the fact.[6] This is especially prevalent if they remain in the military where any recorded "mental health problems" on a soldier's medical records will severely curtail their future promotion and/or redeployment prospects, if not their entire military career.

In addition to these traumatic reactions, combat duty can trigger episodes of manic-depression, paranoia, and other forms of illness, especially if there is genetically based family history of such problems. They can also trigger previously dormant medical problems or worsen existing problems. The research illustrates that many illnesses are stress related, including allergies, heart conditions, skin problems, asthma and bronchitis, and urinary or bladder problems. The repeated trauma and unending stress of a combat deployment breaks down the human immune system, leaving the soldier more vulnerable to illness. Although PTSD and depression are commonly viewed as emotional problems, they also have a strong physiological component, with recent studies finding that survivors of military combat and other traumas suffer more from physical health problems than people who have never been traumatised. However, the traumatic reactions described here are normal reactions to an abnormal amount of stress, not necessarily signs of insanity or severe mental illness.[7] The few soldiers who do not develop some form of stress reaction to combat at some point in their lives are often sociopaths with little conscience or capability to care about others.

In the 1970s, research on combat stress began to switch away from World War II veterans to the more recent veterans of the Vietnam conflict. Initially, the medical personnel in Vietnam defined that stress was a reaction to combat, and this was later called Post-Traumatic Stress Disorder (PTSD), with this definition resulting from an individual's exposure to combat or combat-related conditions.[8] In 1980, the APA's *Diagnostic and Statistical Manual* (DSM) recognised PTSD and in the 4th edition the APA determined that for PTSD to be present and to be a correct diagnosis, two conditions had to be present (APA, 1994). First, the person experienced, witnessed, or was confronted with an event or events that involved actual or threatened death or serious injury, or a threat to the physical integrity of others. Second, the person's response involved intense fear, helplessness or horror (APA, 1994). In 2007, the U.S. Joint Operational Analysis Centre defined PTSD as an individual having symptoms that resulted in a clinically significant impairment in social and occupational functions. Specifically this was if Acute PTSD, symptoms lasted less than 3 months; Chronic PTSD, symptoms lasted more than 3 months; or Delayed-onset PTSD, initial symptoms manifesting more than 6 months after the traumatic event (Kettell, Moiser, Orthner, and Schymanski, 2009).

During the research into PTSD, a number of changes in memory functioning have been identified that are comparable with studies of depressed patients. These tend to show a bias toward enhanced recall of the trauma-related incident and difficulties in retrieving memories of specific incidents. In some studies, high levels of emotion are associated with the more vivid and long-lasting memories, while in others, they are associated with memories that are vague, lacking in detail and error prone. The DSM-IV (American Psychiatric Association, 2000) describes PTSD as characterised by high-frequency, intrusive memories and by amnesia for the details of the event. The other notable feature of memory in PTSD is the experiences of "flashbacks" to the trauma, which include vivid visual images. Lemyre and Tessier (2013) found that "flashbacks," either on their own or in combination with other images and thoughts, were reported as the most frequent intrusive cognition by 43% of their PTSD patients, by 9% of the depressed patients, and not by other patients. These findings support the claim that "flashbacks" are a distinctive feature of PTSD.

Pettera, Johnson, and Zimmer (2009) defined "dissociation" as any kind of temporary breakdown in what we think of as the relatively continuous, interrelated process of viewing the world around us, remembering the past, or having a single identity that links our past with the future. Mild dissociative reactions are common under stress with the most common symptoms being emotional numbing, de-realisation, de-personalisation, and "out-of-body" experiences.[9] These were related to the severity of the trauma, fear of death, and/or a feeling of helplessness. In contrast to fight-or-flight reactions, in which the heart rate significantly increases, dissociation has been linked with a decrease in heart rate.

Consistently, PTSD research has found that a general increase in negative beliefs about self, others, and the world has been found in trauma victims with PTSD compared to victims not suffering from PTSD. Higher levels of anger with others, also reported by PTSD patients, is consistent with the loss of belief in the good intentions of others. There is now extensive evidence that attempts by PTSD patients to suppress unwanted thoughts are usually ineffective, as afterwards the thoughts return more strongly. Other research has confirmed the importance of the individual's beliefs about themselves as PTSD is associated with the belief that trauma has brought about a negative and permanent change in them and their circumstances.[10] These negative beliefs do not have to occur during the trauma itself and may represent the outcome of a separate appraisal process that only begins after the danger has passed.

More recently, research studies have found that there are other methods that can assist the individual soldier in avoiding PTSD, and this is Eye Movement Desensitisation and Reprocessing (EMDR). This is an innovative therapeutic treatment discovered by Dr. Francine Shapiro, San Diego, U.S.A. in 1987, and it has been so successful that over 50,000 practitioners worldwide are using it today.[11] As a result of this treatment by Dr. Shapiro, it was found that a specific traumatic memory or disturbing situation may be resolved in as few as one to three sessions. Grossman and Christensen (2008) in their own research findings recommend such techniques as EMDR, as it could be used to confront and defuse the individual's trauma.

However, not all soldiers magnify the enemy's capabilities, as many see the enemy as being like themselves, simply soldiers facing the stress associated with having to take other soldiers' lives. In this regard, Grossman (2009) claimed that the burden of killing was so great that in many circumstances, soldiers in combat would die before they could overcome their intense resistance to killing another human being. To reinforce this view, Gabriel (2010) sights a survey of wounded combat veterans in the European theatre during World War II where of 277 soldiers interviewed, 65% of the soldiers admitted having had at least one experience in combat in which they were unable to perform adequately due to intense fear. However, Sheppard (2008) identified that fear could be mitigated through certain factors, but that there was no single absolute way to reduce fear, and so he advocated that soldiers needed a variety of tools to deal with fear as they each react individually to combat situations. Nye (2009) stipulated that if military leaders are to understand how fear affects their units' effectiveness, they cannot lead and fight relying solely on rigid precepts from manuals and procedures. They need to take measures to integrate the effects of fear into a unit's preparations for combat operations.

Solomon, Shklar, and Mikulincer (2013) recently published their 20-year longitudinal evaluation research study report into the front-line treatment of combat stress reaction. The purpose of the study was to evaluate the long-term (20-year) effectiveness of front-line treatment provided to combat stress reaction casualties. A longitudinal quasi-experimental design was employed. The participants were Israeli Defence Force (IDF) combat stress reaction casualties from the 1982 Lebanon War who received front-line treatment (n=79), comparable combat stress reaction casualties who did not receive front-line treatment (n=156), and matched soldiers who did not experience combat stress reaction (n=194). The participants were asked which of the front-line treatment principles (proximity, immediacy, expectancy) were applied in their treatment, whether or not they returned to their unit after front-line treatment, and if so, whether they returned before or after they felt completely recovered. Outcome assessments included measures of post-traumatic and psychiatric symptoms and of social functioning.

The results from the study proved that 20 years later, war traumatised soldiers who received front-line treatment had lower rates of post-traumatic and psychiatric symptoms, experienced less loneliness, and reported better social functioning than similar traumatised soldiers who did not receive front-line treatment. This treatment consisted of rest and comfort, as well as psychotherapy methods such as explanation, persuasion, and suggestion, aided by the physical methods of baths and massage, but rest of the mind and body was seen as being essential in all cases.[12] In addition, a cumulative effect of application of front-line treatment principles was documented and found that the more principles that were applied, the stronger the positive effect on psychiatric outcomes. The conclusions of the 20-year study were that front-line treatment was associated with improved outcomes even two decades after application.[13] However, there was now a requirement for an equivalent study to be conducted concerning this treatment's effectiveness for non-military (police and fire service) personnel.

As already discussed, fear triggers many split-second changes in the body in order to defend against danger or avoid it, and this fight-or-flight response was a normal reaction designed to protect the individual from harm. However, those individuals who suffer from PTSD may feel stressed or frightened even when there was no longer any danger. As a result, scientists are currently focusing on the genes that play a role in creating fear memories. In this regard, Orb, Eisenhauer and Wynaden (2012) have published their research study findings, which indicate that the understanding of how fear memories are created would refine or find new interventions for reducing the symptoms of PTSD. During their research, they identified Stathmin, which is a protein needed to form fear memories, and Gastin-Releasing Peptide (GRP), which is a signalling chemical released by the brain during emotional or stressful events. They also found a version of the 5-HTTLPR gene, which controls levels of serotonin, a chemical in the brain that fuels the fear response.

Orb et al. (2012) found that individual differences in these genes set the stage for PTSD without causing the symptoms. They also found that environmental factors, personality, social factors and/or cognitive factors influenced how individuals reacted to fear, stress and/or trauma. As critically, their logical deduction from these findings was that more research may show what combinations of these factors could be used to predict who will develop PTSD following a traumatic event. This rapid progress in research on the mental and psychological foundations of PTSD has led scientists to focus on prevention, rather than cure, as a realistic and important goal.

Following on from this research, Dohrenwend (2013) and his colleagues at the New York State Psychiatric Institute confirmed that traumatic experiences during combat predicted the onset of PTSD. However, more critically, the findings showed that other factors such as pre-war psychological vulnerabilities were equally important for predicting the onset of the disorder. Data from a sub-sample of 260 male veterans from the National Vietnam Veterans Readjustment Study were examined. Dohrenwend focused on the roles of three primary factors: severity of combat exposure (life-threatening experiences or traumatic events during combat), pre-war vulnerabilities (childhood physical abuse, family history of substance abuse) and their involvement in harming civilians or children during the war. The data indicated that stressful combat exposure was necessary for the onset of PTSD but that combat exposure alone was not sufficient to cause the PTSD syndrome.[14] Among the factors that were found to contribute to the onset of PTSD were childhood experiences of physical abuse or a pre-Vietnam war psychiatric disorder other than PTSD.

Age also played an important role as the men who were younger than 25 when they entered the war were seven times more likely to develop PTSD compared to the older men. Dohrenwend (2013) also found that soldiers who inflicted harm on civilians or prisoners of war were much more likely to develop PTSD. The combined data from these three primary factors: combat exposure, pre-war vulnerability, and involvement in harming civilians or prisoners revealed that those veterans who had experienced all three factors had a 97% likelihood of suffering from the onset of PTSD syndrome.[15] Therefore, the findings from this research have important implications for future policies aimed at preventing cases of combat-related PTSD, as with this new knowledge soldiers suffering from these three factors should be identified and de-selected from service in combat operations. So, given the seemingly potent interaction between combat exposure and pre-combat vulnerabilities, these results emphasis the need to keep the most vulnerable soldiers out of the most severe combat situations.

The research indicates that PTSD is associated with a wide range of disturbances to the psychological processes including attention-deficit, memory-loss/impairment, cognitive-affective reactions, coping strategies, and beliefs. It appears that what is unique to PTSD, compared to other psychological disorders, is the inconsistent and unusual memory phenomenon centred on the event itself. It is clear that the emotions involved in PTSD are not by any means restricted to fear, helplessness, and horror, or to what was actually experienced at the time of the trauma. Beliefs to are not restricted to those concerning the event but may involve much more general aspects of the person, their social world, and their future. Therefore, theories of PTSD need to incorporate explanations of process that are specific to PTSD as well as process that are relatively automatic (helplessness and dissociation) or relatively strategic, such as the choice of coping strategy.[16]

As regards the British Army, a recent research study by Mulligan, Jones, and Woodhead (2010) assessed the mental health, which included the PTSD rates, of British forces deployed in Iraq between December 2008 and June 2009. The target sample size was 611 personnel, which represented about 15% of the deployed force. Of the participants, 20.5% were diagnosed with PTSD, and 3.4% were assessed as having possible PTSD. The findings validated that there was a higher risk of psychological distress associated with younger age, female gender, weaker unit cohesion, poor leadership, and non-receipt of a pre-deployment stress brief. An increased incidence of reporting PTSD symptoms was associated with junior rank, having felt in danger of being killed, and a higher rate of exposure to combat stressors. Those personnel who reported sick for any reason were significantly more likely to report symptoms of PTSD than those who had never reported sick.

Significantly, the report identified that of those 26% who reported having experienced a significant stressful combat experience, only 40% reported having received any assistance. This assistance was most commonly received from a comrade, 45%; the chain of command, 24%; chaplains, 18%; and medical professionals, 13%. The findings also found that soldiers serving in the most forward and vulnerable areas to enemy attack significantly increased the risk factor for PTSD. Of significance, the study participants who received a pre-deployment brief reported significantly better mental health than those that did not receive the briefing. A similar finding was demonstrated by the U.S. Army Health Advisory Team, who also found that those who received standardised pre-deployment educational packages had better mental health than those that did not have the benefit of the briefing. This positive influence of the pre-deployment briefings to soldiers on the likely effects that they will experience from combat stress have also become more refined and focused as the wars have progressed and lessons on the prevention of PTSD have been incorporated.[17]

During the 20th century, many definitions of the word "stress" have been put forward, but none have encompassed all the usages of the term – even in the scientific community. This is understandable, as stress is not an agreed concept as it is a concept of interacting variables that included the brain, the body, and the complexities of the world at large. Stress was described by Foa and Riggs (1993) as a transition between each individual's unique biology and their environment while being subjected to a multitude of psychological and social processes. Based on his findings, Selye (1956) came to the conclusion that stress was a biological process of the human body to any challenge, whether external or internal. In order to differentiate the process of stress as a reaction to a challenge, he conceived the term "stressor" for the instrument that created the stress response. Therefore, the stressor is the challenge, and stress is the process by which any organism adapts to the stressor. Selye termed this predictable pattern of biological response to stressors of all kinds the general adoption syndrome.

After discovering the biological stressor response (general adaptation syndrome), Selye went on to study how it evolved and altered over time. He found that the general adaption syndrome was a process that took time to develop in response to a stressor, consumed energy, and could not be sustained indefinitely. Then Selye divided the time course for the general adaption syndrome into three phases. Initially there was the "alarm" phase, where the organism mobilised its resources to respond to the challenge. In this phase, initially its performance worsens under the impact of the stressor, but then the adaptive changes occur and the organism's performance improves. This is when the second phase of "resistance" to the negative effects of the stressor occurs. Then the final and third phase is "exhaustion," where the adaptive resistance to the stressor is lost and a period of recovery may be required before another adaptive response can be mounted to the same stressor. Selye (1956) further identified that depending on the nature of the particular stressor and the biological system that responded to it, the three phases of adaption may be short or long, with the time dimension representing adaptive alterations that occur over minutes, days, or months.[18] To relate these findings to this study, the response of the soldier in a kill-or-be-killed firefight with enemy combatants in close-quarter ground combat over minutes would have the same effect as a year-long operational deployment.

The responses to stress that are most characteristic of human beings are those mediated by conscious decision-making and effort. This in turn accounts for much of the variation in adaptive styles amongst individuals, including individual susceptibilities and vulnerabilities to stress. These conscious components of coping with stress are the ones most responsive to modification through education, training and leadership in military units. Lazarus (1999) defined coping as constantly cognitive and behavioural endeavour in order to manage specific external and/or internal demands that are assessed as exceeding the resources of the person. He also felt that the goal of coping was not only problem solving, but also maintaining one's human emotions while managing self-esteem, and keeping a positive outlook in the most difficult of situations.[19] Therefore, the soldier's aim in coping with stress is not to merely survive the experience but to eclipse it through courage and creativity.

Soldiers during combat deployments have been found to be extremely innovative in their development of coping strategies relying heavily on contact made with loved ones at home through letters and e-mails, thereby assisting in them making sense of their battlefield experiences. Also, their relationships that have been forged in battle with comrades in many cases will prove to be the most enduring of all their life experiences. Many soldiers also experience a re-birth of their religious faith that can neutralise some of the toxic effects of combat stress. The first step in the process of a soldier coping with stress is the correct appraisal of the perceived enemy threat. It has long been established in cognitive psychology that conscious appraisal is the crucial determinant for an individual's behavioural and emotional responses to stressors.[20] This is why individual differences in appraisal of stressful situations accounts for how individuals adapt differently to the same stressor.

Therefore, in order to build resilience in soldiers, their appraisal of operational stressors needs to be modified through education, training, and leadership. On the other hand, it is also critical for the military to identify soldiers with the highest risk of adverse stress reactions, as these will be the most vulnerable to a combat environment.[21] Effective military leaders can promote adaptation to extreme stress in their subordinates, and Grossman (1995) likened this to the leader being a "well of fortitude" into which subordinates would continuously dip in order to restore their own flagging courage.

As mentioned earlier, each soldier faces potential traumatic stressors with a different set of pre-dispositions that are activated by a traumatic event. Whether or not the stressors, or series of stressors, will trigger PTSD depends not only on its severity but also upon its dispositional factors at the time of the experience, the environmental factors, and the interaction with the soldiers pre-disposing factors. As an example, about 25% of soldiers who are exposed to traumatic threats to life or physical injury as a result of combat develop PTSD, which is a much higher percentage than the 10% for all other potential types of trauma.[22] In 2005, the U.S. National Center for PTSD reported that some 30% of combat veterans suffer from PTSD at some point in their lives, a phenomenon that has been explained as a result of killing another human being. These findings were confirmed by Gabriel (2010), who found when examining Afghanistan and Iraq war veterans that the killing of another human being was the most pervasive and traumatic experience of war.

Understandably, physical combat is a significant traumatic stressor as it exposes the soldier to situations that involve killing, as well as the constant possibility of being killed. When investigating the maintained high levels of anxiety in soldiers suffering from PTSD, it needs to be remembered that military action does not occur in a vacuum but within a network of complicated cultural interactions.[23] Also, PTSD is but one of several stressors and traumas and once exposed, the rest of the soldier's continuity is shattered. There may be the loss of coping skills, networks, and values, with resiliency and recovery occurring quickly or never. These psychological disorders resulting from war include brain injury and loss of limbs or body function. Lemyre and Tessier (2013) refer to traumatic brain injury from the concussive force of improvised explosive devices as "the signature wound" of the Afghanistan and Iraq wars.

Therefore, a review of the existing epidemiological research findings reminds us that adaptation to combat and operational experiences is an unfolding dynamic, as little is known about the different "trajectories" of responses to war stressors.[24] Unfortunately, the research to date has been primarily cross-sectional, which restrains causal inference and fails to provide useful primary and secondary prevention information. However, it was found that most soldiers recover due to their resourcefulness with the high rate of enduring resilience being due to education, training, leadership, cohesion, and pride. The studies to date suggest that 18-20% (Siddle, 2009) of soldiers who have served in combat have probable PTSD following deployment, with this prevalence not diminishing in time. Consistent with the wealth of prior research, there is a defined association between the cumulative burdens that soldiers endure from repeated combat and operational stressors, and probable PTSD.

In conclusion, PTSD was not defined as a health condition before 1980, at which time the American Psychiatric Association officially included PTSD in its diagnostic guidebook and established explicit diagnostic criteria. Although there has been academic and medical acknowledgement that post-combat trauma is as a debilitating condition, there has been at best only a grudging acceptance of this by the military authorities. So, the conceptual framework for this study will be based on fulfilling an integrated function between highlighting theories that offer explanations of the issues under investigation and providing a platform within which strategies for the research design can be determined and fieldwork undertaken. It will give coherence to this research by providing traceable connections between theoretical perspectives, research strategy and design, fieldwork, and the conceptual significance of the evidence.

# CHAPTER SIX

# *Military Education and Training*

Bamberger and Hasgell (1995) addressed the issue of the military as a "total institution" and highlighted the instructor's role in the training of infantry soldiers. However, the Army, as the largest part of the "total institution," has never been examined relative to its provision of pre-combat education and leadership training for infantry soldiers who were about to deploy on combat operations. Zurcher (2009) found that human beings develop a mental process that assisted them in making decisions that resulted in responses to a variety of social stimuli with this process being constructed as they learn social customs, values, and beliefs. Grossman (2009) identified that the killing of another human being was considered an unnatural act in the civilian environment. Grossman further explained that the reverse was true in the military, but especially in the infantry, where the defined aim of the infantry was to close with and kill or capture the enemy in any climate, weather, or terrain.[1]

During World War II, U.S. Army Brigadier General S.L.A. Marshall researched how individual soldiers behaved in combat by interviewing thousands of soldiers in more than 400 infantry companies immediately after they had been in close contact with German or Japanese troops. Marshall (1947) found that on average, only 15-20% of soldiers actively engaged the enemy and these findings proved to be consistent during the whole time that the soldiers were engaged in active ground combat. However, those that did not fire did not run away and instead often exposed themselves to more danger by rescuing wounded comrades, carrying ammunition, or running messages. The question of why these soldiers did not fire at the enemy, even to protect themselves and/or their comrades, is that human beings have an intense resistance to killing other human beings.[2]

As a result of these findings, armies have been forced to develop sophisticated methods of overcoming soldiers' innate aversion to killing their own species, and this has resulted in a firing rate of 55% in Korea and 90-95% in Vietnam. However, this achievement of higher firing rates by infantry soldiers has come at a price with a sharp increase in the magnitude and frequency of post-traumatic responses among veterans. Some historians, writers, and soldiers have used this disparity to claim that S.L.A. Marshall was wrong, for the average military leader finds it hard to believe that a significant number of soldiers will not do their duty in combat by actively engaging the enemy.[3] However, those harbouring such doubts do not give credit to the revolutionary measures that have been introduced into infantry training over the past century.

Since World War II, a new epoch has emerged that has artfully created a new era of psychological cohesion in order to have soldiers overcome their innate resistance to killing other human beings. These methods have included operant conditioning, desensitisation, and denial defence mechanisms. Holmes (1985) in his research traced the introduction of the glorification of killing the enemy and found that it was not present during World War I, was rare in World War II, increasingly present in Korea, and completely institutionalised in Vietnam.[4] This glorification of killing desensitised the soldiers to the enemy and at the same time indoctrinated them into believing that their sole purpose was to kill enemy combatants.

However, this desensitisation process also masks the conditioning of soldiers, which is the most important part of the training. As an example, gone are the days of the soldier at a field firing range lying on a grassy firing mound engaging a bull's-eye target with his rifle. Instead, the current training technique is for the soldier to stand for hours in a slit trench, carrying full combat equipment, and then engage man-shaped pop-up targets as they appear at various distances to the front of the trench. To further enhance the reality of killing, the man-shaped enemy targets are filled with red paint or dye, thereby giving positive reinforcement to the soldier when the target is hit. The training is not only realistic, but it is also designed to instil the instinctive act of aiming and pulling the trigger when the enemy is sighted, that is this form of training is "conditioned stimulus."[5] Therefore, in this and other training exercises, the modern infantry soldier is conditioned and rehearsed in every aspect of killing on the battlefield. As a result of rehearsing this process so many times, the soldier is able through this conditioning to automatically kill the enemy.

But this ability to increase the firing rates in modern infantry soldiers has come with a hidden cost, as severe psychological trauma arises when military training overrides the natural human instinct not to kill another human being. As an example, in the war in Vietnam, where 90-95% of soldiers fired their weapons at the enemy, some 52% of the 3.1 million military personnel who served in that conflict suffer from PTSD, which is twice as high as in previous wars.[6] This epidemic of PTSD among Vietnam veterans has caused a significant increase in suicides, drug abuse, alcoholism, criminality, domestic abuse, unemployment, and divorce. The most recent research found that the victims of PTSD are almost all veterans who participated in high-intensity ground combat operations. Concerning these PTSD symptoms, the findings show that soldiers who were in non-combat situations in Vietnam were statistically indistinguishable from those that spent their complete enlistment at home in the USA.

In their critical analysis, Grossman and Christensen (2008) found that within the infantry, the killing of other human beings who have been defined as the enemy, without being killed yourself, was the total focus of all training. However, a fact rarely acknowledged by the military was that these interventions were designed to make the individual infantry soldier the "total killing machine," thereby enhancing their own likelihood of survival, while at the same time advancing the units probability of achieving its operational mission. As critically, Bartlett (2009) found that it was essential that when civilians are inducted into the infantry, they were converted from a human set of values and beliefs based on "thou shall not kill" into an infantry set of values and beliefs based on a "kill-or-be-killed" mentality. A fact that was further hidden from the public at large was that, as stated by Cohen (2009), the accepted civilian principles, which exist within all civilised societies, are counter-productive for the training and leadership of infantry soldiers.

In short, the military system was designed to meet the majority of the criteria that were identified in the "total institution" model. Siddle (2008) described how the individual's entire being was initially devoured, then remodelled, and finally totally subverted to this military ethos. Siddle found that the environment of the "total institution" destroyed the individual's individuality and dignity before creating a regimentation that significantly restricted the options for military personnel until they were either discharged or they died in combat. He also highlighted that within the "total institution" there are varying degrees of regimentation, discipline, esprit de corps, and institutional expectations among the various branches of the military.[7]

The undeniable fact is that the military identity is timeless, as the reason for its existence never alters. It was Clausewitz (1832) who in his theory considered that the military as an institution had one primary purpose, and that was to deliver war as an extension of the political will of the nation state. Therefore, he saw the aim of war as being the furtherance of the nation's political aim through the military defeat of the enemy, thereby preventing the enemy from waging any further wars. The character of war has altered dramatically since the end of World War II, and now we are faced with an asymmetrical battlefield where the aim is to remove a nation's will to fight.[8] However, this has made little difference to the role of the infantry soldier, as the very nature of war underpins the organisational identity of the infantry, which remains to close with and kill or capture the enemy in any weather, terrain or climate. Therefore, infantry education and training prepares the recruit solely for war fighting, which is totally immersed in the infantry organisational identity. This identity is based on its primary rules of obligation that are deeply inculcated in its social structure. These are the unwritten codes and laws that underpin the traditions and expected behaviours of every infantry soldier.

Grossman and Christensen's (2008) study findings demonstrate that the values, attitudes, and beliefs of recruits raised in modern British society differ vastly from the expected values, attitudes, and beliefs of the infantry. The "total institution" is a dynamic identity that reshapes and redefines each recruit's individual identity so that they reconstruct a new reality within which they learn to function.[9] Individuals will adapt their social identity to the situation that they find themselves in by adding and removing identities in order to conform with their current environment. The recruits construct a new reality that is their existence within the infantry training centre and adjust their social identity in order to encompass their new infantry identity.

However, it is not surprising that a third of the recruit population were unable to adapt to military life as the military and especially the infantry identity forms a society of its own. These values and beliefs challenge the individual's established civilian beliefs, and in the process create psychological turmoil and cognitive dissonance. The fact is that the military, and particularly the infantry, sit on the edge of the nation's social and cultural identity, as they cannot afford to reflect the values and norms of the wider society. What is important is the realisation that organisations are built on the values and goals that form their identity, and to move away from these will create a weakness in the identity and create conflict within the organisation.[10] The role that an organisation's identity plays in the achievement of its aims cannot be underestimated. These organisational beliefs are based on the organisation's cultural assumptions and so the organisation's identity involves those cultural assumptions that are self-defining for the organisation. Therefore, if these cultural assumptions are eroded, then the organisation loses its organisational identity.

As a result, the infantry identity is fundamental and so the institution within which the infantry soldier is trained has to be strictly maintained in order to achieve its aim. Therefore, it has to be accepted that the "total institution," which are the infantry training centres are necessary to accomplish this organisational aim. The problem is that British society has become more risk adverse, and so the military reflects society even less. This means that the recruit must re-categorise their social identity in order to adopt a new military identity. In this process, the recruit re-establishes the hierarchy of their social categories based upon a sense of belonging to the infantry social group.[11] It is this difference in these identities that forms the basis for the one-third attrition rate in infantry training, as many recruits fail to cross the gap between the two identities.

The military expects the recruit to adapt their civilian cultural values in three areas. These are physical, emotional, and social. The first is physically where the military has identified that physical fitness leads to better fighting efficiency. However, surprisingly it has been found that it is not the lack of physical ability that caused recruits to fail, but rather their inability to psychologically cope with the physical demands of the military. That is the military expects a high degree of physical output at a point where the recruit feels they cannot continue. This is where this generation of recruits lack the "mental discipline" to keep going when as described in the military they are "running-on-empty."[12] That is, when physically exhausted, there needs to be the mental toughness to continue through the physical pain barrier. This ability not only relies on the individual but also upon teamwork and the cohesion within the unit, where each individual encourages each other.

Secondly, recruit failure also indicates a lack of emotional maturity that would allow the individual to make the transition from civilian to soldier. That is the recruit's inability to make the cultural transition and is a result of their perceived loss of prior emotional and social support. This emotional transition period creates psychological stressors and cognitive disassociation as they try to make sense of the totally new situation while also attempting to develop a coping strategy. Thirdly, these opposing identities create unease for the recruit as they attempt to adopt to the hierarchical military organisation within their own social identity. This causes the individual to feel psychological disassociation due to the multiple individual and organisational demands that the military demands.[13]

Therefore, it argued that the military provides a perfect example of the "total institution" that has the potential to be harmful to some recruits when they experience the initial shock of induction into the cloistered military system. It has been further argued that the recruit, upon entering this "total institution," is subject to a change of self-concept, with the recruit after admission not being the same person as prior to admis-

84

sion, as the recruit has adopted an infantry self-concept. Thereby the recruit redefines their social identity within the military organisation as they struggle with the psychological challenges that being a new member brings. Within this Army organisation, this process of induction has a fine line between integration and alienation. It has been found that it is the inability of the recruit to cope with the psychological impact of the cumulative training demands made by the infantry that causes the failures.[14] Therefore, the challenge for the Army is to assist those individuals that have the potential to successfully transit recruit training and achieve a new set of values, attitudes, and beliefs. To achieve this aim, the recruit needs to be provided with a bridge to cross the divide between the social identity of a civilian and that of an infantry soldier.

A current argument is that an individual's pattern of avoidant behaviours and a failure to succeed repeat themselves in adult life, as they lack the psychological and social maturity to achieve success. This question of psychological and social maturity comes into more focus when it is realised that the British Army has noted, reviewed, and refined their recruiting methods in three decades. However, the British schooling system and its approach to discipline and competition have altered dramatically. The conclusion is that the Army needs to reassess if the current generation of recruits have the emotional social maturity, as well as the life-experiences to endure infantry training. A view that is gaining increasing currency is that some recruits may not be able to commence recruit training initially, but instead will require an preliminary period of pre-training and socialisation into the life of an infantry soldier.

The next question is whether it is possible to predict an individual's likelihood of passing the initial infantry recruit training by using various psychological, physiological, and personality indicators. Watson and Gardiner (2013) focused on the relationship between the recruit's antecedent biographical details and their ability to integrate into the infantry. Their results indicated that there were four factors associated with increasing a recruit's likelihood of passing infantry recruit training. These were pre-enlistment participation in demanding outdoor activities, being a solid citizen, participation in group team sports, and the pursuit of intellectually demanding activities. The study identified that there were pre- and post-enlistment patterns of behaviour with the most prominent factor contributing to a recruit failing was an inability to cope with the nature of the "total institution," personal identity crisis, cognitive disassociation, and a poor expectation of military life.[15] These patterns of behaviour were evident pre-enlistment and simply repeated themselves once the recruit joined the Army. Therefore, as a matter of urgency, the ability to predict the likelihood of failure in military training, based upon the personal biographical details gathered upon the recruit pre-enlistment, need to be quantified and implemented in the pre-screening and pre-selection process.

In this regard, certain patterns of behaviour such as the recruit being considered a "soldier citizen" were indicative of training success and low attrition. Then it has been found that those recruits with developed communications skills, who were more personable, and able to develop new friendships within the new military environment, were found to be able to cope with the new environment more successfully. Also if the recruit spent two to five evenings at home per week prior to enlistment, it was found that this also decreased the odds of failure by a half. That is, those recruits who maintained a balance between nights at home and nights out prior to enlistment had a greater chance of success. Next was the fact that attending three or more schools doubled the odds of failure during recruit training.[16] The current level of attrition at the various British Army infantry training centres has proved unacceptable due to the financial and human cost occasioned by an approximately 30% failure rate. As a result, it is recommended that the Army introduces various measures designed to refine and focus the current recruitment and enlistment criteria.

First, the current recruiting process has been identified as providing the potential recruit with an unrealistic expectation of what the infantry training centre curriculum will entail. This idealised image of life in the infantry that is provided to the potential recruit has proved not to be matched by reality. As a result, upon arriving at the infantry training centre, the recruit experiences a large degree of cognitive disassociation

that leads to failure. Therefore, it is essential the potential recruit is provided with an accurate description of what the training will entail and
the physical and mental demands that will be required in order to pass
the training. This must include information about the environment, living conditions, instructional techniques, and the training programme that
the recruits will encounter.[17] The provision of this accurate information
is dependent upon the Army careers officers being issued with amended
guidance so they can portray accurate information to the potential recruit.

Second, the enlistment process is where it is believed that the most impact can be made in reducing the recruit failure rate. This study suggests
that there are two areas where the current intervention strategies can be
improved; these are the enlistment phase and the training phase. The goal
being to achieve minimal training attrition and maximum training success, thus reducing the financial and human cost of failure. As the enlistment phase is immediately followed by the sudden impact of the training
phase, which often overwhelms the recruit, it is recommended that this
transition is conducted in a more graduated approach; that is the recruit
is eased into the new environment and the new training regime that will
be followed during the course of the recruit training. This familiarisation
phase would be over several days and would lead into a two-week pre-
training induction course.[18] This familiarisation would include an introduction to military training through adventure training, team building,
and socialisation skills. Then the goals, values, beliefs, and culture of the
infantry would be explained to the recruits, which would be a natural introduction into explaining the requirements of the training. During this
period, the recruit would be able to assess whether they want to pursue an
infantry career, and if not, they would be able to leave at any time should
they so decide. At the same time, the infantry instructors can make an
informed judgement as to whether a recruit is suitable for infantry training prior to enlistment.

This integrated approach would be designed to give the recruit the time
to integrate the military beliefs, values, and aims of the infantry while
at the same time allowing them to adjust their personal and social identities to the new environment. This gradual integration would also be

designed to allow the recruit to more successfully retain their ties with family and civilian friends. This whole process would be designed to let the recruit make a gradual psychological and physiological adjustment to life in the infantry prior to enlistment. Additionally, this approach would allow those who were clearly unsuitable for the infantry to have the opportunity to deselect themselves and request either termination of their enlistment or transfer to another arm or service.[19]

The second recommendation for the enlistment phase is the introduction of a targeted-intervention strategy where the instructors monitor the recruits for suitability for service within the infantry. This process would be aided by the instructors examining each recruit's biographical data in order to predict those that may have difficulty with the training by identify behavioural traits that are associated with failure. All recruits who suffer physical injuries during their initial training are placed in a "holding platoon" where they are given time to recover to full fitness. As with this case, it is further recommended that recruits who are suffering from psychological adjustment problems are placed in a separate "holding platoon" where additional support from trained instructors, counsellors, and psychologists would be used to assist the recruits mentally adjust to life in the infantry.[20]

Finally, as indicated previously, it is recommended that each recruit's biographical details are examined for the mental, emotional, and physical traits that would predispose their failure during the initial training. The refinement by the British Army of the current psychometric test would, it is believed, enable the instructors to more accurately predict the occupational fit between the recruit and an infantry lifestyle. As the current approximately 30% failure rate is due mainly to emotional and psychological problems, this future research should amalgamate the current psychometric testing, biographical data, and emotional susceptibility scale into one measure that would more accurately measure the individual's likelihood of success or failure. This would allow the recruit's emotional responses to previous life experiences to be measured against their likely responses to the psychological demands of infantry life. However, as indicated by the current research, the three major factors that determine a recruit's success during initial training remain motivation, mental discipline and physical resilience.

Grossman and Siddle (2010) discovered there were four concepts that were crucial to the "total institution" if the individual was to be successfully socialised into the military. Their first concept was the obedience of all soldiers to all the orders and instructions issued by their superiors, as this would allow for the assigned mission to be completed. Their second concept was that of discipline, which was essential to correctly mould and perfect the mental faculties and character of each soldier. They found that without discipline, soldiers in critical situations would have difficulty completing their mission and so endless and repetitive training, until the soldier's reaction became second nature, were designed to produce the necessary high levels of discipline. Their third concept was survival, as this meant the soldier would have the commitment to facilitate the continuation of life, or for those involved in combat operations the adoption of a "by any means necessary philosophy."[21] By surviving, the benefit was not only for the individual soldier but also for the unit's survival and its success in achieving its assigned mission. Their fourth and final concept was sacrifice, as during the "total institution" training soldiers were required to sacrifice their individuality, and in combat to make the ultimate sacrifice by giving their own lives if required.

In his study into recruit training, Zurcher (2009) found that in preparation for the ultimate challenge, which is war, military educational institutions established a series of benchmarks that had to be met and maintained. The soldier's ability to meet and maintain these benchmarks was measured at various stages of the selection and training process. Zurcher identified that the ultimate aim of the military training process was to produce soldiers who would respond to orders without question and then perform their duties in an exemplary manner. This, he found, was achieved by the continuous repetition of the training subject matter. The more training received by soldiers, the more likely it would be that their responses were automatic. Zurcher found that this socialising training would by necessity bring profound changes in the individual during their transition from civilian to soldier.

Today, the infantry soldier is required to achieve a series of more de-manding training benchmarks in order to become a qualified infantry soldier. This cycle commences with an initial 60-day infantry recruit course where the basic skills of weapon handling, navigation, physical fitness, tactics, movement, and patrolling are taught. This is then fol-lowed by a 30-day combat training course where the tactical require-ments of surviving and winning in close combat on the battlefield are taught. These include marksmanship, bayonet/knife fighting, and un-armed combat where the infantry soldier is taught how to kill effectively and if required silently. At the completion of this intensive training cycle, the infantry soldier has gained the knowledge and ability to successfully operate in a combat environment as a basic rifleman, and to effectively carry out those duties under fire and in close contact with the enemy. It was Knowles (1968), in his adult learning theory that developed the as-sumption that there are significant, identifiable differences between adult learners and learners under the age of eighteen. The primary differences he identified were that adult learners are more self-directed, having a rep-ertoire of experience, and are more internally motivated to learn subject matter that could be applied immediately. This adult learning theory was reflected in the military during the transitional training of entry-level recruits from basically trained infantry soldiers to combat-ready infantry soldiers.[22]

In his earliest research study, Grossman (1995) explained that the train-ing of soldiers in the use of weapons was a primary function of the mili-tary with the aim being to inculcate in the individual soldier an instinct to use a weapon instantaneously in time of peril. As a result of his latest research, Grossman (2009) found that the ability and willingness to fire a weapon at an enemy soldier had escalated over the recent years. He began his research with General Marshall's study of soldiers in World War II, where it was found that only 15-20% of soldiers fired their weapons at the enemy (Marshall, 1947).[23] This rate increased to 55% during the Korean War, and further increased to 90-95% during the Vietnam War. Based on these findings, Grossman argued that the soldier's instruments were the same from World War II to the Vietnam War in that they used rifles, pistols, and automatic weapons. In this critical analysis, Grossman argued that what had altered was that the education of the individual soldier had become more advanced with the introduction of refined and focused training techniques, and these had significantly improved the likelihood of the soldier firing his weapon. He concluded that in combat, the soldiers target is an enemy soldier, and so ultimately the willingness to kill another human being has been significantly enhanced.

It has been found that adversaries will continue to use fear as a weapon, especially in the asymmetrical conflicts such as Afghanistan and Iraq, and as a result, it is education and training that lessen the effect of fear on unit effectiveness within military organisations. The understanding of the psychological advantage that effectively led, well-trained, and cohesive organisations have over an opponent must be based on commanders training their unit to recognise and overcome fear. Controlling fear is in the grasp of every well-trained unit that has undertaken realistic and demanding training, as it provides a soldier with an advantage in the struggle to overcome the desire for self-preservation against real or perceived threats. Holmes (1985) contended that the stress of battle stemmed from its puzzling and capricious nature, but that battle drills, commonly referred to as training in infantry minor tactics, assisted the soldier in his own mind to minimise the randomness of battle by providing familiar points of contact in an uncertain and dangerous environment.

Mastery of the fundamentals through education and training results in a heightened level of confidence in soldiers that they could overcome challenging situations on the battlefield due to their military professionalism. By incorporating the realistic battlefield stimuli of the sights, sounds, and smells of combat in training, the commander makes the training as real as possible. As combat affects soldiers violently, they must be conditioned to deal with fear, and it is through training that a soldier is taught to kill and to overcome fear. The key is not desensitisation but sensitisation, as soldiers need to know how their minds and bodies will react to fear, thereby developing a combative mind-set that mitigates against the physiological and psychological effects of fear.[24] Experiential learning is critical in sensitising soldiers to the bedlam of combat by leaders creating unpredictability in their training events while accepting that failures will occur. This creating of sensory chaos in training teaches soldiers how they and their comrades respond to stress and anxiety. They must then be given the opportunity to discuss their emotional responses in after-action reviews.

Therefore, leaders have the responsibility in training to understand and prepare for the human aspects of war by recognising their soldiers' limits, needs, and motivations while remaining tactically and technically proficient. This means that young officers must manage their own fear in combat while at the same time channelling their subordinates' fears into achieving the unit's mission. Many great commanders considered that the setting of a composed example to their subordinates was a critical factor in time of crisis as was the passage of information to their soldiers in order to reduce uncertainty and anxiety.[25] The absence of information is one of the conditions that fosters panic in soldiers, as uncertainty creates fear and apprehension. The message is that fear can be reduced through training, but there is no single, absolute way to eliminate fear, as soldiers all react differently to combat situations with soldiers being brave one day and afraid the next. It must be realised that soldiers are not machines but human beings who must be led in combat and handled differently. To sense this and arrive at a correct psychological solution is part of the art of command.

In conclusion, throughout the period of the wars in Afghanistan and Iraq, there was no evidence that soldiers have been provided with adequate pre-combat training interventions to prepare them for the detrimental physiological and psychological effects of combat operations.[26] The research-based justification for this study was derived from the previous research that has confirmed that higher rates of trauma are associated with increased exposure to intense infantry ground combat.[27] So, by examining the current literature, we are able to distinguish what has been and still needs to be learned and accomplished in regard to the topic of pre-combat education programmes and leadership training for infantry soldiers.

# Chapter Seven

## *Leadership Theory*

To compare and contrast the various theories applicable to the field of military leadership would appear at first to be a fairly straightforward endeavour, especially as leadership and the military are inseparable, being intertwined with each other so tightly that it is impossible to distinguish between the two. To support this view, the U.S. Army's official vision statement unambiguously states, "We are about leadership; it is our stock in trade, and it is what makes us different."[1] In this regard, it has been said that there are probably as many different definitions of leadership as there are roles for leaders. As a result, there are "at least ten different theories of military leadership and ten times ten books defining leadership styles and traits."[2] However, the fact is that even today, military leadership remains the most elusive of arts, as we still do not know exactly what makes a soldier stand up to attack the enemy and go forward into the face of almost certain death on the order of his commander. [3] Until we understand this phenomenon, then military leadership will remain one of the highest and most elusive of qualities. It will remain an art.

However, despite this intricacy of defining military leadership, there is one absolute fact, a necessity common to all those who would achieve success in combat. This is their ability to manage crises due to the fact that they possess the necessary qualities to remain composed and operative when others are consumed by complex and deadly situations. Therefore, military leaders need to possess not only refined skills of leadership, but also, the ability to use those skills in times of extreme physical danger and psychological challenge.[4] So, as it involves the ultimate struggle between life-and-death, the art of military leadership has been seriously studied for millennium. In fact, the greatest philosophical writings from Plato and his *Republic* to Plutarch and his *Lives* have explored the question "What qualities distinguish an individual as a military leader?"

As indicated, there are at least ten different theories of military leadership, and of these, the six most important ones for the military will now be compared and contrasted. Initially it must be realised that military leadership is widely defined as "organising a unit of soldiers to successfully achieve a defined mission"[5] and so military leadership theories have been produced involving traits, situations, interactions, functions, behaviours, power, vision, values, charisma, and intelligence, among others. The search for the characteristics or traits of leaders, as they are now called, has been ongoing for centuries and the earliest theory was based on the characteristics that certain individuals possessed. This was known as the "trait theory of leadership," and it concluded that military leadership was inherited and leaders were born.[6] The researchers of this theory went on to define a number of characteristics that they believed distinguished between military leaders and non-leaders. These included intelligence, courage, dominance, adaptability, persistence, integrity, and confidence, for example.

The trait approach has several identifiable strengths. It is intuitively appealing, as the image in the community is that leaders are a special kind of people who are different, and their difference resides in the special leadership traits they possess. The second strength is that it has a century of research, and so no other theory has the breadth and depth of studies conducted on the trait approach.[7] Thirdly, the trait approach highlights the leader component in the leadership process, and as such, it provides us with a deeper and more intricate understanding of how the leader's personality relates to the leadership process. Finally, the trait approach defines what traits the leader should possess, enabling the individual's strengths and weaknesses to be identified, leading to an improvement in leadership effectiveness.

However, by the mid-19th century, the "trait theory of leadership" was being challenged, as new research had shown that individuals who were leaders in one situation were not necessarily the leaders in other situations. So, leadership was thought to be no longer reliant on enduring individual traits. Instead, leadership was dependent upon the particular situation at the time.[8] This "situational theory of leadership" dominated the next decades with its premise being that different situations call for different characteristics, so no single optimal psychographic profile of a military leader existed.[9] This theory identified that what an individual did when acting as a leader was largely dependent upon the particular situation in which the leader was functioning.

The situational approach has several strengths, as it is perceived by organisations to be offering a credible model for training people to become effective leaders. The second strength is its practicality, as it is easy to understand, intuitively sensible, and easily applied in a variety of settings. Closely akin to the strength of practicality is the third strength of the situational approach, which is its prescriptive value, in that it tells you what to do in various contexts. A fourth strength of situational leadership is that it emphasises leadership flexibility and stresses that the leader must change their style to meet the requirements of the situation.[10] Finally, situational leadership reminds us to treat each subordinate differently based upon the task at hand, while at the same time nurturing each individual to become more confident in their ability to achieve their military mission.

As with the trait approach, the "skills theory of leadership" takes a leader-centred perspective. However, in the skills approach, there is a shift away from personality characteristics to an emphasis on skills and abilities that can be developed by the leader. So, even though personality is accepted as playing an integral role, it is suggested that knowledge and abilities are fundamental to effective military leadership. In this regard, researchers of this theory have identified three basic personal skills: technical, human, and conceptual, with it being argued that these skills are quite different from the traits or qualities of leaders. Skills are what leaders can accomplish, while traits are the leader's innate characteristics.[11] Technical skill is knowledge and proficiency in a specialised area, analytic capacity, and the ability to use these techniques. Human skill is the knowledge and ability to work with subordinates, or what is popularly referred to as "people skills." Conceptual skill is the ability to work with ideas and concepts. Therefore, it is believed that leadership capacity can be developed over time through education and experience.

The skills approach contributes positively to our understanding of military leadership, as it is a leader-centred model that stresses the importance of developing particular leadership skills. Secondly, the skills approach is intuitively appealing, as it describes competencies that everyone can learn and develop. Thirdly, the skills approach is expansive in that it incorporates a large variety of components that encompass a multitude of factors, including problem-solving, social skills, knowledge, individual attributes, career experiences, and environmental influences. Finally, the skills approach provides a structure that frames the curricula of military leadership education and development programmes.[12]

As a result of the earlier criticism of the trait approach, theorists also began to research military leadership as a set of behaviours and identified broad leadership styles. This became known as the "style theory of leadership" in which the behaviour of the leader was all-important. This distinguished it from the trait approach, which emphasised the personality characteristics of the leader.[13] So, the style approach focuses exclusively on what the leader does and how they act toward their subordinates in various contexts. The research into this theory determined that leadership is composed of two kinds of behaviours: task and relationship behaviours. Task behaviours facilitate mission accomplishment, and relationship behaviours help subordinates feel comfortable with themselves, with their peers, and with the situation in which they find themselves. The central theme of the style approach is to explain how leaders combine these two behaviours in order to motivate their subordinates in their efforts to complete the mission.

It is important to realise that this theory does not limit the leader to one style in a given situation and, with the nature of the battlefield today and tomorrow, being able to adapt to appropriate styles will lead to successful mission accomplishment. Therefore, a leader's judgement, intelligence, cultural awareness, and self-control "play major roles in helping to choose the proper style and the appropriate techniques for the task at hand."[14] Therefore, a leader's effectiveness depends on being able to assess the unit's readiness level and then being able to adapt the appropriate high probability leadership style, and communicate that style to influence behaviour effectively. The leader then assesses results and reassesses the accomplishment of the mission, determining if further modification in leadership style is warranted.

The "contingency leadership theory" tries to match leaders to the appropriate situation as it suggests that a leader's effectiveness depends on how well the leader's style fits the particular setting at the time. Within the contingency approach, leadership styles are described as either "task motivated" or "relationship motivated,"[15] with the leader either focusing upon achieving the mission or with developing close interpersonal relationships. Then the contingency theory suggests that situations can be described in terms of, "leader-member relations, task structure, or position power."[16] The leader-member relations focus on the unit's group dynamics and the confidence and loyalty that the soldiers feel for their commander. The task structure is the degree to which the requirements of the mission are completely defined and then clearly stated to all the leader's subordinates. Then the third characteristic is position power, which defines the amount of power the leader has to reward or punish subordinates.

The contingency theory has several major strengths, the first being that it is supported by a great deal of empirical research with many researchers having found it to be a valid and reliable approach to explaining how effective military leadership can be achieved.[17] Secondly, contingency theory has focused on the importance between the relationship between the leader's style and the demands of the situation. Thirdly, contingency theory is predictive in that it provides information as to how effective a certain type of leadership will be in a particular context. Fourthly, contingency theory matches the leader and the situation but does not demand that the leaders fit every situation. Finally, contingency theory provides data on leader's styles that could be useful to organisations in their development of leadership profiles.

Then finally, we will examine the "transformational theory of leadership," which is one of the current approaches that the military has increasingly adopted, as it provides a new leadership paradigm where "more attention is given to the charismatic and affective elements of leadership."[18] After the invasions of Afghanistan (October 2001) and then Iraq (March 2003), the Coalition forces have increasingly been embroiled in two long and costly wars, and it has been increasingly identified that transformational leadership fits the needs of today's soldiers, as it inspires and empowers in times of uncertainty.[19] As the name implies, transformational leadership changes and transforms subordinates as the leader motivates the unit to be effective by imparting a vision that motivates the unit to achieve its mission.

The term "transformational leadership" describes "the linking of the roles of leadership and followership,"[20] where the leader exploits the motives of subordinates in order to better achieve the unit's mission. In transformational leadership, the commander engages with subordinates and creates a connection that raises the level of motivation in both the commander and subordinates. The transformational leader is attentive to the needs and motives of subordinates and tries to help them reach their fullest potential. Authentic transformational leadership is socialised leadership that is concerned with the collective good, and it is where the leader transcends their own interests for the sake of others.

So, having now compared and contrasted six theories that are applicable to effective military leadership, it is clear that leadership principles are timeless, even though the models that examine those theories may evolve with time. The transformational leadership theory offers one of many good ways to examine leadership, and it is considered to be ideally suited for the profession of arms.[21] Therefore, due to its current importance to all our armed forces, "transformational leadership" is the theory that has been selected to explain how it will add to our understanding of military leadership. Today, "transformational and charismatic leadership occupies one third of all leadership research,"[22] as it is now widely accepted that it is a process that alters and transforms both commanders and subordinates. This theory is primarily concerned with emotions, values, ethics, standards, and goals, while at the same time assessing subordinates' motives, satisfying their needs, and uniquely treating them as human beings. So, transformational leadership involves an exceptional form of influence that motivates the subordinates within a unit to achieve the unachievable. It is designed to harnesses the full power of charismatic and visionary leadership, which results in the commander and his subordinates being inextricably bound together in the transformational process.

According to recent research, there are two basic categories of leadership, and these are now widely described as transitional and transformational. The distinction between the two being that ordinary transitional leaders exchange tangible rewards for the work and loyalty of their subordinates, while extraordinary transformational leaders engage with subordinates, focusing on higher order intrinsic needs to achieve specific outcomes. Initially researchers believed that transitional and transformational leadership were opposites on a continuum. However, new research now puts forward the argument that transitional and transformational leadership are simply two separate concepts and that effective military leaders demonstrate characteristics of both.

The theoretical base of work on leadership that prevailed in the 1970s was founded in explorations into the effective military leader's traits, behaviours, and situations (contingency theories), but it is now realised that these failed to account for some "untypical qualities of leaders."[23] As a result, transformational leadership was seen as a redefinition of subordinates' mission and vision, a renewal of their commitment and a restructuring of their systems of goal accomplishment. So, transformational leadership fosters capacity development and creates higher levels of personal commitment amongst subordinates to organisational objectives. Transformational leaders elevate individuals from low levels of need, based on survival, to higher levels of motivation that transcend their own interests in order to achieve a collective purpose. Transformational leaders engender trust, admiration, loyalty, and respect amongst their subordinates.

Therefore, transformational leadership theory stresses that outstanding leadership involves providing subordinates with assignments that are intellectually challenging, thereby fostering growth and development. It is further argued that the leader must treat subordinates with "individualised consideration."[24] In other words, it is not enough to be considerate of one's subordinates in some generic or well-meaning way. Instead, it is necessary for the leader to approach each subordinate as an individual and provide support, encouragement, and direction that is tailored to that individual's needs at their stage of development.

So, most researchers in the field of leadership now propose that there are four factors that make up effective transformational leadership. The first of these is "idealised influence," which is about building confidence and trust, while at the same time providing a role model that subordinates seek to emulate. This confidence in the leader provides an essential foundation for subordinates to accept radical organisational modifications, and this is where charismatic leadership becomes part transformational leadership.[25] This link between charismatic and transformational leadership is clearest during times of crisis within an organisation.

Secondly, there is "inspirational motivation," which unlike charisma, which is held to inspire the individual, this is about inspiring the whole organisation, for instance to follow a new vision or idea that has been put forward by the leader. To achieve this, transformational leaders provide an appealing vision of the future, offer subordinates the ability to see meaning in their tasks, and go on to challenge them with achieving high standards in these endeavours. So, these leaders encourage their subordinates to become part of the organisation's culture and environment. Through motivational speeches and conversations with individuals, the transformational leader encourages their subordinates to imagine and contribute to the development of the unit's mission.

Thirdly is "intellectual stimulation," which involves arousing and altering subordinates' awareness of problems and their capacity to solve those problems. Therefore, transformational leaders question long-held assumptions, challenge the status quo, and then encouraging subordinates to be innovative and creative. This in turn encourages subordinates to propose new and controversial ideas without the fear of punishment or ridicule.

Finally, there is "individualised consideration," where the leader responds individually to the unique needs of subordinates so that they are included in the transformational process of the organisation. The leader treats individuals differently based upon their talents, knowledge, and potential, with the intention of allowing them to reach the highest levels of achievement. This will take expression through the leader undertaking individualised career counselling, mentoring, and professional development activities. So, the transformational leader not only has an overarching vision for the organisation but also understands the things that motivate followers individually.[26]

Together, these four dimensions of effective transformational leadership are interdependent, co-existing together and creating performance yields that are beyond the expectations of the organisation with which they are associated. As a result, these leaders achieve unexpected improvements in mission, strategy, structure, and culture through a focus on the intangible qualities of vision, values, ideals, and relationship building. In short, the transformational leader gives significance to diverse activities in order to ensure that individuals and groupings work together towards the larger organisational objectives.

Having now identified the four domains of transformational leadership, it is now important to identify the four stages of organisational change under the transformational leader. Firstly, it is necessary to "make a compelling case for change," and here the transformational leader makes a convincing argument based upon heightening followers' sensitivity to existing environmental challenges and by questioning the status quo. Secondly, it is important to "inspire a shared vision" and this needs to be cast in ideological terms through coaching and conscious role modelling strategies. Thirdly, the "change needs to be led" and a sense of urgency must be instilled, with collaboration being encouraged and the self-confidence of followers must be increased. Finally, it has been identified that the "change needs to be embedded" in the organisation by monitoring progress, changing appraisal and reward systems, and hiring staff that are committed to collaboration.

However, despite the recent popularity and advocacy for adoption of transformational leadership, there remains controversy and unanswered questions related to the theory. One criticism is that it lacks conceptual

clarity, as "it covers such a wide range, including creating a vision, motivating, being a change agent, building trust, giving nurture, and acting as
a social architect, to name a few..."[27] So, the argument is that it is difficult to exactly define the parameters of transformational leadership. As an
example, transformational and charismatic leadership are often treated
synonymously even though in some models of leadership charisma is
only one component of transformational leadership.

Also the morality of transformational leadership has been questioned,
as it has the potential for the abuse of power. The fear is that transformational leaders motivate their followers by appealing to strong emotions regardless of the ultimate effects, and that some leaders may have
narcissistic tendencies, thriving on power and manipulation.[28] Moreover,
some followers may have dependent characters and so form strong and
unfortunate bonds with their leaders. Also, transformational leadership
lacks the checks and balances of countervailing interests, influences, and
power that may assist in the avoidance of dictatorship and oppression of
a majority by a minority.

However, these criticisms of transformational leadership have been addressed by the argument that to be a true transformational leader, you must
have moral foundations, which foster the values of honesty, loyalty, and
fairness, as well as the end values of justice and equality. The point is that
transformational leadership, or pseudo-transformational leadership has a
potential immoral and unethical dimension that could be exploited by an
unscrupulous leader inflicted on naive and unsuspecting subordinates.

It is clear that the "authentic transformational leader" must forge a
path of congruence of values and interests among stakeholders while
avoiding the pseudo-transformational traits of deceit, manipulation, self-
aggrandisement, and power abuse.[29] Then there is also the concern that
transformational leadership may be seen as immoral in the manner that
it moves subordinates to sacrifice their own interests and desires for the
organisation's needs. As stated earlier, even though transformational leadership may be viewed as being double-edged, it is believed that with high
moral values such as ethics being espoused by both leader and led, the
dark side will be mitigated in favour of the forces for good.

However, related to this criticism, it is also argued that transformational leadership suffers from a "heroic leadership"[30] bias, as the theory stipulates that it is the leader who moves subordinates to achieve exceptional goals. The feeling is that by focusing primarily on the leader, researchers have failed to give attention to shared leadership or reciprocal influence, where followers can influence leaders just as leaders can influence followers. In this regard, transformational leadership theory assumes that the leader can accurately assess the subordinates' needs and abilities. However, a significant question regarding the theory concerns factors that affect a leader's ability to accurately judge an individual's emotional needs or intellectual capabilities.

As a result, transformational leadership provides a broad set of generalisations of what is typical of military leaders who are transforming, and unlike other leadership theories, it does not provide a clearly defined set of assumptions about how a leader should act in a particular situation in order to be successful. Instead, transformational leadership requires that leaders be aware of how their own behaviour relates to the needs of their subordinates and the changing dynamics within their organisations. Thus, the goal of transformational leaders is to inspire their subordinates to share the leader's values in order to connect with the leader's vision. It is suggested that transformational leadership can be taught at all levels in an organisation, and that as a result, it can positively improve performance.

It has been shown that within the military, leaders will exhibit a mix of transformational and transactional leadership depending on the demands of the situation, their leadership abilities, and the quality of relations between them and their followers. In fact, research into the relations among military leaders and followers shows that those in a position of command can exert transformational leadership over some followers while simultaneously providing transactional leadership to others. It has also been shown that it is possible that some leaders will be more inclined to transformational leadership, some will be more comfortable with transactional leadership, and others will be able to provide both styles of leadership.

In conclusion, there are many leadership theories and models to choose from, and transformational leadership is not the only theory that military leaders should examine, but it is one of the more important ones. As a result, it warrants serious consideration, as it provides concepts and example behaviours for leadership, and so it provides guidance at all levels of the military chain of command on how the leader should project their vision and thereby achieve the mission. This is arguably the central goal of any military leader. Furthermore, in the important areas of leadership research and development, the transformational leadership model has proved valuable in developing leadership potential in military commanders.

# CHAPTER EIGHT

## *Leadership Approaches*

It is often stated that the military is timeless because its existence has not altered for millennium, and this statement was famously reinforced by Clausewitz (1832) and his theory, in which he stated that war was simply the extension of politics designed to further the interests of the nation state. The nature of war is enduring, as it always involves violence, destruction, and death. However, the nature of war has altered over the last decades as witnessed by the recent war in Afghanistan and Iraq, where what is now described as the asymmetric battlefield has emerged as the new paradigm. As a result, the military is heavily involved in developing new strategies across the spectrum of doctrine, organisation, training, material, personnel, and administration. These transformations require a new breed of leaders who are not only tactically and technically proficient, but who possess the character and competencies to lead in the new asymmetric battlefield. More than ever, the effective military leader is a source of power for infusing a culture of professionalism, cohesion, imagination, and courage within military organisations at all levels within the chain of command. Now more than ever it has been recognised that the degree to which subordinates adopt and internalise the values of their military organisation is directly affected by the level of trust the soldiers have in their leader.

As a result, military organisations and researchers have been obsessed over the last decades with leadership as they have attempted to deconstruct the phenomenon into a universal set of measures.[1] The critical analysis of this literature shows that what is now proposed is that effective leaders are differentiated from other leaders through the exercise of a relatively small range of skill or competence areas.[2] However, King (2013) suggested that the way in which these skills and competencies were exercised was not prescribed but was instead the function of the underlying personality of the leader.[3] This relatively simple statement has significant implications for the way in which we view leadership as it is becoming evident that leadership is personal. That is, the personality of the leader plays an important part in the exercise of leadership. Building on this view, King suggested that these areas of effectiveness needed to be exercised in a way which was congruent with the underlying personality of the leader.

Somewhat contrary to these findings, Verljen (2011) found that there is a dynamic relationship between the leader and the organisational context. He postulated that it was reasonable to see that the organisational factors that impacted leadership comprised its strategy, culture, policies, and practices, as well its ability to learn as an organisation.[4] As critically, Yeakey (2008) discovered that the relationship between the leader and the organisation was potentially a dynamic one, as different organisational strategies may require changes in the behaviour of the leader. However, in order to balance this argument, Yeakey also found that it was feasible that a change in leadership behaviour could lead to a different approach being adopted by the organisation.[5] The relevance of these pieces of work was seen by Hesselbein and Shinseki (2010), who defined that the essence was that a change in context required a change in the way in which the leader operated in the organisation.[6]

Dalessandro (2009), in his *Army Officer's Guide,* identified in depth that the trait approach had several identifiable strengths, as it was intuitively appealing, as the image in the community was that leaders were a special kind of people who were different, and their difference resided in the special leadership traits they possessed. The second strength that he stipulated was that the trait approach had a century of research and so no other theory had the breadth and depth of the studies conducted on it. Third, he believed that the trait approach highlighted the leader component in the leadership process, and as such, it provided a deeper and more intricate understanding of how the leader's personality related to the leadership process. Finally, he saw the trait approach as defining what traits the leader should possess, thereby enabling the individual's strengths and weaknesses to be identified, which would lead to an improvement in leadership effectiveness.[7]

However, as Hesselbein and Shinseki (2010) found, by the mid-19th century, the trait theory of leadership was being challenged, as new research had shown that there were gaps in the previous research because individuals who were leaders in one situation were not necessarily the leaders in other situations. Their findings were that leadership was no longer reliant on enduring individual traits, and instead it was dependent upon the particular situation at the time.[8] This situational theory of leadership dominated the next decades with its premise being that different situations called for different characteristics, so no single optimal psychographic profile of a military leader existed. This theory identified the gap in the previous research as what an individual did when acting as a leader was largely dependent upon the particular situation in which the leader was functioning.

Therefore, the trait approach focused exclusively on the leader and not the followers, while at the same time suggesting that organisations would work better if those in managerial positions had designated leadership profiles. The trait approach strengths were that it was intuitively appealing, it had a century of research to support its theory, and by focusing exclusively on the leader, it was able to provide some deeper understanding on how the leader's personality was related to the leadership process. Its weaknesses were that it failed to delimit a definitive list of leadership traits, and even more importantly, it failed to take the situation into account.[9] This approach also resulted in highly subjective determinations of the most important leadership traits. It could also be criticised for failing to look at traits in relationship to leadership outcomes. Finally, it was not a useful approach for the training and development of leadership, as it reasons that traits are relatively fixed psychological structures.

As Northouse (2009) found in his research, the situational approach had several strengths, as it was perceived by organisations to be offering a credible model for training people to become effective leaders. The second strength was its practicality, as it was easy to understand, intuitively sensible, and easily applied in a variety of settings. Closely akin to the strength of practicality was the third strength of the situational approach, which was its prescriptive value, in that it trained the soldier in a particular context. A fourth strength was that it emphasised leadership flexibility and stressed that the leader must alter their style to meet the requirements of the situation. Finally, Northouse found that situational leadership stressed the need to treat each subordinate differently based upon the task at hand, while at the same time nurturing each individual to become more confident in their ability to achieve their military mission.[10]

The situational approach was centred on the idea that leaders move forward and backward along a development continuum. So, to be effective, the leader must diagnose where subordinates are on the continuum and then adapt their style accordingly. In this model, it is the situation, or the readiness and development level of the subordinates, that determines the appropriate leader style. The strengths of the situational approach were that it was well known and frequently used, it was intuitively simple, practical, and was based on sound theories. The weakness of the situational approach was that there have been only a few research studies conducted in order to justify the basic assumptions behind the approach. The concept of the subordinate's readiness or development level was ambiguous, and the match of the leader style and the subordinate's readiness level was also criticised.[11]

Nye (2009) found that, as with the trait approach, the "skills theory of leadership" took a leader-centred perspective. The critical finding was that in the skills approach, there was a shift away from personality characteristics to an emphasis on skills and abilities that could be developed by the leader.[12] Krames (2008) in *The U.S. Army Leadership Field Manual* further identified that even though personality is accepted as playing an integral role, he suggested that knowledge and abilities were fundamental to effective military leadership. Critically, Krames then listed three basic personal skills: technical, human, and conceptual with it being argued that these skills were different from the traits or qualities of leaders. To add breadth to previous studies, he stipulated that skills are what leaders could accomplish, while traits were the leader's innate characteristics. He further added depth to his study, as he identified technical skill as being knowledge and proficiency in a specialised area, analytic capacity, and the ability to use these techniques. A further revelation at the time was that he saw human skill as the knowledge and ability to work with subordinates, or what is popularly referred to as people skills. Finally, he defined conceptual skill as being the ability to work with ideas and concepts. Unlike previous research, he found that leadership capacity could be developed over time through education and experience.[13]

The skills approach describes leadership from a skills perspective, thereby providing a structure for effective leadership. It contended that leadership outcomes were the direct result of the leader's competencies in problem solving, social judgment, and knowledge. Also that environmental influences and career experiences played a direct or indirect role in the leader's performance. The strengths of the skills approach were that it was a leader-centric model that stressed the development of skills, and it conceptualised and created a structure for this process. It was also intuitively appealing as it made leadership available to everyone.[14] The weaknesses of the skills approach were that the breadth of the approach extended beyond the boundaries of leadership, such as motivation, personality, and critical thinking, with this making it more general and less precise. It also had a weak predictive value, as it did not explain how variations could affect performance. Additionally, it claimed not to be a trait model, but major components of the model included trait-like attributes, such as personality variables.

As a result of the earlier criticism of the trait approach, Shalikashvili (2008) began to research military leadership as a set of behaviours and identified broad leadership styles. This became known as the style theory of leadership in which the behaviour of the leader was all important. This distinguished it from the trait approach, which emphasised the personality characteristics of the leader. So, the style approach focused exclusively on what the leader did and how they acted towards their subordinates in various contexts. Critically, the research into this theory by Shalikashvili determined that leadership was composed of two kinds of behaviours:

task and relationship behaviours. Task behaviours facilitated mission accomplishment and relationship behaviours assisted subordinates to feel comfortable with themselves, with their peers, and with the situation in which they found themselves. He believed that the central theme of the style approach was to explain how leaders combine these two behaviours in order to motivate their subordinates in their efforts to complete the mission.[15]

However, in order to broaden the original research, Yeakey (2008) identified that it was important to realise that this theory did not limit the leader to one style in a given situation and, with the nature of the battlefield today and tomorrow, being able to adapt appropriate styles would lead to successful mission accomplishment. Therefore, Yeakey found that a leader's judgment, intelligence, cultural awareness, and self-control played a major role in helping to choose the proper style and the appropriate techniques for the task at hand. He concluded that a leader's effectiveness depended on being able to assess the unit's readiness level, and then being able to adapt the appropriate high-probability leadership style, and communicate that style to influence behaviour effectively. The leader then assessed results and reassessed the accomplishment of the mission and determined if further modification in leadership style was warranted.[16]

However, the style approach is not a refined theory that has an organised set of prescriptions for effective leadership; instead it provides a framework for assessing effective leadership.[17] It reminds leaders that their actions towards their subordinates are at both the task and relationship levels. The strengths of style approach were that it broadened the scope of leadership research to include the behaviour of leaders and what they did in various situations. The style approach ascertained that a leader's style was composed primarily of two major types of behaviour: task and relationship.[18] The weakness of the style approach was that it had not adequately shown how the leader's styles were associated with performance outcomes. It also failed to find a style of leadership that could be effective in almost every situation, as it implied that the most effective leadership style was the high-task and high-relationship style.

In 2011, Verljen postulated that the contingency leadership theory tried to match the leader to the appropriate situation, as it suggested that a leader's effectiveness depended on how well the leader's style fitted the particular setting at the time.[19] He went on further to describe that within the contingency approach, the leadership styles were described as either being task motivated or relationship motivated, with the leader either focusing upon achieving the mission or with developing close interpersonal relationships. However, it was Pendry (2009) who from his research found that the contingency theory had several major strengths, the first being that it was supported by a great deal of empirical research with many researchers having found it to be a valid and reliable approach to explaining how effective military leadership can be achieved. Secondly, he found that contingency theory had focused on the importance between the relationship between the leader's style and the demands of the situation. Thirdly, contingency theory was predictive in that it provided information as to how effective a certain type of leadership would be in a particular context. Fourthly, contingency theory matched the leader and the situation but did not demand that the leader fit every situation. Finally, contingency theory provided data on the leader's styles that could be useful to organisations in their development of leadership profiles.[20]

The contingency approach advocates that by measuring certain variables, it could be predicted whether a leader will be effective in a certain situation. So, once the nature of the situation had been determined, the fit between the leader and situation could be evaluated, with the realisation that all leaders will not be effective in all situations.[21] The contingency theory represented a major shift in leadership research from focusing only on the leader to considering a situational context. The strengths of the contingency approach were that it was supported by a great deal of empirical research, and as a result it forced the consideration of the impact of situations on leaders. The weakness of the contingency approach was that it failed to explain fully why individuals with certain leadership styles were more effective in some situations than others. It also failed to explain adequately what organisations should do when there is a mismatch between the leader and the situation in the workplace.[22]

The transformational theory of leadership is the current approach the military has increasingly adopted, as it provides a new leadership paradigm where more attention is given to the charismatic and affective elements of leadership.[23] After the invasions of Afghanistan and then Iraq, the Coalition forces have increasingly been embroiled in two long and costly wars, and it has been increasingly identified that transformational leadership fits the needs of today's soldiers because it inspired and empowers in times of uncertainty.[24] As the name implies, transformational leadership changes and transforms subordinates as the leader motivates the unit to be effective by imparting a vision that motivates the unit to achieve its mission.

In their research, Kouzes and Posner (2010) used the term "transformational leadership" to describe the linking of the roles of leadership and followership, where the leader exploited the motives of their subordinates in order to better achieve the unit's mission. They found that within transformational leadership, the commander engaged with subordinates and created a connection that raised the level of motivation in both the commander and the subordinates. They further found that the transformational leader was attentive to the needs and motives of their subordinates and tried to help them reach their fullest potential. They broadened their research by concluding that authentic transformational leadership was socialised leadership that was concerned with the collective good, and so it was where the leader transcended their own interests for the sake of others.[25]

However, one of the most important conceptual issues for transformational and charismatic leadership is the extent to which they are compatible, as it is now common to consider the two as being interchangeable. This view has been challenged by Bass (1985), who postulated that charisma was an essential element of transformational leadership but noted that a leader could be charismatic without being transformational. Other theorists have identified that a leader can be transformational without being charismatic, and still others consider that the two forms of leadership are in fact incompatible.[26] The most current research seems to indicate that there is little likelihood that the traits of transformational leadership will naturally result in the leader becoming charismatic. This view is reinforced when it is accepted that the role of the transformational leader is to empower their subordinates, and so it is unlikely that they will attribute charismatic values to that leader. Therefore, the least likely outcome is for the leader to remain both transformational and charismatic, as this combination requires that the leader sustains their subordinates' dependence by displaying exceptional and unique expertise over a considerable period of time.

The descriptive accounts of famous charismatic leaders in military organisations provide added perspectives as some examples exist of leaders who are both charismatic and transformational. However, these are rare, as these leaders are good at managing their own public image and prestige rather than in providing empowerment to their subordinates. Therefore, it is apparent that charismatic and transformational leadership theories provide some important insights; however, with the caveat that the major theoretical weaknesses need to be corrected in order to make the theories more relevant. That is, internalisation is more important to transformational leadership while personal identification is more important to charismatic leadership. Therefore, at the present time, it seems best to hypothesis that the two types of leadership are distinct but at the same time partially overlapping.

As regards the development of leadership approaches within the military, it has been recognised that the effective leader must be able to adapt to the ever-changing nature of military operations in a modern asymmetric battlefield. To be able to do this, the military leader needs to have the knowledge of the various leadership approaches, and then must be able to apply these to diverse combat situations by matching their leadership style to the setting. To this end, the military has undertaken numerous studies throughout the recent decades and has developed an approach based upon the "five-factor personality model,"[27] which has been designed to examine the fundamental leadership traits of intelligence, self-confidence, determination, integrity, and sociability.

The "five-factor personality model" is a psychological theory that has been designed to identify the characteristics that make up an individual's personality. These characteristics are extraversion, openness, agreeableness, conscientiousness, and neuroticism, with researchers attempting to determine whether there is any correlation between these characteristics and effective leadership.[28] These studies found that those who displayed high levels of extraversion and agreeableness positively predicted transformational leadership. Openness was also found to be positively related to effective leadership when it was paired together with these two previous traits. However, conscientiousness and neuroticism were found to be unrelated to predicting effective leadership.

This newly rediscovered interest in the trait approach by the military has led to their introduction of personality assessment instruments to determine whether a potential leaders will display effective leadership within a specific unit. However, the military has also been re-examining the skills approach, which is similar to the trait approach in that it is a leader-focused evaluation with the three main skills that a leader must possess being technical, conceptual, and human.[29] The leader needs to possess all these skills, but at varying levels of leadership different skills are more essential than others. As an example, the infantry section commander must be highly skilled in technical infantry minor tactics, camouflage, concealment, marksmanship, and close-quarter combat. The infantry platoon commander must possess knowledge of these skills while at the same time possessing the conceptual skills that are essential to be effective leader in an asymmetric and constantly altering modern battlefield. Finally, at the highest levels of the military chain of command, the brigade and divisional commanders need to have not only high conceptual skills but also refined human skills as they determine which of their subordinate units is able to most effectively fulfil a particular mission.

Therefore, this new military leadership approach is designed to match the leader's technical, conceptual, and human skill-sets with their military rank and responsibilities. That is, at the very highest levels of military command, very little technical skill is required, as the role of the senior commander is focused on the overall management of their subordinates and sub-units who are actually engaged in the overall ground combat. This approach to leadership has several advantages, as it allows leaders to analysis and then improves their skills and abilities. It also defines that there are two forms of behaviour with these being the leader's task behaviour and relationship behaviour. The task behaviour defines how the leader acts in order to achieve the unit's mission, while the relationship behaviour identifies how the leader builds unit cohesion. The military has also been looking at how specific situations dictate whether the leader utilises a directive or supportive leadership style. This situational approach takes into consideration the circumstances at the particular time, and these dictate how flexible the leader must be in adopting their leadership style.

In conclusion, the transformational theory has many contradictions, as it was a broad-based approach that encompassed many facets and dimensions of leadership. It set out to empower followers and to nurture them; it raised their conciseness, and transcended their own self-interests for the sake of others. The relevance of this approach is that leaders become strong role models with a highly developed set of values, self-determined sense of identity, confident, competent, and articulate. The strength of the transformational approach was that it had a strong intuitive appeal, as it emphasised the importance of followers in the leadership process. However, the weakness of the transformational approach was that it lacked clarity, as it covered many aspects such as creating visions, motivation, change agent, trust, and social architects. It was also implied that transformational leadership had trait-like qualities, since these leaders were often seen as visionaries. It has also been criticised as being elitist and undemocratic because the leader creates the vision, which has the potential to be abused, as this is concerned with altering the follower's values and moving them to a new vision.

# Leadership Application

The style theory focuses exclusively on what the leader does and how they act toward their subordinates in various contexts. As a result, this theory has guided and informed leadership practices within the military for decades, determining that leadership is composed of two kinds of behaviours: task and relationship behaviours.[1] Task behaviours facilitate mission accomplishment, and relationship behaviours assist subordinates feel comfortable with themselves, with their peers, and with the situation in which they find themselves. The central theme of the style approach is to explain how leaders combine these two behaviours in order to motivate their subordinates in their efforts to complete their assigned mission.

The main issues involved in translating the style theory into practice is that it is emphasised within the military that effective leaders must be able to adjust their leadership style to their current situation, as well as to the particular group of subordinates they are commanding.[2] Leaders are not limited to one style in a given situation and, with the nature of the battlefield today, and tomorrow, being able to adopt appropriate styles will lead to success. Traits from different styles are used to motivate subordinates and accomplish the mission. Therefore, a leader's judgement, intelligence and cultural awareness play major roles in helping them to choose the appropriate style for the task at hand.

It is taught that every military leader has two roles, the task specialist and the social specialist, with the ultimate aim being the defeat of the enemy in combat. In the role of task specialist, being likeable is less important than being more professional, competent, and intelligent than the subordinates you command. Then as a social specialist, the military leader's main role is in preserving good personal relationships within the unit, maintaining morale and ensuring unity of command. In a military unit, the functions of a successful social specialist reduces low morale, absenteeism, desertion, malingering, and crime. Also, the social function achieves cohesion as a team or unit, with the ideal military leaders combining excellence as a task specialist, with an equal flair for social leadership.[3]

It is also taught that military leadership styles are influenced by attitudes, values and past experiences. Situational factors along with the abilities and competencies of the military leader's subordinates also influence the leader's style. Consequently, the military leader must correctly assess situational factors and adapt the most appropriate and effective leadership style to that situation.[4] The situational leadership model rests on two concepts. The first is that the leader's effectiveness results from using a behavioural style that is appropriate to the demands of the environment, and secondly that the leader's effectiveness depends upon learning to diagnose that environment. Diagnosing the environment is the first of the three competencies of leadership. Adapting to the environment with the appropriate leadership style and then communicating that style to subordinates are the other two military leader competencies.

Environmental influences have two major components, these being style and expectations. Style is defined as the consistent behaviour that the leader uses when working with and through his subordinates. Expectations are defined as the perceptions of appropriate behaviour for the leader's role, or the roles of others within the organisation. These define what individuals in organisations should do in various circumstances, and as specifically, how they think others should act in their positions.[5]

During the past fifty years, scholars have conducted more than 1,000 studies into leadership in an attempt to determine the definitive styles of great leaders. This mass of research seems to confirm that effective military leaders have certain "core styles" in common.[6] However, it must be noted that the mere possession of these leadership styles, without a deep understanding of them will not automatically make an individual a leader. Therefore, it is essential that a military leader comprehend the meaning of leadership, and the styles required to become successful.

Today these "core values" are emphasised by all military services worldwide, and so they appear at the top of the lists of styles that are emphasised in military training. As Krames (2008) says, people will trust and willingly follow a leader. To this end, there is no better example of an individual pursuing effective military leadership styles than that of General Dwight D. Eisenhower during the liberation of Western Europe 1944-45, as the single theme that characterised his assumption of command was the maintenance of Allied unity. He famously said:

> *"Dealing with the enemy is simple and straight forward matter when contrasted with securing close cooperation with an ally."*[7]

He had great self-awareness, which facilitated "both empathy and self-management," thereby creating effective relationship management. This was reflected in one of his statements, where he said that, "It was no longer a British war or an American war, it was an *Allied* war."[8] However, it was after the D Day landings and during the battles for France and Germany that Eisenhower's effective military leadership styles were put to its greatest test. His ability to remain neutral even during the most vehement of debates between competing British and U.S. generals was truly remarkable. During these months, Eisenhower remained the voice of reason, displaying great resonance, whilst at the same time providing conciliation to both countries' political and military leaders. This was a unique achievement, and this defined him as having outstandingly effective military leadership style, which have defined him as one of the great military leaders in history.

While determining and evaluating effective military leadership styles, it is appropriate to re-examine the American Civil War exploits of Joshua L. Chamberlain, as described in the book *In the Hands of Providence,* written by A.R. Trulock in 2007. Chamberlain illustrated and continually demonstrated that primal leadership operates at its best through effective military leadership styles, whereby the successful leader creates resonance.[9] As the Lieutenant Colonel of the 20th Maine and as the campaign continued, it was interesting to see how Chamberlain was never a conceited leader.

During this period, he was in his element when the weather was brisk, and when asked why he chose to sleep under the sky when he had a whole regiment to build him a shelter, he replied, "I hate to see a man always on the spring to get the best of everything for himself... I prefer to take things as they come, and I am as well and as comfortable as anybody, and no one is the worse for it."[10] This is a prime example of how Chamberlain led by example and suffered the same hardships as everyone else and even more in order to be an inspirational leader.

At the Battle of Fredericksburg, 13-16 December 1862, we again witness Chamberlain's personal courage and galvanising leadership based on personal example. During the charge toward the Confederate lines, a high board fence halted the right wing of his regiment. Chamberlain ordered his men forward to dismantle it, but they hesitated as they were under heavy fire, so Chamberlain immediately sprang forward and began to pull the barrier apart himself, calling to his hesitant men, "Do you want me to do it?"[11] Upon seeing this, his men rushed forward and dismantled the obstacle.

Due to his record and proven leadership ability, on 20th May 1863, Chamberlain was promoted to Colonel and became the commander of the 20th Maine. The stage was now set for the greatest battle of the American Civil War and Chamberlain's greatest test, and triumph as a leader – the Battle of Gettysburg.

At the commencement of the battle, Chamberlain and the 20th Maine were placed on the exposed left flank of the Union line on Little Round Top. His orders were to, "Hold that ground at all hazards."[12] This situation was made worse by the fact that the regiment's left flank was "in the air,"[13] it being the last unit on the whole Union left flank. The regiment was also severely under strength, only having 28 officers and 358 men. So as the Confederate attack on the Union left flank was imminent, the position the 20th Maine was critical if the whole Union line was not to be rolled up, which if this had occurred would have resulted in a Confederate victory.

As he waited for the Confederate attack, Chamberlain concentrated on what he called "the possible and the probable"[14] of the impending attack in order, as any good commander should, to meet any possible contingencies. Then he went "up and down the line,"[15] giving encouragement to the men in his regiment, whilst at the same time maintaining a calm exterior, in order to inspire confidence in all those he commanded. At the height of the Confederate attack, when it seemed that the 20th Maine would be outflanked, he ordered the regiment to "refuse the line,"[16] a particularly difficult manoeuvre, especially when under intense fire. Due to his effective military leadership style, combined with training and discipline, the manoeuvre was carried out faultlessly, and the Confederate attack was checked.

However, then came the greatest test of Chamberlain's leadership as his regiment began to run out of ammunition and the Confederates, who still outnumbered him 2-1, were preparing for a final charge, which he knew his line could not resist. As all leader's well know, desperate times call for desperate measures, and Chamberlain, realising his dire situation, ordered, "Bayonet."[17] The 20th Maine charged down the hill into the larger Confederate force, completely routing them and taking over 400 prisoners, thereby ensuring that the Union won the battle of Gettysburg.

Due to his outstanding leadership and courage, on the 26th August 1863, Chamberlain was given permanent command of the 5th Brigade. Next, at the Battle of Spotsylvania on 21st May 1864, Chamberlain, while under tremendous fire, ordered his men to lie down while he himself stood exposed to enemy fire. When several of his officers urged him to take cover, he replied, "I am in no more danger than any other person would be here. It is necessary to know what is going on."[18] Chamberlain did not normally expose himself to danger unnecessarily, but he did not hesitate to incur risk if his duty dictated it, in this case, that he must be able to observe the battlefield. As we have seen, effective military leadership relies on the style that allows the emotionally intelligent leader to create resonance by tuning into people's feelings, and then by guiding them in the right direction.[19]

Finally, at the Confederate surrender at Appomattox, it was General Grant that chose Chamberlain to command the surrender ceremonies of the infantry of the Confederate Army. During the ceremony, as Major General Gordon, at the head of the Confederate Army, reached the Union guard, Chamberlain ordered a rifle salute in honour of a valiant foe. Then as the last of the Confederate flag bearers surrendered their flag, one colour bearer burst into tears. As Chamberlain knew what the banner meant to him, he said, "I admire your noble spirit and only regret that I have not the authority to bid you keep your flag, and carry it home as a precious heirloom."[20] Not surprisingly, Chamberlain's kind words and obvious empathy with the Confederate soldier were widely reported throughout the Confederate Army and also became widely known throughout the South.

Chamberlain displayed effective military leadership styles to the fullest possible extent within his personal philosophy of leadership, and he completely utilised emotional intelligence so that he as a leader could manage his subordinates effectively. Through the achievement of the five principles of ethical leadership – being, *Respects Others, Serves Others, Shows Justice, Manifests Honesty and Builds Community* – he became one of the most effective military leaders in the history of warfare. [21]

As a leader within a military organisation, it is essential that when determining and evaluating your own effective military leadership styles, you inspire a shared vision. As a component of abstract reasoning and analysis, logical intelligence is most widely used to predict success within any society. Then systematic thinking, coupled with abstract reasoning and analysis, is critical in providing the strategy of vision. Creativity and the unconscious always lead us to assess what we are doing and how we could do it better, thereby providing continuous improvement. Then awareness and possibilities refer to our reflections into possible new vistas that can be incorporated into our own military leadership styles.

Appropriate leadership style is determined by the leader's assessment of his subordinates' competence level relative to the task at hand; once this is identified he can identify the appropriate style. Fundamental to this theory is the leader's ability to adjust his style, with the indication that the leader is using the appropriate style being based on the unit's performance. True military leadership encompasses the willingness to transcend the ordinary in order to achieve the extraordinary. In so doing, the leader inspires and motivates subordinates, knowing when to listen and when to speak, whilst at the same time respecting the uniqueness and individuality of each soldier within one's command.

When developing any effective military leadership style, it has been found that most military leaders agree that *Vision, Values, Care for your Subordinates, Promoting Leader Development, Managing Change, Empowering Diversity* and a *Sense of Humour* are all indispensable.[22] The significance of this for the military leader is the attainment of an integrated and comprehensive view of life that provides a foundation for all other issues. Therefore, it incorporates one's belief in human nature and so defines your understanding of human behaviour.

To create a vision for any organisation, the leader must first co-create it with the group as a whole, thereby involving each individual in a study of themselves and the organisation.[23] This then builds resonance and sustainability within the organisation, creating a mental model of the future condition of the organisation. The vision of the organisation must also include the attributes of appropriateness, purpose and direction, while at the same time, and in all things demanding standards of excellence. So as seen by Bolman and Deal (2009), the best visions must be ambitious, but at the same time they must also be easily articulated and understood. The vision is the mental image of what you want the organisation to look like in the future, how you can accomplish this transformation, and what the organisation should look like at the end of the process.

As stated by Kolenda (2006), the critical factor is that one's subordinates share and understand the vision and actively act to support its implementation, otherwise success will be minimised. So any style of leadership relies on the same concepts of shared purpose, specific methodology, and shared objective. However, after commencement of the implementation of the vision, the leader at some intermediate point on the journey may need to adjust or revise the vision to ensure that the organisation remains adaptable to change. The fact is that as circumstances alter, one's initial vision may prove to be only a waypoint along the road. It is Siddle (2008) who sees that even in a stable environment, senior leaders must focus their attention on setting a vision that precludes the inherent inertia that preoccupies them, and so while they are managing the present, they must also be constantly revising their vision.

In this regard, Pendry (2009) sees setting the vision as being the establishment of a purpose or setting organisational goals. While Kolenda (2006) believes that leader's at all levels guide their organisations by looking forward, with the "most effective leader's providing a vision and a plan of action, a set of synchronized programs, to attain the vision."[24] This combination of vision and planning is what sets apart the most effective military leaders. As described by Nye (2009), it the master tactician's ability to achieve a special vision that makes him unique, that "acute sense of the possible,"[25] which they recognise when they are about to make a critical decision. So effective military leaders do need to express a coherent and compelling vision, and as Krames (2008) says, the leader must articulate a vision clearly, compellingly, and simply.

In the evaluation of effective military leader's styles, it is considered that the maintenance of values must be a central tenet, as within the military these form the basis on which the leader serves the nation. Although many values have been articulated, when considering service to a nation, it is considered that seven values are fundamental. These are *Loyalty, Duty, Respect, Selfless-Service, Honour, Integrity and Courage.*[26] These values must serve as a moral compass for every soldier, from the rank of private to that of general, and the leader must embrace them as an integral part of his style. These must then be discussed with subordinates in terms of relevance and applicability within each organisation.

As stated by Gray (2008), the leader faces many challenges and must speak out and act on values and ethics that are morally correct. Then Kolenda (2006) reinforces this view seeing that the creation of a performance-based culture within an organisation is only possible after establishing and communicating a "value-based" purpose. The General of the

Army Douglas Mac Arthur at the Thayer Award Address in May 1962 articulated it as:

> *"Duty, Honour, Country. These three hallowed words reverently dictate what you ought to be, what you can be, what you will be."*

Malone (2010) believes that leaders who desire to maximise the performance of their organisations need to start to focus on the fundamentals of their trade, these being the inculcation of proficiency in basic skills and the "values that embody the organisations moral ethos."[27] It is believed that despite some views to the contrary, that "core values" can and must be taught. In his work, Gray (2008) identifies that these values can be learned and inculcated by the individual into what can be described as a positive learning experience.

It has been said that the two main leadership requirements within the military are "mission accomplishment" and "caring for your soldiers and families"[28] and as a result of the latter, in the last decades, many nations have adopted, within their military forces, an aggressive soldier's welfare programme. In this regard, Kolenda (2006) believes that although the imperative of caring for soldiers embraces a wide variety of issues, he suggests that the issues include quality of life, the provision of proper training and equipment, family support, and timely recognition when a job is well done. These serve as the "essential catalyst that creates unit bonding, coalescence and morale, which eventually lead to *esprit de corps.* "[29]

On this point, Chapman (2011) considers that a leader should possess human understanding and consideration for others. Soldiers are intelligent, complicated beings who will respond favourably to human understanding and consideration. Adopting these means the leader will gain maximum commitment from each soldier, as well as their loyalty. It is pointed out by Asken, Grossman and Christensen (2010) that loyalty is two-way, not only going downward, but also upwards.

When evaluating effective military leadership styles, it is considered that there are three essential leader development requirements, these being formal military courses, leader training within each organisation and then empowerment through delegation. As Grossman (2009) correctly observes, leader development is a lifetime process that is never-ending, lasting from initial enlistment to retirement. In any military career leader, development programmes must blend education, training and experience in what is a continuous process.[30]

However, the last consideration, but perhaps the most important for leader development, is the empowering of one's subordinates. As it has been said "delegation is the art of command,"[31] however, this is one of the harder tasks for senior leaders to master, as they are often reticent to lose what they perceive as their control. Despite this, a leader must learn to delegate to their subordinates in order to encourage individual leader development within their organisation. It is Chapman (2011) who identify that "empowerment is a powerful tool in providing every individual with a sense of pride, the power to make decisions, and the opportunity to demonstrate their ability."[32]

Inevitably, when considering effective military leadership styles, the management of change, which is not always easy, but is inevitable, must be one of the essential elements. As identified by Huse (2009), a leader's ability to manage change is a critical skill and will certainly be an increasing one for the future. Logically thinking senior leaders can chose to manage change, as they identify it as being inevitable, thereby striving to master the implications. It is Bartlett (2009) who sees that if a leader only sits back and is not pro-active, then change will inevitably engulf that organisation.

So the successful management of change in any organisation is totally reliant upon the leader and the members of the organisation. As Siddle (2008) stresses, for the leader to successfully manage change, he or she must initially articulate the reason for the change and how it is pertinent and beneficial to the organisation and its mission and purpose. Nye (2009) correctly identifies that this simple act of communicating the reason for change is not enough, as soldiers resist change for a variety of reasons. Further to this, Kolenda (2006) sees that "most people are perfectly content with the status quo and have an innate fear of change, as it tends to threaten their self-esteem."[33] As tellingly, Brinkerhoff (2010) views change as "requiring the powerful to admit that they were wrong."[34] Therefore, it is essential that leaders address change in their personal leadership style and then explicitly explain why the change is warranted, what the benefits will be, and how the organisation will successfully manage the change.

Today more than ever, diversity, which is often overlooked, needs to be included as part of the leader's style, as long gone are the days when military formations and units were made up of a homogeneous group of soldiers that shared the same culture, ethnicity, and religion. As elaborated by Gray (2008), the increasing transition to multicultural, ethnic, and religious societies has inevitably led to national armed forces reflecting this mix, as any army is the identical reflection of the population that it protects. So according to Kolenda (2006), leaders everywhere must confront the fact that profound social, political, economic, and technological changes are occurring at a blistering pace within all military organisations. So leaders must see that empathy is the fundamental competence of social awareness that makes resonance possible.

Also, leaders must be able to grasp their subordinates' feelings and perspectives by understanding their social, ethnic, and religious backgrounds. Then the leader, through his or her leadership style, must articulate to the members of the organisation that each member is valued and will be listened to equally. Empathy, as elaborated by Nye (2009), is a critical skill for getting on with other members of the organisation that come from other cultures. It is also critical that as a leader, your subordinates know that you will not tolerate those that do not value diversity within the organisation.

The maintenance of a sense of humour is perhaps not a requirement that is readily recognised as part of effective military leadership style. However, it develops a positive and healthy command atmosphere. Nye (2009) believes that "a good sense of humour helps build personal rapport and a greater spirit of cooperation". The simple fact is that when your subordinates are in a good mood, they will view events in a more positive light, and it will also make them work to the best of their ability.

Good moods prove especially important when it comes to military organisations, where the effective military leaders can energise the group into an enthusiastic and cooperative mood, which can determine its success. Conversely, emotional conflicts within the group will detract from the group's shared task and so the performance will falter. Perkins, Holtman, Kessler and McCarthy (2009) stipulate that a leader displaying emotional intelligence can create a friendly and effective climate that lifts the individual's spirits. This is achieved by the leader keeping cooperation high, thereby focusing the group on the task at hand, while at the same time continuing to maintain the quality of the relationships between the members of the organisation.

So, within any military organisation, the leader and their subordinates must quickly harmonise together, and to do this, they must fully understand the "style leadership theory" and its scope. In this regard, the most appropriate mechanism for one's subordinates to come to quickly understand you and your leadership is through the establishment of effective military leadership styles. These must be written from the heart and in the leader's own words, where the priorities, goals and areas of emphasis of the organisation are clearly and concisely presented. Ultimately, the leader must apply an accurate understanding of the theory that he has chosen and never deviate from their tenets, thereby becoming what Kouzes and Posner (2010) call a credible leader.

The key to unleashing the potential in others and then to actualise the vision rests with the effective military leader who creates the right climate in the organisation. Subordinates who are uninspired by the nature of their work, lack confidence in their skills, are uncertain about their responsibilities, are concerned with being criticised for making mistakes, and who rarely get feedback on their performance will not display high performance or innovation. Members of the organisation need to believe that the work they are doing is essential, they themselves must be competent, understand what is expected of them and how their work fits into the overall plan. So the leader must communicate the purpose and clarify the goals so that each member of the organisation knows what they are to contribute. So, the reasoning linking the application and theory are sound, thus enabling the effective military leader to lay the foundations for the creation of a high-performance unit.

Within any military organisation, the art of implementing an inspired and shared vision is to touch the soul of each individual, to then mould the organisation together as one team, whilst at the same time uplifting their collective spirits. The effective military leader must make full use of the power of oratory in order to communicate and instil a shared ideal, and inspired vision. They must express everything in such concrete terms that they make these visions, impressions, and representations become real to each individual.[35] These leaders are enthusiastic and have a genuine belief in the capacity of their subordinates to achieve the impossible. So effective military leaders strengthen people through their inspired and shared vision, and they then supply the means to achieve the vision, remaining committed, and passionate, despite the obstacles that will be encountered along the path to success.

In conclusion, when evaluating effective military leadership styles *Vision, Values, Care of Subordinates, Leader Development, Managing Change, Diversity* and a *Sense of Humour,* are fundamental "core values." However, these alone will not be a panacea for all the issues that the leader and the organisation will face, instead they will be a solid starting point from which the leader's style can be further crafted and refined through time and experience. It must be foremost in the mind of every effective military leader that true leadership encompasses the willingness to transcend the ordinary, in order to achieve the extraordinary and in so doing inspire, and motivate your subordinates. The effective military leader must know when to listen and when to speak, whilst at the same time respecting the uniqueness and individuality of each soldier within one's command.

# CHAPTER TEN

# *Leadership Research*

The five empirical articles from peer-reviewed journals that this author has identified as being critical to his understanding of his specialisation of effective military leadership, but in particular, the analysis and recommendations for developing strong leadership skills in infantry combat are as follows:

Horey, J. D. & Fallesen, J.J. (2009, November).
**Leadership Competencies.**
*The Military Conflict Institute, 189*(22), 101-141.

This research identifies the problem that leadership competency modelling is an inexact science and that many frameworks present competencies that mix functions and characteristics, have structural inconsistencies, and so may be confusing to potential users. The authors see that the challenge is to establish a common language for discussing leadership concepts, ensuring consistent assessment, development, reinforcement, and feedback processes are in place for maintaining leadership across our military forces. The current problem is that even after decades of research, dozens of theories, and the vast expenditure in funding, we still have vastly different visions of leadership and leadership competencies across our various military services.[1] The authors' view is that defining leadership must be the first step toward establishing how it should be conducted within the military. However, a simple definition is insufficient for describing the nature, boundaries, contexts, and desirable manifestations of leadership. So, enter the evolution of competencies.

The research purpose is to link existing U.S. military leadership competency frameworks and identify similarities and differences in terms of their content and structures.[2] In this regard, behavioural scientists and organisational development professionals have sought to improve individual and group work processes through the application of systematic procedures and research-based principles. The techniques of job-analysis, and to a lesser extent competency modelling, have long been used to establish the requirements of jobs and positions throughout organisations. They have also provided input to selection, training, and management practices. Competencies have become a more prevalent method of identifying the requirements of supervisory, managerial, and leadership positions rather than job or task analysis techniques, as they provide a more general description of responsibilities associated across these positions.[3]

The authors' design examined several existing U.S. military and civilian leadership competency frameworks and attempted to link the core constructs across the frameworks in order to identify similarities and differences in terms of their content and structure. They used data analysis to create tables that represent many of the traits and characteristics commonly found in leadership competency frameworks. As a result, they created constructs that included values (principles, integrity), cognitive skills (inquiring, thinking), interpersonal skills (caring, enthusiastic, communicating), diversity components (tolerance, respect, empathy), and change orientation (open-minded, risk taking).[4] As a result, they were able to design a sample leadership competencies table that demonstrated the universality of their leadership competency profile.

The authors identified that a threat to the validity in their research study was the fact that components of competency frameworks are as varied as the competencies themselves. They further identified that competencies are generally no more than labels that require additional detail to communicate how they relate to leadership and behaviour. The authors also prefaced their study by admitting that it was not appropriate to judge any frameworks by surface comparison of the labels and definitions/descriptions of the competencies and components. The authors further stipulate that a more accurate analysis of these frameworks would involve an elemental analysis of each framework construct, but that this was beyond the scope of their study.

The authors' findings were designed to implement and/or improve sound competency modelling procedures for the future. They recommended the defining of leadership and the establishment of boundaries considered in the organisation's leadership framework. The establishment of consistent parameters that defined the tasks, functions, actions, and behaviours those leaders were to perform. That these organisations seek to eliminate redundancy in competencies and clearly indicate how actions and behaviours are linked to task completion.[5] The authors further recommended the involvement of behavioural scientists as well as leaders at all levels of the organisation in the development and validation of the model/framework.

The article serves as a coherent and relevant source of information and guidance for the development of military leadership competency modelling procedures. The value of the article is that it identifies that thoroughly trained soldiers led by competent leaders reduce the inherent risk to life and limb and motivate each soldier to put forth the maximum effort needed for victory on the battlefield. The relevance of this article is that the authors describe how a soldier's willingness to fight is based on confidence in their leaders, confidence in the effectiveness of their training, and in knowing that the effort of each soldier in the unit is working together toward the same end.

Huse, T. D. (2009, November-December).
**Transformational Leadership in the Era of Change.**
*Military Review,109*(5), 82-117.

The research problem is based upon the fact that the U.S. Army is currently in the midst of unprecedented transformation, with weapons, vehicles, technology, and most importantly, soldiers, being the focus of the Army's reorganisation. As a result, it has been identified that understanding the relationship between soldiers and change is a definite leadership challenge. By combining emerging technologies with soldiers and change, future leadership challenges increase immeasurably. There-fore, the problem is how do Army leaders at all levels enhance leadership through this rapidly changing environment?[6]

The research purpose is to show how transformational leadership is about leading an organisation through change, as in its purest form, it is the ability to guide and direct those within a given organisation, focusing on one clear, directed vision through the application of the components of transformational leadership. The purpose of this research is to high-light that as the U.S. Army continues to change and progress through the 21$^{st}$ century, it will without doubt need transformational leaders to spearhead this change and to serve as "agents of change." The purpose of this research is to determine the applicability of transformational leader-ship within the U.S. Army through analysis and comparison of transfor-mational leadership styles and techniques based upon selected evaluation criteria. The fundamental question underlying this research is whether the U.S. Army should adopt transformational leadership at all levels of command within the Army.

The design of the case studies was an analysis of previous renowned military leaders who possessed exceptional transformational leadership ability through periods of true change and transformation within the history of the U.S. Army. The case studies apply the principles of trans-formational leadership to these leaders' abilities, decision-making, and overall leadership proficiency, with it being illustrated how the skills and attributes of these selected leaders compare using this researches evalua-tion criteria.[7] Initially, the author identifies the flow and framework of the research, and identifies the selected criteria used in evaluating the effectiveness of transformational leadership. Next, the author defines transformational leadership and its components by focusing on the four major components of transformational leadership: idealised influence, inspirational motivation, intellectual stimulation, and individualised consideration. Additionally, the author discusses the use and relevance of the Multi-factor Leadership Questionnaire, in conjunction with the Leadership Development Plan.

The author identifies the threats to validity as being the basic understanding of transformational leadership and how it works, as this must begin early with the individual's initial training and education. This early introduction to the components of transformational leadership will allow leaders at all levels of the military hierarchy to continually develop their leadership style. The U.S. Army has taken the initial steps in this area with the implementation of transformational leadership courses that are attended by all commissioned officers, regardless of their branch. It is further identified that positive reinforcement of transformational leadership traits and characteristics must be throughout the individual's career. This is designed to be achieved through either formalised professional development (career courses), and/or at the informal, personal level (mentoring, coaching).[8]

The findings from the research focus on the premise that transformational leaders are effective and are needed within the U.S. Army. Moreover, the research recommends that the transformational leadership style should be the primary leadership style taught to leaders at all levels of the U.S. Army. The recommendations from the research suggest possible solutions for implementing transformational leadership through the effective application of counselling, mentorship, training and education, attitude, and a personal leadership development plan.

The author of this article identifies that although leadership is a widely discussed and often studied discipline, little agreement exists among scholars or practitioners about what defines leadership. Concepts of leadership are either disarmingly similar or awesomely complex. The value of the article is that it defines that to understand leadership, one must understand its essential nature, which is the process of the leader and followers engaging in reciprocal influence to achieve a shared purpose.[9] The relevance is that the author explains transformational and transforming leadership, which involves strong personal identification of followers with the leader. The findings are that effective military leaders are alike in one crucial trait in that they have what has come to be known as "emotional intelligence."

Kertsh, K.G. (2010, May/June).
**How High-Performance Organisations Develop Leadership.**
*Military Review, 81*(9), 76-118.

Each year, the U.S. Air Force spends tremendous resources on pro-grammes to develop military leaders that will guide it to success in com-ing decades. In this regard, there is little question that classroom and other formal development programmes have benefit for leadership de-velopment. However, it is considered that these will have more impact when based on and supported by a pervasive commitment to leadership development, positive leadership by example, and adherence to values. The problem is that the U.S. Air Force has found it difficult to identify that the best development of leaders comes through a "mastery of the fundamentals," which if adopted, could be a significant improvement in its ability to develop new leadership competencies.[10]

The research purpose is based on the fact that there is little question that classroom and other formal development programmes benefit their mili-tary participants, and it is believed that three things lie at the foundation of developing leadership abilities. The author of this research study describes these as a "mastery of the fundamentals," and these are a top-down com-mitment to developing leaders, exceptional leadership by example, and an integrated value set that guides organisational and individual actions.

The research design was based on case studies of five high-perform-ing organisations, and in order to provide a broad sample set, the study included public, private, big, small, and military organisations.[11] These organisations were Everdream, PeopleSoft, Cisco Systems, the Social Security Administration, and the U.S. Marine Corps. Selection of the study participants was limited to those organisations that consistently outperformed expectations and are thus considered leaders in their fields. Once an organisation agreed to participate, interviews and organisational research were then used to answer a series of questions on how leadership abilities were developed in each organisation.

Specific effort was made to interview individuals representative of mul-tiple levels of leadership within the organisation. In this regard, in this study, a leader was defined as an individual that effectively provides direction, identifies and obtains results, manages relationships, and anticipates and responds to the internal and external environment of the organisation. This definition was derived by the author of the research following discussions with senior consultants in the management /leadership field and served as a common frame of reference during the case study interviews. Comments and insights were then summarised into the case studies.

Threats to validity were based on the fact that there were limited resources for the study, resulting in a small sample size of five organisations, and this raises the potential for error when the findings are applied to other high-performing organisations. However, the consistency of the findings suggests that this is not the case. Also, the final group of five organisations was neither comprehensive nor necessarily representative of all high-performance organisations, but the author still considers that it provides a solid foundation for the study. Once the organisations were selected for the study, the author conducted personal interviews with members of each organisation.[12] However, it was found difficult to interview individuals that were representative of multiple levels of leadership within each organisation.

The findings were based on the case studies of the five high-performance organisations examined in this research study, and the author concludes that success in building leaders has its roots more in the "mastery of fundamentals" than in extensive, formal leadership development programmes or commercial education. The author identifies that when an organisation makes development of leaders a top priority, and when actions of leaders at all levels exemplify that commitment, then leadership abilities are successfully developed and extraordinary results can be achieved. When examining these five high-performance organisations the author further identified the existence and adherence to a set of core values that members could easily connect with, both emotionally and conceptually. It was the adherence to and integration of those values into the organisations daily activities that developed individual's ability to lead.

The compelling case from the article is that the aim of leadership is not merely to find and record failures in men, but instead it is to remove the causes of those failures. It further identifies that effective military leaders enable their subordinates to routinely accomplish the extraordinary, as they realise that in a life-threatening situation, individuals cannot be managed, instead they must be led. It is the effective military leader who successfully builds and leads amazing organisations that achieve their mission ethically, honestly, and humanely.[13] This is achieved by the leader communicating the objectives, while at the same time ensuring that the aim is known and the purpose understood. The author explains in detail each meaning of objective, aim, and purpose as these tenets are essential to achieving effective military leadership.

Bartone, P. T. (2010, April).
**Leadership and Personality in the Military Organisation.**
*Defense Issues, 83*(52), 27-76.

Military organisations have long emphasised the importance of leadership and have sought to train and develop highly effective leaders in a multitude of ways. The problem is that as roles and missions have expanded in the post-modern military, demands on the military leader have increased substantially. Today, our forces are called upon to serve in a broader and more complex range of missions, which have proved that much more challenging in the severe environments of Iraq and Afghanistan. In this context, understanding the full range of factors that contribute to effective military leadership is critical to mission success.[14] Unfortunately, there is considerable speculation, and answers too often rely on anecdotes and hearsay. Historically, social scientists who have tried to address the question empirically have tended to focus on intelligence and various mental abilities, while personality factors have drawn considerably less attention. So, it is believed that there is a requirement to examine personality variables as predictors of leader performance, as this understanding will enhance the quality of leadership in all military services.

The purpose of this research study is to understand the range of factors and personal qualities that contribute to effective military leadership.

However, the author believes that the real problem in defining military leadership lies in specifying what is meant by leadership, and then applying it to the military case. If certain individual characteristics, attributes, or skills are associated with effective leader performance under various conditions, then a vital question for the military is how to develop these characteristics. The research purpose was designed in recognition that effective development of leaders must involve not only skills acquisition, but also personal growth, and increasing individual maturity.[15]

The author's research design investigates the influence of personality factors on effective military leadership by conducting a meta-analysis of 14 samples. These explore the relations of the five-factor model to military leadership. As indicated in his research study, the author identifies that the five-factor model is one of the major developments in personality psychology over the recent years.[16] These five factors are neuroticism, extraversion, openness to experience, agreeableness, and conscientiousness. While the five-factor model represents an important scientific advance in the field of personality, the author considers that it does not describe the sum total of normal personality.

Threats to validity are based on the fact that as the proportion of women military leaders continues to rise in the U.S all-volunteer force, the author should have placed more importance on understanding gender differences as a factor in influencing leader style and performance. This observation is based on the fact that research evidence shows that women tend to be higher in transformational leadership style than men. Studies also suggest that more "feminine" (concerned leadership, individualised attention) approaches lead to better performance in modern organisational cultures that tend to emphasise cooperation and collaboration within relatively flat and flexible structures. These are compared to "male" task-orientated approaches which are characterised by instrumental strategies in a more hierarchical and rigid structure.[17]

The major findings of the research study was that simple training, no matter how elaborate or intensive, is not likely to produce the kind of sophistication and breadth of perspective that the military requires in its leaders. Reflecting this trend, West Point has recently incorporated an explicitly developmental philosophy into its overall leader's development programme. Another trend is the increased attention to personality and cognitive factors that are related to effective military leadership. Both these developments reflect a recognition of and appreciation for abiding individual differences, and at the same time an understanding that leadership growth occurs across the individual's lifespan. It is now clear that personality variables merit serious consideration in the selection and training of military leaders in order to ensure their ability to perform in rapidly altering and high-risk circumstances.[18]

The author's findings relate to the fact that adaptive leadership in the military is increasingly important in the complex and ambiguous military environment of today. Therefore, he believes that the effective military leader must not be limited to one leadership style in a combat situation. He considers that an effective military leader must be adaptive in their own leadership style in order to move towards participative leadership and so empower their subordinates through the delegation of authority. This situational leadership is a widely used model that emphasises using more than one leadership style in order to develop subordinates in the military.[19] The author considers that as subordinates gain training, experience, and guidance, they will be better prepared to accomplish the goals of the organisation with less leader influence. Therefore, his premise is that the effective military leader must be constantly training, developing, and mentoring their subordinates in order to develop a core of competent and professional subordinate leaders who are totally conversant with the orders of the leader.

Vore, K. J. (2010, September/October).
**Senior Leader Decision-Making.**
*Military Review,* 75(19), 12-52.

The problem is that many governmental leaders, leaders of industry, and military officers have failed to succeed when placed at higher levels of responsibility. So, understanding how to solve problems at increasingly higher levels of dynamic complexity is fundamental to the success of the military at large. Being able to discern a complex situation, seizing upon the facts and what is critical to the situation, knowing at a glance what is occurring and understanding what is important, and then making the correct decision are critical aspects of senior military leaders decision-making process. The fundamental truth is that our military resources are rarely sufficient to overwhelm an enemy everywhere and continuously. As a result, the military leader's ability to "divine a path to success," which maximises leverage over the enemy at the least cost to our own forces, is imperative for success in long-term military operations.

The author's research purpose is based on the fact that he considers there is only one way to explore this vital issue, and it is through the examination of the thoughts and decisions of those who have been thrust into complex decision-making situations and proved to be eminently successful.[20] Therefore, the purpose of the research is to examine the decision-making methods used by successful military commanders with respect to patterns and anomalies, singular evaluation, and leverage points.

The research design for this study sampled 27 different authors with respect to decision-making, with 14 of these authors devoting their works specifically to decision-making. The research includes an additional 13 sources that address the topics of intuition, creative intelligence, critical thinking, and senior command decision-making. The author during the course of his research identified that there was a considerable overlap between the sources devoted strictly to decision-making theory and the sources in the other categories, despite their titles.[21]

The author identifies as a threat to validity the fact that conventional decision-making follows a four-step process; these are problem definition, course of action generation, course of action analysis and evaluation, and course of action selection and execution. This is known as "rational choice strategy," and its major disadvantage is that it is time-consuming to determine and evaluate all the options to any given problem. So, the author postulates that a rigorous, analytical approach cannot be used in a dynamic and rapidly developing situation. Therefore, he gravitates toward a "naturalistic" decision-making process where there is time pressure, high stakes, ill-defined problems, dynamic conditions, and inadequate information with which to work. Unfortunately, within this research study, the author fails to recognise the critical importance of expertise and of intuition in any decision-making assessment. Therefore, this is the Achilles' heel for any commander using the "naturalistic" process who does not possess either of these traits.

The author's findings from this research study determined that successful military leaders use patterns and anomalies to an extent, that they do not use singular evaluation (instead preferring to generate and choose from among multiple options), and that they overwhelmingly make ingenious use of leverage points. In addition to their decision-making prowess, successful military leaders possessed a tremendous ability to envision the current state, the desired future state, and to be able to devise a way to move from one to the other with the least cost to their own command.[22] All possessed incredible willpower in prosecuting their decisions. However, these successful military leaders were not infallible; all made numerous mistakes, either missing a prompt decision, or failing to see an opportunity. However, all adapted quickly, decided on an alternate course of action and restructured their winning ways before the enemy had a chance to seal a victory.

This article's findings describe and examine military leadership within conflict and describe combat leadership as both an art and a science. The author sees it as a science, as it works in a deliberate and rational way to achieve a given end, which in military terms is called the mission. The author then describes combat leadership as an art, as the commander relies on persuading his subordinates to engage willingly in an irrational behaviour, where each individual is in a kill-or-be-killed situation.[23] He further considers effective military leadership relies on the transformation of data into information, analysis, decision-making, resource allocation, and communications in order to give rationale direction to the operation. The author believes that it is in leadership that the military commander meets the ultimate test of inspiring individuals to perform their duties and so to effectively contribute to the accomplishment of the mission.

The article that this author has selected, to assess how he might have conducted the research study differently, is "Leadership and Personality in the Military Organization" by Paul T. Bartone. This author's research study would be based upon the nature of effective military leadership, but in particular, the analysis and recommendations for developing strong leadership skills in infantry combat.

The research purpose of this study would be to understand the nature of effective military leadership and in particular, to analyse and make recommendations for developing strong leadership skills in infantry combat.[24] It is considered that this would allow the current and next generations of soldiers to successfully confront and defeat those that are perpetrating worldwide terrorism. At this stage in the research, the realities of infantry combat can be generally defined as both an art and a science, where the effective military leader is able to harness the four emotional intelligence domains, thus creating a shared vision in their subordinates that will inevitably lead to success in combat.[25]

The theoretical perspective for this research design and elements of design would be based on the study of "organisational leadership theories,"[26] which would provide a basis for this study. Additionally, in order to facilitate this theoretical perspective for this research topic, "critical theory perspectives" would be utilised (Schram, 2006), which focus on empowering individuals to overcome the constraints placed upon them by race, class, and gender. It is considered that a scientific method, which begins with a theory, collects data that either supports or refutes the theory and then makes necessary revisions before additional tests are made, will be pertinent to this research study.

The strengths and weaknesses of the envisioned design and methods are based on the fact that at the outset, it must be realised that research questions are in most cases the result of an interpretive design process rather than being the starting point for that process. The fact is that research questions will give specific shape to the stated purposes and this will make explicit that which needs to be learnt. In this case, it has been decided that this line of inquiry is "best served not by one but by several research questions."[27] These questions would build on each other in a linear and logical sequence, thereby complementing each other. In order to achieve this aim, five preliminary questions would be asked, with the goal being to draw out a key question from the process. Throughout there will be a sharpening of the focus, so that increasingly there are less and less peripheral issues to be concerned with, leaving that which is of fundamental concern to be studied in the greatest detail.[28]

The means of ensuring the quality of the findings would be reliant on a scientific method, which begins with a theory, collects data that either supports or refutes the theory, and then makes necessary revisions before additional tests are made, will be pertinent to this study. The fact is that knowledge found in research is always imperfect and fallible, so the researcher is in a constant process of making claims and then refining or abandoning them for other claims that are more strongly affirmed. As data, evidence, and logical considerations shape knowledge being objective is an essential aspect of this research.

The justification for choosing this design and method is that it is believed that critical theory perspectives will allow more room in the study for innovation and to work more within researcher-designed frameworks. That is as they relate to marginalised individuals within the Army chain of command with a view to creating equal opportunities based upon the adoption of accepted organisational leadership principles. The assumption is that collecting diverse types of data best provides an understanding of a research problem as it is founded on actions, situations, and outcomes rather than on precursory conditions.[29] So, this research would not be committed to any one system of philosophy or actuality. This also means that the qualitative methods, approaches and procedures of research best demonstrate validity, ethical principles, and integrity for this study. It is believed that research always occurs in a social, historical, and political context. Therefore, this study will be open to considering multiple methods and different hypothesis, as well as different forms of data collection and analysis.

The methods of data analysis and the reporting plan would be based on this study of organisational leadership theories, which would provide a basis for this research study. Additionally, in order to facilitate this theoretical perspective for this research topic, "critical theory perspectives" would be utilised. In this regard, it is considered that a "case study approach,"[30] which begins with a theory, collects data that either supports or refutes the theory, and then makes necessary revisions before additional tests are made, would be pertinent to this research topic. A case-study approach would be chosen, as it is considered that the reporting plan would provide a means for exploring and understanding the meaning that individuals or groups ascribe to a social or human problem. Then the raw data would be collected, a case record constructed, and a final case study narrative written.

The data that is collected would answer the research question and contribute to theory, as within the Army there are 5.5% officers, 10.7% warrant officers, 19.3% non-commissioned officers, 62.2% soldiers, and 2.3% recruits, and these percentages will be duplicated within the sample. Additionally, as 9.1% of all Army personnel are females, it will be ensured that this percentage is represented in the sample. The survey design will sample these individuals randomly and will target serving male and female Army personnel, as well as those that have retired within the last two years. An instrument will be specifically designed for his research based upon content validity, predictive or concurrent validity, and construct validity. During this process, the survey will be validated.

# CHAPTER ELEVEN

## *Research Ethics*

It is the responsibility of all doctoral researchers to conduct their research with integrity, in a responsible manner, and in accordance with high ethical standards. They must be constantly aware that "scientific integrity"[1] defines the commitment of researchers to adhere to the fundamental rules of good scientific practice. Truth and transparency, self-discipline, self-criticism, and fairness are inseparable for behaviour of integrity. They represent the basis of all scientific activity and are pre-conditions for the credibility and acceptance of science. The present guidelines for research integrity and good scientific practice define the authoritative rules that apply to all doctoral researchers. These guidelines are intended to serve as the defining principles for the planning, execution, presentation, and assessment of research studies.

Ethical issues are present in any kind of research, as the process creates tension between the aims of the research and the rights of the participants to maintain privacy. Therefore, in planning and conducting research, as well as reporting research findings, the researcher must fulfil several obligations in order to meet the required ethical standards.[2] First, the research project must be planned so that the chance for misleading results is minimised. Second, the research study must be structured so that it meets ethical acceptability. Any doubts the researcher may have regarding questionable ethical procedures or methods must be resolved through peer review or through consultation with appropriate parties such as the IRB. Third, steps must be taken to protect and ensure the dignity and welfare of all participants, as well as those that may be affected by the results of the research study.[3]

Once the research topic has been identified, the researcher can begin searching for related literature on the topic. This literature review accomplishes several purposes. It shares with the reader the results of other studies that are closely related to the one being undertaken, and it sets the current research study within a conceptual and theoretic context. Therefore, the literature review is one of the most important steps in a research study, as there is almost no topic that is so new or unique that there is no relevant or related information.[4] However, the researcher needs to concentrate on the scientific literature by concentrating on the most credible research journals that use a peer or juries review system. Also, the researcher needs to commence the literature review early in the research process, as this will assist in defining the parameters of the study.

The important fact is that the researcher acknowledges the importance of reading, reviewing, and understanding the literature on the topic prior to conducting the data collection. The aim is to be as familiar with the topic as possible, as the literature review will demonstrate that our understanding of the topic in question is somehow incomplete. Therefore, the role of the literature review is to document our current understanding of the topic and share with the reader the results of other studies that are closely related to the one being undertaken.[5] It relates the study to the larger, ongoing dialogue in the literature, filling in the gaps and extending prior studies. Importantly, it provides a framework for establishing the importance of the study as well as defining a benchmark for comparing the results with other findings.

When conducting research, the fact is that a good researcher is an ethical researcher, and this is a lifelong learning process because we always have more to learn about the ethical implications of our actions. In this regard, there are four principles that are widely accepted as being essential to mastering the ethics of research. Firstly, "do no harm"[6] by making sure that you have permission to observe, and that those with whom you are working do not suffer in any way from the research. Here, informed consent is the key to ethical conduct in research. Second, "be open," do not observe subjects without their knowledge and also inform them why you have used the material in a particular way. Third, "be honest," do not lie to your subjects or use material without their permission. Finally, "be careful," by making sure that you have correctly documented all the research so that others can readily follow an audit trail through you work.[7] All this documentation must not compromise the confidentiality of the subjects or the settings.

The principle of "voluntary participation" requires that subjects not be coerced into participating in the research, and closely related to this principle is the requirement of "informed consent."[8] These dictate that prospective research subjects must be fully informed of the procedures and associated risks involved in the research and must give their consent to participate. There are two standards that are applied to protect the privacy of research subjects, and these are "confidentiality and anonymity."[9] That is, in order to protect their confidentiality, the subjects are assured that all identifying information will not be made available to anyone not directly involved in the study. The stricter standard of anonymity essentially means that the subjects will remain anonymous throughout the study, even to the researchers themselves. However, even when there are clear ethical standards, at times the need to do accurate research conflicts with the rights of the potential subjects. In this case, the Institutional Review Board (IRB) will review the research study proposal with respect to the ethical implications and decide if additional actions need to be taken to assure the rights of subjects. The IRB also has an important role to protect the organisation and the researcher against accusations of neglecting the ethical rights of the subjects (Resnik 2010).

The purpose of qualitative research is to describe a phenomenon from the subjects' point of view through interviews and observations. However, qualitative research methods make it difficult to predict what data will be collected, and this leaves the researcher with the obligation to anticipate the possible outcomes and to weigh both benefits and potential harm. So, researchers need to protect their research subjects; develop a trust with them; promote the integrity of the research; guard against misconduct and impropriety that may reflect on their organisations or institutions; and cope with new, challenging problems.[10] However, it is important to note that ethical practices involve much more than merely following a set of guidelines, and so researchers need to anticipate and address any ethical dilemmas that may arise during the course of their research.

When writing the dissertation manuscript, the researcher will be expected to follow very formal and explicit analytical procedures in order to produce a scholarly monograph with careful attention to methodological rigour.[11] The researcher will be expected to report in detail on all aspects of the methodology, including discussion of analytical procedures, problems, and limitations. When considering data collection based on surveys, standardised tests, and experimental designs, the lines between data collection and analysis are clear. The ideas for making sense of data that emerge while still in the field constitute the beginning of analysis. Such overlapping of data collection and analysis improves both the quality of the data collected and the quality of the analysis. That is as long as the researcher does not allow these initial interpretations to overly confine analytical possibilities. Instead of focusing additional data collection entirely on confirming preliminary field hypotheses, the researcher should become sensitive to looking for alternative explanations and patterns that could invalidate initial insights.[12]

When the data collection has formally ended, it is time for the researcher to begin the final analysis. In this regard, the researcher has two primary sources to draw from in organising the analysis. These are firstly the questions that were generated during the conceptual and design phases of the study prior to the fieldwork, and secondly the analytic insights and interpretations that emerged during the data collection. However, once the writing of the dissertation manuscript has commenced, the fieldwork may not be over as gaps or ambiguities found during the analysis may require more data collection.[13] Therefore, subjects may be re-contacted to clarify or deepen responses, or new observations may be made to enrich the findings. If additional fieldwork is not possible, the researcher must note any gaps and unresolved ambiguities as part of the final report.

However, in addition to conceptualising the manuscript writing process, the researcher needs to anticipate the ethical issues that may arise during the process. The fact is that the ethical issues do not end with data collection and analysis as they apply as well to the actual writing and dissemination of the final study report. As an example, the researcher must not use language or words that are "biased against persons because of their gender, sexual orientation, racial or ethnic group, disability, or age."[14] Other ethical issues in writing the research will involve the suppressing, falsifying, or inventing of findings to meet the researcher's needs. Also, in planning a study, it is important for the researchers to anticipate the repercussions of conducting the research on certain audiences, ensuring not to misuse the results to favour one group or another.

Another important issue when writing the dissertation manuscript is not to exploit colleagues, ensuring authorship to individuals who have substantially contributed to the research study. Then, it is important for the researcher to present the details of the research with the study design, thereby allowing the readers themselves to determine the credibility of the study.[15] Finally, researchers must not engage in duplicate or redundant publication in which authors publish papers that present exactly the same data, discussions, and conclusions, not offering new material. By adopting these measures, the researcher will ensure that the dissertation manuscript is written with care and integrity in order to meet the ethical standards of scientific research.

Authors who present the words, data, or ideas of others as if they were their own, without attribution in a form appropriate for the medium of presentation, are committing theft of intellectual property, and so may be guilty of plagiarism, and thus of research misconduct. Not only does plagiarism violate the standard code of conduct governing all research, but in many cases, it could constitute an infraction of the law by infringing on a copyright held by the original author or publisher. Therefore, the work of others must be cited or credited, whether published or unpublished and whether it had been written work, an oral presentation, or material on a website. One particularly serious form of plagiarism is the misuse of privileged information taken from a grant application or manuscript received from a funding agency or journal editor for peer review.[16] In such a case, the plagiarism is a serious matter of theft of intellectual property as it deprives the original author of appropriate credit by citation, it could also pre-empt priority of first publication or use of the original idea to which the source author is entitled.

Then there is the question of whether a researcher using a ghost-writer to assist complete the research studies dissertation manuscript is ethical. A ghost-writer is a professional writer who is paid to write books, articles, stories, reports, or other content, which is then credited to another person.[17] Politicians, executives, and celebrities often hire ghost-writers to draft or edit autobiographies, magazine article, or other written material. The division of work between the ghost-writer and the credited author varies a great deal. In some cases, the ghost-writer is hired to polish and edit a draft or nearly completed manuscript, in which case the ideas and language in the finished book or article are primarily those of the credited author. In the other cases, a ghost-writer would do most of the writing, using concepts provided by the credited author. At a minimum, the credited author usually provides a basic framework of ideas at the beginning or provides comments on the ghostwriter's final draft.

By many accounts, ghost-writing has been around for as long as the written word, with some claiming that the book of Genesis was ghost-written, and that the Latin poets supplied Caesar's greatest lines. However, does this fact make ethical ghost-writing, which some consider "the cannibalisation of writing and publishing."[18]

So, a public speaker, writer, or researcher should not be able to use another person's research, ideas or actual written words to communicate a message. In this regard, it is in fact stated in the "Academic Integrity at NCU: Basic Definitions" that:

"NCU considers it a violation of Academic Integrity to knowingly submit another person's work and present it as that of the Learner's without properly citing the source of the work."

Unfortunately, in academic circles there is an ever-increasing problem where university students hire ghostwriters to write essays, papers, theses, and dissertations. Since the beginning of this millennium, many "essay mills"[19] have begun, offering students the sale of previously written essays and more recently even customised essay writing for a higher price.

This academic fraud has required universities to "develop strategies to combat the widespread incidence of cheating."[20] These include comparing student essays against databases of known plagiarised essays and the giving of oral examinations where it is believed that a student's essay is ghost-written. That the NCU has had to introduce an Academic Integrity Tutorial, which includes having all students read NCU's Academic Integrity Policy, and then complete the mandatory NCU Academic Integrity Questionnaire, in order to confirm the students "understanding and acceptance of that policy," supports this view.

Risk assessment involves consideration of physical and psychological risks along with protection of privacy. The researcher must develop procedures that reduce and minimise any risks to human subject participants. No more than minimal risk exists when the probability and magnitude of harm or discomfort anticipated in the research are not greater than those ordinarily encountered in daily life or during performance of routine physical or psychological examination or tests. Therefore, research studies must involve anonymous data to be considered no more than minimal risk. More than minimal risk exists when the possibility of physical or psychological harm, or harm related to a breach of confidentiality, or invasion of privacy is greater than what is typically encountered in daily life.[21]

There are various types of risks, with the main ones being physical and psychological risk, and then there are risks due to invasion of privacy and/or breach of confidentiality. Exercise other than that ordinarily encountered in daily life by that participant would be considered more than minimal risk. So, the researcher must consider the physical characteristics of potential research participants as well as the type of exercise involved in the study. The ingestion, tasting, or smelling of a substance that poses any health risk are considered more than minimal risk. As regards psychological risks, a research activity such as a survey or questionnaire that could potentially result in emotional stress would be considered more than minimal risk. The researcher must also consider whether any activity could potentially result in negative consequences for the participant due to invasion of privacy or breach of confidentiality.[22] However, these risk levels can be reduced by collecting data that is anonymous and uses data-collection procedures that make it impossible to link any identifying information to a particular participant.

Informed consent refers to the process of ensuring that potential human subjects understand that they may choose whether or not to participate in the study. Individuals must never be forced or coerced into participating in a research study. The IRB reviews both the protocol and the informed consent document ('Consent Form") that potential subjects must sign before participating in any research study.[23] Subjects must be informed that they can withdraw from a research study at any time. In this regard, research subjects already participating in a protocol by virtue of signing an approved consent document must be informed of any information regarding risks and benefits of study participation when such data becomes available as the study progresses. If a consent document states that subjects will be informed of research outcomes, the researcher must honour that commitment and so inform the subjects. Any proposed amendment in the research protocol or consent document must be approved by the IRB in advance of its implementation.[24] Every protocol submitted to the IRB must include a plan for data and safety protection and the confidentiality of information related to each individual must be respected and maintained.

Informed consent protocols and opening statements in interviews typically cover such issues as the purpose of collecting the information, who is the information for and how will it be used, what will be asked in the interview, how will the responses be handled, and what risks/benefits are involved for the participant. The researcher provides this information in advance of the interview with the statement of purpose being simple, straightforward, and understandable. Ethical standards also require that the researcher not put participants in a situation where they might be at "risk of harm"[25] as a result of their participation. Harm can be defined as both physical and psychological.

The researcher and the IRB must consider whether any activity could potentially result in negative consequences for the subject due to invasion of privacy or a breach of confidentiality. However, risk levels can be reduced by appropriately protecting confidentiality, by collecting data that is anonymous, and by using data-collection procedures that make it impossible to link any identifying information with the subject's responses. The protection of privacy and confidentiality involves taking careful measures to ensure that research data and/or responses are not disclosed to the public or unauthorised individuals. Whenever possible, researchers should collect data anonymously. If the research involves data from the same subject on multiple occurrences, the data or survey would need to be labelled with an identifier.

The question of confidentiality often raises a dilemma in qualitative research, as ethical tensions are to be expected. Going into the field and dealing with things as you find them will always be complex, and some of that complexity will be ethical. Day-to-day issues or "ethics in practice"[26] is particularly important in order to go beyond the standard protections that we seek through consent forms and other devices. The researcher needs to be ethically sensitive by being reflexive over practices and by being alert to ethical issues as they arise on a daily basis. The fact is that qualitative research often has to discard findings, as reporting those findings might reveal the identity of the informant. So, as qualitative research deals with more complex settings, it should be expected that the researcher's ethical responsibilities are equally more complex.

In order to preserve accurate documentation of observed facts, with which later reports or conclusions can be compared, every researcher has the obligation to maintain a clear and complete record of data acquired. Meticulous record-keeping is a sound scientific practice which provides an accurate account of observations that become a permanent reference for the researcher, who otherwise might not remember later exactly what had been observed, or what methods had been used. An accurate record also serves others who may want to replicate the observation or to apply the same method to other situations.[27] In addition, it is an aid in allowing the eventual sharing of information with others and as documentation that can disprove any subsequent allegation of fabrication or falsification of data.

The research in social sciences poses specific problems, as the protection of human subjects requires that data be used, stored, and disclosed in a way that ensures the privacy of individual research subjects. Furthermore, for purposes of analysis, this data is coded and entered into computer files with only code numbers identifying the individual subjects. This primary data, that may include clinical or laboratory records, questionnaires, tapes of interviews, and field notes, must be available for review. Also, where possible, questionnaires should be stored without identifiers, using only code numbers to link them to computerised files. Records, including transcripts of taped interviews, must have the names and key identifiers removed.

The correct handling of research data requires the researchers to acquaint themselves with the relevant quantitative methods available for processing data, including graphical and tabular methods of presentation, error analysis, and tests for reliability. The fact is that research integrity requires not only that reported conclusions are based on accurately recorded data or observations, but that all relevant observations are reported. In this regard, it is considered a breach of research integrity to fail to report data that contradicts or fails to support the reported conclusions, including the purposeful withholding of information about confounding factors.[28] Any intentional or reckless disregard for the truth in reporting observations may be considered an act of research misconduct.

Since any research study may be a cooperative endeavour encompassing many individuals who now or in the future may pursue related research interests, and since it is in the interests of all to rely on the contributions and findings of others, every researcher has an obligation to the general scientific community to cooperate by sharing data. Other virtues of sharing data include the facilitation of independent confirmation or refutation of reported outcomes. It is generally accepted that the data underlying a research publication should be made available to other responsible researchers upon request after the research results have been published or accepted for publication.

Data should be stored securely for at least five years after completion of the study, submission of the final report, or publication of the research, whichever comes last. Some types of data are expected to be deposited in a national or international data bank. A list of websites for social science archives is available to researches and in some research fields, authors are encouraged to create their own websites on which they may store extensive data sets for general access.

The reporting of suspected research misconduct, mistakes, and/or negligence is a shared and serious responsibility of all members of the academic community. Any person who suspects research misconduct, mistakes, and/or negligence has an obligation to report the allegation to the appropriate authorities.[29] If a finding of an error, either intentional or inadvertent, or of plagiarism is made subsequent to the publication of a research study, the investigator has the obligation to submit a correction or retraction in a form specified by the editor or publisher. Ethical researchers do not fabricate or falsify data, do not present work of others as their own, or do not fail to give appropriate credit for the work of others through citations. The researcher needs to avoid careless mistakes and negligence by carefully and critically examining their own work, keeping accurate records of research activities, such as data collection, research design, and correspondence with agencies or journal.

There are some circumstances in which conflicts of interest could compromise the integrity of the research findings or even lead to research misconduct. The annual disclosures of outside interests by researches, which are reviewed by academic administrators, are intended to avoid the escalation of conflicts into improper behaviour or misconduct.[30] A notice of conflicting financial interests must be included, possibly as a footnote in publications, in research proposals and reports, and in clinical research protocols. Many journals and funding agencies require such disclosures. When asked to enter into peer review of a manuscript or proposal, a researcher must disclose any conflict of interest with respect to the matter under review. Conflict of commitment must be avoided in order not to threaten the researcher's primary professional allegiance and responsibility to NCU.

The research shows that graduate students who are mentored by faculty increase their academic self-confidence and course completion rates. Mentors assist graduate students in selecting and building a research area and then in developing research skills. At the graduate level, the focus of mentoring is on finishing the course on time and in accordance with the academic advisor's expectations. The mentor also provides support in publishing and building a résumé for the learner's post-graduate employment.[31] However, peer support and peer mentoring is also an important component of mentoring and should be encouraged. The members of faculty who mentor graduate students who are from a different gender or ethnic identity need to educate themselves in term of cultural and racial perspectives in order to be more effective mentors.

Then peer mentoring and support is also an important component of mentoring and should be encouraged, such as women's groups or minority groups, as well as matching younger students with more experienced students. Adequately mentoring graduate students is also beneficial to tenure-track faculty with part of the evaluation process for tenure involving looking at the success rate graduate students under a faculty's direction. Another important part of the mentor's role is to promote students in gaining employment and creating professional connections for the student. Furthermore, mentoring on how and where to publish the students research study and the review process are important to future research career progression.

The Northcentral University requirements for IRB approval are guided by ethical principles regarding research involving human subjects and states that:

"In accordance with federal regulations (Title 45, Part 46, Code of Federal Regulations) and Northcentral policy, all research involving human subjects or other living creatures (including studies of institutions, organisations, or other entities that involve human participation) that is conducted by Faculty Mentors, Core Faculty, Staff, and Learners, including unfunded as well as funded projects, must be reviewed and approved by an appropriately constituted IRB Committee before such investigations are undertaken. This includes not only all dissertations, but all other research endeavours." (NCU Dissertation Handbook, Version 04/15/2011, p. 41).

In conclusion, as well as conceptualising the writing process for a proposal, doctoral researchers need to anticipate the ethical issues that may arise during their studies. The researcher must realise that the research does involve the collection of data from people that is about people. So, researchers need to protect their research participants; develop a trust with them; promote the integrity of the research; guard against misconduct and mistakes; and successfully cope with the day-to-day problems that will occur throughout the research study. Furthermore, the doctoral researcher must be constantly aware that ethical practices involve much more than merely following a set of academic research guidelines, they must also anticipate and address any ethical dilemmas or conflicts of interest that may occur during their research. It must be remembered that ethical issues are not confined to data collection and analysis as they apply just as importantly to the actual writing and dissemination of the final doctoral research study report.

*Deployment*

*Air Assault*

*Thunder Run*

*In Contact*

*Colatoral Damage*

*Suicide Bomber*

*Incinerated*

*Aftermath*

*Returning Fire*

*Overwhelming Force*

*Close and Personal*

*Out-Going*

*No Escape*

*Bunker Protection*

*Innocence of Youth*

*Humanitarian Aid*

*On Patrol*

*Desolation*

*Shock and Awe*

*Loneliness*

*Spy-in-the-Sky*

*Sentry Duty*

*Dusk Patrol*

*Death of a Comrade*

# Chapter Twelve

## *Soldiers' Pre-Combat Training*

The conflict in Afghanistan has now been ongoing for over a decade, even surpassing Vietnam as America's longest undeclared war.[1] Even after all this time, the Afghanistan conflict persists with no identifiable political or military solution, and casualties continue to increase within the U.S. and Coalition forces.[2] In addition, in 2014, Coalition forces seem likely to become involved in the renewed conflict in Syria and Iraq, which will inevitably see the further deployment of infantry soldiers on combat operations. The U.S. Department of Veterans Affairs (2013) official estimates indicated that of the 1.64 million service members who have served in the recent wars in Afghanistan and Iraq, 20% or 328,000 are experiencing depression, anxiety, stress, or PTSD. In the British military the total number of personnel deployed to the Afghanistan and Iraq wars from October 2001-June 2014 was 219,420 soldiers.[3] However, statistics from the MoD confirmed that there are over 11,000 serving members of the military currently diagnosed with combat stress mental conditions, including PTSD.

However, despite this new research, there still remain no effective pre-combat education programmes or leadership training that addresses the negative effects of combat on infantry soldiers.[4] Researchers have confirmed that higher rates of stress and trauma are associated with increased exposure to intense infantry ground combat and are researching auditory exclusion, intensified sound, tunnel vision, and post-traumatic stress responses.[5] The purpose of this qualitative case study was to document infantry soldiers' experiences and perceptions of the negative physiological and psychological effects of combat and their recommendations for effective pre-combat education programmes and leadership training to prepare soldiers to counter the negative effects of combat.

This study used a qualitative case study methodology, as it was believed that this approach allowed for greater depth and understanding of the participants perspective and points of view. In this regard, a semi-structured interview process allowed the researcher the flexibility to modify questions or to ask follow-up questions that added depth, breadth, and substance to the study. Also, the questions were open-ended to allow the participants the freedom to develop their answers and to allow for additional probes or questions of clarification from the researcher. Interviews were conducted until saturation was achieved, and as expressed by Yin (2009), this is the point where the information the researcher learns becomes redundant. These research questions guided the study.

Q1. According to infantry soldiers' combat experiences, what types of pre-combat education programmes and leadership training were provided to soldiers, pre-tour of duty, to help them cope with negative physiological and psychological effects of combat?

Q2. According to infantry soldiers' combat experiences, what were the negative physiological and psychological effects that soldiers experienced during and after combat?

Q3. According to infantry soldiers' combat experiences, what types of pre-combat education programmes and leadership training interventions could be effective in helping soldiers cope with the negative physiological and psychological effects of combat?

The qualitative case study findings are presented through the analysis of the data collected from the soldier volunteers and triangulated with the pre-combat training programmes they received prior to deployment on operations in Afghanistan. Data analysis and interpretations of the findings for the three research questions are reported in the next chapters of this book. The chapter concludes with a summary of the key points deduced from the data analysis.

## Results

The pseudonyms of A to J were assigned to all the soldier participants in the study to protect their confidentiality and maintain their anonymity. It is important to acknowledge the soldiers' role in this research and to comprehend the context of their experiences of combat, and how those experiences changed their lives. The soldiers' responses gave a sense of who they are and how they individually dealt with the stresses of combat in their personal and subsequent lives. Each individual was different and unique, and as a result, their physiological and psychological reaction to the stresses of combat was individual, different, and unique. All of the soldier participants were selected based upon their having experienced combat within the previous two years.

The research questions for this qualitative case study focused on the common elements for all participants in their understanding of the physiological and psychological effects of combat on infantry soldiers. The findings are presented using the information gathered from each participant's interview transcript and include the researcher's field notes, observations, and additional documentary evidence regarding pre-deployment education programmes and leadership training. This was done to accurately represent the experiences and perspectives of all the participants. The accuracy of the transcripts was verified through member checking and peer-reviewed by a fellow colleague, a retired British Army Lieutenant Colonel who had widespread combat experience in the recent Afghanistan and Iraq wars.

The confidentiality and anonymity of each participant was protected, with each participant being assigned a pseudonym, such as Soldier A, B, C, etc.[6] Also, the study data will be kept in a locked, secure location for five years, with the password known only to the researcher, and then after five years, all records will be destroyed. Demographic information on each participant was collected during the interviews and included rank, age, gender, years in the Army, unit, and dates of operational service in Afghanistan as shown in Table 5.

**Table 5**

*Demographics of Participants*
*(All Served a Combat Tour in the Last Two Years)*

| Soldier | Rank | Age | Gender | Years in Army Time of Study | Planned Stay in Army at Time of Data Collection |
|---------|------|-----|--------|-----------------------------|------------------------------------------------|
| A | Cpl | 28 | M | 9 yrs 6 mos | Finish 22-yr Engagement |
| B | L/Cpl | 23 | M | 4 yrs 8 mos | Finish 6-yr Engagement |
| C | Pte | 21 | M | 3 yrs 11 mos | Finish 6-yr Engagement |
| D | Lt | 24 | M | 6 yrs 3 mos | Finish 16-yr Engagement |
| E | Sgt | 31 | M | 12 yrs 7 mos | Finish 22-yr Engagement |
| F | Pte | 20 | M | 2 yrs 7 mos | Finish 6-yr Engagement |
| G | WO2 | 36 | M | 17 yrs 2 mos | Finish 22-yr Engagement |
| H | Pte | 21 | M | 3 yrs 9 mos | Finish 6-yr Engagement |
| I | Pte | 22 | F | 4 yrs 5 mos | Finish 6-yr Engagement |
| J | S/Sgt | 33 | M | 15 yrs 5 mos | Finish 22-yr Engagement |

*Note:* Rank from lowest to highest: Pte=Private, L/Cpl=Lance Corporal, Cpl=Corporal, Sgt=Sergeant, S/Sgt=Staff Sergeant, WO2=Warrant Officer Class 2, Lt=Lieutenant.

The Army ranks of the participants ranged from Lieutenant to Private, and years of service ranged from 2 years and 7 months to 17 years and 2 months. The soldier participants' ages ranged from 20 to 36 years old. Nine soldiers were male, one was female, all were Caucasian, 4 soldiers were married, and 6 were single. The following steps describe the method the researcher used to analyse the research data:

1. Recorded the transcript of the participants' interview.
2. Examined the transcripts for combat experiences that created physiological and/or psychological stress.
3. Formulated a composite textual description.
4. Formulated a structural-based description of all the participants' combat experiences.
5. Examined the composite textual and structural descriptions for themes within the participants' combat experiences.
6. Employed computer software programme to confirm themes.
7. The pre-deployment training programmes were reviewed and compared with the participants' interview responses in order to validate the findings.

The data analysis conducted in this study was a constant comparison between the pre-deployment training programmes and the participants' interview responses.[7] The interviews were all digitally recorded. The data were then reduced into smaller identifiable segments where the data were organised and coded for easier reference. When the data were coded, this allowed the data to be placed into similar groups allowing the themes to emerge. This constant comparative analysis assisted the researcher in identifying the themes between the pre-deployment training and the participants' actual combat experiences where physiological and psychological stress had occurred.

**Q1. According to infantry soldiers' combat experiences, what types of pre-combat education programmes and leadership training were provided to soldiers, pre-tour of duty, to help them cope with negative physiological and psychological effects of combat?**

Six interview questions were asked of participants to collect data to answer research *Question (1)*. Nine themes that emerged from the participants' answers are shown in Table 6.

**Table 6**

*Pre-Combat Programmes and Training Themes that Emerged in Response to Research Question (1).*

| | Participants | | | | | | | | | | | |
|---|---|---|---|---|---|---|---|---|---|---|---|---|
| Themes | A | B | C | D | E | F | G | H | I | J | Total % of Affirmative Responses | n |
| Military training as indoctrination | Y | Y | N | Y | N | N | Y | Y | Y | Y | 70 | 7 |
| Builds soldier's reliance on camaraderie | N | Y | Y | Y | Y | Y | N | Y | Y | Y | 80 | 8 |
| Trainers explain programmes and training goals | Y | Y | Y | N | N | N | Y | Y | Y | Y | 70 | 7 |
| Acknowledges soldiers' fears of killing enemy combatants | N | Y | Y | Y | N | Y | Y | Y | Y | Y | 80 | 8 |
| Prepares soldiers for injury or death of comrades | Y | Y | Y | Y | Y | Y | Y | Y | Y | Y | 100 | 10 |
| Incorporates soldiers' previous experiences in instruction | Y | Y | Y | Y | Y | Y | N | Y | N | Y | 80 | 8 |
| Incorporates trainers' previous combat experiences | Y | Y | N | Y | Y | N | N | Y | Y | Y | 70 | 7 |
| Provides evaluation of instruction for programme feedback | Y | Y | Y | Y | Y | Y | Y | Y | Y | Y | 100 | 10 |
| Programmes and training are inadequate | Y | N | Y | Y | Y | Y | Y | Y | Y | N | 80 | 8 |

***Military training as indoctrination.*** All the participants stated that the military culture aimed to turn young civilians into operationally effective infantry combatants by inculcating blind conformity and obedience to the military system. This was encapsulated in what Soldier D described as: "There was an unquestioning obedience to superior's orders, no matter what the circumstances." All the participants stated that pre-deployment training included the traditional teaching of military skills such as shooting and field-craft with the main objective being to re-model how the recruits thought and behaved. Soldier A explained it in another way and said: "The training was designed to shape the recruits' minds by indoctrinating them into believing in the values of the military system by rewarding obedience and punishing non-conformity." Soldier H went further, stating: "The whole aim of the military system was to dispose the recruits of their civilian identities and instead build a new self-image in each recruit." Soldier B said: "This was achieved by creating distance from the recruit's civilian life from the first day of training by confining recruits to their barracks where your thoughts, movement, personal appearance, and choices were dictated by the military system."

***Builds soldiers' reliance on camaraderie.*** Soldier B stated: "The training was designed to create peer camaraderie that was seen by the military as being the most valued benefit of a military career." However, Soldier I believed: "This camaraderie served the purposes of the military system as peer group pressure assured the successful imposition and maintenance of military values and behaviours." Soldier H said: "The training was further designed to overcome the recruit's natural revulsion to killing at close quarters by conditioning their minds to obey orders without hesitation." Soldier C went further, stating: "The recruit training aimed to overcome the individual soldier's fear of killing by stressing the importance of protecting the other soldiers in your unit and becoming one of the team." Soldier E believed: "This unquestioning obedience to orders and acceptance of military discipline was the essential factor in any military system." To reinforce this statement, Soldier E added: "This factor was especially important within the infantry where the instant response to orders was often the factor that decided between life and death in combat."

Then Soldier J raised the point: "The maintenance of the highest levels of physical fitness and the development of mental toughness were essential when conducting infantry operations." This point was reinforced by Soldier D, who stated: "Once the soldier accepted this military ethos, there was a natural tendency to strive for recognition from your peers by receiving verbal praise from superiors, awards, and promotion." Soldier D also said: "An integral part of a military life was the provision of support for comrades in their time of need along with an acceptance of long periods away from your family and civilian friends." Soldier G was even more forthright, stating: "As a soldier, you had to accept the ethical judgements of the military and to repress all your moral doubts, while being brave in face of the enemy, and accepting both physical and mental hardships."

In general, the participants said that a number of these demands, such as peer support, preparedness, personal achievement, physical fitness, and stoicism were responsible for minimising the physiological and psychological effects of combat on infantry soldiers. However, other factors, such as loss of autonomy, restrictions, suppression of guilt, and distance from family and friends were considered by the participants to increase their vulnerability to the physiological and psychological effects of combat. Soldier E believed: "The effects of combat, which included the possibility of instant death, produced a dramatic range of mental and physical responses in soldiers." These he saw as resulting in a significant denigration in soldiers' abilities to carry out routine tasks when engaged in a combat environment.

***Trainers explain programmes and training goals.*** At the outset, the participants in the study stated that their instructors told them that the programmes' goals were to teach them the basic information, techniques, and skills to make them effective members of an infantry unit. Soldier C stated: "The instructors indicated that we would be educated and trained physically, psychologically, and technically, with the aim of ensuring that we were prepared to become an effective team member within an infantry combat unit." Soldier F observed that during this process, the instructors stressed that re-socialisation was an important aspect of the induction into military service. This re-socialisation was described as a sociological process of mentally and emotionally re-training a soldier so that they could operate in a combat environment.

Soldier D indicated that the instructors assisted the adult soldiers in developing an early and appropriate mental discipline for the forthcoming learning programmes by providing an overview of the course objectives and a description of future activities. Soldier G said: "The early introductory exercises in the instruction allowed us to express our learning goals and concerns." In these exercises, the participants were given the opportunity to express their learning goals, aims, hopes, desires, fears, and concerns. The instructors then used this information to ensure that their instruction was cognisant of these elements and was sensitive to the individual participants.

Soldier A stated: "In order to increase the participants' motivation, the instructors provided clear instructional goals and learning outcomes that created a strong learning interest in us all." To capitalise on this positive learning interest, the instructors explored ways in which each participant's level of learning could be incorporated into each session. This included the examples the instructor gave the class regarding problems soldiers might personally encounter when faced with combat stress during operational deployments. Soldier C said: "The learning activities were self-paced and tailored to the participant's individual rate (level) of learning." The instructors realised that part of an adult soldier's preparation to learn was determined by the perceived benefits to the individual of that learning, as well as the disadvantages of not learning. In this case, Soldier J indicated: "The benefits of learning were that we would have a better chance of surviving combat."

Soldier H said: "The instructors indicated that they realised that each of us preferred to be treated as an individual who had particular combat experiences." He further indicated that the instructors realised that as adult soldiers, they learned better when new material was presented through a variety of instructional methods. Therefore, the instructors' goal was to appeal to the participants' different learning preferences. Soldier I observed: "The learning styles were based upon the senses that were involved in processing information." The instructors' goal was to have the participants learn the new instruction by simultaneously processing the information through multiple senses. Therefore, as experienced by Soldier B, the presentations were multi-sensory as they used visual and auditory components and these in combination with interactive activities increased learning and retention by the participants.

Soldier J identified: "During this transition, from the life of a civilian member of society to one of a soldier, we were trained to only follow the commands of our superiors." Soldier G, a Warrant Officer Class 2, a rank just below Lieutenant, described three types of training techniques they underwent, these being classical conditioning, operant conditioning, and role modelling. Soldier G reported that the military conditioned soldiers to become effective in classical conditioning, where the goal was to associate a desired behaviour with a reward. He said that in operant conditioning, the soldiers were trained in simulated environments in order to develop an automatic response during combat. Finally, he observed that role modelling in the military was reliant upon the instructors demonstrating aggression while maintaining discipline, thereby providing soldier recruits with a model for their own behaviours. It should be noted that Soldier G, who was a Warrant Officer Class 2, had previously spent a three-year posting at the Infantry Training Centre, Warminster before returning to his battalion for their operational tour of Afghanistan. Soldier A said: "Through these techniques, we were effectively trained to accomplish the military goal of killing enemy combatants without question or hesitation."

***Acknowledges soldiers' fears of killing enemy combatants.*** The first interview questions asked specifically about the pre-combat education programmes and leadership training that were provided to soldiers pre-tour of duty. However, the soldiers answered in much more detail than expected, to the point that further themes emerged from their answers to the first interview question, including this and other themes. This was particularly apparent when interviewing Soldier G, who was a Warrant

Officer Class 2 with 17 years and two months' experience, and Soldier J, who was a Staff Sergeant with 15 years and five months experience. Also of note was the clarity of the answers to the interview questions provided by Soldier D, who was a Lieutenant with 6 years and three months experience, and who had completed a three-year Bachelor of Arts (BA) university course before joining the British Army.

In speaking about pre-deployment training, Soldier H said: "All soldiers have a fear of killing, and so the leader must be made aware that this fear of killing another human being is a natural human reaction. When armed with this knowledge, the leader can then make sure that he particularly observes the soldier who has just experienced this shock of killing another human being in order to identify any negative reactions." He believed that once an infantry soldier had personally taken another life, had seen the enemy die before his eyes, then that soldier was changed for life, with no possibility of going back. Soldier J elaborated, believing that the reality of killing an enemy combatant in close combat was completely different from a fighter pilot that destroys an enemy plane, a tank gunner who destroys an enemy tank, or an artilleryman who fires a shell five miles to kill an enemy soldier. He went further to say: "None of these (pilot, gunner or artilleryman) physically sees another human being at close range, and then makes the calculated decision to kill them with their rifle, bayonet, or bare hands, witnessing their life drain away in front of their eyes." He concluded by saying: "Infantry close combat is like no other; it is not a video game, you are so close to your enemy in combat that you can smell him, and when you kill him, and approach him to make sure that he is dead, you can hear his breath fade away as he dies in front of your eyes. These are the experiences that change who you are forever."

Soldier I when relating his own combat experience said: "When I saw an enemy soldier at close range for the first time and looked at him in the eye, an overwhelming fear gripped me, my heart began to pound, and I froze in place. It was only after the enemy soldier fired at me and missed that I was jolted out of my inaction and was able to throw myself on the ground to escape his fire." Soldier G identified that along with this reaction of being "frozen by fear." He found that he hesitated when faced with an enemy soldier in his sights, as he felt a resistance to killing his own kind. Both these soldiers when relating their own experiences said that they found that the only way to override their own human instincts was by continuous training, which inculcated the soldier to killing by making the act of pulling the trigger an unconscious decision. The participants stated that the only way to overcome this resistance to killing was by operate conditioning, which is designed to make the killing of an enemy combatant a conditioned reflex.

Soldier B went further in stating: "If a soldier is not prepared emotionally for the act of killing ahead of time, the magnitude of the trauma can be significant, as the soldier will be left living with something that he felt was not correct and was something that he did not want to do." Soldier C identified that: "If the soldier was convinced that the act of killing was justified and correct, if society said that the soldier was killing an enemy combatant and was not committing murder, he would not have any problems with remorse." However, he went further to say that if the soldier felt some doubt about the legitimacy of the act of killing and killed without conscious thought, then there was the potential that the soldier would be devastated and psychologically destroyed by the act. In this regard, Soldier D believed that: "One of the most important roles of the commander, both during and after combat, is to be aware that the act of killing enemy combatants will have an inevitable effect on soldiers and that afterwards they will need moral support, understanding, and perhaps counselling."

***Prepares soldiers for injury or death of comrades.*** As regards friendly casualties, Soldier F witnessed that the death or injury of a comrade would lead the soldier to have a feeling of deep personal lose, and this could well affect that soldier's ability to carry out his tasks, especially during the stress of combat. Soldier B felt that the noise and sight of combat had a traumatic effect on soldiers' senses, which caused confusion and a sense of chaos that could be particularly unnerving. In this regard, Soldier E was convinced that pre-combat education programmes and leadership training must attempt to prepare the soldier for such experiences, thereby creating and understanding by the leader of how to lessen the debilitating effect of combat on soldiers. Finally, Soldier H saw that after intensive pre-combat training, there was always the apprehension from infantry soldiers that they would "not measure-up as a soldier under fire and would let their buddies down." As a result, he believed that all commanders, during their leadership training, must be made aware that this possible fear could be detrimental, especially if these apprehensions ultimately overcome the soldiers' desire to be an effective member of the unit.

*Incorporates soldiers' previous experiences in instruction.* It was identified by the vast majority of the participants that the instructors showed regard or esteem for those soldiers who already had operational combat experiences, which created a climate in the learning environment that conveyed respect. This meant that the participants were more open to learning, as they felt respected and were not being talked down to, patronised, or otherwise denigrated. Soldier D considered that: "The instructors fostered a comfortable and productive learning climate by showing respect for the soldiers' individuality and experiences." Soldier H identified that: "The instructors were open to different perspectives, treated each soldier as an individual, and adopted a caring attitude." Soldier J stated: "In the longer term, the instructors established a learning climate that displayed mutual respect and mutual trust." The participants reported that the principal that the instructors followed was that adult soldier learners needed positive reinforcement, as they were self-directed, only preferring to know how their efforts were measuring up when compared with the objectives of the instructional programme.

Soldier F indicated that: "Our instructors identified that one of the most significant qualities unique to adult learning was each individual's combat experiences, and that these offered them a meaningful advantage in the learning process of how to cope with the effects of combat." Soldier I considered that these experiences provided many reference points for exploration, new applications, and new learning. The instructors realised that all learning began with experience and that real learning began when a response was called for in relationship to an experience. The instructors indicated that new experiences needed to be experimented with, evaluated, reflected upon and reasoned about for the most effective learning to take place. These post-combat behaviours were seen as being the best and highest form of learning where experience was the best teacher.

Instructors also indicated to Soldier C that: "It was possible that the negative experiences of combat could be avoided if a soldier learned from another soldier who had already encountered and experienced a negative combat experience." That is the learning from an older and more experienced soldier mentor provided a valuable learning forum and support network. The listening and learning from a mentor's combat experiences could assist and expand another less experienced soldier's knowledge base and so shorten the learning experiences required. Soldier C said: "The instructors believed that personal combat experiences provided the most effective form of learning."

Soldier B stated: "The instructors felt that adult soldiers brought to the learning situation a background of experiences that was beneficial for themselves and others." Therefore, the instructors placed greater emphasis on discussion methods, case studies, and problem-solving exercises, which utilised the accumulated combat knowledge and skills of the participants. The instructors then expanded upon and refined this prior knowledge that the adult soldiers brought to the programme. Soldier A said: "The instructors also identified soldiers' experiences so that they could better tailor their instruction to meet their needs. Soldier A went on to say that it was stressed that all the participants came to the learning situation with unique combat operational experiences. However, all combat experiences were different from those of the other participants and that these combat experiences also included misconceptions, biases, prejudices, and preferences. In general, the instructors found that those participants who had the broadest experience of combat were the ones who most readily accepted and assimilated new ideas and skills. This was as a result of the veterans realising that even the smallest advantage that they could gain over the enemy may be the one factor that saved their lives when they were next involved in combat.

***Incorporates trainers' previous combat experience.*** The majority of participants described how the instructors appealed to them through the power of arousing their interest in the combat skills that the instructors had themselves adopted. Soldier B described this as: "The instructors gave us examples of their own combat experiences, as these were the problems that we were most likely to encounter when faced with combat during our own operational deployments." Soldier F said: "The instructors aroused our natural motivation to learn as we came to believe that what we were learning was something new that we needed to know if we were to survive in combat." Soldier I said: "The instructors gave us the knowledge regarding the problems that we would personally encounter when faced with combat and how we could overcome those dangers. As a result, one particularly experienced old veteran, who had completed multiple tours in Afghanistan and Iraq, was christened the 'prophet.'" Soldier H said that: "The instructors stressed that combat was the most frightening event they had ever experienced, as they had felt an overwhelming sense of fear, anger, and anxiety." However, of all the physiological and psychological effects they experienced during combat, the instructors stated that the single most traumatic event was the act of killing an enemy combatant.

***Provides evaluation of instruction for programme feedback.*** All the participants found that the army had a comprehensive and systematic process for the evaluation and review of adult soldier training, which was completed at the end of each programme to provide the instructor with course content feedback. This validation system used information provided by recruits, instructors, and programme designers at various stages of the programmes. These monitored the implementation of the training at various stages of the programmes and identify any improvements that were required. As an example, Soldier G had been involved in gaining feedback from adult soldiers who had recent operational experience and saw that this was incorporated into the ongoing training programmes where appropriate. Soldier F believed that: "This new training contributed to the enhanced combat effectiveness of the infantry soldier and a higher survival rate when engaged in combat operations." However, post-programme evaluations continued in order to further enhance the adult learning aspects of infantry combat training.

At the completion of every training programme, the instructors had all the participants complete a course evaluation form that asked for the positive and negative aspects of the course, as well as for any recommendations for improvement in the course. As a result of this feedback, there were alterations in various courses based upon this soldier's feedback. Soldier B stated: "As I and my colleagues brought our own combat experiences to the programme, this was acknowledged and respected by the instructors in their training setting." Soldier E said: "It is now recognised that adult learning is enhanced by hands-on experience, which effectively involved the soldiers in the learning process." Soldier J added: "As adult learners we were more likely to accept and retain an idea when we had arrived at the conclusion ourselves." Therefore, when training adult soldiers, the presentation of structured activities generated the students' ideas and concepts, which facilitated more effective learning than by simply giving the adults information to remember. Soldier D also found: "The introduction of humour by the instructors was an important tool for effectively promoting a comfortable learning environment." Soldier I indicated that: "By being involved in the learning process and understanding how this new learning would enhance our likelihood of surviving in combat, we all gained a new motivation." The soldiers said that what they did with the new information was dependent on them being given the opportunity to practice the new skills, which increased the likelihood of retention and application when faced with a combat situation.

The evaluations that the participants completed at the end of each programme led Soldier A to the conclusion that all learning began with experience. This was explained as all new experiences needed to be experimented with, evaluated, reflected upon, and reasoned with for the most effective learning to take place. These post experience behaviours culminated in the best and highest form of learning, where change and increased experience occurred. Soldier D observed that: "The aim of the instructors was to have us avoid negative combat experiences by learning from other soldiers who had already experienced the stress of combat." This listening and learning from soldier mentors successes, failures, and mistakes was found to expand adult soldiers knowledge base and shorten the learning cycles personal experience alone would require. Soldier G saw that this had better equipped him and his colleagues to succeed in combat by avoiding so many of the pitfalls experienced by the uninitiated.

***Programmes and training are inadequate.*** The participants identified that, despite the variety of training and education regimes they underwent prior to their combat deployments, these initiatives did not adequately prepare them for all the physiological and psychological effects of combat. In this regard, Soldier D said: "In the current environment, military commanders at all levels were learning how to lead their units through lectures, tutorials, books, manuals, and simulators." However, he further indicated that as the future leaders of infantry soldiers, they were not being educated and instructed in the reactions, thoughts, hopes, and fears they should expect of front-line infantry soldiers when they came face-to-face with the enemy.

The study participants went further to identify that the current pre-combat education programmes and leadership training did not specify all the likely sources of fear that the infantry soldier was likely to face in combat. These include the possibility of being killed, wounded, or captured as this was a natural fear that was always present in infantry soldiers. Soldier E stipulated: "The leader must be aware of this fact, as it could lead soldiers to freeze in combat or to carry out irrational actions while engaging the enemy." This he said would endanger the unit's mission and the soldiers within the unit. He went on to say that currently there was no way for the leader to be able to identify which soldiers may be more susceptible to these reactions until they were faced with a combat situation. The consensus from the participants was that the leader must be able to identify the soldiers that were demonstrating the symptoms of fear that could lead to irrational behaviour that would endanger other soldiers within the unit.

Soldier D identified that: "Training needs to be as realistic as possible with the combat simulation scenarios ensuring not only physical and mental engagement by soldiers, but also an emotional engagement." All the participants stated that realistic training, which creates emotional stress, should be designed to create within the soldier feelings that are similar to those that they would experience in real combat situations. Soldier F stated: "In my view, the emotional issues that are brought about by combat are not being effectively addressed as indicated by the ever-increasing number of soldiers who are now experiencing growing emotional difficulties as a result of those experiences." He further illustrated this fact by highlighting the number of medical reports that suggest that the incidence of "Vietnam-levels" of combat-related stress and PTSD has been found in an increasing numbers of military personnel returning from the recent Afghanistan and Iraq wars.

# Chapter Thirteen

## *Soldiers' Combat Experiences*

The research study asked the participants the following second question:

**Q2. According to infantry soldiers' combat experiences, what were the negative physiological and psychological effects that soldiers experienced during and after combat?**

Four interview questions were asked of participants to collect data to answer research *Question (2)*. The three major themes that emerged were that soldiers suffered significant negative physiological and psychological effects from combat, and afterwards they experienced the long-term effects of combat after their return home. The soldiers' physiological and psychological sub-themes are shown in Tables 7 and 8. A total of 11 physiological combat stress symptoms were recorded by the researcher from the participants' answers as shown in Table 7.

***Circulatory and respiratory problems.*** A common trait experienced by all the participants who repeatedly experienced high levels of stress over long periods of time found that their hearts beat more rapidly, and this caused a significant increase in their blood pressure. Soldier E stated: "When in combat and you experienced anxiety or fear, it was natural to feel a rapid heartbeat, a sense of pressure in the chest, occasional skipped beats, and chest pains were common." Hyperventilation was identified by Soldier D as being rapid respiration, shortness of breath, dizziness, and a sense of choking. He said that this was often accompanied with tingling and cramping of fingers and toes. These reactions occurred in tandem

**Table 7**

*Physiological Themes that Emerged in Response to Research Question (2).*

| | Participants | | | | | | | | | | | |
|---|---|---|---|---|---|---|---|---|---|---|---|---|
| Themes | A | B | C | D | E | F | G | H | I | J | Total of % Affirmative Responses | n |
| Circulatory and Respiratory Problems | Y | N | N | Y | Y | Y | N | N | Y | Y | 60 | 6 |
| Hearing Problems | Y | Y | Y | N | Y | N | Y | N | Y | Y | 70 | 7 |
| Hyper-alertness | Y | Y | N | Y | N | Y | Y | Y | Y | Y | 80 | 8 |
| Digestive and Urinary Problems | Y | N | Y | Y | N | Y | N | N | Y | Y | 60 | 6 |
| Muscular Tension | N | Y | Y | Y | N | Y | N | Y | Y | Y | 70 | 7 |
| Partial Short-Term Paralysis | N | Y | Y | N | Y | N | N | Y | Y | N | 50 | 5 |
| Perspiration and Dehydration | Y | Y | N | Y | Y | Y | Y | N | Y | Y | 80 | 8 |
| Physical Fatigue | Y | Y | Y | Y | N | Y | Y | N | Y | Y | 80 | 8 |
| Shaking and Tremors | N | Y | Y | N | N | Y | Y | Y | Y | Y | 70 | 7 |
| Sleep Disturbance | Y | Y | Y | N | N | Y | Y | Y | Y | N | 70 | 7 |
| Vision Problems | Y | N | N | Y | Y | N | Y | Y | Y | N | 60 | 6 |

with generalised muscular weakness, lack of energy, physical fatigue, and extreme stress when engaged in combat. Soldier I indicated that in his experience, soldiers who experienced frequent intense and long-term combat stress suffered from digestive problems, urinary complications, and a weakened immune system.

***Hearing problems.*** Soldier E believed that stress and anxiety affected the body completely, with this also including the ability to hear. He witnessed in his comrades that these hearing problems included the inability to hear orders or nearby conversations, and in extreme cases his comrades had complete short-term deafness occur. However, he found that the most common issue was the difficulty focusing on sound or conversation. During periods of intense anxiety, which was brought about by the stress of combat, Soldier J reported that: "It was not uncommon for me to 'zone-out' my thoughts, fears, and apprehensions when I was in combat." However, he further indicated that this meant that he was unable to hear anything that anybody was saying to him, and he believed that this was not because he was not hearing, but rather that his brain was not processing the information. This anxiety he felt also caused soldiers to be more prone to being "on-edge," which meant that they would start noticing all of the sounds and noises that they had not noticed before. Those soldiers with this increased anxiety often found that these new noises created more anxiety and fear.

*Hyper-alertness.* All the participants found that in response to a threat in combat, the brain sent out warning signals causing the body to become fully aroused. Soldier H found that this alerting system became finely tuned, allowing him instant focus and immediate reaction to any threat. Some of the participants referred to being "hyper-alert," and this referred to them being distracted by any external stimuli that could signal danger. However, this "hyper-alertness" state also meant that they over-reacted to things that were in fact safe. Soldier C witnessed that when in combat, some soldiers experienced a "startle reaction," which was an increased sensitivity to minor external stimuli and leaping, jumping, cringing, jerking, or other forms of involuntary self-protective responses to sudden noises were common. He went on to state that: "I found that any sudden noise, movement, or light caused a "startle reaction" in me, which led me to misinterpreting reassuring information as threats, so causing me to react without adequately thinking."

***Digestive and urinary problems.*** Soldier C's experience was that those soldiers experiencing high levels of psychological stress over a long period of time were more likely to develop medical problems in their digestive and urinary systems. Soldier A experienced a feeling of nausea when under stress and vomiting when under extreme combat stress. Soldier F said that: "I experienced a lack of appetite as a reaction to stress, and this became a significant problem for me, as I did not eat a sufficiently balanced diet to keep my muscles and brain supplied for sustained operations." Soldier J suffered from acute abdominal pain during combat and also urinated frequently, especially at night. He further stated that during combat, the inability to control bowel and/or bladder functions was not uncommon.

*Muscular tension.* Soldier J found: "When on prolonged periods of combat operations, I began to suffer from muscular tension, which the medic in our platoon informed me was the most common physical symptom of anxiety." Soldier D saw from his comrades that those suffering from anxiety found it harder for that tension to dissipate naturally. Soldier B said: "During combat, my muscles all tightened up, and even after the danger had passed, my body was still tense. To reinforce this phenomenon, Soldier C found: "It seemed that the muscular tension would never end, and it caused continuous pain that resulted in me having trouble with my mobility, especially as we were carrying combat loads of 50+ pounds and were traversing steep rocky terrain."

*Partial short-term paralysis.* Soldier H believed that stress-related blindness, deafness, loss of other sensations, and partial, short-term paralysis were not physical injuries but physical symptoms that unconsciously enabled the soldier to escape or avoid a seemingly intolerable stressful situation. He further indicated: "Often soldiers with these physical conditions were unaware of the relationship between these physical signs and their inability to cope with stress." Soldier B witnessed during combat: "My paralysis or loss of sensation was usually confined to one arm or leg, with prickling sensations or rigidity of my joints occurring." However, he also witnessed that some soldiers became completely immobile for a period of time.

*Perspiration and dehydration.* Soldier J stated: "It was quite normal to experience either mild or heavy sweating or sensations of chilliness under combat stress." He further indicated that the severity of this sweating could vary from time to time and would come and go depending upon the presence of triggers such as anxiety, stress, and traumatic experiences. Soldier A indicated: "The various types of stress experienced in combat caused a general and increased sweating in soldiers that led to dehydration." Several of the participants stated that what is referred to as "cold sweats," which in medical terms is diaphoresis, does not come from heat or exertion, but from the body's response to stress, called a fight-or-flight response. Soldier F indicated that this fear and anxiety caused anything from panic to heightened tension and "cold sweats," which was one of the signs that a soldier was under severe psychological distress.

*Physical fatigue.* All participants gave personal and comrade examples of significant symptoms of combat stress. But they stated that combat and operational stress reactions were expected and predictably, including emotional, intellectual, physical and/or behavioural reactions from the exposure to stressful battlefield experiences. Moderate stress physiological reactions included fatigue, sweating, difficulty sleeping, jumpiness, rapid heartbeat, dizziness, slow reaction times, dry mouth, muscular tension, nausea, vomiting and/or diarrhoea. They also indicated in different ways that physical fatigue significantly contributed to the onset of fear, and as soldiers became exhausted, their ability to reason began to deteriorate. Soldier H identified that: "My most common reaction to fatigue was slow reaction time, a difficulty sorting out priorities and a difficulty in starting new tasks." Soldier A stated: "When I was tired, I became preoccupied with the completion of familiar and routine jobs, to the detriment of completing new tasks, and this led to a point where I became lacking in motivation."

*Shaking and tremors.* During combat, Soldier G said: "I experienced unintentional shaking and tremors in my body, and this made it extremely difficult for me to reload my rifle with a fresh magazine even though at the time the enemy was firing at us." Soldier F further reported that these symptoms rapidly appeared and then disappeared depending upon the level of combat stress and tension that was being experienced at the time. These tremors usually affected the arms and hands, although he reported that it also affected the head, face, tongue, trunk, and legs. Soldier B witnessed that during some instances, a soldier's voice also sounded shaky. The majority of the participants reported that if the soldier experienced continuing combat stress and anxiety, then the shaking and tremors would gradually get worse. These would eventually becoming so severe that the carrying out of normal activities would become initially difficult and finally impossible, thereby rendering the soldier inoperative in a combat environment.

*Sleep disturbance.* Soldier H stated: "After experiencing combat, I could not sleep even when the situation permitted, and when I did fall asleep, I frequently woke up and had difficulty getting back to sleep." Soldier C said that sleep disturbances came in the form of terror dreams, battle dreams, and nightmares, and these were all part of the coping process. Some of the participants stated that even when awake, they sometimes re-experienced the memory of a stressful combat experience as a "flashback." These participants went onto say that these "flashbacks" were normally triggered by a smell, sound, or sight which was related to the combat experience. Several of the participants in command positions noted that their soldiers who exhibiting a need for excessive sleep could well be showing the symptoms of combat stress, while persistent insomnia was found to be a common indicator for depression.

*Vision problems.* One common side effects of combat stress leading to anxiety was reported by Soldier H as being distorted vision. He personally had comrades who suffered from vision problems including blurred vision, double vision, difficulty in focusing, or total blindness. He believed that these symptoms were related to the surge of adrenaline in the body that accompanied anxiety. As well as these individual observations, many participants commented that they experienced vision problems due to combat stress, and then these vision problems increased their anxiety, especially as this impairment reduced their ability to observe the enemy. To highlight this observation, Soldier B said: "You often hear the term expressed 'the fog of war,' and this describes the smoke caused by the explosions that obscure the battlefield. But this is not half of it, as when I was in direct combat, I found that I was seeing double and was having difficulty focusing. Some of my chums in the platoon had the same problem, and this distorted sight made it very difficult to accurately aim your rifle at the enemy."

A total of 10 psychological combat stress symptoms were recorded by the researcher from the participants' answers as shown in Table 8.

**Table 8**
*Psychological Themes that Emerged in Response to Research Question (2).*

| | Participants | | | | | | | | | | | |
|---|---|---|---|---|---|---|---|---|---|---|---|---|
| Themes | A | B | C | D | E | F | G | H | I | J | Total of % Affirmative Responses | n |
| Altered Behaviours | Y | Y | Y | N | Y | Y | Y | Y | Y | Y | 90 | 9 |
| Anxiety | Y | Y | Y | Y | Y | Y | Y | Y | Y | Y | 100 | 10 |
| Depression | Y | Y | Y | N | Y | Y | Y | Y | Y | N | 80 | 8 |
| Disruptive Reactions | Y | Y | N | Y | N | N | Y | Y | Y | Y | 70 | 7 |
| Fear | Y | Y | Y | Y | Y | Y | Y | Y | Y | Y | 100 | 10 |
| Irritability | Y | Y | N | Y | N | Y | Y | Y | Y | N | 70 | 7 |
| Loss of Adaptability | Y | Y | N | N | Y | Y | Y | N | Y | N | 60 | 6 |
| Mental Fatigue | Y | Y | Y | Y | Y | Y | Y | Y | Y | Y | 100 | 10 |
| Substance Abuse | Y | N | N | Y | N | N | Y | N | Y | N | 40 | 4 |
| Suicidal Thoughts and Behaviours | N | Y | N | Y | N | N | N | Y | N | N | 30 | 3 |

***Altered behaviours.*** Combat stress reaction is a term used to describe acute behavioural disorder resulting from the results of combat trauma.[1] The participants felt that combat stress was the expected emotional, intellectual, physical and/or behavioural reactions by soldiers who had been exposed to the horrors of combat. Soldier I identified that these combat stress reactions had some overlap with acute stress reaction and so could be a precursor to the development of PTSD. The participants believed that many of the initial symptoms of combat stress reaction were as a result of an extended activation of the fight-or-flight response as the body released a flood of adrenaline to prepare the muscles for action. They witnessed that the fight-or-flight response normally ended when the fear or threat had disappeared. However, in the combat zone, Soldier E stated that: "I constantly felt that I was in mortal danger, and so I considered that I remained under constant threat." Soldier D believed that the human body responded to this extended period of stress by becoming more resistant to the stresses triggered by the fight-or-flight response during combat. He went on to say that he witnessed that during this period, the physical and mental symptoms of combat stress reaction were reduced as the body attempted to cope with the continuing stress. However, he concluded by saying that this long-term combat involvement depleted the body's resources and triggered long-term damage, notably to the cardiovascular system and gastrointestinal tract.

Soldier G said: "In my experience, the symptoms of combat stress reaction were based upon the soldier's unique experiences when involved in combat and then the amount of support that they received after the event." These symptoms he stated could occur immediately after a stressful event, but could take days, months or even years to appear, with some veterans first noting the symptoms after returning home from an operational deployment." The participants summarised these reactions as withdrawing from others, being hyper-vigilant, angry outbursts, self-destructive behaviours, an alteration in eating/sleeping patterns, crying, staring into space, and being startled easily. The participants observed that soldiers suffering from combat stress reaction, if treated immediately at the front line, were more likely to return to duty. This treatment was not therapy, but rather was designed to simply restore the soldiers' coping skills by ensuring sleep, water, hygiene, food, encouragement, counselling, and the involvement in simple work details.

The participants all thought that a great deal of self-care could be done to alleviate combat stress reaction, and this included reminding themselves that the feelings they were experiencing were normal in the circumstances. They also consciously looked for sudden changes in their comrades' behaviours, as this could be an early indication of combat stress reaction. If these concerns for their own well-being or those of their comrades did not dissipate, they alerted their next superior in the unit as to their observations and fears. However, for this "self-help" and "buddy-system" to be successful, the participants stressed that the leader needed to be fully conversant with the physiological and psychological effects of combat on their soldiers. This meant that the leader had been fully trained to be able to identify the first indications of combat stress and then to have the first line of psychological medical support readily available.

***Anxiety.*** Soldier G witnessed that primary and secondary forms of anxiety had different effects. He saw that primary anxiety was that part that energised the soldier to deal with a threat, as the body was flooded with adrenaline, sugars, fats, and other hormones to allow action to be taken. However, he believed that secondary anxiety by contrast had no particular focus, as it manifested itself in terms of concerns over whether certain tasks were within the grasp of the individual soldier. Soldier G said that: "This secondary anxiety was hard to control, as it interfered with the soldier's performance with it causing physical symptoms such as shaking, a difficulty with walking, nausea, giddiness, and sight distortions." Additionally, Soldier I witnessed that a common feature of anxiety in soldiers was increased vigilance with them being unable to relax and constantly staying alert in anticipation of what they perceived as being an immediate enemy attack. This constant anticipation of combat increased this stress within the soldiers, who could never completely sleep, rest, or even relax. This vigilance affected all the senses and the soldiers became sensitised to any slight movement, and, over time, this and the strain on the other senses caused muscular tensions and headaches.

Soldier D stated that fear of death, pain, and/or injury caused him severe anxiety reactions. After witnessing the loss of a comrade in combat, he lost confidence and felt overly vulnerable and incapable. In some instances, he witnessed that soldiers confronted with extreme stress and daily anxiety tended to dissociate from those threats instead of becoming more vigilant. Soldier F witnessed his comrades and stated that: "When a soldier was under extreme stress, he developed symptoms of post-trauma, and this can be identified by what we called 'the thousand-yard stare,' that is he was present in body but his mind was somewhere else and he just stared into space." He also experienced that those with severe anxiety often found that they were easily upset and their tempers became difficult to control. Soldier B believed that this anxiety was brought about by the soldiers trying to control their panic attacks, which caused negative emotions that made it more difficult to cope with the pressures of daily life, let alone the stress and trauma of combat. He further witnessed his comrades grappling with these feelings of anxiety 24 hours a day, which in turn made it that much more difficult for them to cope with any additional battlefield stress.

*Depression.* Soldier C witnessed that during combat, depression was a serious medical condition that affected a soldier's behaviour, thinking, emotions, health, and performance. He believed that a common cause of depression was the build-up of stress and anxiety caused by combat experiences on the battlefield. He witnessed how soldiers responded to depression with protective defensive reactions against painful experiences that resulted in a numbing of normal responsiveness. He personally experienced that: "I found that I was increasingly ineffective, lacked the ability to think clearly, and was constantly tired, but despite this constant exhaustion, I could not sleep." Soldier H added: "During my periods of depression, I found that the emotions of pride, shame, grief, and gratitude no longer mattered. I became less talkative and was unable to enjoy relaxing with my buddies." This included continuous and long mood swings, when he changed from feeling happy to despairing, sorrowful, angry, or irritable. The things that had given him enjoyment now left him numb and uninterested. He felt despair that he could not escape and so withdrew from or avoided colleagues. He also had a feeling of exhaustion, a lack of energy, an inability to concentrate, and a lack of interest in carrying out his duties.

*Disruptive reactions.* All participants indicated that individual soldiers could panic, become confused, and rush around without self-control, and a soldier suffering from these symptoms could compromise both their and their comrades' safety. Soldier J saw that: "One day, while on operations up in the mountains, one of my close friends all of a sudden could not complete assigned tasks, appeared dazed, and wandered around aimlessly. It was so bad that he had to be CASEVACED (Casualty Evacuation)[2] by helicopter, and I never saw him again." Other participants described how some soldiers appeared confused or disorientated and exhibited either a complete or partial memory loss. Also some soldiers, in a desperate attempt to escape the danger that they perceived was about to engulf them, would panic and became confused. Soldier E further identified that: "Some soldiers' mental ability became impaired to the degree that they could not think clearly or follow simple commands." He saw that a soldier in panic was virtually out of control and needed to be protected from injuring himself. If this panic was not quelled early, it would easily spread to other soldiers within the unit. Soldier G witnessed that during periods of extreme combat and operational stress, vengeful thoughts occurred in individuals or groups of individuals within a unit. These feelings led to violent and uncontrolled reactions unless the leaders at all levels were able to identify the risk factors and behaviours that could lead to such actions.

*Fear.* The participants found that there were some specific sources of psychological fear that were brought about by combat. First was the natural fear of being killed, wounded, or captured by the enemy. Second was the fear of having to kill an enemy combatant, as this was against their social and religious beliefs. Third, there was the fear that was generated in them by the chaos of war and the sights and sounds of combat. Four, they felt the fear of apprehension about not being able to measure up when under fire. Finally, fatigue caused their reasoning abilities to deteriorate to a point where they became indecisive and slow in carrying out orders. Soldier E said that: "During close combat with the enemy, I experienced a pounding heart, and no matter how many times I was in combat, the same thing happened; your body could never adjust to the expectation of sudden death." The participants identified that the other automatic body reactions to fear were trembling, irrational laughter, sweating, tunnel vision, auditory exclusion, and a fight-or-flight response.

Soldier C said that: "When I was afraid in combat, I found that I would became obsessed with minor details, was unable to make decisions, and became lacking in self-confidence." Soldier I witnessed that the three extreme reactions to fear were aggression, rage and freezing when under fire. Soldier B also observed that the unexpected actions of the enemy had a significant impact on soldiers as they began to sense that they did not have control of the situation. Soldier G also found that the unknown was a source of fear for soldiers, as the less they knew about the enemy, the more they exaggerated the enemy's capabilities, and the more fearful they became. The majority of participants said that they developed a feeling of helplessness if they felt they did not control the situation and that none of their actions affected the outcome. Finally, all the participants identified that fear was infectious, as it would spread through a unit and destroy its effectiveness if not actively checked by the commander.

*Irritability.* Soldier D witnessed that irritability was a common symptom of anxiety as soldiers struggled to manage their anxiety by themselves. He said that irritable reactions ranged from angry looks to sharp words but could also progress to more serious acts of violence. He witnessed that sporadic and unpredictable explosions of aggressive behaviour and/or violence occurred with little or no provocation. On this topic, Soldier G stated: "When under stress, my buddies had short attention spans and found it difficult to concentrate and follow orders; this of course was a nightmare for our commander, who was trying to keep the unit focused." He also witnessed that the soldiers had difficulty understanding what others were saying, in aiding others and/or performing unfamiliar tasks. After these experiences, he believes that there are two different types of close irritability. The first is physical closeness, when the soldier becomes irritable when someone is nearby, as this creates a feeling of having no space. The second type is emotional closeness, when the soldier becomes irritable around those soldiers they care about, driving a wedge between them and their colleagues.

*Loss of adaptability.* Soldier F stated that in his experience, a common reaction to combat stress included uncontrolled emotional outbursts such as crying, yelling, or laughing. However, on the other extreme, he also saw that some soldiers became withdrawn, silent, and tried to isolate themselves from their comrades. Many of the participants saw that uncontrolled reactions appeared singly or in combination with a number of other symptoms, and in this state, the soldier became restless and unable to keep still. The participants also witnessed that soldiers felt rage or fear, which was demonstrated by aggressive acts, angry outbursts, and/or irritability. This loss of adaptability caused anxiety, irritability, complaining, and difficulty in paying attention or remembering details. There was also an identifiable difficulty in thinking, speaking, and communicating. Soldier B stated: "I experienced severe sleeping difficulties; I grieved constantly, and often cried for the friends that I had lost." The vast majority of the participants said that they had a feeling of guilt, anger, and resentment after they returned from operations. And these feelings were reinforced once they returned home only to find that nobody cared or was interested in their sacrifices.

***Mental fatigue.*** All participants indicated in different ways that mental fatigue significantly contributed to the onset of fear, and as soldiers became exhausted, their ability to reason began to deteriorate. Soldier E indicated: "I suffered from an excessive concern with seemingly minor issues and had difficulty in focusing attention on my tasks." Soldier C believed that as soldiers became increasingly tired, they became indecisive and slow in carrying out orders. If confronted with the daily stress of combat, and if this was coupled with fatigue, participants stated that they developed a feeling of helplessness and an inability to continue fighting. In this regard, Soldier I witnessed that no matter how well soldiers were led, they could only take so much combat stress as physical fatigue, hunger, disease, and thirst all contributed to breaking the soldiers' will to continue fighting.

These mid-stress reactions adversely affected and/or slowed soldiers' performances in carrying out routine tasks. However, severe-stress reactions prevented soldiers from performing their duties and created safety concerns. These symptoms included constant movement, severe startle response, shaking or trembling, paralysis, exhaustion, immobility, acute abdominal pain, impaired speech, heart palpitations, hyperventilation, and/or insomnia. Soldier D stressed that: "I found war to be physically exhausting, as I was constantly tired and struggled with recurring dreams and nightmares that did not permit me any rest." Soldier G stated: "I was totally tired the whole time I was in Afghanistan, as my senses were heightened in order to increase my chances of survival." These heightened senses led to an increase in blood pressure and heart rate that only gradually subsided once the participant was safely home.

*Substance abuse.* All the participants felt that the life of a soldier was frequently stressful due to having a life of frequent change, regular danger, difficult living conditions, and potential stress and trauma caused by combat experiences. As a result, soldiers tended to use substances such as alcohol or other drugs as a means of escaping combat stress. Unfortunately, Soldier A witnessed that those suffering from substance abuse problems found that this in turn produced new traumatic event experiences which led to even worse substance abuse, and so forth. As an example, he believed that PTSD and depression occurred frequently among soldiers with substance abuse disorders and vice versa. He said that: "My experiences after I returned from operations have led me to believe that traumatised soldiers are more likely to abuse drugs before and after being diagnosed with PTSD." In this regard, Soldiers D stated: "Since my return from operations, a number of my former buddies have sought escape through either alcohol or substance abuse, and as a result, a number of them have been forced to leave the Army."

*Suicidal thoughts and behaviours.* Soldier H believed that some behaviours and symptoms were not only signs of combat stress reaction but also a signal for potential suicide risks. Soldier D witnessed that some of the common symptoms that indicated that a soldier may be contemplating suicide were sleep problems, impulsiveness, and the inability to sit still or concentrate. He also saw that the soldier would have a feeling of worthlessness, guilt, and a feeling of being trapped. The majority of the participants believed that combat veterans are not only more likely to have suicidal thoughts, often associated with PTSD and depression, but that they were more likely to act on a suicidal plan.

Soldier B stated: "In my experience serving, soldiers and veterans are less likely to seek help, as they feel that they can handle the problem, often through alcohol or drugs, but when these measures do not work they are also more likely to carry out a successful suicide." Most of the participants felt that these suicidal feelings were related to a belief that they did not belong with other people and that they were a burden on others and society. Soldier E felt that: "Once you are a combat veteran, you can more easily acquire the capability to overcome the fear of pain associated with suicide." All the participants identified that a soldier in this sort of distress would demonstrate a range of uncharacteristic behaviours that were different from their normal character.

***Long-term effects of combat.*** The third major theme that was identified by the participants' responses to research *Question (2)* was that the soldiers experienced the long-term effects of combat after their return home. All of the participants, upon returning from their combat deployment, reported that upon arriving home, their first emotional reaction was one of profound relief that they had survived the experience. However, Soldier C reported that: "My relief at returning home safely was short-lived, as my mind returned to the war that was still being fought and to other British soldiers that I knew that were still engaged in the war. I also had a feeling of guilt when I remembered the friends that I had lost." Soldier G indicated that he struggled with intense moments when he found himself reliving the horrors of war. These feelings often provoked anger and irritability in Soldier J, who felt a feeling of inadequacy for not having done enough. These emotions often left Soldier A feeling alone and overwhelmed by the feelings of guilt and remorse. He believed that these emotional reactions were the symptoms of post-combat stress.

The incidence of post-combat stress significantly and profoundly altered the way the participants thought, as the memories of their combat deployment dominated their minds and made it difficult for them to concentrate on anything else. Soldier H reported that: "When I returned home, I felt confusion, lacked good judgement, and became forgetful." This led to a preoccupation with the combat experiences, which in turn led to a loss of objectivity, resulting in increasing self-criticism. Soldier E also reported a breakdown in his value system, as he had witnessed first-hand the horrors of war and the results of close combat, all of which changed his perceptions of life.

Soldier G felt that the mental reactions he experienced after returning from Afghanistan were as a result of him suffering from mild traumatic brain injury (TBI), which is defined as "an injury with loss of consciousness or altered mental status (dazed or confused)." He further stated that amongst his comrades, about 9% had been diagnosed with TBI, and of these, 85% were suffering from some form of mental health disorder. On this point, Soldier J witnessed that: "As the tour continued, the symptoms of stress became more common amongst the soldiers in my platoon who had previously suffered from blast injuries, with them having flashbacks and nightmares." Soldier H said that: "I found that I was suffering from headaches, dizziness, and memory loss as a result of a mine blast that severely damaged the armoured vehicle I was in while I was on patrol." On this subject, Soldier C reported that his own TBI had been associated with his continuing hearing and visual impairments. He had also witnessed that blast induced TBI had created hearing loss, eardrum perforation, and dizziness amongst his comrades.

Although most of the participants upon returning from Afghanistan did not have any behavioural health conditions and did not experience any traumatic brain injuries, all experienced a period of readjustment as they reintegrated into life with family, friends, and community. They reported that upon returning from their combat deployment, they experienced a variety of psychological symptoms including sleeplessness, nightmares, and feelings of sadness, rejection, abandonment, and/or hopelessness. The participants also struggled to concentrate, some engaged in aggressive behaviour, and some used alcohol, tobacco and drugs excessively. The intensity and duration of these and other psychological symptoms indicated a more serious problem that required professional treatment. The participants reported that this complex interaction between the physical, emotional, and mental reactions to post-combat stress produced negative behavioural reactions.

Upon returning home, most of the participants were looking for relief from their stressful combat experiences, some through reckless or aggressive behaviour. As an example, Soldier C described that: "While I was in Afghanistan, we had nothing to spend our money on, as there were no shops outside Camp Bastion in Helmand Province. So, when I got home I spent all my saved-up wages on a new sports car. However, I drove it too fast when I was drunk one night, got pulled over by the police, was convicted of DUI, and lost my driving license for 6 months – a really dumb move!" Other participants said that they immersed themselves in work in the hope that being busy would lessen the painful memories of combat. Soldier H found that: "When I got home, the memories of Afghanistan were with me constantly, and so to get my mind of things, I volunteered for the Special Air Service (SAS) selection course. I figured that all the pre-course physical training and practice in cross-country navigation, at night, with a 50-60lb. pack would take my mind off my experiences." A further common reaction was for the participants to socially withdraw from friends, colleagues, and even their own family. Some of the participants experienced that these symptoms worsened over the first year after a veteran returned home due to readjustment to civilian life, employment and more restricted access to military health care. Some participants said that when considering PTSD, it was often associated with co-occurring disorders such as depression and traumatic brain injury (TBI), which complicated a correct medical assessment and treatment.

# Chapter Fourteen

## Soldiers' Post-Combat Recommendations

The research study asked the participants the following third question:

**Q3. According to infantry soldiers' combat experiences, what types of pre-combat education programmes and leadership training interventions could be effective in helping soldiers cope with the negative physiological and psychological effects of combat?**

Two interview questions were asked of participants to collect data to answer research *Question (3)*. The eleven major themes that emerged from the participants' answers to research *Question (3)* are shown in Table 9.

*Combat training.* The participants emphasised that the introduction of realism into training was an important element in preparing soldiers for combat. Soldier J went further, suggesting that: "During training exercises, all movement of soldiers needs to be done tactically as should be the re-supply of rations, water, and ammunition." Soldier B reinforced this point by recommending that as well as this tactical training there should also be the use of camouflage and concealment at all times, when moving and when static. Soldier F further elaborated that throughout the pre-deployment, training leaders within the chain of command, from the unit commander down, should be made "exercise casualties" so that subordinates need to be trained in the higher command functions in preparation for when real casualties occurred on combat operations. Soldier I identified that: "In order to realistically practice fire and movement, laser engagement systems should be used in order to teach soldiers the use of cover and concealment."

**Table 9**

*Programmes and Training Themes that Emerged in Response to Research Question (3).*

| | Participants | | | | | | | | | | | |
|---|---|---|---|---|---|---|---|---|---|---|---|---|
| Themes | A | B | C | D | E | F | G | H | I | J | Total % of Affirmative Responses | n |
| Combat Training | Y | Y | Y | Y | Y | Y | Y | Y | Y | Y | 100 | 10 |
| Daily Survival Requirements | N | Y | Y | Y | N | Y | Y | Y | Y | Y | 80 | 8 |
| Education Programmes | Y | Y | Y | Y | Y | Y | Y | N | Y | Y | 90 | 9 |
| Mental Survival | Y | Y | Y | Y | Y | N | N | Y | Y | Y | 80 | 8 |
| Physical Survival | Y | Y | Y | N | Y | Y | Y | Y | Y | N | 80 | 8 |
| Leadership Training | Y | Y | Y | Y | Y | Y | Y | Y | Y | Y | 100 | 10 |
| Morale | Y | Y | Y | Y | Y | Y | Y | Y | Y | Y | 100 | 10 |
| Motivation | Y | Y | Y | Y | N | N | Y | Y | Y | Y | 80 | 8 |
| Discipline | Y | Y | Y | Y | Y | N | Y | Y | Y | Y | 90 | 9 |
| Proficiency | N | Y | Y | N | Y | Y | Y | Y | Y | Y | 80 | 8 |
| Esprit de corps | Y | Y | Y | Y | Y | Y | Y | N | Y | Y | 90 | 9 |

Soldier G believed that the replication of the sights, sounds, and conditions of combat during training would better prepare soldiers for actual combat. He also stipulated that: "This type of training must be conducted during day and night as well as in all climates, weather, and terrain, as these were the conditions that we faced when in combat."

The participants identified a number of training techniques that they believed should be utilised during pre-combat training exercises. These were designed to prepare infantry soldiers for the negative physiological and psychological effects of combat:

> *a.* Ensure that soldiers are properly trained in infantry minor tactics skills and drills.

*b.* Ensure that training includes an understanding of combat stress and how to deal with the effects.

*c.* Place welfare of subordinates before personal welfare.

*d.* Ensure that soldier get as much rest as possible.

*e.* Ensure that the best possible shelters are available.

*f.* Ensure soldiers are well supplied with food, water, and other essentials.

*g.* Provide mail, news, and other information sources.

*h.* Provide the best medical, logistic, and other support.

*i.* Maintain high morale, unit identity, and esprit de corps.

*j.* Ensure that experienced unit members mentor new members.

*k.* Ensure continuity by keeping the same unit members together where possible.

For all of the participants, the witnessing of comrades being killed or wounded had a traumatic impact on themselves, their comrades, and the leader within the unit. Soldier F found that this led some soldiers to develop fear and apprehension that it would happen to them, and this in turn increased their reluctance to take risks and obey orders. Soldier I identified that: "How soldiers respond after their unit had received casualties indicated the effectiveness of their training, preparation, and self-discipline." To this end, Soldier C believed that the leader must be trained to be able to ensure prompt and effective medical treatment and/or evacuation for the unit's casualties, as this would positively affect morale. To facilitate this, he said that the leader and the second-in-command must constantly be aware of which soldiers become casualties and where they are located.

The participants articulated that the use of live-firing exercises would give soldiers the opportunity to use live ammunition as realistically as possible in artificial combat situations where all the personal weapons and support weapons are fired. They believed that the use of live-firing exercises will teach soldiers to have confidence in themselves, their weapons, and their comrades when firing live ammunition. Soldier F found: "The conduct of live-firing exercises will teach the difference between in-coming and out-going artillery and mortar fire." During this phase, enemy weapons would be fired so that soldiers when engaged in combat could recognise the sounds of friendly and enemy fire. Soldier A also felt: "During training, soldiers should be subject to live overhead fire, as this further reinforces the individual's battlefield inoculation, as noise is one of the most frightening aspects of combat." Finally, he witnessed that the use of artillery and mortar simulators, pyrotechnics, explosive charges, and smoke increases the realism of the training and provides soldiers with an idea of the "fog-of-war" that they would experience in actual combat.

*Daily survival requirements.* Most of the participants experienced situations where a reduction in caloric intake during continuous operations led to both physical and mental fatigue and degraded performance. Therefore, Soldier A suggested that soldiers must be trained and then supervised to ensure that they eat all the main items in their 24-hour combat rations to ensure that they got a balanced diet. Soldier H believed that eating regularly was important during continuous operations, as was the provision of hot meals when operations permit. He personally described how an inadequate diet had degraded his own and his comrades' performances, reduced their resistance to disease, and prolonged their recuperation from illness and injury. However, Soldier D felt that: "It was part of the leaders' command function to provide and maintain an adequate supply of food that enabled the soldiers to cope with the increased stresses of combat." He believed that it was part of all leaders' tasks to ensure that their soldiers ate and drank properly.

Soldier F identified that the excitement, stress, and rapid pace of combat also caused soldiers to forget to drink liquids, which resulted in dehydration. He described how the relative lack of moisture in 24-hour combat rations contributed to the development of dehydration. Soldier J further witnessed how he and his comrades when experiencing dehydration lost their appetite and reduced their food intake, which led to degraded performance. In concluding, Soldier E stipulated that: "In training, each soldier must be trained to realize the importance of being hydrated prior to combat and that additionally leaders must monitor their soldiers' fluid intake at all times."

According to the participants, the lot of infantry soldiers was to endure conditions of wet, cold, hunger, thirst, and tiredness, and as a result, they build up a resilience and tolerance to the extremes of weather. However, at a certain point, Soldier A witnessed that: "Every soldier in my platoon in Afghanistan at some point became unable to continue due to the onset of various physical problems and/or mental exhaustion. It was at these times that his buddies rallied around and distributed his load amongst ourselves, taking such items as the extra ammunition belts, spare radio batteries, night-viewing devices etc." Soldier H witnessed that every day an infantry soldier is enduring one form of discomfort or another, and so he felt that the leader must be constantly aware of this danger and be trained, where and when possible, to provide dry clothing, food, water, and protection from the elements to his soldiers.

The "hurry-up-and-wait" phenomenon in many military operations was, according to the participants, aptly called "hours of boredom," whereas the transition to combat was deemed to consist of "moments of terror." The inadequate recognition of the implications resulting from long lull periods, combat pulses, and the need to recover from stress could lead to dysfunctional soldiering as well as poor individual and small unit performance. Soldier G stated that the management of such time-based transitions effected the psychological state of soldier combatants, and so it was important to conduct resilience training for small group leaders and their soldiers. Soldier D believed that: "A little appreciated fact is that boredom and inactivity have a negative impact on soldiers, who can become complacent and ineffective." He recommended that to alleviate the effects of boredom, the leader needed to be trained to instigate briefings, rehearsals, and training events that kept the soldiers occupied and their thoughts away from themselves and home.

***Education programmes.*** The participants stated that pre-combat education programmes should be designed to give the infantryman an insight into the negative physiological and psychological effects of combat. The aim would be to get each individual infantry soldier to begin thinking about the stresses of combat so that they understood the challenges, characteristics, and fear associated with combat. Soldier J felt that the essential message to each soldier must be that they do not have to actually experience combat in order to understand the essential requirements for enduring and winning in combat operations. Soldier C further elaborated that each soldier must realise that combat is an extreme test of their morale, mental, and physical stamina where they will experience danger, fear, and exhaustion. However, Soldier E stressed that the effects of combat varied for every soldier and the conditions that broke one soldier may only lead to fortifying the resolve of another soldier.

The participants explained that commanders and soldiers need to know a host of details about the enemy forces. The more accurate the picture the better the commanders can prepare their operational plans. Soldier A stressed that: "All soldiers during pre-deployment training must be taught their own capabilities and characteristics, as well as the strengths and weaknesses of their enemy, as this dispels their fear of the unknown." Also, training must include knowledge of the enemy's weapons, tactics, and vehicles, as this contributes to success in combat. Soldier C stated: "When I was first in contact with the enemy, the fact that I had heard the sound of an AK47 firing during pre-deployment training allowed me to identify the direction from which the enemy was advancing on our defensive position."

The participants also stated that as important as knowing the enemy is the need for accurate information during training and briefing in the field on the capabilities, limitations, and locations of friendly forces, as it was often difficult to maintain a clear picture of the other Coalition operations that were taking place at the same time. Soldier D found that: "There was confusion regarding other friendly forces, especially the Afghan National Army (ANA),[1] that is where they were and what they were doing, and this problem was made worse by the language barrier and poor communications." Soldier G reinforced this point by saying that: "When you were in a fire-fight, it was critical to know where your flanking units were located so that a "blue-on-blue" situation did not arise. We all remembered the incident where the NFL football star, Sergeant Tilman,[2] is accidentally killed by his own unit when they incorrectly identified him as the Taliban." In this regard, Soldier J felt that it was critical that soldiers are taught the capabilities and characteristics, as well as the strengths and weaknesses of their own and Coalition forces. He believed that this will allow for the identification of any weaknesses in the friendly forces leadership, training, equipment, and experience as this will allow realistic tactical planning to be conducted.

***Mental survival.*** Most of the participants emphasised that mental fitness was just as important as physical fitness. However, they noted that this type of training was largely ignored prior to their own operational deployments. When discussing mental fitness, Soldier D noted it as the ability to achieve it through emotional health, where a series of exercises that helped the soldier slow down, decompress, and boost a flagging memory were practised prior to deployment. Soldier E had followed a technique of achieving a sense of calm through imagery, which reduced tension in both his body and mind. This controlled his feelings of self-confidence and optimism, while at the same time boosting his emotional well-being and calming him mentally. Therefore, the consensus arrived at by the participants was that soldiers must be both mentally as well as physically fit before operational deployment in order to cope with the stresses of combat operations.

All the participants stressed that the implementation of realistic training is a primary stress-reduction technique, as it can reassure soldiers by developing maximum confidence in their skills and beliefs that their leaders were doing their best for their units. In this regard, Soldier I identified that: "It is essential that the leaders within each unit encourage and support their soldiers in their efforts to cope with stress." He further indicated that this would have a decisive effect in ensuring that soldiers endured combat exposure, while at the same time accomplishing the unit's combat mission. Soldier A expressed a view that stress-coping indoctrination needed to be part of every unit's combat training, as controlling stress required practice. To this end, Soldier B believed that: "The stress training had to be under conditions as similar to combat as possible." Soldier G further stressed that a unit's ability to cope with stress in combat depended primarily on how rigorously and realistically the pre-deployment training is conducted.

The participants stressed that during pre-deployment training, every soldier within each unit must be trained to effectively sustain combat performance in continuous operations. Soldier F believed that the gaining of this capability went beyond the achievement of a high level of proficiency in combat skills and technical specialties. He felt that instead it meant being able to identify the adverse physical and mental conditions of continuous operations in order to cope with them and then overcome their negative effects. As part of this process, Soldier H stressed: "Each soldier must be trained in how to slow the rate of performance loss as adverse conditions and continual combat stress are constantly eating away at each soldiers' military effectiveness." However, Soldier D believed that the rate of performance decline could be slowed if pre-combat training in safety, food intake, and physical fitness loss had been undertaken. He believed that this requirement for safety training was necessitated by fatigue as overtired soldiers were more vulnerable to injury than those who were rested. In this regard, Soldier B witnessed with his own comrades that: "After 72 hours of continuous combat, there became a tendency to seek short cuts, and as a result, accident rates increased significantly." In order to alleviate this problem, Soldier G suggested the inclusion of additional training in safety operating procedures, which was to be accompanied by increasing the supervision of soldiers during extended periods of combat stress.

***Physical survival.*** Most of the participants emphasised that good physical conditioning delayed fatigue, built confidence, and shortened recovery times from illness and injury. They also believed that it prepared soldiers to better cope with the physical demands of combat-related stress. In the experience of Soldier I, physical fitness, which includes aerobic fitness, muscular strength, and endurance, needs to be developed in soldiers in order to strengthen their ability to rebound from exhaustion. He also believed that aerobic fitness increased a soldier's work capacity and ability to withstand stress. Soldier I also found that: "The pursuit of physical exercise helped the mind, as physical activity increased the flow of oxygen to the brain and increased your mental alertness." Soldier G also found that: "Those in good physical condition tended to enjoy a higher level of mental resilience." When in combat, he had witnessed how the prior pursuit of vigorous exercise had helped both him and his comrades to cope with combat-induced depression, to gain a more positive outlook, and to help beat stress. Further to these observations, Soldier C stated: "It was very apparent that even though the feelings of depression and moodiness accompanied tiredness, aerobically fit soldiers were affected less than the unfit."

Soldier A emphasised that it should be ensured that the soldier is physically fit for the stresses of combat operations, as the demands were extreme and varied depending upon the environment in which the operations were being conducted. He believed that routine physical training did not prepare soldiers for the rigors of oppressive heat, extreme cold, or the lack of oxygen when operating at altitude. His conclusion was that: "In my experience, wherever possible soldiers need to arrive in the operational theatre several weeks early to allow the essential acclimatisation while carrying out demanding physical training such as carrying heavy loads (50-60 lbs.), at speed, over undulating and hilly terrain."

The participants believed that the leader must aim to minimise the physiological and psychological effects of combat on soldiers, and to do this he must be aware that the main sources of stress for soldiers is boredom, fatigue, discomfort, and friendly casualties. The participants recommended that in order to lessen these effects on soldiers, the leader must be trained to carry out the following:

*a.* Assure every effort is made to provide for the troops' welfare.
*b.* Instil confidence in each soldier and his equipment, unit, and leadership.
*c.* Be decisive and assertive by demonstrating competence and fair leadership.
*d.* Provide sleep and/or rest, especially during continuous operations, whenever possible.
*e.* Ensure sleep periods are enforced, but especially for decision-making personnel.

*f.* Set realistic goals for progressive development of individual soldiers as well as the unit and then test these goals.

*g.* Recognise that battle duration and intensity increases stress.

*h.* Be aware of environmental stressors such as light, temperature, and precipitation.

*i.* Recognise that individual soldiers and units react differently to the same stress.

*j.* Learn the signs of stress in yourself and others.

*k.* Recognise that fear is a normal part of combat stress.

*l.* Rest minor stress casualties briefly, keeping them with their unit.

*m.* Be aware of background stress sources prior to combat such as family concerns, separation, and economic problems.

*n.* Provide an upward, downward, and lateral information flow to minimise stress due to lack of communication.

*o.* Practice stress control through cross-training, task allocation, task matching, and task sharing.

*p.* Look for stress signs and a decreased ability to tolerate stress.

*q.* Practice and master stress-coping techniques.

*r.* Acknowledge combat stress, as it is unhealthy to deny the stresses of combat.

**Leadership training.** All the participants believed that the leadership skills applied to troop welfare and war-fighting need to be taught to be used to reduce and/or prevent combat stress reactions. They felt that it was the leader's responsibility to take preventative actions and address stress symptoms as they appeared in their soldiers. Soldier B felt that: "In order to reduce stress, the commander needs to lead by inspiration and not fear or intimidation." In this regard, Soldier I said that the leader needed to be taught this in training so that they could initiate and support stress-management programmes and provide information in order to focus stress positively. Soldier C recommended that leaders need to be taught to check that each soldier has mastered at least two stress-relaxation techniques – a slow one for deep relaxation, and a quick one for immediate stress management. Importantly, Soldier H identified that: "Each unit commander experiences the same risks and fears as their soldiers, but these have to be overcome in order to provide effective leadership that would lead to success in combat." Soldier E stated that in order to lead soldiers effectively, soldiers need to believe that the leader is aware of the conditions that stimulate and inspire courage in the soldiers. He further stipulated that in order to do this, the leader must be taught to understand the conditions that will stimulate fear, which he saw as being the unexpected, the unknown, and a feeling of helplessness.

Soldier F described how the unexpected was often instigated by surprise enemy action, which had a powerful impact on soldiers, as they began to doubt whether they had control of the situation, which created the danger of the soldiers panicking. Soldier D stated that: "During these times, the commander is responsible for exerting strong leadership in order to maintain control of the soldiers within the unit." Soldier A witnessed that: "Our fear of the unknown was ever-present, and we often attributed greater strength and ability to the enemy than was warranted." He felt that it was at this time that the leader needed to provide guidance as to the enemy's true strengths and capabilities, thereby dispelling any exaggerations.

In many cases, the participants identified that the leader must be taught to prevent feelings of helplessness pervading the unit by acting to direct and inspire the response against the enemy. Soldier H witnessed that in a large part, this is aided by the leader ensuring that all soldiers are carrying out their assigned tasks, as soldiers being busy prevents this condition from taking hold within the unit. Soldier H experienced the first shock of combat, which he felt was a powerful factor that soldiers would initially face until they became confident when functioning under fire. In this regard, he said that: "The leader must provide the decisive example that transforms soldiers' fears into aggression." On this point, Soldier G stated that the presence of the leader had tremendous value in overcoming soldiers' fears, as it is at these times that soldiers tend to feel alone and isolated.

All the participants saw effective leadership as reducing the impact of stress when the leader understands the causes of combat stress and how soldiers would react to these fears. The participants contributed their recommendations as to how the leader should be trained to successfully manage combat stress problems so that they did not spread throughout the unit as follows:

    *a.* The leader is trained to focus soldiers on completing the assigned mission.

    *b.* The leader is trained to ensure that all soldiers perform their assigned duties.

    *c.* The leader trains their soldiers to remain calm and in control at all times.

    *d.* The leader is trained to inform their soldiers that their reactions to combat are normal.

    *e.* The leader is trained to keep soldiers active and productive through various training regimes.

    *f.* The leader is trained to ensure that soldiers maintain the highest levels of personal hygiene.

    *g.* The leader is trained to supervise that soldiers eat, drink, and sleep correctly.

    *h.* The leader is trained to allow soldiers to express their views and give practical advice.

Soldier I said: "The confidence of soldiers is based upon the technical and tactical competence demonstrated by their leaders, and this confidence was one of the strongest defences against combat stress." Therefore, he believed that the development of both individual soldier and unit confidence must be a major goal for every military leader. Soldier B went on to say that soldiers must believe in themselves, their leader's competence, their equipment, other unit members, and their training. He believed that each of these beliefs must be instilled and reinforced at every opportunity in training and combat. Soldier D witnessed that: "All soldiers within a unit will naturally build confidence, integrity, and cohesion when the leader is competent."

The participants observed that as soldiers became increasingly tired, they lost their ability to make rapid and rational decisions as they became more confused, disorientated, and eventually ineffective. Therefore, the participants were unanimous in their view that it was essential that the leaders understood and were trained on the effects of fatigue on themselves and their soldiers. Soldier J indicated that the main indicators that a soldier was suffering from fatigue was a reckless disregard for the safety of themselves and their comrades, or conversely, excessive caution or an unwillingness to expose themselves to risk, failure to fire at the enemy, a lack of concern for weapons and/or other equipment, and a lack of concern for personal cleanliness. Soldier F identified that: "To avoid unnecessary symptoms of fatigue, the leader needed to be trained to ensure that everyone received a minimum of four hours of sleep per-day, as when on combat operations, this reduces unnecessary casualties from occurring."

***Morale.*** Morale was seen by the participants as the mental and emotional condition of an individual soldier or group of soldiers, and that the leader who harnessed this resource in the unit would ultimately prevail. Soldier E believed that: "Morale could be described as the enthusiasm and determination with which the soldiers were totally engaged in the unit's success." While Soldier B described morale as: "A function of cohesion and teamwork." In the military, the participants mentioned that the terms "morale" and "motivation" were often used interchangeably. However, they further stipulated that "morale" highlighted the condition of the unit, while "motivation" principally described the attribute of the individual soldier.

All the participants believed that within the military, morale and motivation were the foundations of discipline, esprit de corps, and professionalism, all of which led to success in combat. This was reflected in the confidence, resolution, and courageous attitude of soldiers within the unit who were determined to accomplish the assigned mission. Soldier A believed that this morale was based upon the soldiers' pride in the unit, confidence in their leader, a sense of participation and belonging to the unit, and faith in the unit's ultimate success. However, he also observed that this maintenance of morale within the unit was the leader's constant concern, as ultimately it was the foundation of discipline.

The participants in general identified that there were specific indicators of morale that the leader had to be aware of and needed to be taught in leadership training, and these were: responses to shortages, care of weapons and equipment, rumours, excessive quarrelling, personal hygiene, standards of military courtesy, personal conduct, and appearance. Soldier J believed that: "The leader always needed to be aware if the unit suffered shortages, but particularly in food, water, clothing, ammunition, or medical supplies, as this would adversely affect morale." In this regard, Soldier H found that in a unit with high morale, the soldiers automatically divided equally what was available and that this unconscious act maintained unit cohesion. On this point, Soldier D found that: "The failure of soldiers to properly maintain weapons and equipment was an indication of the loss of discipline within a unit."

Soldier G witnessed that a lack of accurate information was common in combat, and so rumours abounded, and these had to be refuted by the leader issuing accurate and timely updates as to the situation. Soldier E found that the incidence of excessive quarrelling jeopardised cooperation, trust, and confidence within the unit, and so the leader needed to identify and correct the source of irritation so that unit efficiency was not affected. He also found that the standard of soldiers' personal hygiene within the unit was always maintained by the leader, as poor hygiene was an indication of poor discipline within the unit, which in turn affected the unit's morale. In his experience, Soldier D found that: "Units with a high level of morale and motivation maintained levels of military courtesy, and so poor standards of military courtesy indicated poor discipline and morale." Soldier I found that the leader had to always monitor each soldier's personal conduct, as any sudden and unexplained change in a soldier's behaviour may indicate personal problems. Finally, Soldier E believed that: "The personal appearance of soldiers was an indication as to the levels of morale and motivation within that unit."

Soldier I believed that soldiers demonstrated discipline through initiative, self-control, self-resilience, and obedience. This leadership was based upon: "A concept of trust and confidence in each other's initiative and self-discipline." While Soldier E saw that: "Self-reliance and self-control enabled soldiers to endure the horrors of combat." Finally, Soldier C witnessed in his unit that: "Obedience to the leader's orders during combat were essential, as this allowed the unit to respond as a team."

***Motivation.*** As seen by the participants, motivation is a by-product of morale, and when soldiers are enthusiastic about being part of a unit and have confidence in their leader, then they have the incentive to win in combat. Therefore, they believed that the training of military leaders at all levels of command in combat motivation was a key factor, and they indicated that on numerous occasions, quantitatively inferior forces had prevailed due to their fighting spirit, aggressiveness, and high morale. In fact, the participants believed that there was a strong relationship between cohesion, soldiers' level of morale, and combat efficiency. Soldier J believed that: "The motivation of soldiers was developed and maintained by an emphasis on professionalism and training." Nevertheless, Soldier H considered that: "Unit cohesion and pride were essential factors in the maintenance of high combat motivation."

In explaining what motivates a soldier in combat, the participants stressed that unit cohesion, tradition, commitment, aggression, and patriotism all motivated the soldier to persevere in battle. They believed that cohesion of the unit was perhaps the strongest motivating factor in combat, and this was built on common experiences and shared hardships, which fostered closeness among individuals in the unit. They also found that the traditions of the unit with its values, traditions, and attitudes needed to be constantly stressed in pre-deployment training in order to foster unit esprit de corps. Soldier G stressed that: "Motivation was based on commitment, which was founded on mutual respect, confidence, discipline, and shared dangers." Finally, Soldier A stressed that the leader needed to foster an aggressive fighting spirit within the unit but also had to show compassion for a defeated enemy or non-combatants when appropriate. Therefore, he felt that: "The patriotism of the soldiers within the unit served as the foundation for their motivation."

The participants felt that one of the most effective pre-combat leadership initiatives that countered the detrimental effects of combat on infantry soldiers was the building and maintaining of morale and motivation. Soldier D described how he had learned in his own officer training four ways of building morale and motivation, and these are: instilling confidence, allocating assignments, provision of adequate rest food and shelter, and showing concern for the welfare of soldiers. Soldier H considered that: "The leader could instil confidence by maintaining a positive attitude, while at the same time cultivating the soldiers' trust and confidence." Soldier C believed that this could be reinforced by the leader "leading from the front" and by so doing demonstrating a willingness to take the same risks as their soldiers. Soldier G insisted that when the leader was allocating tasks within the unit, they must alternate assignments and rotate dangerous duties in order to share the burden equally within the unit. Soldier J considered that: "The lack of food and inadequate sleep would erode the morale and motivation within a unit." He went on to identify that as well as providing food, rest, and shelter, the leader must also check soldier's welfare and that they were carrying out their duties correctly.

Soldier G described the five ways of maintaining motivation, and they were to establish a positive, optimistic, and realistic attitude, know your soldiers, provide a break in the routine, keep the soldiers informed, and tend to administrative matters. The participants also identified other factors that affected combat motivation as being: (1) tenacity of purpose, (2) responsibility, (3) creditability, (4) personal example, (5) professionalism, (6) discipline, (7) comradeship, and (8) sense of mission. Soldier B also highlighted that combat motivation was enhanced by soldiers having confidence in their immediate leaders, which depended on the commander's professional capability, creditability as a source of information, and the amount of care and attention he paid to his subordinates. Soldier G had witnessed within units in which he served that: "Motivation was based on psychology factors, with a soldier's commitment and pride in their unit being the reason why they fought.

**Discipline.** Discipline was defined by the participants as bringing soldiers under control. The leader achieved this in order for soldiers to disregard the natural tendency for self-preservation and when required place themselves in danger in order to complete the unit's mission. Soldier A found that: "My unit leaders understood the human dimension and anticipated our reactions to stress." Soldier E identified that an essential element in combat was discipline, as this held the unit together, and then resilience and competence enabled the unit to complete its mission. Soldier H believed that: "Discipline led to unit cohesion, and this was achieved through personal bonding and a strong sense of responsibility to the unit and its soldiers." According to Soldier I, this discipline was the binding force that kept the soldiers within a unit together and achieving the mission despite the danger of death or injury. This was seen as being the result of soldiers knowing and trusting their leaders and comrades and understanding their dependency on one another. Soldier B witnessed that: "Discipline ensured that soldiers promptly and willingly carried out their unit leader's orders." Soldier J considered that: "The morale and motivation within a unit provided the foundation for discipline, which was an essential condition that allowed soldiers to overcome the extreme fear and fatigue of combat." In this regard, Soldier D identified that there were three types of discipline, and these were self, unit, and imposed. Self-discipline was an important quality that the leader developed within the soldiers, as it fostered a sense of duty to the unit and fellow comrades within the soldier's unit. Unit discipline was based on the expectations of the soldiers within the unit for all their comrades to complete their mission. Imposed discipline was exercised by the leader and was utilised in dangerous and difficult situations.

***Proficiency.*** Proficiency in the opinion of the participants referred to the leader being proficient in all the aspects of commanding the unit, as a leader's professional competency was the primary leadership factor that soldiers said decreased their stress in combat. In this regard, Soldier F personally witnessed that: "Our boss often showed personal bravery in the face of the enemy, and this personal example inspired the rest of us in the platoon." Soldier C believed that another important role for the leader was that of information provider for the soldiers within the unit, as communication and trust were crucial to lessening the soldier's fear of the unknown. Soldier B also saw the leader as the link between the higher command elements that were geographically removed from the battlefield and the soldiers within the unit who were required to fulfil the mission. In his unit, Soldier J observed that: "My boss demonstrated a genuine concern for taking care of our physical and emotional needs, and this resulted in us carrying out our tasks more willingly and without supervision." Soldier I observed that this legitimacy of the leader within the unit and the trust in leader's professionalism was only developed through a constant face-to-face relationship with the soldiers within the unit.

*Esprit de corps.* All the participants agreed that esprit de corps was the common spirit reflected by all members of the unit, and that as a result, it provided group solidarity. It implied devotion and loyalty to the unit and its history and traditions. Soldier F considered that: "It is the unit's personality, as it is based on the soldier's satisfaction at belonging to the unit, their attitudes towards their comrades and their leaders." The participants stipulated that the ways for the leader to instil esprit de corps were by training their soldiers as a team, developing a team-spirit, instructing the soldiers in the history and traditions of the unit, developing the highest levels of physical fitness and military proficiency, reinforcing all unit successes, using competition to develop a team concept, and employing the unit according to its capabilities. Soldier A believed that this was accomplished through education and training, which once achieved developed self-confidence in the soldier. He considered that this in turn built and strengthened morale, motivation, discipline, and esprit de corps.

*Triangulation.* A review of the transcripts from the participants' answers to research question one were triangulated with the British Army Directives' pre-deployment training syllabus. The purpose of the review was to compare what the pre-deployment training syllabus stated with what the participants experienced in pre-deployment programmes and training. The essential assumption from this study is that the validity of inquiry findings is enhanced when two or more methods of data collection are implemented in order to validate and corroborate the findings.[3]

The participants' answers to the interview questions, when compared to the British Army pre-deployment training directives, indicated that they experienced the syllabus as described. In the British Army, the syllabus is a descriptive outline and summary of the topics to be covered in an education or training course. The six checks for triangulation of participants' answers with British Army syllabi are shown in Table 10.

**Table 10**

*Participants' Pre-deployment Training Statements Triangulated with British Army Directives Pre-deployment Training Syllabi.*

| Statements | A | B | C | D | E | F | G | H | I | J | Total % of Affirmative Responses | n |
|---|---|---|---|---|---|---|---|---|---|---|---|---|
| Participants received full pre-deployment training. | Y | N | Y | Y | N | Y | Y | Y | N | Y | 70 | 7 |
| Pre-deployment training included the possibility of physiological stress caused by combat. | Y | Y | Y | Y | N | Y | Y | Y | N | Y | 80 | 8 |
| Pre-deployment training included the possibility of psychological stress caused by combat. | Y | Y | Y | Y | N | Y | Y | Y | Y | Y | 90 | 9 |
| Pre-deployment training was relevant to the physiological stresses experienced in combat. | Y | Y | N | Y | N | Y | Y | Y | N | Y | 70 | 7 |
| Pre-deployment training was relevant to the psychological stresses experienced in combat. | Y | Y | Y | Y | N | Y | Y | Y | N | Y | 80 | 8 |
| The pre-deployment training syllabus addressed all of the types of physiological and psychological stress faced in combat. | N | Y | N | Y | N | Y | N | Y | Y | Y | 60 | 6 |

# Chapter Fifteen

## *Evaluation of the Findings*

Throughout the study, the psychological cost borne by the participants who had experienced infantry combat was apparent, as they stated that the killing of enemy combatants was a traumatic and psychologically damaging experience that altered their lives forever. This finding is congruent with the most recent research into combat stress and PTSD, which has shown that psychological breakdown has become so prevalent that there is now a greater likelihood of becoming a psychiatric casualty of war than being killed or wounded by the enemy.[1]

This study found that there were two key stressors that caused psychological breakdown of the participants either during or after combat. The first was the trauma caused by being a soldier in a close-quarters, inter-personal, and life-threatening, deadly aggressive situation. The second was the trauma associated with the responsibility of killing another human being at close range, as an average healthy person will resist killing his/her own kind. Therefore, the infantry soldier is inserted into a psychologically traumatic environment from which the only escape is to become killed or wounded, by becoming a deserter, or by becoming a psychiatric casualty. This study also produced a number of other key findings based on the three questions posed to the participants.

There will now be a detailed examination of the findings based upon the research data derived from the three research questions that were posed to the participants during this case study.

**Q1. According to infantry soldiers' combat experiences, what types of pre-combat education programmes and leadership training were provided to soldiers pre-tour of duty to help them cope with negative physiological and psychological effects of combat?**

Several significant findings emerged from the participants' answers to *Question (1)*. All the participants stated that the military culture aimed to turn young civilians into operationally effective infantry combatants by inculcating blind conformity and obedience to the military system. In this regard, Bartlett (2009) also found that it was essential that when civilians are inducted into the infantry that they were converted from a human set of values and beliefs based on "thou-shall-not-kill" into an infantry set of values and beliefs based on a "kill-or-be-killed" mentality. A fact that was further hidden from the public at large was that, as stated by Cohen (2009), the accepted civilian principles, which exist within all civilised societies, are counterproductive for the training and leadership of infantry soldiers. In short, the military system was designed to meet the majority of the criteria that were identified in the "total institution" model. Siddle (2008) described how the individual's entire being was initially devoured, then re-modelled, and finally totally subverted to this military ethos.

The findings from this study indicated that the participants' training was designed to create peer camaraderie that was seen by the military as being the most valued benefit of a military career. This camaraderie served the purposes of the military system, as peer group pressure assured the successful imposition and maintenance of military values and behaviours. This view of camaraderie mirrors Asken, Grossman, and Christensen (2010), who found that in order to subvert this instinct of self-preservation, peer camaraderie was identified as being one of the most essential factors that forced soldiers to do their duty in order not to let his comrades down during combat. Earlier, Grossman (2009) had also identified what military battles had in common was the human behaviour of men struggling to reconcile their instinct of self-preservation with their sense of honour, and the achievement of their mission, over which other men are ready to kill them.

## Evaluation of the Findings

Findings also indicated that the soldiers would be educated and trained physically, psychologically, and technically, with the aim of ensuring that the soldier was prepared to become an effective team member within an infantry combat unit. The participants observed that during this process, the instructors stressed that re-socialisation was an important aspect of the induction into military service. This re-socialisation was described as a sociological process of mentally and emotionally re-training a soldier so they could operate in a combat environment. Knowles (1968), in his adult learning theory, identified significant differences between adult learners and learners under the age of eighteen. The primary differences were that adult learners are more self-directed, having a repertoire of experience, and are more internally motivated to learn subject matter that could be applied immediately. This adult learning theory is reflected in the military during the transitional training of entry-level recruits from basically trained infantry soldiers to combat-ready infantry soldiers.[2]

Another finding identified by the research was that all soldiers have a fear of killing, and so the leader must be made aware that this fear of killing another human was a natural human reaction. Participants stated that when armed with this knowledge, the leader can then make sure that he particularly observes the soldier who has just experienced this shock of killing another human being in order to identify any negative reactions. If a soldier is displaying negative reactions, it is normally caused by fear, which is a natural human reaction to the battlefield. However, if not controlled by the leader, fear can destroy not only the ability of the individual, but can spread throughout the whole unit. In this instance, the leader must take control of the situation and issue direct orders to the soldier who is exhibiting negative reactions. In this way, the soldier will become refocused on achieving the new task, thereby minimising the fear.[3] Then the leader must encourage the other soldiers within the unit to verbally and emotionally support the soldier that is having a negative reaction to a combat situation. This "moral support" by fellow soldiers will further reduce the fear, as the unit teamwork will replace the individual's negative concerns. These measures will be further reinforced by the leader inculcating confidence by personally leading the soldier forward by their own example.[4]

That the death or injury of a comrade would lead the soldier to have a feeling of deep personal loss that often affected a soldier's ability to carry out his tasks, especially during the stress of combat, was another significant finding. These findings fall in line with the findings from the U.S. Army's Mental Health Advisory Team (2008) that conducted post-combat surveys and interviews with 652 soldiers and marines returning from Operation Iraqi Freedom (OIF) during 2005-2007. Over 75% reported being in situations where their personal safety was at risk and where there was a likelihood of personal injury or death. They all indicated in the survey that they experienced "intense fear, helplessness," and/or horror when they witnessed the death or injury of a comrade. This "intense fear or helplessness" are also the exact terms used by the American Psychological Association (APA) in their determination of the symptoms that must be present for PTSD, or some form of combat-related stress, to be diagnosed by medical professionals.[5]

It was identified by the vast majority of the participants that the instructors showed regard or esteem for those soldiers who already had operational combat experiences (combat veterans), which created a climate in the learning environment that conveyed respect. This meant that the participants were more open to learning, as they felt respected and were not being talked down to, patronised, or otherwise denigrated. Watson and Gardiner (2013) also found that stress levels, psychological distress, and life events could be all reduced by instructors showing regard and respect for combat veterans. Stress, individual traits, adverse life events, and psychological distress were found to be all interrelated. Significantly, findings showed that these detrimental effects could be reduced by instructors showing consideration, which in turn enhanced the veterans' willingness to learn.[6]

The majority of participants described how the instructors appealed to them through the power of arousing their interest in the combat skills that the instructors had themselves adopted. The instructors gave examples of their own combat experiences, as these were the problems that the soldiers were most likely to encounter when faced with combat during their own operational deployments. These findings expand upon Zurcher's (2009) recruit training study, where he found that in preparation for war, military educational institutions established a series of benchmarks which had to be met and maintained. The soldier's ability to meet and maintain these benchmarks were measured at various stages of the selection and training process. Zurcher identified that the ultimate aim of the military training process was to produce soldiers who would respond to orders without question and then perform their duties in an exemplary manner. This he found was achieved by the instructors themselves relating their own combat experiences and how they had learned to survive on the battlefield. Zurcher found that this socialising training would by necessity bring profound changes in the individual during his/her transition from civilian to soldier.

All the participants found that the army had a comprehensive and systematic process for the evaluation and review of adult soldier training, which was completed at the end of each programme in order to provide the instructor with course content feedback. This validation system used information provided by recruits, instructors, and programme designers at various stages of the programmes. Kouzes and Posner (2010) also described the requirement for accurate and timely review of all instructional techniques and content. They found that by instigating this feedback, the instructors engaged with subordinates and created a connection that raised the level of motivation in both the instructor and the students. By being attentive, the instructor motivated the students to reach their full potential. Kouzes and Posner (2010) concluded that the evaluation and review of adult soldier training had a socialising effect that was concerned with the collective good. The participants identified that, despite a variety of training and education regimes they underwent prior to their combat deployments, these initiatives did not adequately prepare them for all the physiological and psychological effects of combat. Horey and Fallesen (2011) also found that throughout the period of the wars in Afghanistan and Iraq, there was no evidence that soldiers were provided with adequate pre-combat training interventions to prepare them for the detrimental physiological and psychological effects of combat operations.

## Q2. According to infantry soldiers' combat experiences, what were the negative physiological and psychological effects that soldiers experienced during and after combat?

Several significant findings also emerged from the participants' answers to *Question (2)*. Physiologically, participants who repeatedly experienced high levels of stress over long periods of time found that their hearts beat more rapidly, and this caused a significant increase in their blood pressure. This finding is congruent with the physiology that in a fight-or-flight situation the brain directs the body to begin shutting down some systems, while increasing activities for other parts of the body. Blood flow and increased heart rate are two prime examples of how the brain tells the body to prepare for the fight-or-flight.[7]

It was also found that stress and anxiety affected the body completely, including the ability to hear. Participants stated that hearing problems included the inability to hear orders or nearby conversations, and in extreme cases, complete temporary deafness occurred. It was also reported by some participants that the most common issue was the difficulty focusing on sound or conversation. These findings were confirmed by Lemyre and Tessier (2013), who found that stress disorders, including hearing loss or impairment, occurred only as a result of stress of great intensity or long duration, or when pathogenic processes were present.

All the participants found that in response to a threat in combat the brain sent out warning signals causing the body to become fully aroused. It was found that this alerting system became finely tuned, allowing instant focus and immediate reaction to any threat. Some of the participants referred to being "hyper-alert" and this referred to them being distracted by any external stimuli that could signal danger. The findings of Grossman (1995, 2009) also revealed that prolonged exposure to stress or chronic stress increased the risk of cognitive, emotional, or physical illness. His research found that the effects of combat stress could range from hyper-alertness, physically, to memory problems, cognitively, and to depression, emotionally.

The participants also stated that those who experienced high levels of psychological stress over a long period of time were more likely to develop medical problems in their digestive and urinary systems. Soldiers experienced a feeling of nausea when under stress and vomiting when under extreme combat stress. In this regard, the research by McEwen and Lasley (2008) discovered that the stress hormones that interacted within the body caused digestive and urinary problems. More importantly, this critical analysis discovered that chronically elevated levels of these same stress hormones could cause long term damage to the body's vital functions.

Another finding was that on prolonged periods of combat operations, soldiers began to suffer from muscular tension, which was the most common physical symptom of anxiety. Those soldiers suffering from anxiety found it harder for that tension to dissipate naturally. McEwen and Lasley (2008) and Medina (2008) confirmed that stress-inducing moments created the distinct possibility of muscular tension and/or muscular spasms.

Findings also revealed that stress-related temporary blindness, deafness, loss of other sensations, and partial, short-term paralysis were not physical injuries, but physical symptoms that unconsciously enabled the soldier to escape or avoid a seemingly intolerable stressful situation. Often soldiers with these physical conditions were unaware of the relationship between physical conditions and their inability to cope with stress. In regards to the symptoms of combat stress, many research studies have shown that soldiers in combat deal with a daily routine that is often unpredictable, stressful, and out of the ordinary.[8] McEwen and Lasley (2008) identified that these circumstances caused the soldier to lose control, and this lack of control was exactly what the APA (1994) concluded regarding a sense of helplessness leading to combat stress, depression, and PTSD symptoms in soldiers.

Throughout the study, another finding was that it was quite normal for soldiers to experience either mild or heavy sweating or sensations of chilliness under combat stress. The severity of this sweating could vary from time to time and would come and go, depending upon the presence of triggers such as anxiety, stress, and traumatic experiences. It was reported that the various types of stress experienced by soldiers in combat caused a general and increased sweating that led to dehydration. Grossman and Christensen (2008) found that soldiers operating in a stressful environment every day, by forcing their bodies to remain in an automatic stress reaction mode, sweated constantly, which could lead to dehydration especially in harsh desert climates where water was at a premium.

All participants gave personal and comrade examples of significant symptoms of combat stress leading to physical fatigue. However, they stated that combat and operational stress reactions were expected and predictable, which included emotional, intellectual, physical and/or behavioural reactions from the exposure to stressful battlefield experiences. Moderate stress physiological reactions included fatigue, sweating, difficulty sleeping, jumpiness, rapid heartbeat, dizziness, slow reaction times, dry mouth, muscular tension, nausea, vomiting and/or diarrhoea. These findings confirm Morgan's (2011) critical analysis, which found that 37% of deployed forces were suffering from combat-induced stress. The reality is that although figures vary, research shows that there is a significant amount of stress placed on soldiers when engaged in combat.

During combat, another common symptom that soldiers experienced was unintentional shaking and tremors in their bodies and limbs. These tremors usually affected the arms and hands, although it was reported that tremors also affected the head, face, tongue, trunk, and legs. The critical findings by Grossman (2009) confirmed these observations where he reported of soldiers finding themselves with uncontrollable tremors that were so severe they prevented the soldiers from firing or re-loading their weapons.

After experiencing combat, a finding was that soldiers could not sleep even when the situation permitted, and when they did fall asleep, they frequently woke up and had difficulty getting back to sleep. These sleep disturbances came in the form of terror dreams, battle dreams, and nightmares, and these were all part of the coping process. The findings of Shay (2009), based on interviews with 232 Vietnam veterans, found that even 40 years after their combat experiences, they still could not sleep through the night, instead they experienced the nightmares night after night.

Another common side effect of combat stress was distorted vision. These vision problems included blurred vision, double vision, difficulty in focusing, or temporary total blindness. Foa and Riggs (1993) found that distorted vision was one of the most common symptoms, and these finding were later confirmed by Shephard (2008), who further confirmed these earlier findings.

Combat stress reaction is a term used to describe altered behaviours resulting from combat trauma. The participants felt that combat stress was the expected emotional, intellectual, and physical reactions by soldiers who had been exposed to the horrors of combat. The term "stress" was first introduced by Hans Selye (1936), and it is now widely used to describe a state of tension often seen as being related to modern life and so psychological stress concerns the state of "normal" tension, preoccupation, and agitation reported by many people.[9]

Many of the participants witnessed that primary and secondary forms of anxiety had different effects. They saw that primary anxiety was that part that energised the soldier to deal with a threat as the body was flooded with adrenaline, sugars, fats, and other hormones to allow action to be taken. Lemyre and Tessier (2013) confirmed these findings in their general theoretical framework based upon a model of stress that included environmental parameters and individual processes of perception and coping with stressors. They recognised stress as a target construct in the process of adapting to life events and circumstances.

Another major finding was that during combat, depression was a serious medical condition that affected a soldier's behaviour, thinking, emotions, health, and performance. The study participants believed that a common cause of depression was the build-up of stress and anxiety caused by combat experiences on the battlefield. These findings confirmed Gabriel's (2010) findings as he measured the effects of depression on 184 Special Operations soldiers returning from operations in Afghanistan from 2007-2009. The soldiers had been exposed to trauma or stress during that period of time, and he found that 31.2% of them were suffering from depression upon returning from operations.

All participants indicated that individual soldiers could panic, become confused, and rush around without self-control, and soldiers suffering from these symptoms could compromise both theirs and their comrades' safety. A critical examination of these disruptive actions was conducted by Kitayama (2010) with 334 soldier participants. His findings were that a common effect of direct combat with the enemy during ground operations was that during the mental "fight-or-flight" phase of the mental decision-making process, it was not uncommon for soldiers to lose control of their physical actions.

The participants found that there were some specific sources of psychological fear that were brought about by combat. First was the natural fear of being killed, wounded, or captured by the enemy. Second was the fear of having to kill an enemy combatant, as this was against their social and religious beliefs. Third, there was the fear that was generated in them by the chaos of war, and the sights and sounds of combat. Fourth, they felt the fear of apprehension about not being able to measure up when under fire. During their research, McEwen and Lasley (2008) discovered that the stress hormones that interacted within the hippocampus make it possible to etch memorable experiences into our declarative memory. More importantly, this critical analysis discovered that chronically elevated levels of these same hormones could damage the very part of the brain that shuts them off. Therefore, soldiers found that on operational deployments, a sense of fear was part of their environment, which generated stress on a regular basis.

Irritability was also a symptom of anxiety as soldiers struggled to manage their anxiety by themselves. These irritable reactions ranged from angry looks to sharp words, but could also progress to more serious acts of violence. In this regard, studies have shown that soldiers in combat deal with a daily routine that is often unpredictable, stressful, and out of the ordinary. McEwen and Lasley (2008) identified that these circumstances caused soldiers to lose control and become overly irritable.

Another finding was that common psychological reactions to combat stress by soldiers included uncontrolled emotional outbursts such as crying, yelling, or laughing. However, on the other extreme, it was also witnessed that some soldiers became withdrawn, silent, and tried to isolate themselves from their comrades. There have been many contradictions and inconsistencies in the research into stress and this loss of adaptability, but it was Grossman (2009) who discovered that combat stress was a normal human reaction to the combat experience.

All participants indicated in different ways that mental fatigue significantly contributed to the onset of fear, and as soldiers became exhausted, their ability to reason began to deteriorate. Morgan (2011) placed the incidence of mental fatigue at 16-17%, while Kertsh (2010) found it as high as 41%. However, Tanielian (2010) indicated that 26% of returning soldiers were suffering from the consequences of combat-induced stress and mental fatigue. Despite these conflicting statistics, the fact is that there is a significant amount of stress and mental fatigue induced in soldiers as a result of direct combat with the enemy.

A significant overarching finding that was present through the study was that the life of a soldier was frequently stressful due to having a life of frequent change, regular danger, difficult living conditions, and physical stress and trauma caused by combat experiences. To deal with the stresses of combat life, soldiers tended to use substances such as alcohol or other drugs as a means of escaping the trauma they had experienced. On this topic, Stouffer (2010) studied 2,863 U.S. soldiers one year after their return from operations in Iraq and found a direct correlation between physical health problems and substance abuse.

Another major finding was that some behaviours and symptoms were not only signs of combat stress reaction, but also a signal for potential suicide risks. The majority of the participants believed that combat veterans are not only more likely to have suicidal thoughts, often associated with PTSD and depression, but that they are more likely to act on a suicidal plan. The results by Grossman (2009) found that stress levels, psychological distress, and life events were all associated with time and across time. It was identified that the pattern of psychological distress differed between newly recruited soldiers and those soldiers who had experienced combat in previous deployments. Significantly, Watson and Gardiner (2013) found that stress, adverse life events, psychological distress and suicidal thoughts and behaviours were all interrelated.

The final findings that were identified by the participants' responses to research *Question (2)* were the long-term effects of combat. In this regard, all of the participants, upon returning from their combat deployment, reported that upon arriving home, their first emotional reaction was one of profound relief that they had survived the experience. Then the soldiers experience of post-combat stress significantly and profoundly altered the way the participants thought as the memories of their combat deployment dominated their minds and made it difficult for them to concentrate on anything else. On the topic of the long-term effects of combat on soldiers research has identified disparities from the present military conflicts in the published percentages of soldiers suffering from such effects. Northouse (2009) placed the incidence of the long-term effects of combat at 15-18%; Gray (2008) indicated it was 26%; and Morgan (2011) found that more that 34% of deployed forces were suffering from the long-term effects of combat-induced stress. The reality is that although figures vary, research shows that there is an ongoing significant number of soldiers who return home from operations and continue to suffer from the long-term effects of combat.

**Q3. According to infantry soldiers' combat experiences, what types of pre-combat education programmes and leadership training interventions could be effective in helping soldiers cope with the negative physiological and psychological effects of combat?**

Important findings also emerged from the participants' answers to research *Question (3)*. The participants emphasised that the introduction of realism into training was an important element in preparing soldiers for combat and believed that the replication of the sights, sounds, and conditions of combat during training would better prepare soldiers for actual combat. They also stipulated that the type of training must be conducted during day and night as well as in all climates, weather, and terrain as these were the conditions that we faced when in combat. These should be designed to prepare infantry soldiers for the negative physiological and psychological effects of combat. In this regard, Zurcher (2009) found that human beings develop a mental process that assisted them in making decisions that resulted in responses to a variety of social stimuli with this process being constructed as they learn social customs, values, and beliefs.

Most of the participants also experienced situations where a reduction in caloric intake during continuous operations led to both physical and mental fatigue and degraded performance. They identified that the excitement, stress, and rapid pace of combat also caused soldiers to forget to drink liquids, which resulted in dehydration. According to the participants, the lot of infantry soldiers was to endure conditions of wet, cold, hunger, thirst, and tiredness, and as a result they build up a resilience and tolerance to the extremes of weather. Also, the inadequate recognition of the implications resulting from long lull periods, combat pulses, and the need to recover from stress could lead to dysfunctional soldiering as well as poor individual and small unit performance. Grossman (1995, 2009) found that soldiers could be taught daily survival requirements by performing specific actions required for survival without conscious thought. His research showed that whatever was taught and drilled in training would be reflected in the soldiers' actions during combat. He believed that the findings from all this research was that soldiers do not rise to the occasion in combat, rather they sink to their level of training.

The participants stated that any pre-combat education programmes should be designed to give the infantryman an insight into the negative physiological and psychological effects of combat. The aim should be to get each individual infantry soldier to begin thinking about the stresses of combat so that they understood the challenges, characteristics, and fear associated with combat. The participants identified that pre-deployment training needs to be as realistic as possible, with combat simulation scenarios ensuring not only physical and mental engagement by soldiers but also emotional engagement.

All the participants stated that realistic training, which created emotional stress, should be designed to create within the soldiers' feelings that are similar to those that they would experience in real combat situations. World War II training was conducted on standard grassy firing ranges where the soldiers would shoot at a bull's-eye up to 300 yards away from the firing point, after which they would walk forward to check their targets accompanied by their instructor.[10] However, today the military has learnt to use what could be described as B.F. Skinner's operant learning techniques where the training comes as close to stimulating actual combat conditions as is possible. In this battlefield simulation training, the fully combat equipped soldier fires from a slit-trench (fox-hole in U.S. Army terminology) at a man-shaped pop-up target. The man-shaped target "falls-when-hit," thus providing immediate feedback to the soldier. The positive reinforcement is provided when the most successful soldiers are awarded "marksmanship badges," which normally have some form of privilege associated with them such as recognition, praise, and/or additional leave passes. Through this operant learning technique, infantry soldiers develop an instantaneous "shoot-to-kill" response whereby they immediately identify the enemy soldier, aim, and shoot without thinking of the consequences.[11]

All of the participants emphasised that good physical conditioning delayed fatigue, built confidence, and shortened recovery times from illness and injury. They also believed that it prepared soldiers to better cope with the physical demands of combat-related stress. As explained by Vore (2010), the infantry soldier is required to achieve a series of more demanding training benchmarks in order to become a qualified infantry soldier. This cycle commences with an initial 60-day infantry recruit course where the basic skills of weapon handling, navigation, physical fitness, tactics, movement, and patrolling are taught. At the completion of this intensive training cycle, the infantry soldier has gained the mental fitness, knowledge, and ability to successfully operate in a combat environment as a basic rifleman, and to effectively carry out those duties under fire and in close contact with the enemy. Participants also emphasised that mental fitness was just as important as physical fitness. When discussing mental fitness, participants noted that it was a soldiers' ability to achieve it through emotional health, where a series of exercises that helped the soldier slow down, decompress, and boost a flagging memory were practised prior to deployment. However, they noted that this type of training was largely ignored prior to their own operational deployments.

The British Army is by no means alone in the increasing concern with not only the physical demands of combat but also with the problem of addressing the mental dimensions of soldiering. The infantry has increasingly sought to improve performance on the battlefield through mental preparation and this has taken the form of "resilience training," which has been developed in response to extreme psychological pressures that are experienced during combat operations.[12] Specifically, "resilience training" aims at improving the performance of infantry soldiers by identifying the importance of mental fitness training. Four specific tools have been developed, and these involve "goal-setting," "mental rehearsal/visualisation," "self-talk," and "arousal reduction" (i.e., controlled breathing).[13] These mental fitness techniques are designed to augment the standards cycles of training and exercises that precede deployment in order to improve the performance and determination of infantry soldiers during combat operations. The instruction process emphasises that these mental fitness techniques need to be not merely understood but practised regularly. If they are to become effective, these four psychological techniques must be repeated until they themselves become muscle memories in the brain.[14] To illustrate how these techniques overcome the natural reaction to panic in combat, the "resilience training" describes to the soldiers the function and structure of the brain in great detail. It is claimed that by conducting sufficient mental preparation, the frontal lobes and the cortex can ultimately control the instinctive responses in the brain stem and the amygdala from which primitive "fight-or-flight" responses are generated.[15] The aim of the instruction is to strengthen the psychological preparedness of every infantry soldier to the traumas of combat by improving their understanding their own cerebral functioning.[16]

Participants also believed that the leader must aim to minimise the physiological and psychological effects of combat on soldiers, and to do this he must be aware that the main sources of stress for soldiers is boredom, fatigue, discomfort, and friendly casualties. All the participants believed that the leadership skills that applied to troop welfare and war fighting would need to be taught to be used to reduce and/or prevent combat stress reactions. They felt that it was the leader's responsibility to take preventative actions and address stress symptoms as they appeared in their soldiers. They further stated that in order to lead soldiers effectively, soldiers need to believe that the leader is aware of the conditions that stimulate and inspire courage in the soldiers. They also felt that in order to do this, the leader must be taught to understand the conditions that will stimulate fear, which he saw as being the unexpected, the unknown, and a feeling of helplessness. In this regard, Verljen (2011) found that there is a dynamic relationship between the leader and the organisational context. He postulated that it was reasonable to see that the organisational factors that impacted leadership comprised its strategy, culture, policies, and practices, as well as its ability to learn as an organisation. As critically, Yeakey (2008) discovered that the relationship between the leader and the organisation was potentially a dynamic one, as different organisational strategies required changes in the behaviour of the leader.

Another significant finding was how important the participants felt about the need for leaders to foster good morale in the field. Morale was seen by the participants as the mental and emotional condition of an individual soldier or group of soldiers, and that the leader who harnessed this resource in the unit would ultimately prevail. All the participants believed that within the military, morale and motivation were the foundations of discipline, esprit de corps, and professionalism, all of which led to success in combat. This was reflected in the confidence, resolution, and courageous attitude of soldiers within the unit who were determined to accomplish the assigned mission. However, Yeakey (2008) identified that it was important to realise that in order to create morale, the leader must not be limited to only one style of leadership, as being able to adapt appropriate styles would lead to successful mission accomplishment. Yeakey found that a leader's judgement, intelligence, cultural awareness, and self-control played a major role in developing morale within a unit. He concluded that a leader's effectiveness depended on being able to assess the unit's readiness level and then adopt the appropriate high probability leadership style and communicate that style to create morale.

As seen by the participants, motivation is a by-product of morale, and when soldiers are enthusiastic about being part of a unit and have confidence in their leader, they have the incentive to win in combat. Therefore, they believed that the training of military leaders at all levels of command in combat motivation was seen as a key factor. They indicated that on numerous occasions, quantitatively inferior forces had prevailed due to their fighting spirit, aggressiveness, and high morale. In fact, the participants believed that there was a strong relationship between cohesion, soldiers' levels of motivation, and combat efficiency. In this regard, Verljen (2011) postulated that the leadership theory adopted must match the leader to the appropriate situation, as it suggested that the leader's effectiveness depended on how well he/she motivated the soldiers within the unit.[17]

The need for discipline was also another finding. Discipline was defined by the participants as bringing soldiers under control of the leader's direct orders. The leader achieved this in order for soldiers to disregard the natural tendency for self-preservation, and when required place themselves in danger in order to complete the unit's mission. Participants believed that this discipline was the binding force that kept the soldiers within a unit together and achieving the mission despite the danger of death or injury. However, discipline and the threat of judicial sanction under "The Articles of War" has, within a professional Army, become less necessary, as soldiers have been imbued with a sense of professional honour. This when accompanied with unit morale, motivation, cohesion, and esprit de corps has reduced the requirement for military discipline, as soldiers have become self-motivated.[18]

Also, the emergence of totally professional armies has resulted in the institution of new training regimes in which soldiers are trained individually and collectively to a higher level than was ever possible with a volunteer or conscripted army. Therefore, within the British Army soldiers are increasingly self-disciplined by their individual commitment to professional competence. This has meant that the threat of disciplinary action against a soldier, though ever-present, has become the leader's action of last resort.[19]

In addition to discipline, in the opinion of the participants, proficiency referred to the leader being proficient in all the aspects of commanding the unit, as a leader's professional competency was the primary leadership factor that soldiers said decreased their stress in combat. These findings are congruent with the transformational theory of leadership, the current approach that the military has increasingly adopted, as it has provided a new leadership paradigm, where more attention is given to the charismatic and affective elements of leadership.[20] After the invasions of Afghanistan and then Iraq, Coalition forces were embroiled in two long and costly wars. It has been increasingly identified that transformational leadership fits the needs of today's soldiers, as it inspired and empowered in times of uncertainty.[21] As the name implies, the researcher notes that transformational leadership changes and transforms subordinates as the leader motivates the unit to be effective by imparting a vision that motivates the unit to achieve its mission.

All the participants also agreed that esprit de corps was the common spirit reflected by all members of the unit, and that as a result, it provided group solidarity. It implied devotion and loyalty to the unit and its history and traditions. They believed that this was accomplished through education and training, which once achieved, developed self-confidence in the soldier. Siddle (2008) described how during initial training, the individual's entire being was initially devoured, then re-modelled, and finally totally subverted to this military ethos. He found that the environment of the "total institution" destroyed the individual's individuality and dignity before creating esprit de corps that was based on regimentation and unswerving obedience to the leader. He also highlighted that within the "total institution," there are varying degrees of regimentation, discipline, esprit de corps, and institutional expectations among the various branches of the military.[22]

## Summary

The conflicts in Afghanistan and Iraq have led to heightened interest in the welfare and health of soldiers upon their return from combat deployments. More than 245,000 soldiers were deployed twice to either Afghanistan or Iraq, with a better than 50% increase in the incidence of combat-related stress as the numbers of deployments increased.[23] Each year in the U.K., about 24,000 men and women leave the British armed forces and enter civilian life. There is an increasing international recognition, both within the military and within civilian society of "post-conflict dysfunction," including, but not limited to, PTSD in ex-service personnel, particularly in recent years.[24] The large-scale U.K. studies of veterans of the 1991 Gulf War, Bosnia, Afghanistan and Iraq found that the most common mental health problems are depression, anxiety, adjustment, mood, personality disorders, and alcohol misuse/dependence.[25]

Those studies agree with the findings of this study that identified a number of important findings regarding the physiological and psychological well-being of British Army soldiers while deployed on operational combat tours. Significant physiological findings of combat stress were: circulatory and respiratory problems, hearing problems, hyper-alertness, digestive and urinary problems, muscular tension, partial short-term paralysis, perspiration and dehydration, physical fatigue, shaking and tremors, sleep disturbance, and vision problems. Significant psychological findings of combat stress were: altered behaviours, anxiety, depression, disruptive reactions, fear, irritability, loss of adaptability, mental fatigue, substance abuse, and suicidal thoughts and behaviours.

# CHAPTER SIXTEEN

## *Implications*

The problem to be addressed in this study was that the minimalist pre-combat education programmes and leadership training given to British Army infantry soldiers to help them cope with the negative physiological and psychological effects of combat were proving to be increasingly inadequate.[1] According to infantry soldiers, throughout the period of the wars in Afghanistan and Iraq there is no evidence that soldiers were provided with adequate pre-combat education programmes or leadership training interventions to prepare them for the negative physiological and psychological effects of combat operations.[2] The purpose of this qualitative case study was to document infantry soldiers' experiences and perceptions of the negative physiological and psychological effects of combat and their recommendations for effective pre-combat education programmes and leadership training to prepare soldiers to counter the negative effects of combat.

A single qualitative case study research design was employed to investigate the lack of pre-combat education programmes and leadership training interventions designed to negate the negative physiological and psychological effects of combat on infantry soldiers. Consequently, this case study focused on a contemporary phenomenon within a "real-life" context.[3] The size of the sample was 10 serving British Army personnel who returned from operational service in Afghanistan within the previous two years – men and women who were all over 18 years of age. The reason for choosing two years was that greater than two years and subjects may lose clarity of their experiences. This study used open-ended interviews for data collection and compared the participant's transcribed answers to training manuals that were used prior to deployment.[4]

A case study design allowed for the retention of the holistic and meaningful characteristics of the real-life events as soldiers experienced the physiological and psychological effects of infantry combat. The natural setting for evidence collection involved serving soldiers from British Army bases in the U.K. and Western Europe. This cloistered and secure military environment is normally inaccessible to researchers for interviews or observations. Therefore, such conditions justified the use of a case study on the grounds of its revelatory nature.[5]

When interviewing the soldiers, the researcher was cognisant of and recorded observations of any non-verbal behaviour that could possibly be attributable to combat stress. In this study, the researcher identified that the negative physiological and psychological effects of combat and effective pre-combat education programmes and leadership training as the unit of analysis. The use of multiple sources of evidence allowed the researcher to develop "converging lines of inquiry," a process of triangulation that allowed the comparison of data from the participants' interview answers to each other and to the training documents.[6] There was an examination of the unit's pre-combat education programmes, and leadership training frameworks in order to ascertain what measures had been undertaken to lessen the soldier's physiological and psychological trauma when engaged in combat operations. Then there was an examination of the unit's archives and in particular the "War Diary," which details all the activities, operations, missions, and tasks that had been undertaken by the unit during the course of every operational tour. Finally, the researcher ensured that the interpretations of the findings were based on the identification and examination of rival explanations for the research findings.[7]

As with most qualitative studies, the creditability of this study was dependent on the perspectives, personal combat experiences, and military backgrounds of the participants. This limitation, outside the researcher's control, limited the study's findings.[8] Also, as purposive sampling was the method used for selecting the participants, the selection of material-rich study participants became the overriding concern over any attempts to have equal representation with respect to age, gender, ethnicity, or branch of service. In this regard, as the combat arms of the British Army are primarily male-only career fields, this study did not have equal gender representation.[9] The final limitation was, as Gobo (2008) cautioned, that there may have been a "Hawthorne Effect" where the presence of a researcher affected the behaviour of the observed. In conclusion, the findings of the study are limited by the accuracy and truthfulness of the participants' interview responses.

In regards to Ethical Assurances, for this study, adherence to the concept of moral rights was an essential component of respect for the dignity of individuals. The rights to privacy, self-determination, personal liberty, and natural justice were of particular importance to researcher, and he had the responsibility to protect and promote these rights in his research activities. As such, the researcher developed and followed procedures for valid consent, confidentiality, anonymity, fair treatment, and due process that were consistent with those rights. Given this level of respect, the researcher explained the nature of the research to which the participants were being asked to contribute and realised that individuals could choose not to be involved in the research. This researcher was also aware of his personal and professional responsibilities and was alert to the possible consequences of unexpected outcomes of the research with the aim of avoiding potential risks to the psychological well-being, mental health, personal values, or dignity of the participants.

In accordance with the *Guidelines for Responsible Conduct of Research,* Office of Research Integrity (2011), this researcher ensured that every person from whom data were gathered for the purpose of this research had consented freely to the process on the basis of adequate information. The participants during the data-collection phase were able to freely withdraw from the study at any time. Also, the data are stored in a secure location for five years and will then be destroyed. As this research involved the collection of data using digital recording, additional detail was added to the informed consent procedures. The researcher ensured that the protocol followed for seeking recording consent was appropriate to the nature of the research.

In this regard, two standards were applied to protect the privacy of the research participants. First, the research guaranteed the participants confidentiality, and to this end, they were assured that identifying information would not be made available to anyone who was not directly involved in the study. Second, the stricter standard of anonymity was maintained, which meant that the participants remained anonymous throughout the study. To guarantee these two standards, the researcher considered all relevant ethical issues in formulating the research plan, approval of which was gained from the NCU Institutional Review Board (IRB) before any data collection commenced. As well as seeking NCU IRB approval, the researcher sought and received approval from the MoD Research Ethics Committee (MoDREC), and from the British Army commanders in the U.K. and Western Europe in order to gain access to military bases to interview the soldier participants. The process of informed consent involved informed consent protocols and opening statements in interviews that covered the issues of the purpose of collecting the information, who the information was for, how it was to be used, what would be asked in the interview, how the responses would be handled (including confidentiality), and what risks and/or benefits were involved for the person being interviewed. This researcher provided this information in advance of the interview and then again at the beginning of the interview.

This chapter is structured so that the data collected and each of the three research questions are discussed for interpretation of the results. A description of the purpose of each research question is provided. A discussion of the findings and supporting literature is provided. The implications of the research findings will now be discussed in the next section of this chapter. Then, recommendations for applications to pre-deployment education programmes and leadership training will be discussed, as well as recommendations for future research. Finally, the conclusions or summary of the research study will be presented.

## Implications

Implications were drawn using the sources from the literature review conducted prior to data collection and the answers given by the participants. The study results are supported by a number of identified research references. Implications are addressed per each research question answered.

## Q1. Types of pre-combat education programmes and leadership training provided to soldiers pre-tour of duty.

The first research question asked the participants what types of pre-combat education programmes and leadership training was provided to them, pre-tour of duty, to assist them cope with the negative physiological and psychological effects of combat. The purpose of this question was to accurately ascertain the education and training regimes that were used by the British Army to prepare their infantry soldiers for combat deployments. The findings that emerged from the participants responses to the first research question supported and reinforced the existing literature by Grossman (1995), Grossman and Christensen (2008), Siddle (2009), Grossman and Siddle (2010), and King (2013).

All the participants stated that the military culture was shaped to turn young civilians into operationally effective infantry combatants by inculcating blind conformity and obedience to the military system. This training was designed to create peer camaraderie, which was seen by the military as being the most important factor in ensuring unit cohesion, morale, motivation, and esprit de corps. As indicated in the literature review, these points are the basis of the research by Grossman (1995). Therefore, the implications of the findings are that the British military culture is geared to turning men and women into soldiers, as is required for war.

However, the majority of participants identified that their pre-combat education programmes and leadership training initiatives did not adequately prepare them for the physiological and psychological effects of combat. Those participants who were in command positions stipulated that as the leaders of infantry soldiers, they were not being educated and instructed in the reactions, thoughts, hopes, and fears they should expect of front-line infantry soldiers when they came face to face with the enemy. The study participants went further to identify that the current pre-combat education programmes and leadership training did not specify all the likely sources of fear that the infantry soldier was likely to face in combat. The implication from this finding is that realistic training was currently lacking, and that what was needed was training that created emotional stress within the soldier, which are feelings that were similar to those that soldiers would experience in real combat situations.

As an example, soldiers naturally have a fear of killing, and so the leader must be made aware that the fear of killing another human being was a natural human reaction. Therefore, the implication is that if soldiers are not trained and prepared emotionally for this act of killing, the magnitude of the trauma could be significant, as the soldier would be left living with something that they would regret forever. However, if the soldier was trained and convinced that the act of killing was justified and correct, if society said that the soldier was killing an enemy combatant and was not committing murder, he would not have any problems with remorse. These findings are consistent with prior study findings Grossman and Christensen (2008), Grossman (2009), and Siddle (2010), with the implication that soldiers must be prepared emotionally for the act of killing before going into combat.

All the participants then further described how the sights of comrades being killed and injured along with the noise, sights, sounds, and smell of combat had a traumatic effect on soldiers' senses, which caused confusion and a sense of chaos that could be particularly unnerving. As a result, the participants were convinced that pre-combat education programmes and leadership training must attempt to prepare the soldier for such experiences, thereby creating an understanding by the leader of how to lessen the debilitating effect of combat on soldiers. The implications of these findings are that the infantry soldiers' reactions to the trauma and stress of combat has not altered for millennium, a view that all the previous literature supports, as war is still perhaps the most challenging situation that a human being can experience.[10]

The physiological, psychological, emotional, and cognitive demands of a combat environment places enormous stress on even the best-trained infantry soldiers. These stressful experiences, which have been a characteristic of the recent wars in Afghanistan and Iraq, have produced an ever-increasing number of soldiers suffering from psychological health conditions, which in a significant number of cases have developed into PTSD.[11] The implications of these findings is that in 2013, the British Ministry of Defence (MoD) reported that 11,934 active duty personnel had been diagnosed with either PTSD or depression, which is a significant proportion of the 177,000 active duty personnel.

As to the findings regarding current education programme goals and explanations, the participants in the study stated that their instructors told them that the programme goals were to teach them the basic information, techniques, and skills to make them effective members of an infantry unit. The instructors indicated that they would be educated and trained physically, psychologically, and technically, with the aim of ensuring that they were prepared to become an effective team member for an infantry combat unit. During this process, the instructors stressed that re-socialisation was an important aspect of the induction into military service. The implication of this finding is that re-socialisation, which was described as a sociological process of mentally and emotionally re-training a soldier, is required to ensure they can successfully operate in a combat environment. The findings are consistent with the previous study by Moon, Tracey, and Schama (2011).

While examining the findings of incorporating soldiers' previous experiences in instruction, it was identified by the vast majority of the participants that the instructors showed regard or esteem for those soldiers who already had operational combat experiences, which created a climate in the learning environment that conveyed respect. This is consistent with the adult learning theory as presented by Knowles (1968). This meant that the participants were more open to learning as they felt respected and were not being talked down to, patronised, or otherwise denigrated. The vast majority of the participants considered that the instructors fostered a comfortable and productive learning climate by showing respect for the soldiers' individuality and experiences. The participants reported that the principal that the instructors followed was that adult soldier learners needed positive reinforcement, as they were self-directed, only preferring to know how their efforts were measuring up when compared with the objectives of the instructional programme. The implications of these findings are that the military would do well to continue to respect soldiers' prior deployment experience through the continuing utilisation of the adult learning theory recommended by Knowles (1968).

As to the finding of instructors discussing likely problems soldiers would encounter during combat, the majority of participants described how the instructors appealed to them through the power of arousing their interest in the combat skills that the instructors had adopted themselves. The method of instruction that was implemented was that the instructors gave the soldiers examples of their own combat experiences, as these were the problems that they were most likely to encounter when faced with combat during their our own operational deployments. The instructors aroused the soldiers' natural motivation to learn, as they came to believe that what they were learning was something new that they needed to know if they were to survive in combat. This technique is consistent with the research of Merriam and Caffarella (1999). The implication from the finding, which the instructors stressed, is that combat is the most frightening event they had ever experienced, as they felt an overwhelming sense of fear, anger, and anxiety. However, of all the physiological and psychological effects they experienced during combat, the instructors stated that the single most traumatic event was the act of killing an enemy combatant.

Another recurring finding was the evaluation of instruction for programme feedback, as at the completion of every training programme, the instructors had all the participants complete a course evaluation form that asked for the positive and negative aspects of the course, as well as for any recommendations for improvement in the course. As a result of this feedback, there were alterations in various courses based upon this soldiers' feedback. As the participants brought their own combat experiences to the programme, this was acknowledged and respected by the instructors in their training setting. In this regard, it became obvious to the participants that the instructors realised that adult learning is enhanced by hands-on experience, which effectively involved the soldiers in the learning process. As adult learners, the soldiers were more likely to accept and retain an idea when they had arrived at the conclusion themselves. This is a theme that is consistently stressed by Brinkerhoff (2010) and Shapiro (2012). The implication of these findings are that when training adult soldiers, the presentation of structured activities generated ideas and concepts from the students, which facilitated more effective learning than by simply giving the adults information to remember.

## Q2. Negative physiological and psychological effects during and after combat.

The second research question asked the participants about the negative physiological and psychological effects they experienced during and after combat. The purpose of this question was to accurately identify the negative physiological and psychological effects that combat had on infantry soldiers. The foundation for the understanding of combat-related stress is based on the research by Rivers (1917), a British psychiatrist during World War I who studied the phenomenon of shell-shock. The implication is that both mental and physical fatigue significantly contributed to the onset of fear, and as soldiers became exhausted, their ability to reason began to deteriorate.

The participants also reported that when on prolonged periods of combat operations, they began to suffer from muscular tension, and these tremors usually affected the arms and hands, although they also reported that it affected the head, face, tongue, trunk, and legs. It was also reported that it was quite normal to experience either mild or heavy sweating or sensations of chilliness under combat stress. Those soldiers repeatedly experiencing high levels of psychological stress over a long period of time were more likely to develop medical problems in their digestive and urinary systems. Another common symptom that was experienced by all the participants was that during combat, they found that their hearts beat more rapidly, and this caused a significant increase in their blood pressure. The implications from these findings are consistent with the research findings of Grossman and Christensen (2008), Grossman (2009), and Siddle (2010).

A further finding experienced by the participants was that sleep disturbances came in the form of terror dreams, battle dreams, and nightmares and these were all part of the coping process. Some of the participants stated that even when awake, they sometimes re-experienced the memory of a stressful combat experience as a "flashback." They stipulated that stress-related blindness, deafness, loss of other sensations, and partial paralysis were not physical injuries, but physical symptoms that unconsciously enabled the soldier to escape or avoid a seemingly intolerable stressful situation. One common side effect of combat stress leading to anxiety was reported as being distorted vision with soldiers suffering from visual problems including blurred vision, double vision, difficulty in focusing, or temporary total blindness. The participants also reported that stress and anxiety also affected hearing, and these problems including the inability to hear orders or nearby conversations and in extreme cases, temporary total deafness occurred. However, the most common issue was the difficulty focusing on sound or conversation. These findings reinforced the previous research studies by Grossman (1995), Grossman and Christensen (2008), Siddle (2009), and King (2013), all of which have serious implications for leaders as they attempt to successfully achieve their allocated combat missions.

All the participants found that in response to a threat in combat, the brain sent out warning signals, causing the body to become fully aroused. This alerting system became so finely tuned that it allowed a soldier instant focus and immediate reaction to any threat. Some of the participants described being "hyper-alert" and this referred to them being distracted by any external stimuli that could signal danger. The participants identified that the other automatic body reactions to fear were trembling, irrational laughter, sweating, tunnel vision, auditory exclusion, and a fight-or-flight response. This fear of death, pain, and/or injury caused soldiers to have severe anxiety reactions, and if they witnessed the loss of a comrade in combat, they lost confidence and felt overly vulnerable and incapable. It was reported by the participants that irritability was a common symptom of anxiety as soldiers struggled to manage their situation by themselves. These irritable reactions ranged from angry looks to sharp words, but could also progress to more serious acts of violence. Once again, these findings were consistent with prior study findings of Siddle (2009), Grossman and Siddle (2010), and King (2013) and have serious implications for the operational commander on the battlefield.

Another significant finding was that during combat, depression was a serious medical condition that affected soldiers' behaviour, thinking, emotions, health, and performance. All the participants felt that the life of a soldier was frequently stressful due to having a life of frequent change, regular danger, difficult living conditions, and potential stress and trauma caused by combat experiences. As a result, soldiers tended to use substances such as alcohol or other drugs as a means of escaping combat stress. The common reactions to combat stress included uncontrolled emotional outbursts such as crying and laughing. All participants indicated that individual soldiers could panic, become confused, and rush around without self-control, and a soldier suffering from these symptoms could compromise both theirs and their comrades' safety. A serious implication was that some of these behaviours and symptoms were not only signs of combat stress reaction but were also a signal for potential suicide risks. In this regard, the participants witnessed that some of the common symptoms that indicated that a soldier may be contemplating suicide were sleep problems, impulsiveness, and the inability to sit still or concentrate.

All the participants stated that combat and operational stress reactions were expected and predictable emotional, intellectual, physical and/or behavioural reactions from the exposure to stressful battlefield experiences. Mild stress physical reactions included fatigue, sweating, difficulty sleeping, jumpiness, rapid heartbeat, dizziness, slow reaction times, dry mouth, muscular tension, nausea, vomiting and/or diarrhoea. A concerning implication from the findings was that these combat stress reactions had some overlap with acute stress reaction and so could be a precursor to the development of PTSD. Also, the participants believed that many of the initial symptoms of combat stress reaction were as a result of an extended activation of the fight-or-flight response as the body released a flood of adrenaline to prepare the muscles for action. All of the participants, upon returning from their combat deployment, reported that upon arriving home, their first emotional reaction was one of profound relief that they had survived the experience.

The subsequent research assumptions into this phenomenon have indicated that stress affects both learning and cognitive functions.[12] This evidence has suggested that the psychological impact of multiple operational deployments, which often involves repeated exposure to combat stress, will be disproportionately high in comparison to the number of physical injuries sustained during war.[13] Soldiers who are exposed to the stresses of combat experience physical and emotional reactions, many of which sharpen their abilities to survive. However, the implication is that other reactions produce disruptive behaviours that may threaten the soldier, and as a result the unit's cohesion, which in turn may adversely affect the unit's ability to successfully fulfil its mission.[14]

## Q3. Types of pre-combat education programmes and leadership training needed to effectively help soldiers cope with the negative physiological and psychological effects of combat.

The third research question asked the participants what types of pre-combat education programmes and leadership training interventions could be effective in helping soldiers cope with the negative physiological and psychological effects of combat. The purpose of this question was to ascertain from infantry veterans what their suggestions were for improving the pre-combat education programmes and leadership training interventions.

All the participants stressed that the implementation of realistic training was a primary stress-reduction technique, as it reassured soldiers by developing a maximum confidence in their skills and a belief that their leaders were doing their best for their unit. They contributed to a list of training techniques that they believed could be utilised during pre-combat exercises to prepare infantry soldiers for the negative physiological and psychological effects of combat. The participants also stressed that every soldier within each unit must be trained to effectively sustain performance in continuous operations. It was believed that the gaining of this capability went beyond the achievement of a high level of proficiency in combat skills and technical specialities. The implication from the findings is that soldiers need to learn to identify the adverse conditions of continuous operations in order to cope with them and then overcome their negative effects.

Most of the participants experienced situations where a reduction in caloric intake during continuous operations led to both physical and mental fatigue and degraded performance. Therefore, the participants suggested that soldiers must be trained and then supervised to ensure that they eat all the main items in their 24-hour combat rations to ensure that they got a balanced diet. Most of the participants emphasised that good physical conditioning delayed fatigue, built confidence, and shortened recovery times from illness and injury. The implication from this finding is that most of the participants emphasised that mental fitness was just as important as physical fitness. However, they experienced that this type of training was largely ignored prior to their own operational deployments.

The participants further emphasised that the introduction of realism into training was an important element in preparing soldiers for combat. They articulated that the use of live-firing exercises was an opportunity for soldiers to use live ammunition as realistically as possible in artificial combat situations where all the personal weapons and supporting weapons were fired. They believed that this use of live-firing exercises taught soldiers to have confidence in themselves, their weapons, and their comrades when firing live ammunition. These findings are also consistent with prior study findings of Siddle (2009), Grossman and Siddle (2010), and King (2013), which have implications for the methods of training the future generations of infantry combat soldiers.

The participants also explained that a commander needed know a host of details about the enemy forces, as the more accurate the picture, the better the commander could prepare their operational plans. The participants recognised that as important as knowing the enemy was the need for accurate information on the capabilities, limitations, and locations of own friendly forces, as it was often difficult to maintain a clear picture of the other Coalition operations that were taking place at the same time. All the participants believed that the same leadership skills that applied to troop welfare and war fighting should be used to effectively reduce and/or prevent combat stress reactions. They felt that it was the leader's responsibility to take preventative actions and address stress symptoms as they appeared in their soldiers. All the participants saw effective leadership as reducing the impact of stress when the leader understood the causes of combat stress and how soldiers would react to them. They contributed their suggestions as to how leaders could manage combat stress problems and keep them from spreading throughout the unit by implementing various actions. These findings reinforce those of King (2013), and these have implications for the future training of combat leaders.

The participants also believed that the leader must aim to minimise the physiological and psychological effects of combat on soldiers, and to do this he must be aware that the main sources of stress for soldiers is boredom, fatigue, discomfort, and friendly casualties. They observed that as soldiers became increasingly tired, they lost their ability to make rapid and rational decisions as they became more confused, disorientated, and eventually ineffective. Therefore, the participants were unanimous in their view that it was essential that the leader understood the effects of fatigue on themselves and their soldiers. According to the participants, the lot of an infantry soldier was to endure conditions of wet, cold, hunger, thirst, and tiredness, and as a result they built up a resilience and tolerance to the extremes of weather. For all of the participants, the witnessing of comrades being killed or wounded had a traumatic impact on themselves, their comrades, and the leader within the unit. The implication is that this led some soldiers to develop fear and apprehension that it would happen to them, and this in turn increased their reluctance to take risks and obey orders. These findings reinforce the previous study findings of Grossman (1995), Grossman and Christensen (2008), and King (2013).

The "hurry-up-and-wait" phenomenon in many military operations was, according to the participants, aptly called "hours of boredom," whereas the transition to combat was deemed to consist of "moments of terror." The inadequate recognition of the implications resulting from long lull periods, combat pulses, and the need to recover from stress could lead to dysfunctional soldiering as well as poor individual and small unit performance. Morale was seen by the participants as the mental and emotional condition of an individual soldier or group of soldiers, and that the leader who harnessed this resource in the unit would ultimately prevail. As seen by the participants, motivation was a by-product of morale, and when soldiers were enthusiastic about being part of a unit and had confidence in their leader, then they had the incentive to win in combat. The implication is that discipline was defined by the participants as bringing soldiers under control. The leader achieved this in order for soldiers to disregard the natural tendency for self-preservation and when required place themselves in danger in order to complete the unit's mission. These findings are also consistent with previous study findings of Grossman (1995), Siddle (2009), and Grossman and Siddle (2010).

Proficiency in the opinion of the participants referred to the leader being proficient in all the aspects of commanding the unit, and a leader's professional competency was the primary leadership factor that soldiers said decreased their stress in combat. All the participants believed that within the military, morale and motivation were the foundations of discipline, esprit de corps, and professionalism, all of which led to success in combat. This was reflected in the confidence, resolution, and courageous attitude of soldiers within the unit who were determined to accomplish the assigned mission. In explaining what motivates a soldier in combat, the participants stressed that unit cohesion, tradition, commitment, aggression, and patriotism all motivated the soldier to persevere in battle. Discipline and esprit de corps were significant factors that the participants identified that the leader needed to develop in their soldiers, as along with morale and motivation, these influenced success in combat. The participants felt that one of the most effective pre-combat leadership initiatives that countered the detrimental effects of combat on infantry soldiers was the building and maintaining of morale and motivation. The implication from this finding was that there were four ways of building morale and motivation and these are instilling confidence, allocating assignments, provision of adequate rest food and shelter, and showing concern for the welfare of soldiers.

# CHAPTER SEVENTEEN

## *Infantry Selection and Screening*

During combat, it has been demonstrated continually that there is a connection between poor leadership and the breakdown of unit cohesion, with the failure of combat leaders when the unit is under enemy fire, inducing panic and the disintegration of unit cohesion.[1] Based upon these studies, it can be seen that the problem the Coalition forces faced in the war in Iraq and are still facing in the war in Afghanistan is that we are sustaining avoidable combat casualties and taking longer than necessary to win the war, as the soldiers assigned to the infantry units do not represent a fair cross-section of the nations' manpower.[2]

The combat role of the infantry is to engage, fight, and kill or capture the enemy at close range using a firearm, edged weapon, or bare hands, in close-quarter combat. The physical, mental, and environmental operating demands of the infantryman are extreme, with combat loads weighing 60-80lbs, foot patrols of 20-25 miles a day being common, and in temperatures ranging from +30 degrees to -30 degrees Celsius. These conditions demand the highest levels of physical endurance and mental determination.[3] Therefore, there are clearly defined areas where further research or alterations to the current selection criteria require a better understanding of what the 21st Century infantry soldier is expected to achieve. When considering the asymmetric battlefields of Afghanistan and Iraq, where the threat to the individual infantry soldier is from 360 degrees, during 24 hours a day, and over 365 days of the year, the combat stress levels can finally be realised. However, as will be demonstrated, in the British Army, we do exactly the opposite by allocating those with the lowest aptitude test results to the infantry.

A further factor when considering infantry selection is that medical researchers have found a version of the 5-HTTLPR gene, which controls levels of serotonin, a chemical within the brain, which is related to mood and fuels the fear response in humans.[4] Also, the latest scientific research findings indicate that, as with other mental disorders, many genes, each with small effects, are at work in creating combat stress and PTSD (Orb, Eisenhauer, and Wynaden, 2012).[5] Findings indicate that individual differences in genes and brain area set the stage for combat stress and PTSD without causing the symptoms.[6] This means that soldiers with these genes will be more susceptible to combat stress. New research also shows that environmental factors, such as childhood trauma, head injury, or a history of mental illness, will further increase the risk.

The study by Dohrenwend (2013) showed that identifying soldiers for behavioural-health problems before they deploy to a combat zone through screening and then coordinating care for those soldiers while they are deployed could reduce suicidal thoughts, psychiatric disorders, and other mental problems. His findings indicate that individual differences in genes and brain area set the stage for combat stress and PTSD without causing the symptoms. This means that soldiers with these genes will be more susceptible to combat stress, and as a result, through the introduction of a robust selection and screening process, should not be selected to serve in infantry combat units.[7] The new research also shows that environmental factors, such as childhood trauma/abuse, head-injury, or a history of mental illness, will further increase the risk, and so soldiers who have experienced any of these pre-war vulnerabilities must also not be selected for service in infantry combat units. However, it is also considered that the combat stress resilience training, as previously described, could logically be broadened to include emotional assessment at the time the individual is recruited into the military. That is, prospective infantry soldiers would be subjected to a series of challenging combat-related emotional environments and situations that they would expect to encounter during combat operations. This would allow for the prediction of their potential risk for developing mental health difficulties or PTSD based upon their physiological, psychological, verbal, behavioural, and hormonal reactions recorded during their virtual combat simulated engagements.[8]

These new research findings by Dohrenwend (2013) found that the pre-war vulnerabilities of individual soldiers was just as important a factor as the actual combat-related trauma in predicting whether a soldier would become a psychological casualty. The research re-examined data from a sample of 260 Vietnam veterans from the National Vietnam Veterans Readjustment Study.[9] In his research, Dohrenwend concentrated on the role of three primary factors, which were the severity of the combat exposure, the existence of pre-war vulnerabilities, such as physical abuse/family history of substance abuse, and involvement in harming civilians and prisoners. The findings showed that stressful combat exposure was necessary for the onset of PTSD, as 98% of the veterans who developed PTSD had experienced at least one traumatic combat event.[10]

However, the most significant revelation from the study was that traumatic combat exposure was not in itself enough to cause PTSD, as of the soldiers who had experienced a traumatic combat exposure, only 31.6% developed PTSD.[11] After gaining these unexpected findings, Dohrenwend sought to tighten the parameters of his study by limiting his analysis to only soldiers who had experienced the most severe traumatic combat exposures. But even after this new criteria was introduced into the study, there was still 30% of the soldiers who had experienced the most severe combat exposures that did not develop PTSD. Therefore, the logical conclusion from these findings was that there were other factors at work that had made a significant percentage of the soldiers resilient to PTSD even after the severest combat exposures, while other soldiers were vulnerable to PTSD after only minor exposure to combat stress.

Among the factors that made soldiers more susceptible to PTSD were having experienced childhood physical abuse or having a pre-enlistment psychiatric disorder. Then age played a significant role, with men who were younger than 25 when they were deployed being seven times more likely to develop PTSD when compared with older men.[12] The research also found that soldiers who inflicted harm on civilians and prisoners of war were more likely to develop PTSD. The combined data from the three primary factors of severity of combat exposure, pre-war vulnerability, and involvement in harming civilians or prisoners revealed that PTSD reached 97% for veterans high on all three factors.[13] These findings reinforce the earlier studies that found that the severity of the exposure to combat trauma was the strongest predictor of whether a soldier would develop PTSD. However, more significantly it also found that pre-war vulnerabilities increased the likelihood of the onset of PTSD after even the most minor exposure to combat stress. The logical conclusion from these findings is that, given the potent interaction between combat exposure and pre-war vulnerability, the most vulnerable soldiers must be excluded from the most severe combat situations.[14]

However, currently within the British Army when infantry soldier candidates present themselves, their aptitude is assessed by the British Army Recruit Battery (BARB) test, the results of which generate the General Trainability Index (GTI) score. The GTI score is used to determine which roles are available to prospective soldiers. The maximum score for the BARB test in its current form is 80 points.[15] The roles and associated GIT scores are divided into:

   *a.* Combat Troops (The armour and infantry).
   *b.* Combat Support (The artillery, engineers, signals, and air corps).
   *c.* Combat Service Support (The logistics, electrical and mechanical engineers, medical corps, and intelligence corps).

The BARB test is a computer-based, psychometric assessment that was developed by the Defence Evaluation and Research Agency (DERA) and Plymouth University. It is a series of timed questions which assess a candidate's ability to absorb information quickly, logically, and accurately. The computer-based system automatically calculates the candidates score based upon the number of correct answers and the time taken. This final score is what is referred to as the candidates "GTI score." All potential recruits are required to take the BARB test on application to join the British Army.[16] It consists of seven different tests and takes about 30 minutes to complete, with the tests being:

- *a.* Reasoning (12 questions)
- *b.* Letter checking (16 questions)
- *c.* Number distance (20 questions)
- *d.* Odd one out (20 questions)
- *e.* Symbol rotation (12 questions)
- *f.* Maths (% grade)
- *g.* English (% grade)

The BARB test determines the candidate's ability to solve problems and retain information, and when completed, the GTI allows the Army to match the candidate to suitable roles. The higher the score the candidate attains, the more roles that are available to them. The GTI minimum scores by role are as follows:

- *a.* Armour – 44 points
- *b.* Infantry – 26 points
- *c.* Artillery – 38 points
- *d.* Engineers – 47-55 points (depending on specialisation)
- *e.* Signals – 48 points
- *f.* Air Corps – 48 points
- *g.* Logistics – 42-55 points (depending on specialisation)
- *h.* Electrical and Mechanical Engineers – 48 points
- *i.* Medical Corps – 50-58 points (depending on specialisation)
- *j.* Intelligence Corps – 55 points

The significance of this table is that the infantry are allocated recruits with the lowest BARB test results of 26 points, with recruits needing at least 38 points to be allocated to the artillery, which is the next lowest category. Also of note is the fact that the British Army has long had a policy where recruits are placed into specialisations that match their civilian employment or educational background/qualifications.[17] This policy finds computer technicians being allocated to the signals, builders to the engineers, students to the intelligence, electricians to the electrical and mechanical engineers, etc. These measures simplified the requirement for technical training within the Army, but the problem of combat training was rendered that much more difficult, as the infantry is left with a percentage of available, sub-average recruits. The fact was that higher grades on the GTI disqualified recruits from being allocated to the infantry and this resulted in the lower categories of recruits being over-represented in the infantry.[18] As a result of this allocation of recruits to the infantry who are in the lowest GTI aptitude and intelligence categories of 26 points, field commanders at all levels have complained that they have been receiving recruits of such a low level of mental ability that they are unable to be trained.[19] Obviously, this disproportionate allocation of recruits to the infantry also affected the ability to select and train leaders for subunit command, as the right material for infantry leaders was scarce.

Although the BARB test is relatively useful at identifying an intellectual and physical capacity of training, it does not appear to predict organisational fit. That is the test identifies those behavioural characteristics that are associated with training, but does not have the ability to identify those emotional factors that are associated with training failure. It has been found that emotional factors are the most prominent causes of recruits failing initial training, and so future research should seek to amalgamate the current psychometric BARB test with a biographical questionnaire and a scale that measures emotional factors. Currently, the U.S. military uses a non-cognitive two-scale test battery which includes an assessment of individual motivation and a biographical inventory questionnaire.[20] The U.S. biographical questionnaire interestingly includes the candidate completing a self-report that is related to reactions to specific life-events that are indicative of the targeted personal characteristics. That is they have identified the need for emotional robustness as well as mental discipline within their soldiers and are attempting to measure these traits in relation to the candidates' previous life-experience reactions.[21] As the British Army has become ever more reliant on predictive tools, it is recommended that the development of a multiple scale recruitment battery be pursued.

Therefore, this study recommends that each individual who applies to become an infantry soldier should be selected and screened for not only their suitability for a combat environment but also for their resilience or susceptibility to combat stress. As a result of the findings from this study, it is recommended that three types of screening tests are utilised to assess the suitability of candidates to become infantry soldiers. The first of these is the Wonderlic Cognitive Ability Test, which is an intelligence test that can to be used to assess the aptitude of a candidate for learning and problem solving in the military. It consists of 50 multiple choice questions to be answered in 12 minutes,[22] with a score of 20 indicating average intelligence. The test, as a vocational and intelligence test, falls under the field of organisational psychology, and as a personnel test, it is used to gauge a candidates employment, educational, and training potential.[23] The tests are divided into four different sections, and these are skill, cognitive, behavioural, and personality. The scores are predictors of the possible conformity that a candidate has within the field for which they are applying.

The skills test measures the candidate's skill in areas such as maths and English where the individual's ability to answer numerical and alphabetic details with accuracy is assessed. The cognitive test measures the candidate's capacity to solve problems and to learn. The behavioural test is an assessment of the candidate's potential to engage in counterproductive or unethical behaviour within an organisation or community, e.g., theft. As such, the test profiles the candidate's three behavioural traits, with these being neuroticism, agreeability, and conscientiousness. Finally, the personality test measures the candidate's personal characteristics that are widely accepted as being predictive of an individual's expected employment performance. This test can be designed to align with the particular demands of a particular employment position, thereby reducing recruitment costs and employee turnover. This test uses the five primary dimensions of an individual's personality, with these being extroversion, agreeableness, conscientiousness, emotional stability, and openness to experience. [24]

The second screening test that is recommended to assess the suitability of candidates to become infantry soldier is the Minnesota Multiple Personality Inventory (MMPI).[25] The MMPI is the most widely used and researched standardised psychometric test for adult personality and psychopathology that is currently available. The test is used by psychologists and other mental health professionals to amongst other tasks screen candidates during the personnel selection process for various employments. The MMPI first became available in 1943 and was replaced by an updated version, the MMPI-2, in 1989. Subsequently, an alternative version of the test, the MMPI-2 Restructures Form (MMPI-2-RF) became available in 2008.[26] This MMPI-2-RF adopts a different theoretical approach to personality test development by utilising the PSY-5 (Personality Psychopathology Five Scales), which measure dimensional traits of personality disorders, with these being aggressiveness, psychoticism, constraint, negative emotionality (neuroticism), and positive emotionality (extroversion).[27] This PSY-5 identifies the following traits in individuals:

a. *Aggressiveness* – Measures a person's tendency towards overt and instrumental aggression that typically includes a sense of grandiosity and a desire for power.

b. *Psychoticism* – Measures the accuracy of a person's inner representation of objective reality.

c. *Constraint* – Measures a person's level of control over their own impulses, physical risk eversion, and traditionalism.

d. *Negative Emotionality (Neuroticism)* – Measures a person's tendency to experience negative emotions, particularly anxiety and worry.

e. *Positive Emotionality (Extroversion)* – Measures a person's tendency to experience positive emotions and have enjoyment from social experiences.

This study further recommends that once this screening by the Wonderlic Personnel Test and the MMPI-2-RF has been completed, then the candidates should then be put through a third set of screening tests based upon a gruelling series of tasks to measure their motivation, fitness, aptitude, intelligence, and ability to work with others under stress. These tests would be undertaken both individually and in groups as the candidates complete demanding command tasks with carefully designed behavioural observations being taken during the completion of each task. A candidate would be able to voluntarily remove themselves from the assessment at any time without any negative consequences, though they could return to re-attempt the assessment at a later date should they so request and be judged by the instructors to be successful at a later date.

At the end of the screening, the instructors and psychologists would review the psychological profiles of each of the remaining candidates. Soldiers with unusual profiles that historically had been associated with poor performance would then individually interviewed by the psychologist, who would attempt to assess each soldier's likelihood for success during the infantry training course. The process is designed to deselect by screening the candidates rather than selecting the most suitable. In particular, the psychologists attempt to identify any potential problems that are likely to interfere with the soldier's success either academically or behaviourally. As an example, a history of poor academic performance, coupled with poor test scores on the Wonderlic Personnel Test and MM-PI-2-RF would indicate a poor likelihood of success. Similarly, histories of arrests or of non-judicial punishment are good examples of future problems with authority. The psychologist's aim is to identify the "whole man"[28] by incorporating the test scores with the complete background and history of each individual. They will then prepare their recommendations for each candidate.

Finally, a board consisting of the officer and senior NCO instructors and the psychologists and medical professionals would review each candidate's performance. The president of the board would be the final arbiter on whether a candidate should proceed to infantry training. The psychologists and medical professionals would provide insightful and carefully documented recommendations, ensuring that the process of selection was based on solid empirical and legal ground. The integration of the psychologists performing the assessments and continually reviewing the entire selection procedure will allow them to conduct extensive normative and predictive research on which profiles are associated with success or failure. This will ensure that the new screening instruments are being constantly validated.

In conclusion, given the findings of this study and the potent interaction between pre-war vulnerability and combat exposure, there is a need to keep the most vulnerable soldiers out of the most severe combat situations. The recommendation is that infantry soldiers are rigorously screened. Further, only those displaying the highest levels of physical endurance and mental determination be selected for their suitability to endure the physiological and psychological effects of combat.

# CHAPTER EIGHTEEN

## *Stress-Management Programmes*

The findings from this study indicated that the incidence of combat stress caused by the physiological and psychological effects of combat on infantry soldiers can be lessened or minimised through stress-management and stress-coping programmes. As a result, it is recommended that education in the form of stress-management exercises be introduced during pre-deployment training. This will be designed to deal with the physiological and psychological effects of combat and will teach soldiers about the stressful phenomena that they will find in combat.[1] Much self-induced stress comes from the lack of education, and so if soldiers are trained before combat about the sensations that they will encounter in combat, it is believed that this will eliminate some causes of stress and reduce the effects of many others.[2]

In this regard, stress-management techniques can include the leader ensuring that every effort has been made to provide for the soldier's welfare. Also, each soldier must be instilled with confidence in their leader, unit, and equipment, all of which can be achieved by the leader demonstrating decisive and assertive leadership.[3] The leader must recognise that each soldier will react differently to stress and each will have a different breaking point when faced with continuous combat operations. As a result, the stress management techniques of cross-training, task-matching, and task-sharing need to be incorporated into the pre-deployment training.[4] The recommendation is to incorporate effective stress-management techniques that are demanding and realistic while at the same time replicating stressful combat environments.[5]

This stress-management training must not only include the traditional military medical professionals and the regimental chaplains, but must be broadened to include military leaders and service members at all levels of the military hierarchy.[6] To achieve this recommendation, leaders must identify the risk factors of combat stress for themselves and their soldiers prior to deployment. This must include educating soldiers in the use of techniques for minimising the effects of combat stress and then the implementation of these methods to reduce stress. As part of this recommendation, the institutionalisation by the MoD of formal stress-management training would reduce the overall combat stress levels suffered by soldiers. This training should encompass officer, non-commissioned officer, and recruit training institutions. Finally, the MoD should implement this stress-management programme to span from pre-deployment to post-deployment of all officers and soldiers.[7]

The experience of close-quarter combat is a physical act and training must increasingly be focused not only on the indispensable physical performance of soldiers but also on their mental resilience. Combat is a brutal and disorientating event even for fully trained soldiers who have experienced combat previously. However, this is even more so during close-quarter combat where the sounds, sights, and smells are intensified by the close range at which the violence is prosecuted. In order to sustain soldier's performance in such an intense arena, a method of mental preparation for close-quarter combat must be devised: that is a "state-of-mind" must be developed for these types of operations.[8] It must be stressed that there is still no substitute for physical training and the mastering of all the essential infantry skill and drills. However, research by Pettera, Holtman, and Zimmer (2009) found that once these skills have been successfully achieved, performance can be improved by mental techniques that employ the techniques of visualisation and attitudinal conditioning.

This visualisation of combat techniques will improve combat execution by sensitising the soldier's responses to external cues while ingraining the physiological reactions of the soldier. The attitudinal conditioning is also involved in developing the correct motivation for combat as during such an experience the natural human response is to simply seek to survive.[9] In close-quarter training, the aim should be to develop the soldier's ability to not only survive but to also prevail over the enemy by developing a different "state-of-mind." Despite the horrible nature of a close-quarter combat situation, the soldier should be trained to remain in a calm mental state while being attuned to their heightened senses. This "state-of-mind" is psychological and exists only in each individual soldier.

In this regard, "resilience" training could also assist soldiers to mitigate extreme operational pressures by identifying the importance of mental preparation. This training would include "goal-setting," "mental rehearsals," "self-motivation," and "arousal reduction." These mental techniques would be designed to augment the standard training and exercise training prior to deployment. This training on resilience would describe the structure and function of the brain in detail, as by conducting this mental preparation, the frontal lobes and the cortex can control the instinctive responses in the brain stem and the amygdale from which the "fight-or-flight" responses are generated.[10] The aim of this training would be to strengthen the psychological preparedness of each soldier to the traumas of combat by improving the understanding of their own brain's cerebral functioning. By identifying the brain as an object of collective concern, it will ensure that mental preparation is undertaken as a part of military training. As a result, there needs to be a standardisation and collectivisation of the soldier's emotional and psychological responses to combat, as these once private domains are now public concerns.

Based on this study's findings, therefore, there is a powerful rationale for developing methods that promote psychological fitness within the military with the same vigour that has been traditionally applied to physical fitness.[11] As a result, it is recommended that there is a pro-active education and training approach for better preparing service members for the emotional challenges that they have to face during combat deployment in order to reduce the potential for later adverse psychological reactions such as combat stress, PTSD, and depression. Through this training, infantry soldiers would be able to exhibit positive adaptation when they encounter significant trauma or other sources of stress. One element of the training should draw from the principles of cognitive behavioural science, which advances the theoretical foundation that it is not the "event" that causes an emotion but rather how a person "appraises" the event that leads to emotion.[12] Based upon this foundation, it can then be postulated that internal thinking or appraisals about combat events can be "taught" in a way that leads to a more robust and measured reaction to traumatic combat stress. This approach does not imply that infantry soldiers with natural and effective coping skills do not feel some level of rational emotional pain when confronted with a combat situation that would normally be stressful to a normal individual. Instead, the aim is to teach infantry soldiers skills that will assist them cope with these disturbing events.

The first phase of this psychological fitness training would be the pre-deployment phase. This phase would focus on education prior to entering a combat environment or conducting operations that increase the likelihood of combat stress. This educating of military personnel on the reasons for combat stress will prepare soldiers and provide a forum to address any fears or concerns.

The second phase would be the deployment phase where the unit deploys to the combat operation. Here, the planning and resource allocation needs to be thorough in order to minimise any likelihood of inducing any additional combat stressors. Those units that experience stressful or traumatic combat situations, or where the unit has been involved in sustained operations against the enemy should have planned rest and recuperation (R&R) periods where the soldiers can decompress.[13] These R&R periods would allow military leaders to take a pro-active role in minimising the effects of combat stress.

The third and final phase is post-deployment, where the focus is on ensuring that soldiers return home in a positive frame of mind.[14] During this phase, the availability of care facilities for soldiers should be emphasised. Here soldiers can conduct reintegration training, receive additional briefings on life after deployment, and attend pre-emptive mental and psychological screenings in order to identify any soldiers suffering from combat stress reactions. It is believed that these interventions could assist future generations of soldiers in minimising the effects of combat stress.

However, despite this additional education, it is realised that stress and PTSD can never be totally eliminated, as almost all soldiers develop some form of combat stress or PTSD after combat operations.[15]

The military training of infantry soldiers has many goals, but the primary aim of the infantry is clear, and that is to close with and kill or capture the enemy in any climate, weather, or terrain. The competencies that the infantry soldier needs to fulfil this mission include not only the knowledge to perform assigned tasks but also the cross-functional skills necessary to succeed in a complex and stressful environment. These skill sets should include adaptability, tolerance to stress, concentration, and perseverance.[16] Unfortunately, these competencies have not traditionally been explicitly incorporated into the training syllabus for infantry soldiers. Despite the current emphasis on training under stress, which is an important component of stress-management training, considerably less attention has been placed on developing behavioural and cognitive skills that facilitate successful performance in combat environment.

The goal of stress-management programmes is to prepare soldiers to perform tasks effectively under high-stress conditions. Here, the term "stress" is used to describe a situation where the environmental demands are so intense that they lead the soldier to feel that the demands required are beyond their ability to successfully complete. This results in the soldier suffering undesirable physiological, psychological, behavioural, or social outcomes. At this point, it is important to distinguish between "training" and "stress training."[17] The primary goal of training is skill acquisition and retention, with these processes being undertaken in an environment that is designed to maximise learning. However, other tasks must be performed in conditions unlike those experienced in the training classroom. The research has shown that for some tasks, normal training procedures do not improve the task performance when the task is expected to be performed under stress conditions. That is, the primary purpose of "training" is to ensure the acquisition and retention of the required knowledge, skills, and abilities, while the primary purpose of "stress training" is to prepare soldiers to maintain effective performance in a high-stress battlefield environment. Therefore, "stress training" is defined as an intervention that is designed to enhance the soldier's familiarity with a battlefield environment in order to teach the skills necessary to maintain effective task performance under these stress conditions.[18]

These stress management programmes (stress inoculation training) should be taught in four component parts or phases: (1) education about human stress responses, (2) behavioural and skill training required to control these responses, (3) provision of the opportunities to practice these skills under replicated battlefield conditions, and (4) review and evaluation of individual outcomes. The stress-management programmes would expose soldiers to just enough stress in order to arouse their defensive coping skills with the exposure not being so great that it overwhelms the individual. Each of the four phases will now be discussed in detail.

The primary goal of phase one is the provision of information to the soldier, and this encapsulates two elements (a) indoctrination or discussion as to why stress training is important, and (b) information describing what sort of stressors are likely to be encountered in a combat environment, the likely effects that the stress may feel, and the likely effects on how the soldier may perform. The indoctrination is designed to increase the soldier's motivation to acquire the skills required to overcome a stressful combat setting. It emphasises the rewards and detriments of an effective compared to an ineffective performance in a stressful combat environment in order to reinforce the importance of stress-management programmes. This is especially important as stress-management programmes are additional to the basic training that a soldier experiences and so "user acceptance" becomes important.[19] That is the soldier must be motivated to undertake the stress-management programmes if they are to be fully effective.

The second element of the phase one training is the provision of the preparatory information as it has been shown that this can lessen the negative reactions to stress experienced by the soldier. The premise is that stress can be reduced by providing the soldier with as much knowledge and understanding as possible regarding possible stressful combat events. Therefore, the stress-management training provides preview of the combat stress environment making it less frightening and unfamiliar. Also, this knowledge can increase predictability that can decrease the soldier's distraction from performing essential tasks. Finally, preparatory information can create a sense of cognitive control over a stressful event by providing the soldier with means to respond to the stress.[20]

The aim is to provide the soldier with a comprehensive preparatory information strategy that addresses how they will feel in a stressful combat situation, describes the events that will occur in the transition from normal to stress condition and provide the soldier with information on how to adapt to the new stress levels. There are three types of preparatory information, and these are "sensory," "procedural," and "instrumental." The "sensory information" relates to how the soldier will feel under stress from a number of intrusive physical and emotional sensations. The typical physical reactions are increased heart rate, shallow breathing, sweating, and muscular tension, while emotional reactions include confusion, fear, and frustration. The "procedural information" describes for the soldier the events that are likely to occur in a combat stress environment, including a description of the setting, the effects the stressors will have, and the types of stressors that will be encountered. Finally, "instrumental information" provides a description of the actions to be undertaken by the soldier in order to counter the undesirable effects of the combat stress.[21]

The goal of the first phase is to increase the infantry soldier awareness of the likely physiological and psychological stressors that they are likely to experience on the battlefield and how this stress will most likely effect their performance. In order to fully engage the soldiers, it is recommended that initially there is an emphasis on the importance of stress training through military case studies, and these can be supplemented by the instructors introducing field experiments. These field experiments would entail the soldier performing a familiar task, such as stripping and assembling their personal weapon under varying levels of stress. These stressors would include the sights and sounds of battle where the soldiers are bombarded by the noise of explosions, the sounds of screaming comrades, the yells of their leaders as they attempt to rally their subordinates, smoke and darkness obscuring their vision, and the battlefield smells of death.[22] All these can be replicated and will provide soldiers with feedback as to their performance so that they can learn how their bodies and minds react to combat stress.

Once the soldiers have a full appreciation of the potential adverse effects of stress, the instructors can begin to discuss specific stressors that are likely to be experienced during combat. It is appreciated that not all stressors will be known, and that different soldiers will react to the same stressor differently. However, it can be argued that by raising the soldiers' awareness of the combat stress environment, we can elicit the cognitive and behavioural skills and responses that are necessary to overcome or at least minimise these stressors. The whole premise to this recommendation is based on the old adage "forewarned is forearmed"[23] where the availability of information and pre-exposure to combat stress will reduce the impact of stressful battlefield environment and increase the likelihood that soldiers will be able to continue functioning effectively, thereby reducing both the physiological and psychological reactivity.

The goal of the second phase of the stress-management programme is to develop cognitive and behavioural skills that facilitate the introduction, maintenance and finally enhancement of the soldiers' performance under combat stress conditions. However, some skills are generic and are as a result applicable to most tasks, such as cognitive awareness strategies, while others are dependent upon the specific task to be performed, such as decision-making. As a result, the specific training to be implemented in this phase is dependent upon the requirements of the task, in this case minimising stress for soldiers experiencing a combat environment. There are various types of stress-exposure skill training that can be described as physical awareness, cognitive awareness, mental application, rote-learning, decision-making, and team-skills. [24]

The physical awareness focuses on controlling the body's reactions to stress by utilising relaxing strategies including controlled breathing, muscle relaxation to reduce tension, constraining of the heart rate, and reducing nervousness. The goal of this relaxation training is to have the soldier control their muscle tension and breathing as relaxation and stress are incompatible. This training is designed to have the soldier respond under stress conditions with control, calmness and relaxation. In order to master these skills, the soldiers need to be monitored by equipment that can provide feedback on their physiological "vital signs," such as heart rate and blood pressure while they are experiencing a simulated battlefield environment. As an example, bio-feedback involves training a soldier to control their physical responses (blood pressure and heart rate) by using external monitoring devices to indicate when a desired change occurs. By using this technique, soldiers can learn to bring their physiological processes under their conscious control.

The cognitive awareness is aimed at increasing the soldiers' attention span and depth of concentration by concentrating on the task at hand, thereby minimising distractions and negative thoughts. There are several training strategies that have been shown to increase cognitive control, reduce anxiety, and maintain performance under stress. The primary emphasis of these interventions is to replace negative or distracting cognitions with positive task focused cognitions. The problem is that soldiers under stress begin to share their cognitive resources between the task and the worrying stressor itself. Therefore, the soldiers' performance suffers as their attention is distributed between the relevant task and the irrelevant cognitions that have been brought about by the combat stressor. The basis of this training is that worrying consumes valuable attention resources that are available to the memory, and that this causes less to be available for processing of the current task. The primary task in cognitive awareness is the training of soldiers to recognise thoughts that are irrelevant to their task and to replace them with task-focused cognitions. Therefore, the aim of this strategy is to eliminate, or at least effectively suppress, the thoughts that are irrelevant to the task, such as fear, thereby significantly decreasing inefficient performance by the soldier when in a combat environment.[25] Training that concentrates directly on enhancing the soldiers' attention focus may assist alleviate the distractions and perceptual narrowing that occur in a combat stress environment.

The mental application has the goal of preparing soldiers for combat by mentally rehearsing all the specific elements, skills, and drills to be utilised in a military mission (task). This mental practice is beneficial when approaching a task that will require a considerable amount of mental (cognitive) effort and is at its most effective when the mental practice is conducted directly before the mission (task).[26] As a prime example of the use of this technique, the members of SEAL Team 6 carried out this strategy before boarding their helicopters for their Osama Bin Laden raid to Abbottabad, Pakistan on 2nd May 2011. The results from the recent research show that in recent meta-analysis, it was concluded that mental practice was an effective means of enhancing performance, but that it was less effective than physical practice. This mental application allows the soldier an opportunity to rehearse behaviours into easily remembered words and images to aid recall.

The rote-learning strategy is designed to maintain the soldiers' skills performance even when under extreme combat stress. Almost all basic military training is designed to reduce the disruptive effects of combat stress through the teaching of repetitive drills and skills. Once again to use the example of the soldier stripping and assembling their personal weapon, this drill must be learnt so repetitiously that a soldier can carry out the skill, as described in Army circles, "while sleeping." That is the action of stripping and assembling the weapon is so ingrained that it becomes "automatic" even in the most stressful combat conditions.[27] Therefore, the soldier is over trained beyond the level of normal proficiency, thereby building up an automatic adaptive response. The premise is that the combat stress environment reduces the attentional capacity of the soldier and so automatic drills will be more resistant to downgrade. When preparing soldiers to perform under combat stress conditions, the conditions provided during training must approximate the stress environment in as much detail as possible.

The decision-making skills are in themselves a strategy to complement a soldier's performance when experiencing combat stress. That is the battlefield stressors of the sounds, sights, and smells of horror are significantly increased when the soldier is exposed to information overload, time-pressure, and multiple tasks to complete. Under certain combat stress conditions, such as increased time pressure, the use of less analytic decision-making strategy will be necessary. The research indicates that this increased time pressure will prevent the use of analytic decision strategies, but that this is of little concern as analytic strategies are rarely used in these circumstances. These combat stress demands can also be reduced to a manageable level by training the soldier in the "combat appreciation" process, where they are taught to make an assessment of the situation, based on the current information, and then make an instant decision as to which course of action to adopt.[28] In this context, which has been termed "hyper-vigilant decision-making," the consideration of only limited options, a non-systematic information search, accelerated evaluation of the available data, and rapid decision-making in a combat critical environment is the most effective response.

Finally, for the infantry soldier, team-skills are particularly important, as teamwork at the section level will often mean the difference between living and dying. The fact is that combat stress situations will cause soldiers to falter and ultimately fail, causing team coordination to become ineffective. The research findings indicate that an individual's focus of attention alters from the broad to the narrow when under stress. This has a significant implication for team cohesion as individuals adopt a narrower "tunnel vision" perspective by shifting from a broader, team perspective to a narrower, individualistic focus. As with the rote-learning strategy already discussed, the team skills at section, platoon, company, and battalion level are essential to the successful completion of the mission. It has also been found that when under extreme battlefield stress, the soldier will immediately revert to their ingrained team skills, and this gives the soldier an immediate focus for the actions that must be accomplished, thus reducing their fear and indecision. Therefore, it is necessary to train and reinforce team skills by providing information on the importance of teamwork skills and how they can be affected by stress, by training in team skills and providing feedback to other team members, and the practice of these skills in a realistic task setting.[29]

The goal of the third phase of the stress-management programme is the provision of the opportunities to practice these skills under simulated battlefield conditions. Training generally occurs in a calm and benign environment, as it is designed to be conducive to learning, while recruit soldiers acquire their basic infantry skills. However, the actual combat conditions under which these skills need to be performed by soldiers are totally unlike those found in a training setting. Therefore, the performing of a well-learned skill or drill in a hostile combat environment will cause the severe degradation of soldiers' performance when compared with their training environment performance. Therefore, in order to maintain soldiers' combat performance, they must be exercised in a stressful environment that replicates a hostile combat environment to every extent possible. This type of training, which allows a degree of pre-exposure to the stressors of an operational environment, will reduce the extent of soldier performance degradation experienced in an operational setting.

The exposure to these stressors allows the soldier to practice and refine their battlefield skills and drills while experiencing information overload, time-pressure, and lack of information due to the "fog-of-war." The soldiers will also have the natural environmental stressors of climate, weather, and terrain. The intensity of the stressors should be increased as the proficiency of the soldiers improves. However, this increasing intensity must be carefully monitored to ensure that the predetermined limits, which will be promulgated prior to the exercise, are observed. The benefits of this strategy are that it allows the soldier to perform tasks in a simulated stress environment and to experience the types of performance difficulties encountered in this type of setting. This will allow the soldiers to adapt their performance to the new combat environment.[30] Also, this pre-exposure to combat-like stressors reduces the uncertainty in the soldier regarding their likely experiences, thus creating confidence in their ability to perform in this setting. Finally, these events that have been experienced during training will be less distracting when faced for the first time in a combat environment.

The goal of the fourth and final phase of the stress-management programme is to review and evaluate individual outcomes. Here the results demonstrate that these stress-management programmes have a significant effectiveness for soldiers drawn from the high-anxiety and normal-anxiety populations. The effectiveness of the training was also found to be dependent on the number of training sessions that the individual soldier undertook. However, the overall results indicated that stress-management programmes resulted in decreased subjective stress and improved performance, and the beneficial effects of stress training were maintained when soldiers entered a combat environment for the first time.

As well as the introduction of these stress-management programme initiatives, it is further recommended that resilience and mental determination training should be implemented in order to create enhanced tolerance to combat stress. It is resilience that provides the soldier with the ability to initially endure and then recover from combat-related traumatic events. The whole premise of these recommendations is that the prevention or minimising of combat stress symptoms is more preferable than the treatment of stress-related medical disorders. In their recent study, Watson and Gardiner (2013) found that resilience could be enhanced by the promotion of four factors, these being:

*a.* Individual factors, including the development of positive thinking, coping abilities, behavioural control, realistic outlook, and physical fitness.
*b.* Family factors, including emotions, communications, closeness, and support.
*c.* Unit factors, including effective leadership, unit cohesion, teamwork, morale, and esprit de corps.
*d.* Community factors, including feeling of belonging, cohesion, connections, and collective concerns. Mental determination.

Mental determination has long been related to the field of professional sports psychology, but it has also been found to reduce the effects of combat stress on soldiers. The traits that should be promoted are self-belief, persistence, coping with failure or adversities, and maintenance of concentration. Also, the early exposure to stress has been found to promote the development of coping mechanisms and stress regulation. The general assessment from the most current research is that physically fit and mentally determined soldiers are more resilient to combat stress, as they experience a much quicker decline in physiological fight-or-flight arousal following the removal of the stressor.[31]

High-intensity and high-stress conditions frequently lead to disrupted performance, as stress affects the soldiers' physiological, psychological, cognitive, emotional, and social processes. When soldiers face combat stressors that disrupt goal-orientated behaviour, the effects will be increased errors, slower responses, and greater variance in performance. As a result, the preparation of soldiers for combat requires that they be highly skilled, be aware of the stress environment they will experience, and be trained in the skills necessary to overcome these high-stress conditions. However, the absolute realism of the stress-management programmes is not possible or totally desirable. The desire by some trainers to re-create a real-life threatening experience for soldiers is not possible, as the trainees will always realise that they are in a safe training environment.[32] However, well-designed simulation training can feel like the real thing without imposing unnecessary high levels of stress, as these may prove detrimental to the training. The research had found that stressors introduced at a moderate level of realism during training will provide a realistic representation of a combat environment.

In conclusion, the findings suggest that there can be an effective strategy for enhancing soldiers' performance when experiencing combat stress through stress-management programmes. These skills include controlling anxiety, positive self-attitude, goal-setting, and a focused outlook. To facilitate this training, as soldiers return from operational deployments the specific nature, range, and intensity of the combat stressors that they experienced require documentation. It needs to be recognised that stress is perhaps the most common element in the life of an infantry soldier, especially as experienced during the recent asymmetric war in Afghanistan and Iraq, where the danger to the soldier is 360 degrees, 24 hours a day, and 365 days of the year. The cognitive abilities and certain personality traits have been found to facilitate some soldiers' resistance to combat stress. However, it has also been found that stress-management programmes will minimise the adverse effects of the combat experience.

# Chapter Nineteen

## *Combat-Simulation Training*

Initially, it is important to realise that training can serve as either a Type 1 or a Type 2 moderator, that is it can intervene either before or after the individual's stress response occurs. Most of the current research on the moderating effects of training focuses on a particular type of training, namely combat-simulation training, in which the infantry soldier is repeatedly exposed to certain stressors and asked to perform a target task under that stressor. This Type 1 moderator training has been found to gradually reduce the soldier's physiological and psychological response to the specific stressor.[1] This stress-exposure training allows the soldier to practice performing complex tasks while being confronted by an external stressor, which leads to task mastery, thereby allowing the soldier to maintain their performance under stress. In addition, stress-exposure training can reduce the soldier's uncertainty involved in stressful situations by allowing the individual to develop expectations regarding the effects that stressors will have on their mental and physical performance.[2]

Therefore, both skill-building and stress-mitigating aspects of the training are important as they can build improved performance when the soldier is under stress by building problem-solving skills, increasing self-efficiency, and enhancing control and coping skills. Grossman (2009) found that combat-simulation training that replicated the combat environment was effective in mediating the effect of the stress responses on the decision-making process. By training in an as-real-as-possible simulated environment, the soldier is able to develop adaptive capabilities that prepare them for the more complex and challenging stressors of the combat environment. As evidence of the importance of this type of training, King (2013) found that combat support and combat service support, as well as reserve units that came under direct enemy fire, were more susceptible to severe stress reactions than infantry soldiers. The obvious conclusion is that the full-time infantry soldiers received additional and specific combat-related training that allowed them to cope more effectively with the more difficult stressors created by direct ground combat with the enemy.[3]

There are many studies that offer empirical evidence of the positive effects of training programmes on reducing the physiological and psychological effects of combat stress. Northouse (2009) examined the effects of relaxation training on performance, with those that received the training reporting lower levels of anxiety and increased self-efficiency, which both acted indirectly in reducing the effects of stress on performance. The research by Gouws (2010) found that even though each single training session was beneficial, there was a significant positive relationship between the number of training sessions and the effect of the training on improving performance and reducing stress-related anxiety. These results suggest that military leaders can utilise combat-simulation training to reduce their soldiers' susceptibility to stressors and further identified that the results were better when the training included some form of behavioural practice, when the size of the training group was small (no more than a 10 person infantry section), and when the training occurred in a field training environment. These results confirmed that effectively structured combat-simulation training moderates the effects of stress on soldiers' performance both when performing mental and physical tasks.[4]

The recommendation from the findings is that there is the introduction of combat-simulation training that increases the sensory fidelity and interactional realism of a virtual environment that will enhance the transfer of training from the simulation to the real world. It was found that learning that which took place under specific physiological and psychological conditions will have a higher probability of being recalled when the initial physiological and psychological states that the learning initially occurred under is present. The findings suggest that if combat-simulation training is to effectively transfer to criterion environments that may engender a range of innate stress reactions, then that training should be conducted while the soldier is experiencing a similar range of emotional states.[5] As military operations are constantly in a state of dynamic change, adult learning theory would dictate that that optimal combat-simulation training should also include a wide range of emotional states in order to counteract the possibility of negative transfer and to promote successful performance in combat environments that may inherently induce a dramatic range of emotional states.

The new technology of virtual reality has been shown to effectively support soldiers' resilience to combat stress, and as the technology has advanced, the virtual images have become more real, giving the soldiers the sense of being there or the sense of being in a different environment. This advancement in virtual reality has already found many applications in psychology, where it helps patients cope with their phobias. The environment so created is real enough to expose the patient to the feared stimuli in a controlled setting. In the military, virtual reality can be used in the same manner by providing the soldier with vivid and customised combat stimuli. Also, prior to deployment, this virtual reality can be used to screen soldiers who may be susceptible to combat stressors or eventual PTSD. Such virtual reality tools offer the potential for use in combat-readiness training and for stress inoculation. Both these approaches can be used to better prepare the infantry soldier for the emotional stress of combat. Studies suggest that virtual reality can be more effective than the traditional field training exercises when considering the cost, time expenditure, stress adaptation and performance level enhancements are considered.[6]

Therefore, there is a powerful rationale for developing methods that promote psychological fitness within the military with the same vigour that has been traditionally applied to physical fitness.[7] As a result, it is recommended that there is a pro-active education and training approach for better preparing service members for the emotional challenges they have to face during combat deployment in order to reduce the potential for later adverse psychological reactions such as PTSD and depression. Through resilience, infantry soldiers will be able to exhibit positive adaptation when they encounter significant trauma or other sources of stress. One element of this programme should draw from the principles of cognitive-behavioural science, which advances the view that it is not the "event" that causes an emotion, but rather how a person "appraises" the event that leads to emotion. Based upon this theoretical foundation, it can then be postulated that internal thinking or appraisals about combat events can be "taught" in a way that leads to a more resilient reaction to traumatic combat stress.[8] This approach does not imply that infantry soldiers with natural and effective coping skills do not feel some level of rational emotional pain when confronted with a combat situation that would normally be stressful to a normal individual. Instead, the aim is to teach infantry soldiers skills that will help them cope with these disturbing events.

The recommendation from this study is that, in order to develop combat-stress resilience, a set of combat simulations need to be created that will be used as contexts for infantry soldiers to experientially learn stress-reduction skills and cognitive-behavioural emotional coping strategies prior to deployment. This approach would involve immersing infantry soldiers into a variety of virtual combat mission episodes where they are confronted with emotionally challenging combat situations. The interaction within such emotionally challenging scenarios would aim to provide a more meaningful context in which to engage with psycho-educational information and to practice stress-reduction techniques and cognitive-coping strategies that will psychologically prepare the infantry soldier for a combat deployment. The virtual reality emotionally challenging events would include such events as seeing/handling human remains, death/injury of a comrade, killing an enemy combatant, and the death/injury of a child.[9] At the point of the emotionally challenging event, a mentor would guide the soldier through stress-reduction, psych-educational strategies and self-management techniques. There would also be the provision of rational restructuring exercises for the appraisal and processing of the virtual experience. All this stress resilience education and training would draw on the experiences and evidence from the recent wars in Afghanistan and Iraq.

In this way, each infantry soldier will be provided with a digital "real-life experiences" that replicate emotionally challenging combat events and situations that can be used to provide context-relevant learning of emotional-coping strategies under very tightly controlled and orchestrated simulated conditions. This combat-simulation training will improve infantry soldiers' generalisation to real-world situations by introducing a state-of-the-art learning component and further develop resilience by leveraging the learning process of latent inhibition. This latent inhibition refers to the delayed learning that occurs as a result of pre-exposure to a stimulus without adverse consequences.[10] Therefore, the exposure to a simulated combat experience is designed to decrease the likelihood of fear, stress, and/or trauma during the actual combat event.

Therefore, the findings indicate that individual differences in genes and brain area set the stage for combat stress and PTSD without causing the symptoms. This means that soldiers with these genes will be more susceptible to combat stress, and these should not be selected to serve in infantry combat units. Also, the new research also shows that environmental factors, such as childhood trauma/abuse, head-injury, or a history of mental illness, will further increase the risk, and so soldiers who have experienced any of these pre-war vulnerabilities must also not be selected for service in infantry combat units. However, it is also considered that the combat-stress resilience training, as previously described, could logically be broadened to include emotional assessment at the time the individual is recruited into the military. That is, prospective infantry soldiers would be subjected to a series of challenging combat-related emotional environments and situations that they would expect to encounter during combat operations. This would allow for the prediction of their potential risk for developing mental health difficulties or PTSD based upon their physiological, psychological, verbal, behavioural, and hormonal reactions recorded during their virtual engagements.[11] This stress-exposure training would provide a framework in which fear is attenuated and tasks can be trained so that a soldier's performance withstands the negative effects of combat. This programme would be a three-phase approach that would be based on the provision of information, skills acquisition, and confidence building.

The research has shown that individuals given information about an impending stressful event will experience a reduction in anxiety when the event occurs. Therefore, phase one of any stress-exposure training would require that the soldier learns about what they are likely to feel during combat, what the actual stressors experienced in combat are, and how those stressors affect the soldier's performance. The soldiers would be taught the full range of emotional symptoms and physical signs of stress, with it being emphasised that such experiences are normal when first exposed to combat. This information will result in soldiers being less likely to overreact to normal anxiety symptoms during combat. The stressors that are present during combat are numerous and include the sights and sounds of comrades being killed and wounded. These stress-creating stimulants should be openly discussed and replicated as accurately and realistically as possible in training. Additionally, soldiers must be made aware of the effects that these stressors have on the individual soldier's performance, such as marksmanship, concentration, and teamwork. This information will give soldiers the ability to successfully counteract the negative consequences of combat stress. Throughout this process, soldiers must be constantly reassured that adhering to tactical training principles will increase their likelihood of survival.[12]

The phase two of the stress-exposure training would deal with the soldiers' skills acquisition during which positive cognitive control strategies would enable soldiers to learn to recognise task-irrelevant thoughts and instead replace them with task-relevant thoughts. That is, they would be taught to focus on the mission-essential tasks while blocking out the non-essential distractions that could impair the successful achievement of their allocated tasks. The development of these skills would improve task performance and reduce anxiety. In addition, soldiers must be taught skills such as marksmanship, not in the calm conditions of a rifle range but while experiencing the noise and moving distractions they will experience during combat. Then as combat requires multiple tasks to be performed by each soldier, such as engaging one target while scanning the battlefield for additional threats, significant improvements in multi-tasking performance would be obtained when the tasks are paired during training. Finally, team and unit skills should be the focus during training, as group coordination deteriorates under the stress of combat, as the individual soldier will tend to concentrate on survival rather than the unit's mission when under stress.[13] Therefore, teamwork must be practised under stressful training conditions that replicate actual combat as accurately as possible.

The third phase of the stress-exposure training would implement confidence building through application and practice, as routine tasks learned under peaceful conditions deteriorate when the same task is performed during stressful conditions. Therefore, if training is undertaken during stressful situations, this will limit the amount and extent of the deterioration. Training under conditions that approximate the stresses of the combat environment will improve the overall performance of the soldier during battlefield conditions.[14] This training will also enhance the soldier's confidence in his and the unit's proficiency, which is essential in limiting incidences of combat stress experienced by soldiers.

It is recommended that combat-simulation training is designed to be an intensive, multi-stage process designed to mould the infantry soldier to become more resilient in stressful combat situations by making them more aware of their cognitive processes. This would be designed to teach soldiers more adaptive cognitive sets of habits to replace harmful thoughts and behaviours. These interventions would be based on three developmental phases. The first phase would be educational, where the soldiers discuss the typical reactions to combat stress and then identify their own reactions to situational stressors. This framework provides a coherent system that promotes the soldiers' understanding and facilitates their desire to complete the training. The second phase would be devoted to the development of specific skills required to lessen the effects of combat stress through their own awareness of stress reactions, thereby developing their own emotional, cognitive, and behavioural-control strategies to combat stressors. The final phase would involve the practice of the new control strategies during realistic combat-simulation training.[15]

This mental readiness approach would be directly integrated into more intense training situations that have a direct operational relevance. This recommendation advocates that instructors devote increasing time to incorporate lessons that address cognitive and emotional control and readiness as well as the traditional technical and physical training. These important instructions in mental readiness will have more impact with soldiers if they are delivered by instructors who have previous operational experience and, as a result, creditability.[16] It is recommended that the instructors encourage soldiers to monitor their own physiological, psychological, and emotional reactions to various combat-simulation training scenarios with these procedures being gradually incorporated into military training courses.

Interestingly, military training increasingly utilises combat simulators as a cost-effective method of inculcating combat-stress resilience in infantry soldiers. A continuing challenge for combat-simulation training that adopts a mental readiness or resilience approach is to determine how to best use the newest simulators or virtual-reality systems so that they duplicate the stress levels of real combat operations in training.[17] In this regard, the training scenarios that are used during the combat-simulation training should be based upon actual after-action reports from recent operations in Afghanistan and Iraq. There must also be some scenario-based training offered to allow soldiers to adopt mental readiness training principles, followed by a debriefing of all aspects of the soldiers' experience, including why various decisions or courses of action were adopted.

This form of combat-simulation training provides the capacity to train, validate (through after-action reports), also to verify the tactics, standard operating procedures (SOPs), and techniques to support training and mission rehearsals.[18] The introduction of "live-simulation" involves soldiers operating their actual equipment and weapons, which provides realism by providing a realistic battlefield environment. This training is conducted in the field and yields outcomes that could be expected on operations. Then virtual-reality simulators involve individuals or groups of soldiers reacting with a virtual environment of varying fidelity.[19] This allows them to evaluate their progress in real-time for immediate after-action analysis by the instructors. This simulation process gives the soldier a 360-degree perspective of the virtual environment and allows the use of dummy weapons to give the same effect as the actual scenario. These systems use highly sophisticated physics modelling, artificial intelligence, total immersion environment, improvised explosive device (IED) simulation, highly developed infrared simulation, and interactive command and control functions.[20] This constructive combat-simulation training for mission rehearsal preparation can be conducted at the local, tactical, operational, or theatre level depending upon the type of training that needs to be imparted to the soldiers.

In conclusion, a common criticism of stress-exposure training is that the stress of combat can never be accurately replicated in training exercises. However, research has shown that the complete and accurate recreation of operational stressors is not necessary. Another criticism is that stress exposure will itself produce such a degree of stress that soldiers become even more afraid than before the training.[21] To avoid this problem, the stressors need to be introduced incrementally in order to allow soldiers to gradually develop the necessary stress-coping skills. Therefore, the recommendation is that the initial learning of tasks should take place in a non-stressful environment, but once learnt, the training should be conducted in ever-more stressful environments, culminating in as-realistic-as-possible combat exercises. These combat simulators allow soldiers to train in tactical operations, to assess their combat readiness, decision-making, and knowledge of vehicles, weapons, language, and various cultures.[22] The training can be conducted in various simulated climates, weather, or terrain, with the light conditions also being varied, as day transits into night and vice versa.

CHAPTER TWENTY

# *Leadership Training*

Today, military operations experienced by infantry soldiers on the new asymmetric battlefield involve them being able to control their fear in order to maintain unit cohesion and operational effectiveness. All military combat missions are similar in that all decisions have life or death consequences and occur against a backdrop of psychological stressors, time pressure, and uncertainty, all of which reduce operational effectiveness. Some of these impairments that soldiers experience are attention lapses, narrowing of focus, short-term memory loss, and biased cognitive processing, all of which can contribute to fatal errors in judgement and/ or performance.[1] Therefore, despite all the recent technological developments, it is still the human being who remains the critical element in all combat operations, and as a result, the infantry soldier is required to maintain their emotional, cognitive, and behavioural control in order to ensure their own and their comrades' safety, as well as their unit's operational effectiveness.

It must be realised that the infantry section is a homogenous living and breathing organism. Once its soldiers have experienced combat together, the unit becomes the strongest human bond on the planet, far outstripping any family bonds. To those in the "outside world," as it was euphemistically called by Vietnam veterans, there is absolutely no concept by those who have not personally experienced the phenomenon of the strength, resilience, and longevity of these bonds that have been forged in the cauldron of life-and-death combat.[2]

The point of this description is to bring out the fact that the first identification of the negative effects of combat upon each individual soldier will always be identified within every military unit by his/her closest comrades and the commander. That is because every military leader is taught that they must know each soldier under their command better than their own family.[3] Therefore, because the environment in which the combat infantry soldier exists is so physically close and personal, even the slightest mood change becomes instantly obvious both to the commander and all the soldiers within the unit. This intimacy of feelings is often described as the intimacy of the relationship that is experienced by a husband and wife. To follow this argument, the findings from this study showed how the early identification of combat stress needs to be done by the commander, and once identified that effective management of that stress must be delivered by the military leader at the lowest possible level. An obvious conclusion that can be drawn from these findings is that military commanders at all levels must bear the responsibility for combat stress control in their units. In addition, their subordinate military leaders, at all levels, are also responsible for continuously implementing their commander's combat stress control policies and procedures.[4]

As a result of the findings from this study, the participants identified a number of stress-management techniques that the unit leader can utilise in order to reduce the negative physiological and psychological effects of combat on infantry soldiers:

*a.* The demonstration of competent, professional, and fair leadership through decisive and assertive actions.

*b.* Create and maintain progressive and realistic improvement goals for both the individual soldier and the unit as a whole, while systematically testing the achievement of those goals.

*c.* Ensure that every effort is made to provide for the soldiers' welfare, including food, water, shelter, medical, logistics, and whenever possible sleep and/or rest.

*d.* Be cognisant that the extended duration and intensity of combat will increase the stress levels amongst soldiers, and be able to recognise the signs of stress in soldiers.

e. Foster the flow of information to soldiers by encouraging upward, downward, and lateral communications, including mail, news, and other public information avenues.

f. Understand that fear is a normal reaction to combat or uncertain situations, ensuring that soldiers are trained to recognise the stressors of operations and how to manage those situations.

g. Ensure realistic training, as it is one of the primary stress-reduction techniques that fosters soldiers' maximum confidence in their personal skills, the effectiveness of their unit, and the professionalism of their leaders, thereby creating high morale, unit identity, and esprit de corps.

h. Inculcate stress control through cross-training, task-allocation, task-matching, and task-sharing, while at the same time ensuring that individual soldiers practice and master personal stress-coping techniques.

i. Endeavour to keep soldiers in the unit together in order to build cohesion and encourage experienced soldiers to mentor the new soldiers in the unit, thereby further enhancing unit identity and cohesion.[5]

The most encouraging findings from this study were that several of physiological and psychological effects of combat on soldiers are potentially modifiable by instituting new training and deployment protocols. New training and deployment protocols include: unit cohesion, education programmes in stress management, leadership training at all levels of command, and the provision of R&R (rest and relaxation) during operational deployments. The findings illustrated that soldiers believe that professional leadership, effective education programmes and strong cohesion between unit members could significantly improve morale, mental health, and military efficiency. These findings further found that social support offered by a cohesive unit, and supportive leadership, diminished physiological and psychological ill health acted as a buffer against the potentially negative effects of combat stress.[6]

It must be understood by military leaders that combat is sudden, intense and life threatening, and that the stresses experienced by their soldiers will be traumatic. The most effective ways to confront combat stress and to reduce psychological breakdown in combat is for the leader to admit that fear is a natural reaction when faced with a life-threatening situation.[7] The leaders must ensure that that the lines of communication are open between them and their subordinates. They must treat combat stress reactions as combat injuries, recognise the limits of their soldiers' endurance, and openly discuss the moral implications of their soldiers' behaviour during combat. In order to reduce stress the leader needs to inspire their subordinates, initiate and support stress-management programmes, ensure that each soldier has mastered at least two stress-coping techniques – a slow one for deep relaxation, and an immediate one to cope with unexpectedly stressful situations.[8]

Therefore, it is recommended that the military leader be designated the responsibility for mitigating the impact of combat stress on their unit and its soldiers. It is believed that this will create one of the missing links, transforming the military from a passive to an active stance in the fight to minimise the short and long-term negative effects of combat stress. Therefore, to achieve this aim, it is recommended that education is expanded past the military medical health professionals and chaplains to include military leaders and soldiers, as they are the individuals directly affected by the physiological and psychological effects of combat stress. Education related to combat stress should be added to officer, non-commissioned officer and recruit courses, commencing at these initial basic courses, but then continuing throughout officers', non-commissioned officers' and soldiers' full military career. That is every course that military personnel attend throughout their 20-30-year careers should contain modules within each that re-educate all ranks on the latest interventions to prevent, identify, and treat combat stress.[9] This will ensure that those military leaders have the requisite knowledge and training to use all the available resources to counter combat stress. However, the effectiveness of this education programme will depend upon Army-wide implementation. What this study recommends is a three-phased prevention plan that is supervised by all military leaders at all levels of the chain of command.

The research findings indicate that individual differences in genes and brain area set the stage for combat stress and PTSD without causing the symptoms. This means that soldiers with these genes will be more susceptible to combat stress, and these should not be selected to serve in infantry combat units. Also the new research also shows that environmental factors, such as childhood trauma/abuse, head injury, or a history of mental illness, will further increase the risk, and so soldiers who have experienced any of these pre-war vulnerabilities must also not be selected for service in infantry combat units. However, it is also considered that the combat stress resilience training, as previously described, could logically be broadened to include emotional assessment at the time the individual is recruited into the military. That is prospective infantry soldiers would be subjected to a series of challenging combat-related emotional environments and situations they would expect to encounter during combat operations.[10] This would allow for the prediction of their potential risk for developing mental health difficulties or PTSD based upon their physiological, psychological, verbal, behavioural, and hormonal reactions recorded during their virtual engagements.

Military leaders must be trained to understand the human dimension and anticipate their soldiers' reactions to combat stress. In order to reduce this stress when preparing for an operational deployment, leaders must be trained to lead by inspiration and not fear or intimidation. They must initiate and support stress-management programmes and provide information to focus stress positively. Finally, the leader must be trained to ensure that each soldier has mastered at least two stress coping techniques, one for deep relaxation and the other for short rests. The leader must consolidate his command position within the unit during the mobilisation phase prior to deployment on operations. This allows the leader to build trust within the unit while it undergoes the rigorous combat skills certification and theatre-specific training. The soldiers' confidence in their leaders, comrades, training, and leadership are key factors in lessening the detrimental effects of combat stressors.[11]

After deployment, the leader must be trained to ease the unit into the mission by initiating daytime operations before embarking on the more difficult operations at night. During this phase, the leader continues to build the leader-to-led relationship by discussing and absorbing critical operational experiences to include assisting soldiers cope with the initial experiences of combat stress. At this time, the leader must be trained to realise that the passage of information within the unit is key to maintaining cohesion, including the information regarding wounded and evacuated comrades. At this time, the leader needs to identify those soldiers with serious mental health issues and direct them to mental health professionals as necessary. Soldiers should be encouraged to relate their combat experiences and inner thoughts, and at the same time, the leader must be trained to identify soldiers showing signs of combat stress and refer them to a psychologist or chaplain as appropriate. Wherever possible, soldiers should have unrestricted access to medical and chaplain support so they can deal with their psychological problems. At all times, the unit commander must be trained to realise that their sound leadership, the unit's cohesion, and the close camaraderie amongst soldiers within the unit are essential to assure expeditious psychological recovery from combat stress.[12]

Now more than ever, it has become apparent that combat leadership is different from all other types of leadership, and as such, commanders at all levels must be trained to deal with this additional dimension. In this regard, the leader's tactical proficiency and professionalism are key to maintaining unit cohesion, as they must execute their mission and make decisions, while motivating their soldiers amidst noise, confusion, dust, explosions, and the screams of the wounded and dying. The leader must realise that discipline holds the unit together, while resilience and confidence, supported by the leader's competence, ensure battlefield effectiveness.[13] It is through training that the leader is able to add unanticipated conditions to the basic stress levels of training to create a demanding learning environment.

Jones (2012) found that the characteristics of the unit's leadership could have a significant impact on reducing the negative effects of stress on the unit's performance in combat operations. King (2013) identified that the leader's characteristics, including effective communication and motivational skill, could limit the influence of stress on team performance and significantly contribute to unit morale and efficiency. Additionally, De Becker (2012) argued that the quality of the leadership and the involvement of the leader with the unit were together able to significantly reduce stress-related performance decrements. Based on these studies, it is recommended that military planners should pay particular attention to developing junior and senior leaders who have the qualities to foster effective performance by their soldiers when under stress.[14] Therefore, in order to achieve this goal, this study recommends that the infantry must be given a fair and equal cross-section of all the available recruit talent rather than being allocated those with a lowest possible 26-point score on the BARB test. There is on old saying that: "a chain is only as strong as its weakest link," and this applies perfectly to the infantry that is based upon the lowest denominator, which is the 10-person infantry section.[15] The section is the foundation of the whole infantry edifice from platoon, to company, to battalion, to brigade, to division, to army. Unless the section is commanded by an effective leader, it will evaporate at the slightest pressure from the enemy, and once it disintegrates, the whole edifice above it will also be destroyed. The answer is the allocation to the infantry of a fair and balanced number of recruits and then the implementation of leadership development courses to ensure that the new generation of military leaders have the skills and abilities to lead in the face of uncertain future combat conditions.[16]

Each military leader must also be trained to realise that unit cohesion is another important moderator of stress at unit level. Unit cohesion, or esprit de corps, is defined as a strong affinity between soldiers within the unit who are committed to each other and the success of the unit. This unit cohesion is also characterised by egalitarianism, sensitivity, and consideration.[17] However, this cohesion will not occur spontaneously, and instead it is the leader's responsibility to create the climate within the unit that will promote growth in unit cohesion. To this end, the leader must be taught to introduce training exercises that encourage the soldiers to work together and build mutual trust amongst themselves and also respect and trust of the leader. Additionally, the leader must be taught that further unit cohesion can be fostered through the creation of shared experiences, the expectation of future interaction, and by the leader adopting a style that encourages soldiers to participate.

Huse (2009) found that there is evidence that successful unit performance increases unit cohesion, which suggests that cohesion and unit performance can operate in both directions. As importantly, his research found that higher levels of unit cohesion are associated with soldiers achieving more effective psychological coping when subjected to combat stressors.[18] Therefore, a cohesive unit provides the optimum support system for the soldiers within that unit during times of crisis, as it provides emotional support, timely information, instrumental assistance, and camaraderie. Gabriel (2010) during his study of the Vietnam War 1965-69 also supports this view that unit cohesion is a significant stress moderator that all levels of military leadership promote. His study examined the difference between units operating under a "unit replacement system" and those operating under an "individual replacement system." He found that those units who moved in and out of the theatre of operations as a formed unit displayed significantly more cohesion after their 356-day tour than units who had individual replacements move in and out of other units when an individual soldier had finished their own particular 365 days in country. This cohesion was apparent due to the incidence of higher reciprocal learning (the buddy system), higher personal morale, and lower levels of reported stress.[19]

Therefore, as the research conclusively demonstrates that cohesion moderates unit performance when soldiers experience combat stress, it behoves the military leadership to actively train the new generation of commanders to grasp the importance of unit training in a field environment. Gray (2008) suggests that the most important aspect of this unit training is an emphasis on communications and information, as this will foster a shared mental model where the soldiers within the unit think of a problem in the same, shared terms.[20] Eliot (2011) examined a specific type of training designated as team adaption and coordination training, which was found to contribute to the ability to perform under stress. The units that received this training and then feedback on their performance achieved the highest performance and teamwork results. The conclusion from this research is that the leader must be taught that in order to moderate the effects of stress on performance, training must include not only instruction, but as importantly, feedback in order for individual soldiers and junior commanders to modify their actions when placed in a combat stress environment.[21]

Finally, leadership training needs to encompass the awareness at all levels of command that a soldier's personality is one of the most significant Type 1 moderators, as those with high-anxiety Type A personalities have significantly more physiological and psychological responses to combat stressors than low-anxiety Type B individuals.[22] A Type 2 moderator is defined as one that affects the relationship between stress and performance. As an example, having additional information can act as a Type 2 moderator by improving a soldier's expectations, and in so doing, enhancing performance on a given task. As regards unit performance, cohesion and effective leadership have been identified as being important moderators of the stress-performance relationship. Therefore, it is the recommendation of this study that ensuring high-quality leadership by allocating to the infantry recruits that are a fair cross-section of all mental and physical abilities, and then fostering unit cohesion the military leadership at the highest levels can reduce the negative performance effects of combat stress.[23]

In conclusion, leadership training acts as a moderator for both soldiers and units, as prior exposure to operational-like situations and challenges will reduce uncertainty and improve a unit's military effectiveness. The importance of leadership training as a moderator is increased by the fact that it can be directly controlled and targeted to reduce the negative effects of combat stressors. Based on the results of this research, the most effective training should include combat-simulation training that is designed to build adaptive skills, promote unit communications, and is followed by feedback from the instructors.

# CHAPTER TWENTY ONE

## *Combat-Stress Teams*

Stress is an inherent part of life, with infantry combat being amongst the most stressful experiences that a human being can experience. A soldier's individual reaction to combat stress varies depending on personality, age, experience, training, and circumstances.[1] However, every soldier has a limit and can become a combat stress causality if exposed to intense and/ or long periods of battlefield exposure. Despite the common misconception, combat stress is not only caused by direct combat and can be affected when a soldier witnesses mass casualties or the death of a comrade. The symptoms can also be caused by non-violent pressures such as loneliness, boredom, and discomfort during extended service in isolated locations.[2] When this personal frustration within the soldier becomes unbearable, it may take the form of misconduct stress behaviours, discipline problems, drug/alcohol abuse or attacks upon fellow soldiers.

It must be stated that combat stress reactions are normal human responses to abnormal circumstances and are not a sign of weakness or cowardice and so should not be a cause of shame. It should also be realised that combat stress control is not primarily a medical problem, as it is a leadership responsibility at all levels of command, which is supported by an array of psychologists, medical professionals, and chaplains.[3] The research has identified that combat stress is better prevented than cured with leaders, aided by medical professionals, identifying and correcting controllable stressors in the unit, thus enabling soldiers to continue with the mission. The role of leaders at all levels of command is to increase their soldiers' resilience to the unavoidable stressors of combat by realistic training, creating unit morale and cohesion, ensuring that soldiers are kept informed, and inspiring them continuously.[4] The leader must also manage the soldiers within the unit in order to avoid, where possible, unnecessarily prolonged combat exposure, sleep loss, and physical or emotional exhaustion.

A key instrument in establishing and conducting an effective combat stress control programme starts with an assessment tool that is designed to determine the health of the unit and to identify key components that may require some level of support. This will allow the unit leadership to monitor the longitudinal health of the organisation and identify any stress-related concerns.[5] The key considerations when utilising this tool would be that the survey is anonymous and that soldiers are confident of their anonymity.

Mobilisation is where individuals or units are alerted for deployment and commence preparations for operational service. The mobilisation stressors that are experienced by soldiers include long working hours, combat-simulation training, fear of the future, and family worries. Signs of poor coping include insomnia, increased use of alcohol, marital problems, bickering within the unit, and irritability.[6] Therefore, during the preparation for deployment, leaders should direct the unit to practice stress-coping and relaxation techniques, and if necessary, the unit's health professional and chaplains can provide additional support. Overloading soldiers with additional tasks and responsibilities is another major source of stress, and as a result, leaders must allocate duties fairly among the available soldiers. Another consideration is family stress. This will add to combat imposed stressors, will cause the soldier to be distracted, and will interfere with their performance of essential tasks.[7]

Deployment, in addition to the normal stress associated with moving to a combat zone, causes soldiers to begin worrying about their survival and performance under fire. At this point, unit leaders should emphasise that stress under these circumstance is an expected natural reaction. Unit leaders should provide as much information as possible, reinforce stress control techniques, and help their soldiers to understand what happens to them when stressors occur. The issuing of warning, operational, and fragmentary orders is critical to ensuring adequate information flow, as it reinforces the importance of the unit organisation and chain of command.[8] This accurate information also reduces the negative effects of rumours, while the accurate knowledge of the unit's mission builds unit cohesion, develops a positive attitude, and reduces the effects of stress.

Medical practitioners who are members of the military health professions are responsible for providing direct treatment for those military service members whose adverse combat stress reactions cannot be managed by their military commanders.[9] Therefore, the recommendation based on the findings from this study is that to improve prevention, "early identification," and optimal management of adverse stress reactions, a closer partnership is needed between military leaders and military mental health professionals who can directly help the soldiers.[10] To treat combat stress, military mental health professionals should be embedded in combat units at the level of battalion/regiment rather than attaching them to specialised external medical health/treatment – hospitals/facilities. Psychiatrists, psychologists, and psychiatric technicians should be organic to the military units that they support in the same way that battalion/regiment doctors, medics and padres are organic to their combat units.

These military medical health professionals should train with their battalion/regiment prior to combat deployment, then accompany their units into forward combat areas during deployment, and continue to provide support to their units after deployment. The aim behind this recommendation is to build a cultural bridge between combat soldiers and military mental health professionals by drawing the latter as fully as possible into the culture and life of the combat unit they are supporting.[11] The prevention, "early identification," and effective treatment at the lowest level possible should be the goals of the military mental health professionals who are serving in battalions/regiments. It is believed that this will achieve more effective care within units, will increase the early access to specialised mental health care, and lower rates of long-term combat-related stress disorders being suffered by soldiers.

Therefore, the recommendation is that, dedicated integral "Combat Stress Teams" (CSTs), which provide prevention and treatment within infantry units and within the normal part of the units' military organisation are established within the Army.[12] The primary responsibility of the CSTs would be the prevention, triage, and short-term treatment of combat stress reaction. These CSTs should consist of a psychologist or psychiatrist, psychiatric nurse, occupational therapist, two mental health specialists, and two occupational therapy specialists. They should be strategically placed with forward units in order to prevent and treat combat stress reaction. By educating the unit commander about the roles and responsibilities of the CSTs, this would enable the leader to more quickly and accurately identify the onset of combat stress within the unit. The CSTs would also be able to apply psychometric and qualitative techniques in order to provide the commander with specific issues that could contribute to decreased morale and, once identified, would provide recommendations for improved unit effectiveness.[13]

The CSTs would also provide preventative education to soldiers through briefings on suicide prevention, stress, and anger management. Another important strategy envisioned for the CSTs would be that members of the team would visit sub-units and talk with soldiers individually and in their own environment. If a higher level of care is identified as being required, then the soldier can be referred to the licensed provider for a more in-depth intervention or additional counselling sessions. Another crucial service would be provided by the CSTs through post-combat debriefings, as after a stressful incident, the health professionals can help soldiers normalise feelings and challenge distressing beliefs.[14] This debriefing would provide a safe environment for the soldiers to process the traumatic or stressful incident on several levels without fear of reprimand or stigmatisation from their command.

The CSTs treatment for soldiers suffering from the symptoms of combat stress would be based upon assurance, rest, and physical replenishment. If a soldier is in need of services greater than the prevention team can provide, the soldier will be sent to the treatment team for as little as one day or several days depending on the severity of the combat stress symptoms. If the soldier is suffering from depression or anxiety symptoms, then psychotherapeutic interventions, such as cognitive or solution-focused therapy can be provided. With proper rest and treatment, the vast majority of the soldiers seen by the treatment team should be able to return to duty. Within the CSTs, it is envisaged that all team members, whether officers or enlisted men, will participate both in the prevention and treatment regimes for the soldiers. In this regard, command consultations, psycho-educational briefs, walkabouts, crisis debriefings, and distribution of informational handouts would be conducted by all CST personnel.[15] The primary functions of the CSTs' members are envisaged as being those of psychiatrist, psychologist, psychiatric nurses, occupational therapist, and mental health/occupational therapy specialists.

The psychiatrists would be responsible for the diagnosis, treatment, and disposition of soldiers with combat stress and psychiatric disorders. As a physician, the psychiatrist would conduct medication consultations and prescribe psychotropic or other medications where appropriate. The psychiatrist would assist with triage by ruling out medical etymologies that may better explain a soldier's clinical condition.[16] Additionally, the psychiatrist would assist in the education of the CSTs personnel and unit leaders regarding the identification and appropriate response to combat stress. When the CST was located near a combat support hospital or medical treatment facility, the psychiatrist would be consulted about soldiers with co-occurring psychiatric symptoms.

The psychologists would be responsible for distinguishing between combat stress and mental health disorders. When undergoing triage, the psychologist would evaluate soldiers using clinical interviewing and psychometric assessment tools. These assessments would enable the identification of combat stress and neuropsychiatric disorders, thereby making recommendations for the prevention and treatment of soldiers.[17] When identified, soldiers with combat stress would be treated with a variety of individual and group psychological interventions and techniques. Additionally, the psychologist would supervise subordinate personnel in the provision of clinical services.

The CSTs' psychiatric nurses would possess clinical skills and expertise that could be drawn upon in various ways, depending on the particular requirements. The psychiatric nurse would assist the psychiatrist with medication consultations as well as assisting in the individual and group treatments. This would include both preventive and treatment interventions.

The physiological and psychological effects of combat on soldiers can result in a number of behavioural anomalies within the individual. When these rise to the level of combat stress, a negative impact on the soldier's military performance will inevitably result. As a result, the occupational therapists would be trained to assess and rehabilitate functional impairments that are negatively affecting the individual's mental well-being.[18] The occupational therapist would assess the soldier's duty task requirements along with the soldier's current capability in order to structure a therapeutic environment that reconditions the soldier and returns them to their place of duty. The occupational therapist would also consult with unit commanders on the ways to minimise the effects of combat stress on the unit's military performance.

Mental health specialists and occupational therapy specialists would be enlisted personnel who have completed specialised training in basic clinical skills and interviewing. In addition to all the preventative activities, these specialists would be trained to conduct interviews, participate in mass casualty interventions, structure and oversee occupational therapy programmes, and escort psychiatric casualties during medical evacuations.[19] Additionally, as enlisted personnel, they would be responsible for all the basic tactical training of the members of the CST.

Therefore, the design of combat stress management would be based upon leaders throughout the chain of command who would be assisted by medical professionals and chaplains as required. As the next level of support, the CSTs would provide medical professionals including psychiatrists, social workers, clinical psychologists, psychiatric nurses, occupational therapists, and enlisted specialists. The CST personnel would be responsible for talking to soldiers in order to identify problems early, advise unit commanders on stress prevention, conduct classes and debriefings, train unit personnel to be able to identify the early onset of combat stress, and assist overstressed soldiers to continue their duties. The CST personnel would provide one-on-one stress-control counselling to overstressed soldiers either forward with the unit or at their own support location. In this regard, the CST will be required to provide tents and staff where soldiers who become stressed can stay in their unit location and get one to three days' rest, including fresh meals and sleep, in order to regain their self-confidence.[20] However, inevitably the CST personnel will identify soldiers who will require more specialised treatment at medical facilities. The forward provision of such support within units is likely to make the identification and treatment of the physiological and psychological effects of combat on soldiers more effective. This would reduce the likelihood of internal stigmas acting as barriers to the reporting of such illnesses, while at the same time ensuring the psychiatric doctrine of operational care for soldiers.

At the moment, British infantry battalions have a regimental medical officer and a medical platoon that provides integral medical support to the unit. Both the regimental medical officer and the medical platoon are an integral part of each battalions "war and peace establishments."[21] As a result, in peace while training for combat, a respect and rapport is built between the regimental medical officer (battalion doctor) and the medical platoon, who operate on a daily basis within the unit's barracks from the Regimental Aid Post (RAP) or battalion medical facility. This is delivered by combat medical technicians or medical assistants who support the unit's medical officer. However, the combat medical technician and medical assistant training does not currently cover the nature of psychological health disorders caused by the negative effects of combat on soldiers. Nor does it prepare them to conduct a psychologically focused consultation.[22] The conclusion from this study is that the training of combat medical technicians and medical assistants at unit level should include the relationship between reporting sick and mental health, combined with training in psychological combat stress symptoms. This will enable the identification of those requiring psychological assistance at the earliest opportunity.

The recommended reorganisation would see mental health personnel as integral in the medical support provided to battalions, brigades and divisions with them being provided with psychiatrists, social workers, and enlisted specialists. Reinforcing the CSTs would be small mobile teams who would be able to deploy forward to company level with a tailored mix of personnel from the five mental health disciplines, including psychiatric nursing and occupational theory. These teams would have their own vehicles in order to be able to move forward and support the tactical units down to company level for one to three days.[23] Each CST would support one division or two to three separate brigades/regiments. The CST would consist of three four-person combat stress control preventative teams that would be able to move forward to brigade support areas when requested. There would also be a CST fitness restoration that could run a combat fitness centre in the division support area or the corps forward area.

All these recommendations are based on the substantial body of research evidence that has found that the effective and immediate treatment of combat stress symptoms, based upon in-field intervention programmes can reduce the long-term effects of stress on the individual soldier. This intervention emphasises four aspects, with these being: proximity (treatment facilities adjacent to unit), immediacy (treat as soon as the symptoms occur), expectancy (tell the soldier that they will recover and return to their unit), and simplicity (offer rest, nourishment, and medical assistance).[24] The further research by Fishback (2008) on this method of treatment intervention has found that soldiers so treated are no more likely to display long-term PTSD than soldiers who never displayed any stress symptoms. Importantly, this method makes use of several moderators, as discussed above, these being unit cohesion, expectations, anticipation, and self-efficacy.[25]

Other unit level moderators are leadership qualities where the leader with good communication skills and motivational characteristics can increase morale and efficiency of their unit and so reduce the effects of stress on unit performance. Then unit cohesion can reduce the negative effects of stress on unit performance by fostering more effective psychological coping. Finally, units that are exposed to combat-simulation training and then receive feedback on their performance reduces the incidence of combat stress symptoms by developing a shared mental model among the soldiers within the unit.

In conclusion, the concept of CSTs is derived from the findings of this study and has as its basis the recognition of the negative effects that combat stress has on soldiers and a unit mission accomplishment. As a result, the creation, development, and refinement of specialised behavioural health teams are recommended. Through the utilisation of both professionals and para-professionals trained in preventing and treating combat stress in soldiers, it is believed that the Army would be better able to maintain unit and mission capabilities.

# CHAPTER TWENTY TWO

## *Future Research*

As a result of the findings from this research study, there are two recommendations for future research, both of which are designed to facilitate the selection and screening of candidates wishing to become infantry soldiers. The first recommendation for future research is that there is a longitudinal study conducted within the military community into the long-term effects of combat on infantry soldiers with randomly selected control and test groups. The second recommendation for future research is that there is a comprehensive study into how the experience of various forms of childhood adversity increases the likelihood that soldiers who experience combat stress will develop the symptoms of depression and PTSD after their operational deployment.

As regards the first recommendation for future research, it is suggested that the study uses the Minnesota Multiphasic Personality Inventory (MMPI), which is the most frequently used psychological test for military PTSD sufferers.[1] Although there are many very high-quality personality tests used by psychologists, the MMPI and its updated versions have been used for over 70 years. The MMPI series is very useful for many types of psychological issues, and the MMPI-2-RF is the most used test by military psychologists when attempting to detect PTSD symptoms.[2]

The MMPI was developed in the late 1930s by psychologist Strake R. Hathaway and psychiatrist J.C. McKinley at the University of Minnesota. It is a psychological test that assesses personality traits and psychopathology. Today, it is the most frequently used clinical testing instrument and is one of the most researched psychological tests in existence. The MMPI is currently administered in one of two forms, either the MMPI-2, which has 567 true/false questions, or the newer MMPI-2-RF, which was only produced in 2008 and has only 338 true/false questions.³ The MMPI is a protected psychological instrument that can only be administered and interpreted by a trained psychologist. The psychological testing is preceded by a clinical interview by the psychologist who will administer the test. Once the test is complete, the psychologist completes a report that interprets the test results in the context of the test recipients personal history and current psychological concerns.

The MMPI-2-RF is designed with 10 clinical sub-scales which assess 10 major categories of abnormal human behaviour, and four validity scales, which assess the test recipients general test-taking attitude, and as a result whether they answered the items on the test in a truthful and accurate manner.⁴ Based upon the results of answering certain questions on the test in a certain manner, the 10 clinical sub-scales are as follows:

 a. **Hypochondriasis (Hs).** This sub-scale has two primary factors and measures poor physical health and gastrointestinal difficulties. The sub-scale contains 32 items.
 b. **Depression (D).** This sub-scale measures clinical depression. The sub-scale contains 57 items.
 c. **Hysteria (Hy).** This sub-scale measures five components. These are poor physical health, shyness, cynicism, headaches, and neuroticism. The sub-scale contains 60 items.
 d. **Psychopathic Deviate (Pd).** This sub-scale measures social maladjustment and the absence of pleasant experiences. The sub-scale contains 50 items.
 e. **Masculinity/Femininity (Mf).** This sub-scale measures interests in vocations and hobbies, aesthetic preferences, activity-passivity, and personal sensitivity. It measures in a general sense how rigidly an individual conforms to very stereotypical masculine and feminine roles. The sub-scale contains 56 items.

*f.* **Paranoia (Pa).** This sub-scale measures interpersonal sensitivity, moral self-righteousness, and suspiciousness. The sub-scale contains 40 items.

*g.* **Psychasthenia (Pt).** This sub-scale measures an individual's inability to resist specific actions or thoughts, which is now called obsessive-compulsive disorder (OCD). This sub-scale also examines abnormal fears, self-criticisms, difficulties in concentration and guilt feelings. This sub-scale contains 48 items.

*h.* **Schizophrenia (Sc).** This sub-scale measures strange thoughts, peculiar perceptions, social alienation, poor interpersonal relationships, difficulties concentrating and controlling impulses, lack of interests, disturbing questions of self-worth and self-identity. This sub-scale contains 78 items and so has more than any other sub-scale on the test.

*i.* **Hypomania (Ma).** This sub-scale measures milder degrees of excitement and examines over activity, both behaviourally and cognitively, irritability and egocentricity. This sub-scale contains 46 items.

*j.* **Social Introversion (Si).** This sub-scale measures the social introversion and extroversion of an individual. The sub-scale contains 69 items.[5]

The MMPI-2-RF also contains four validity scales, and these are designed to measure an individual's test-taking attitude and approach to the test. They are as follows:

*a.* **Lie (L).** The Lie scale identifies individuals who are deliberately trying to avoid answering the MMPI-2-RF honestly by measuring the individual's attitudes and practices. The scale contains 15 items.

*b.* **F (F).** The F scale is intended to detect unusual or atypical ways of answering the test items by examining strange thoughts, peculiar experiences, feelings of isolation and alienation as well as contradictory beliefs, expectations, and/or self-descriptions. The F scale items are scattered throughout the entire test up until around item 360. The scale contains 60 items.

*c.* **Back F (Fb).** The Back F scale measures the same issues as the F scale, but only during the second half of the test. The scale contains 40 items.

*d.* **K (K).** The K scale is designed to identify psychopathology in individual's who would otherwise have normal profiles. It measures self-control, and family and inter-personal relationships. Those who score highly on the scale are often defensive in nature. The scale contains 30 items.[6]

As indicated, the MMPI-2 contains 567 test items and takes approximately 90 minutes to complete, while the MMPI-2-RF contains 338 questions and takes 30-50 minutes to complete.[7] The MMPI can be administered both individually and in groups and has a computerised version available. Due to the increasing sophistication and reliability of the MMPI in 2012, the Department of Defense authorised the MMPI-2-RF to be administered to 251 National Guard soldiers who had recently returned from deployments in Afghanistan. The soldiers were also administered questionnaires to identify PTSD and mild traumatic brain injury (mTBI). As a result of the tests, the soldiers were classified into four groups: 21 soldiers were diagnosed with PTSD, 33 soldiers were diagnosed with mTBI, 9 soldiers were screened positive for both conditions, and 166 soldiers did not screen positive for either condition.[8] These findings support the use of the MMPI-2-RF in assessing PTSD and mTBI in non-treatment-seeking veterans.

It is recommended for future research that the military use scientific methods to gather data on the effects of pre-combat psychological training. A longitudinal study that utilises the MMPI-2-RF would be beneficial for future generations of soldiers who experience the stress of combat operations. The advantage of the MMPI-2-RF is that it is the most used and most researched psychological test in the world.[9] A particular strength of the MMPI-2-RF is its measures of validity. This research can be accomplished within the military community and in order to address the problem of whether combat stress and PTSD can be reduced or prevented through preventative training and effective leadership soldiers would be administered the MMPI-2-RF before deploying on combat operations. The test and control groups would be randomly selected with an infantry battalion being given extensive pre-combat psychological training prior to deployment, and the control group, consisting of another infantry battalion, would receive no more than the current pre-deployment training. Then both infantry battalions would require to be deployed on the same combat operation, at the same time, in order to ensure that the conditions, circumstances and dangers were equally experienced. It is recommended that Army psychologists administer the MMPI-2-RF to all the soldiers within the two battalions before and after their operational deployments.

The results of this study would determine what percentages of soldiers from each infantry battalion (study group) were suffering from combat stress or PTSD. As the symptoms of combat stress or PTSD may develop immediately or in some cases over months or even years, it is recommended that the soldiers are tested immediately after returning home from the operational deployment. Then due to the delayed nature of the appearance of the symptoms in some soldiers, it is recommended that the soldiers are once again tested three months and the six months after their return home, as this will identify the great proportion of the cases. Then tests could be conducted every year for the next five years dependent on the availability of the soldiers through discharge, retirement, and/or unwillingness to continue with the study. It is realised that this recommended study would require authorisation from the relevant MoD authorities and due to the sensitivity of the information and the intricacies of the MMPI-2-RF tests the Army Medical Corps psychological department would be required to manage the whole study.[10]

The second recommendation for future research is that there is a comprehensive study into how the experience of various forms of childhood adversity increases the likelihood that soldiers who experience combat

stress will develop the symptoms of depression and PTSD after their operational deployment. As regards this topic, one previous study by Cabrera, Hoge, Bliese, Castro, and Messer (2007) demonstrated a relationship
between childhood adversity and health outcomes in later life. Also, current research has shown a stable association between childhood adversity
and behavioural difficulties in later life.[11] The research has also shown a
relationship between adults' exposure to combat and mental health outcomes. However, little is known about whether childhood adversity adds
to the risk associated with combat exposure, or if childhood adversity and
combat exposure interact in predicting mental health.

To date, the most comprehensive study of the relationship between
childhood adversity and health was the adverse childhood experience
study carried out by Foa and Riggs (1993). This was a large retrospective
examination of over 8,000 adults queried about their exposure to seven
types of adverse childhood experiences. The results showed a correlation
between these experiences and heart disease, obesity, drug abuse, depression, and suicidal tendencies.[12] Also, other research has shown that adverse childhood experiences were related to other health outcomes such
as alcohol abuse and smoking behaviours.[13]

As regards combat experiences, as demonstrated throughout this research study, it is related positively to depression and PTSD with the lifetime rates among British Army veterans being substantially higher than
those of the civilian population. Also as shown in this study, increases
in these symptoms following combat has also been documented among
U.S. veterans of the recent wars in Afghanistan and Iraq.[14] Finally, combat stress has also been shown to have a significant impact on depression,
and these findings suggests that exposure to war trauma is a critical factor
in fostering mental health impairment.[15]

The study, previously referred to, by Cabrera et al. (2007) examined:
(1) rates of adverse childhood experience in two samples of male soldiers,
one that deployed to Iraq and one that had not, (2) the association between adverse childhood experience and depression and PTSD in the
two samples, (3) the independent predictive value of adverse childhood
experience and combat exposure in the post-Iraq sample, and (4) the

interaction between adverse childhood experience and combat in predicting depression and PTSD symptoms in the post-Iraq sample.[16] The pre-Iraq sample, interviewed in 2003, consisted of 4,529 soldiers who had not deployed to Iraq. The post-Iraq sample consisted of 2,392 soldiers surveyed three months after returning from Iraq in 2004.[17] All the participants were male soldiers serving on active duty in infantry units of combat brigades. The soldiers were recruited for the study under a human protocol approved by the Institutional Review Board of the Walter Reed Army Institute of Research. The written consent was obtained from each soldier and the surveys were anonymous.[18]

In the study, childhood adversity was measured by exposure to six adverse experiences: (1) exposure to a mentally ill person in the family home, (2) exposure to an alcoholic person in the family home, (3) sexual abuse, (4) physical abuse, (5) psychological abuse, and (6) violence directed against the respondent's mother.[19] Depression was measured using a nine-item scale, the Patient Health Questionnaire (PHQ), which has demonstrated excellent psychometric properties and substantial convergent validity. Post-traumatic stress disorder was measured using the 17-item PTSD checklist (PCL). Combat exposure among post-Iraq soldiers was measured using a 29-item scale measured on a five-point Likert-type scale (1="never" to 5="ten or more times"). Examples of these possible combat experiences that the soldiers could have been exposed to included: (1) being attacked or ambushed, (2) handling or uncovering human remains, and (3) shooting at the enemy. The analysis of this data was conducted from 2005-2006. A five-point adverse childhood experience predictor was created that recorded the following: (1) no adverse childhood experiences, (2) one experience, (3) two experiences, (4) three experiences, and (5) four or more experiences.[20]

The results were consistent and among post-Iraq soldiers, the odds of depression rose from 2.2 with one adverse childhood experience to 6.1 for soldiers with four or more adverse childhood experiences. In the analysis of PTSD, the odds of depression rose from 1.6 with one adverse childhood experience to 4.9 for soldiers with four or more adverse childhood experiences.[21] As mentioned, this was the first study to assess the relationship between mental outcomes and adverse childhood experiences among soldiers who had recently returned from combat. The results, which held true for both the pre- and post-Iraq samples, showed that soldiers who reported two or more adverse childhood experiences were at an increased risk of being diagnosed with depression and PTSD. The analysis of the post-Iraq sample showed that adverse childhood experiences were a significant predicator of depression and PTSD above and beyond the effects of combat exposure alone. These findings are significant, as they show that developmental trauma, described in the study as adverse childhood experiences, compound the detrimental effects of combat exposure.[22] Therefore, there is a lack of data on the existence of depression and PTSD relative to the intersection between early childhood trauma when it is followed by combat-induced, adult trauma. Therefore, further research in this field is strongly recommended.

In conclusion, there are two recommendations for future research, both of which are designed to facilitate the selection and screening of candidates wishing to become infantry soldiers. The first recommendation for future research is that there is a longitudinal study conducted within the military community into the long-term effects of combat on infantry soldiers with randomly selected control and test groups. The second recommendation for future research is that there is a comprehensive study into how the experience of various forms of childhood adversity increases the likelihood that soldiers who experience combat stress will develop the symptoms of depression and PTSD after their operational deployment.

# CHAPTER TWENTY THREE

## *Infantry of the Future*

The primary purpose of any military force is to win battles by being successful in combat, as this will be a "war-winner." Simply stated, the objective is to overwhelm the enemy with so much stress that they submit and surrender. However, at the same time, the enemy is also subjecting our own forces to the physical stress of injury and death as well as the emotional and psychological stress that plagues all soldiers involved in combat. Therefore, the loss of soldiers, not through death or injury received on the battlefield, but instead through the physiological and psychological effects of combat on soldiers can be a "war-loser." As a result, a fundamental requirement for any successful army is to have effective pre-combat education programmes and leadership training in place which will lessen and militate against the effects of combat on their infantry soldiers.

This basic premise of this study is that combat forces soldiers to go beyond the paradigms of ordinary life experiences, as when a soldier takes another human life, they are catapulted far beyond the range of "normal" human behaviour. However, to survive and be victorious in combat, soldiers must aggressively seek out and kill or capture the enemy. This has far-reaching physiological and psychological implications, as this "killer instinct" becomes a very real impulse for soldiers in the heat of battle. The fact is that a soldier suffers physiologically and psychologically when the body and mind are triggered to kill another human being, as it cuts across everything the soldier has been taught about "the sanctity of life." So, at the end of each battle, and when the war is over, the images and sounds of combat are still present in the minds of the soldiers involved.

As this study has discovered, many soldiers have deployed to a war zone trained to kill the enemy, but few if any received adequate pre-combat education programmes or leadership interventions that prepared them physiologically and psychologically for the reality of combat. The current reality is that soldiers deploy to war and are expected to be victorious in life or death combat operations never having been trained to physiologically or psychologically withstand the shock of taking a life or losing a close comrade. As one veteran interviewed for this study described it: "I feel that the military expects soldiers to walk through fire without ever getting burned, but the memories of combat that are forever seared in my mind are impossible to avoid."

As shown in the past, the medical profession did not really understand the effects of trauma on soldiers who had experienced combat to the extent that they do today. As a result of the most recent research, which has included in-depth interviews with combat veterans from the recent war in Afghanistan, we now know that battle-hardened veterans are reluctant to talk about their physiological and psychological experiences during and after combat. A part of this reluctance is because of the risk they take in admitting a combat stress related problem when this fact will reflect poorly on their military record. By admitting continuing stress problems, a soldier will most assuredly be immediately "down-graded medically," which will then be followed by a battery of medical and psychological examinations. These could result in the combat veteran not being returned to "active duty" and cleared for further operational deployments. However, even if this is not the case, the soldier will have reports on his medical record indicating that he has suffered from combat stress, and this will be extremely detrimental to his promotion prospects. On the other hand, if there is the slightest doubt raised by the examinations into combat-related stress, then the combat veteran will be "medically down-graded" and categorised as "non-deployable." In this case, the soldier may be "medically discharged" or failing this have his promotion prospects and any possible extension of military service curtailed.

Of course, the practical implication of this recommendation contradict the centuries old popular view that "anyone can be made into an infantryman" and that recruits who do not have the academic and/or technical ability to join the specialised armour, artillery, signals, engineers, intelligence, aviation, for instance are "the dross of society" who will naturally become the next generation of infantry "cannon fodder." Therefore, historically when the allocation to various branches was being made, the brightest and best were allocated to these premier specialised units, and those that were left over and nobody particularly wanted were allocated to "the poor bloody infantry," so named as they always suffer the greatest casualties in any war. However, in the light of the findings from this study, which are based upon the recent war in Afghanistan, the reverse is in fact true, as when the allocation to branches is being made, then those recruits with the best physical stamina and mental resilience, who are able to endure the physiological and psychological stress of combat, must be allocated to the infantry.

Therefore, the major recommendation of this study is for a total re-evaluation by the military, at the highest level of the MoD, in order to address the current glaring omissions in how infantry soldiers are prepared for the negative physiological and psychological of combat. As detailed above, this study has made five recommendations designed to prepare the next generation of British Army infantry soldiers for the new asymmetric 21st century battlefield that they will face when deployed on future combat operations. These recommendations are selection/screening, stress-management programmes, combat-simulation training, leadership training, and the creation of dedicated and integral Combat Stress Teams within infantry units. At this point, it is worth examining this author's criterion for making these five recommendations.

## Infantry Selection and Screening

The combat role of the infantry is to engage, fight, kill or capture the enemy at close range using a firearm, edged weapon, or bare hands, in close-quarter combat. The physical, mental, and environmental operating demands of the infantryman are extreme with combat loads weighing 60+ lbs being normal, foot patrols of 20-25 miles a day in undulating or mountainous terrain being common, and in temperatures ranging from

+30 degrees to -30 degrees Celsius. There also needs to be a realisation of the stress levels that the individual infantry soldier faced on the asymmetric battlefields of Afghanistan and Iraq, where the threat was from 360 degrees, during 24 hours a day, and over 365 days of the year.

These conditions demand the highest levels of physical endurance and mental resilience. However, currently within the British Army when infantry soldier candidates present themselves, their aptitude is assessed by the British Army Recruit Battery (BARB) test,[1] the results of which generate the General Trainability Index (GTI) score.[2] The GTI score is used to determine which roles are available to prospective soldiers. The maximum score for the BARB test in its current form is 80 points. The significance of this score is that the infantry are allocated recruits with the lowest BARB test results of 26 points, with recruits needing at least 38 points to be allocated to the artillery, which is the next lowest category.[3]

Also of note is the fact that the British Army has long had a policy where recruits are placed into specialisations that match their civilian employment or educational background/qualifications. This policy finds computer technicians being allocated to the signals, builders to the engineers, students to the intelligence, electricians to the electrical and mechanical engineers, etc. These measures have simplified the requirement for technical training within the Army, but the problem of combat training has been rendered that much more difficult, as the infantry is left with sub-average recruits. The fact is that higher grades on the GTI disqualified recruits from being allocated to the infantry, and this has resulted in the lower categories of recruits being over-represented in the infantry. As a result of this allocation of recruits, field commanders at all levels have complained that they have been receiving recruits of such a low level of mental and physical ability that they are unable to be trained. The current failure rate at Infantry Training Battalions (ITBs) is an unsustainable 30% of recruits. Obviously, this disproportionate allocation of sub-average recruits to the infantry also affects the ability to select and train junior and senior NCOs at platoon and company level.

A further factor when considering infantry selection is that medical researchers have found a version of the 5-HTTLPR gene, which controls levels of serotonin, a chemical within the brain which is related to mood and fuels the fear response in humans.[4] Also, the latest scientific research findings indicate that, as with other mental disorders, many genes, each with small effects, are at work in creating combat stress and PTSD. The findings indicate that individual differences in genes and brain area set the stage for combat stress and PTSD without causing the symptoms. This means that soldiers with these genes will be more susceptible to combat stress. New research also shows that environmental factors, such as childhood trauma, head injury, or a history of mental illness, will further increase the risk. Therefore, identifying soldiers for behavioural-health problems before they deploy to a combat zone could reduce suicidal thoughts, psychiatric disorders, and other mental problems. The findings indicate that individual differences in genes and brain area set the stage for combat stress and PTSD without causing the symptoms. This means that soldiers with these genes will be more susceptible to combat stress, and as a result, through the introduction of a robust selection and screening process, these soldiers should not be selected to serve in infantry combat units.

## Stress-Management Programmes

The findings from this study indicate that the incidence of combat stress caused by the physiological and psychological effects of combat on infantry soldiers can be lessened, or at least minimised through stress-management and stress-coping programmes. As a result, it is recommended that education in the form of stress-management exercises be introduced during pre-deployment training. This will be designed to deal with the physiological and psychological effects of combat and will teach soldiers about the stressful phenomena that they will find in combat. Much self-induced stress comes from the lack of education, and so if soldiers are trained before combat about the sensations that they will encounter in combat, it is believed that this will eliminate some causes of stress and reduce the effects of many others. The number one priority should be to provide stress inoculation and mental preparation to infantry soldiers in what is now described as "resilience training," which encapsulates the education programmes and leadership training that makes infantry soldiers genuinely more capable in combat by increasing robustness and resistance to mental stressors. These education programmes and leadership training interventions would increase the unit's professionalism and cohesion, while at the same time developing esprit de corps through social and emotional bonding, which will itself increase the psychological resilience of the infantry soldiers within the unit.

High-intensity and high-stress conditions frequently lead to disrupted performance, as stress affects the soldier's physiological, psychological, cognitive, emotional, and social processes. When soldiers face combat stressors that disrupt goal-orientated behaviour, the effects will be increased errors, slower responses, and greater variance in performance. As a result, the preparation of soldiers for combat requires that they be highly skilled, be aware of the stress environment they will experience, and be trained in the skills necessary to overcome these high-stress conditions. However, the absolute realism of the stress-management programmes is not possible or totally desirable. The desire by some trainers to re-create a real-life threatening experience for soldiers is not possible, as the trainees will always realise that they are in a safe training environment. However, well-designed simulation training can feel like the real thing without imposing unnecessary high levels of stress, as these may prove detrimental to the training. The research had found that stressors introduced at a moderate level of realism during training will provide a realistic representation of a combat environment.

## Combat-Simulation Training

There are many studies that offer empirical evidence of the positive effects of training programmes on reducing the physiological and psychological effects of combat stress. The research examined the effects of relaxation training on performance, with those that received the training reporting lower levels of anxiety and increased self-efficiency, which both acted indirectly in reducing the effects of stress on performance. The research found that even though each single training session was beneficial, there was a significant positive relationship between the number of training sessions and the effect of the training on improving performance and reducing stress-related anxiety. These results suggest that military leaders can utilise combat-simulation training to reduce their soldiers susceptibility to stressors and further identified that the results were better when the training included some form of behavioural practice, when the size of the training group was small (no more than a 10-person infantry section), and when the training occurred in a field training environment. These results confirmed that effectively structured combat-simulation training moderates the effects of stress on soldiers' performance both when performing mental and physical tasks.

The recommendation from the findings is that there is the introduction of combat-simulation training that increases the sensory fidelity and interactional realism of a virtual environment that will enhance the transfer of training from the simulation to the real world. It was found that learning that which took place under specific physiological and psychological conditions will have a higher probability of being recalled when the initial physiological and psychological states that the learning initially occurred under is present. The findings suggest that if combat-simulation training is to effectively transfer to criterion environments that may engender a range of innate stress reactions, then that training should be conducted while the soldier is experiencing a similar range of emotional states. As military operations are constantly in a state of dynamic change, adult learning theory would dictate that that optimal combat-simulation training should also include a wide range of emotional conditions in order to counteract the possibility of negative transfer and to promote successful performance in combat environments.

## Leadership Training

It must be understood by military leaders that combat is sudden, intense and life threatening and that the stresses experienced by their soldiers will be traumatic. The most effective ways to confront combat stress and to reduce psychological breakdown in combat is for the leader to admit that fear is a natural reaction when faced with a life-threatening situation. The leaders must ensure that that the lines of communication are open between them and their subordinates. They must treat combat stress reactions as combat injuries, recognise the limits of their soldiers' endurance, and openly discuss the moral implications of their soldier's behaviour during combat. In order to reduce stress, the leader needs to inspire their subordinates, initiate and support stress-management programmes, ensure that each soldier has mastered at least two stress-coping techniques, a slow one for deep relaxation and an immediate one to cope with unexpectedly stressful situations.

Therefore, it is recommended that the military leader be designated the responsibility for mitigating the impact of combat stress on their unit and its soldiers. It is believed that this will create one of the missing links, transforming the military from a passive to an active stance in the fight to minimise the short and long-term negative effects of combat stress. Therefore, to achieve this aim, it is recommended that education is expanded past the military medical health professionals and chaplains to include military leaders and soldiers, as they are the individuals that are directly affected by the physiological and psychological effects of combat stress. Education related to combat stress should be added to officer, non-commissioned officer and recruit courses, commencing at these initial basic courses, but then continuing throughout officers, non-commissioned officer and a soldier's full military career. That is every course that military personnel attend throughout their 20-30 year careers should contain modules within each that re-educate all ranks on the latest interventions to prevent, identify, and treat combat stress. This will ensure that those military leaders have the requisite knowledge and training to use all the available resources to counter combat stress.

## Combat Stress Teams

Medical practitioners who are members of the military health professions are responsible for providing direct treatment for those military service members whose adverse combat stress reactions cannot be managed by their military commanders. Therefore, the recommendation based on the findings from this study is that to improve prevention, "early identification," and optimal management of adverse stress reactions, a closer partnership is needed between military leaders and military mental health professionals who can directly help the soldiers. To treat combat stress, military mental health professionals should be embedded in combat units at the level of battalion/regiment, rather than attaching them to specialised external medical health/treatment – hospitals/facilities. Psychiatrists, psychologists, and psychiatric technicians should be organic to the military units that they support in the same way that battalion/regiment doctors, medics and padres are organic to their combat units.

These military medical health professionals should train with their battalion/regiment prior to combat deployment, then accompany their units into forward combat areas during deployment, and continue to provide support to their units after deployment. The aim behind this recommendation is to build a cultural bridge between combat soldiers and military mental health professionals by drawing the latter as fully as possible into the culture and life of the combat unit they are supporting. The prevention, "early identification," and effective treatment at the lowest level possible should be the goals of the military mental health professionals who are serving in battalions/regiments. It is believed that this will achieve more effective care within units, will increase the early access to specialised mental health care, and lower rates of long-term combat-related stress disorders being suffered by soldiers.

Therefore, the recommendation is that there is the establishment within in the Army of dedicated integral "Combat Stress Teams" (CSTs) that provide prevention and treatment within infantry units, within the normal part of the units' military organisation. The primary responsibility of the CSTs would be the prevention, triage, and short-term treatment of combat stress reaction. These CSTs should consist of a psychologist or psychiatrist, psychiatric nurse, occupational therapist, two mental health specialists, and two occupational therapy specialists. They should be strategically placed with forward units in order to prevent and treat combat stress reaction. By educating the unit commander about the roles and responsibilities of the CSTs, this would enable the leader to more quickly and accurately identify the onset of combat stress within the unit. The CSTs would also be able to apply psychometric and qualitative techniques in order to provide the commander with specific issues that could contribute to decreased morale and once identified would provide recommendations for improved unit effectiveness.

## Future Research

The recommendation from this research has indicated that a future study should be undertaken utilising the MMPI-2-RF technology in order to ascertain if pre-combat education programmes and leadership training will reduce the incidence of combat stress and PTSD. To reinforce this recommendation, there has been a number of case studies on PTSD but never a longitudinal study. A study as described in the recommendations above it is believed will have the potential to alter the way that infantry soldiers are currently educated and trained. The message from this research is that instead of devoting the training of infantry soldiers in the tactical skill of closing with and killing or capturing the enemy, we must first train our infantry soldiers how to understand and then apply the techniques for surviving in combat. The infantry soldier must be trained to efficiently kill enemy combatants, but when that task has been completed, the soldier must have been so inoculated that they do not themselves become the psychological casualties of their own justifiable actions.

In conclusion, it must be stressed that these five recommendations have been designed to lessen or minimise the effects of combat stress on infantry soldiers and are inter-dependent as they overlap, even though each area is unique and distinct. That is each can be considered as a pillar, and each of these five pillars supports, builds, and reinforces steps taken in the other areas. Therefore, to be totally effective, all five pillars must be implemented equally if the maximum reward of lessening and minimising combat stress is to be achieved.

In closing, this research study into the physiological and psychological effects of combat on infantry soldiers has been this author's life work. First during his 41 years (1969-2010) as an active duty infantry soldier and then during this last six years as he has endeavoured to unlock the secrets of how to better prepare our next generation of infantry soldiers for their own first shock of combat. In this regard, this author has never discovered a more appropriate quote about the importance of the infantryman than the one provided by Field Marshal Lord Wavell over 70 years ago. The fact is that soldiers are the nation's most precious of resource and this author would argue that the infantry soldier is the most precious of all:

> *"Let us be clear about three facts: First, all battles and all wars are won in the end by the infantryman. Secondly, the infantryman always bears the brunt of the fighting, his casualties are heavier, and he suffers greater extremes of discomfort and fatigue than the other combat arms. Thirdly, the art of the infantryman is less stereotyped and far harder to acquire in modern war than any other arm."*

Field Marshal Lord Wavell (1945)[5]

# Honours and Awards

Member of the British Empire (MBE)

NATO Meritorious Service Medal (MSM)

British General Service Medal 1962 (bar Northern Ireland)

United Nations Observer Mission in Georgia (UNOMIG) Medal (with Numeral 2)

NATO non-Article 5 Medal (Former Yugoslavia)

NATO non-Article 5 Medal (Kosovo)

British Operational Service Medal (Afghanistan)

NATO non-Article 5 Medal (ISAF)

British Iraq Medal

NATO non-Article 5 Medal (NTM-I)

EU ESDP Medal, HO & Forces (with Numeral 2)

EU ESDP Medal, Planning & Support

Australian Service Medal 1945-75 (bar PNG)

Australian Defence Force Service Medal

Australian Defence Medal

Papua New Guinea Independence Medal

Queen Elizabeth II Golden Jubilee Medal

# Airborne Qualifications

British Military Free-Fall (MFF) (HALO/HAHO)
    Grade 1 – 13 March 1994


STATIC-LINE

Australian Parachute Wings – 18 May 1973

U.S. Parachute Wings (Basic) – 2 April 1985

Canadian Parachute Wings – 11 July 1987

British Parachute Wings – 1 December 1989

U.S. Parachute Wings (Senior) – 13 February 1992

German Parachute Wings – 22 May 1992

French Parachute Wings – 13 August 1992

Belgium Parachute Wings – 22 June 1993

Portugese Parachute Wings – 8 October 1993

Italian Parachute Wings – 23 February 1994

U.S. Parachute Wings (Master) – 30 June 1994

Polish Parachute Wings – 15 September 1994

Russian Parachute Wings – 16 July 1997

Dutch Parachute Wings – 9 November 1997

# Notes

## Chapter 1

1. Kouzes, J.M. & Posner, B.Z. (2010). *The leadership challenge* (4th ed.). San Francisco, CA: Jossey-Bass, p.89.
2. Grossman, D. & Siddle, B.K. (2010, August). Critical incident amnesia: the physiological basis and implications of memory loss during extreme survival situations. *The Firearms Instructor, 237*(21), 56-72, p.63.
3. King, A. (2013). *The combat soldier: Infantry tactics and cohesion in the twentieth and twenty-first centuries.* Oxford, England: Oxford University Press, p.78.
4. Siddle, B.K. (2009). The impact of the sympathetic nervous system on use of force investigations. *Research Abstract, 76*(13), 23-45, p.39.
5. Grossman, D. & Christensen, L.D. (2008). *On combat: The psychology and physiology of deadly conflict in war and in peace.* New York, NY: Warrior Science Publications, p.131.
6. Grossman, D. & Siddle, B.K., op cit, p.101.
7. Stouffer, S. (2010). *The American soldier: combat and its aftermath.* Princeton, NJ: Princeton University Press, p.75.
8. Bartone, P. T. (2010, April). Leadership and personality in the military organization. *Defense Issues, 83*(52), 27-76, p.99.
9. Grossman, D. (2009). *On killing.* New York, NY: Back Bay Books, p.112.
10. Ibid, p.129.
11. Grossman, D. (1995). *On killing: The psychological cost of learning to kill in war and society.* Boston, MA: Little, Brown & Company, pp.203-204.
12. Bartlett, F.C. (2009). *Psychology and the soldier.* Cambridge, England: Cambridge University Press. P.67.
13. Morgan, D. (2011, May 27). Post-traumatic stress soars in U.S. troops in 2007. *Defense Issues, 15*(12), 27-76, p. 39.
14. De Becker, G. (2012). *The gift of fear: and other survival signals that protect us from violence.* New York, NY: Dell, p.174.

15. Gray, J.G. (2008). *The warriors: reflections of men in battle.* New York, NY: Harper-Collins, p.78.

16. Asken, M.J., Grossman, D. & Christensen, W. (2010). *Warrior mindset.* New York, NY: Warrior Science Publications, p.241.

17. Werner, N. (2009). Hippocampal function during associative learning in patients with post-traumatic stress disorder. *Journal of Psychiatric Research, 43* 309-318, p.134.

18. King, A., op cit., p.213.

19. U.S. Department of Veterans Affairs. (2013). *Fifth annual report of the department of veterans affairs undersecretary for health special committee on post-traumatic stress disorder.* Washington, DC: DoD Press, p.337.

20. Ibid, p.398.

21. U.K. MoD, Department of Defence Statistics (2014, 04 June), Freedom of Information Act 2000, Request: FOI2014/01137. London, England: MoD Press, p.4.

22. Ibid, p.6.

23. Grossman, D. & Christensen, L.D., op cit, pp.156-159.

24. Asken, M.J., Grossman, D. & Christensen, W., op cit, p.146.

25. U.S. Department of Defense. (2013). *Department of defense task force on mental health.* Washington, DC: DoD Press, p.155.

26. U.K. MoD, Department of Defence Statistics (2014, 04 June), op cit, p.7.

27. King, A., op cit., p.241.

28. Ibid, p.144.

## Chapter 2

1. Grossman, D. & Siddle, B.K. (2010, August). Critical incident amnesia: the physiological basis and implications of memory loss during extreme survival situations. *The Firearms Instructor, 237*(21), 56-72, p.58.

2. Crump, L.D. (2011). Gestalt therapy in the treatment of Vietnam veterans experiencing PTSD symptomatology. *Jornal of Contemporary Psychotherapy, 14*(1), 96-128, p.132.

3. Kettell, K., Mosier, W., Orthner, W., & Schymanski, T. (2009, June). Combat stress: Post-traumatic stress disorder in the military – Identifi-

cation, diagnosis, and intervention. *Joint Centre for Operational Analysis Journal, 10*(2) 28-40, p.98-101.

4. Fishback, S.J. (2008). *Learning and the brain: What every educator should know.* Thousand Oaks, CA: Sage Publications, p.155.

5. Pavic, L. (2007, February 28). Smaller right hippocampus in war veterans with post-traumatic stress disorder. *Psychiatry Research: Neuroimaging 154,* 191-198, pp.193-195.

6. McEwen, B.S. & Lasley, E.N. (2008). *The end of stress as we know it.* Washington, DC: John Henry Press, p.87.

7. Grossman, D. (1995). *On killing: The psychological cost of learning to kill in war and society.* Boston, MA: Little, Brown & Company, p. 181.

8. Wolfe, P.J. (2001). *Brain matters, translating research into classroom practice.* Alexandria, VA: Association for Supervision and Curriculum Development, p.99.

9. Fishback, S.J., op cit, p.134.

10. McEwen, B.S. & Lasley, E.N., op cit, p.87.

11. Tanielian, T. (2010). *Invisible wounds of war: Summary and recommendations for addressing psychological and cognitive injuries.* Santa Monica, CA: Rand Centre for Military Health Policy Research, pp.124-126.

12. Swank, R.L. & Marchand, W.E. (1946). Combat neurosis: Development of combat exhaustion. *Archives of Neurology and Psychology, 55,* 236-247, p.143.

13. Gabriel, R.A. (2008). *No more heroes: madness and psychiatry in war.* New York, NY: Hill and Wang, p.222.

14. Kosslyn, S. & Koenig, O. (2009). *Wet mind: new cognitive neuroscience.* New York, NY: Free Press, p.84.

15. Lemyre, L.D. & Tessier, R.A. (2013). *Measuring psychological stress.* Montreal, Canada: Montreal Press. P.101.

16. Marlowe, D.H. (2001). *Psychological and psychosocial consequences of combat and deployment, with special emphasis on the Gulf War.* Santa Monic, CA; Rand, p.256.

17. Lazarus, R.S. (1999). *Stress and emotions: A new synthesis.* New York, NY: Springer Publishing Company, p.112.

18. Kosslyn, S. & Koenig, O. (2009). *Wet mind: new cognitive neuroscience.* New York, NY: Free Press, p.76.

19. Gabriel, R.A. (2010). *Military psychiatry: a comparative perspective.* New York, NY: Greenport Press, p.245.

20. Figley, R.F & Nash, W.P. (2007). *Combat stress injury: Theory, research, and management.* New York, NY: Routledge, p.49.

21. Ehlers, A. & Clark, D.M. (2000). A cognitive model of post-traumatic stress disorder. *Behaviour Research and Therapy, 38,* 319-345, pp. 333-334.

22. Dohrenwend, B.P. (2013). The roles of combat exposure, personal vulnerability, and involvement in harm to civilians or prisoners of war – related to post-traumatic stress disorder. *Association of Psychological Science, 81*(22), 25-73, p.66-67.

23. De Becker, G. (2010). *Fear less: real truth about risk, safety and security in a time of terrorism.* Boston, MA: Little and Brown, p.87.

24. Dohrenwend, B.P. (2013). The roles of combat exposure, personal vulnerability, and involvement in harm to civilians or prisoners of war – related to post-traumatic stress disorder. *Association of Psychological Science, 81*(22), 25-73, p.39.

## Chapter 3

1. Keegan, J. (1976). *The face of battle.* Suffolk, England: Chaucer Press, p.12.

2. Marlowe, D.H. (2001). *Psychological and psychosocial consequences of combat and deployment, with special emphasis on the Gulf War.* Santa Monic, CA; Rand, p.84.

3. Thompson, M. (2009, April 16). Broken down: What the war in Iraq has done to America's Army-and how to fix it. *Research Abstract, 21*(9), 13-35, p.27.

4. Stouffer, S. (2010). *The American soldier: combat and its aftermath.* Princeton, NJ: Princeton University Press, p.154.

5. Holmes, T.H. & Rahe, R.H. (1967). The social readjustment rating scales. *Journal of Psychosomatic Research 11,* 213-218, pp.215-216.

6. Grossman, D. & Siddle, B.K. (2010, August). Critical incident amnesia: the physiological basis and implications of memory loss during extreme survival situations. *The Firearms Instructor, 237*(21), 56-72, p.65.

7. Ibid, p.69.

8. Grossman, D. (2009). *On killing.* New York, NY: Back Bay Books, p.132.

9. Foa, E.B. & Riggs, D.S. (1993). Post-traumatic stress disorder. *American Psychiatric Review, 12,* 273-303, p.287.

10. Gabriel, R.A. (2010). *Military psychiatry: a comparative perspective.* New York, NY: Greenport Press, p.141.

11. Shephard, B. (2008). *A war of nerves: soldiers and psychiatrists in the twentieth century.* Cambridge, MA: Harvard University Press, p.215

12. Jones. D. (2009). *Diagnostic and statistical manual (DSM IV) of mental disorders.* Belleville, IL: PPCT Research Publications, p.154.

13. Kosslyn, S. & Koenig, O. (2009). *Wet mind: new cognitive neuroscience.* New York, NY: Free Press, p.245.

14. Keegan, J., op cit, p.119.

15. Grossman, D. (2009). *On killing.* New York, NY: Back Bay Books, p.119.

16. Ibid, p.147.

17. Grossman, D. & Christensen, L.D. (2008). *On combat: The psychology and physiology of deadly conflict in war and in peace.* New York, NY: Warrior Science Publications, p.241.

18. Crump, L.D. (2011). Gestalt therapy in the treatment of Vietnam veterans experiencing PTSD symptomatology. *Jornal of Contemporary Psychotherapy, 14*(1), 96-128, p.114.

19. Grossman, D., op cit, p.161.

20. Artwohl, A. & Christensen, L. (2009). *Deadly force encounters: What cops need to know mentally and physically prepare for and survive a gunfight.* Boulder, CA: Paladin Press, p.251.

21. Asken, M.J., Grossman, D. & Christensen, W. (2010). *Warrior mindset.* New York, NY: Warrior Science Publications, p.301.

22. Artwohl, A. & Christensen, L., op cit, p. 264.

23. Fishback, S.J. (2008). *Learning and the brain: What every educator should know.* Thousand Oaks, CA: Sage Publications, p.325.

24. Klinger, D. (2010). *Into the kill zone: A cop's eye view of deadly force.* San Francisco, CA: Josey-Bass, p.76.
25. Ibid, p.99.

## *Chapter 4*

1. Grossman, D. (1995). *On killing: The psychological cost of learning to kill in war and society.* Boston, MA: Little, Brown & Company, p.129.
2. Holmes, R. (1985). *Acts of war: The behaviour of men in battle.* New York, NY: The Free Press, p.45.
3. Jones. D. (2009). *Diagnostic and statistical manual (DSM IV) of mental disorders.* Belleville, IL: PPCT Research Publications, p.342.
4. Foa, E.B. & Rothbaum, B.O. (1998). *Cognitive behavioral therapy for PTSD.* New York, NY: Guilford Press, p.147.
5. Grossman, D. (1995). *On killing: The psychological cost of learning to kill in war and society.* Boston, MA: Little, Brown & Company, p.139.
6. Grossman, D. (2009). *On killing.* New York, NY: Back Bay Books, p.163.
7. Emerson, G.A. (1976). *Winners and losers: Battles, retreats, gains, and losses.* New York, NY: Harcourt Brace, p.234.
8. Figley, R.F & Nash, W.P. (2007). *Combat stress injury: Theory, research, and management.* New York, NY: Routledge, p.91.
9. Shephard, B. (2008). *A war of nerves: soldiers and psychiatrists in the twentieth century.* Cambridge, MA: Harvard University Press, p.221.
10. Chapman, J. (2011). *Leadership.* Mechanicsburg, PA: Stackpole Books, p.78.
11. Marshall, S.L.A. (1947). *Men against fire: The problem of battle command.* Norman, OK: University of Oklahoma Press, p.341.
12. Grossman, D. & Christensen, L.D. (2008). *On combat: The psychology and physiology of deadly conflict in war and in peace.* New York, NY: Warrior Science Publications, p.135.
13. Grossman, D. & Siddle, B.K. (2010, August). Critical incident amnesia: the physiological basis and implications of memory loss during extreme survival situations. *The Firearms Instructor, 237*(21), 56-72, pp.60-62.
14. Grossman, D. (1995). *On killing: The psychological cost of learning to kill in war and society.* Boston, MA: Little, Brown & Company, p.151.

15. Gray, J.G. (2008). *The warriors: reflections of men in battle.* New York, NY: Harper-Collins, p.88.

16. Jones, N.T. (2012). Leadership, Cohesion, Morale, and the Mental Health of UK Armed Forces in Afghanistan. *Journal of Psychiatry. 75,* 49-89, p.55.

17. Shalikashvili, J. M. (2008, April). The three pillars of leadership. *Defense Issues, 10*(42), 27-76, p. 49.

18. Shephard, B. (2008). *A war of nerves: soldiers and psychiatrists in the twentieth century.* Cambridge, MA: Harvard University Press, p.243.

19. De Becker, G. (2012). *The gift of fear: and other survival signals that protect us from violence.* New York, NY: Dell, p.223.

20. Gabriel, R.A. (2010). *Military psychiatry: a comparative perspective.* New York, NY: Greenport Press, p.61.

21. Stouffer, S. (2010). *The American soldier: combat and its aftermath.* Princeton, NJ: Princeton University Press, p.77.

22. King, A. (2013). *The combat soldier: Infantry tactics and cohesion in the twentieth and twenty-first centuries.* Oxford, England: Oxford University Press, p.268.

23. Shapiro, F. (2012). *Getting past your past: Take control of your life with self-help techniques from EMDR therapy.* New York, NY: Rodale Books, p.138.

24. King's Centre for Military Health Research (KCMHR), King's College London (2014, 27 February), London, England: King's College London Press, p.324.

25. Grossman, D. & Christensen, L.D., op cit, p.166.

## Chapter 5

1. Morgan, D. (2011, May 27). Post-traumatic stress soars in U.S. troops in 2007. *Defense Issues, 15*(12), 27-76, p.33.

2. McEwen, B.S. (2000). Allostasis and allostatic load; Implications for neuropsychopharmacology. *Neuropsychopharmacology, 22,* 108-124, p.121.

3. Lemyre, L.D. & Tessier, R.A. (2013). *Measuring psychological stress.* Montreal, Canada: Montreal Press, p.241.

4. Kosslyn, S. & Koenig, O. (2009). *Wet mind: new cognitive neuroscience.* New York, NY: Free Press, p.145.

5.  Paulson, D.S. 7& Krippner, S. (2007). *Haunted by combat: Understanding PTSD in war veterans including women, reservists, and those coming back from Iraq.* Seattle, WA: Greenwood Publishing Group, p.279.

6.  Mulligan K.J., Jones, N.B. & Woodhead, C.D. (2010). Mental health of UK military personnel while on deployment in Iraq. *The British Journal of Psychiatry. 197,* 405-434, pp.426-427.

7.  Orb, A., Eisenhauer, L.K., & Wynaden, D.L. (2012). What is post-traumatic stress disorder (PTSD). *Journal of the National Institute of Mental Health, 81*(4) 59-86, p.68.

8.  Pettera, R.L., Johnson, B.M., & Zimmer, R. (2009, September). Psychiatric management of combat reactions with emphasis on a reaction unique to Vietnam. *Military Medicine, 134*(9), 673-678, p.675.

9.  Shay, J. (2009). *Achilles in Vietnam: combat trauma and the undoing of character.* Boston, MA: Touchstone Books, p.97.

10. Shephard, B. (2008). *A war of nerves: soldiers and psychiatrists in the twentieth century.* Cambridge, MA: Harvard University Press, p.187.

11. Shapiro, F. (2012). *Getting past your past: Take control of your life with self-help techniques from EMDR therapy.* New York, NY: Rodale Books, p.115.

12. Watson, R.D. & Gardiner, E.C. (2013*). A longitudinal study of stress and psychological distress in soldiers.* Sheffield, England: The University of Sheffield Press, pp.312-314.

13. Solomon, Z.D., Shklar, R.A., & Mikulincer, M.N. (2013). *Frontline treatment of combat stress reaction: A 20-year longitudinal evaluation study.* Tel Aviv, Israel: Tel Aviv University Press, p.256.

14. Stouffer, S. (2010). *The American soldier: combat and its aftermath.* Princeton, NJ: Princeton University Press, p.345.

15. Swank, R.L. & Marchand, W.E. (1946). Combat neurosis: Development of combat exhaustion. *Archives of Neurology and Psychology, 55,* 236-247, p.255.

16. Werner, N. (2009). Hippocampal function during associative learning in patients with post-traumatic stress disorder. *Journal of Psychiatric Research, 43,* 309-318, p.315.

17. Gray, J.G. (2008). *The warriors: reflections of men in battle.* New York, NY: Harper-Collins, p.224.

18. Grossman, D. & Christensen, L.D. (2008). *On combat: The psychology and physiology of deadly conflict in war and in peace*. New York, NY: Warrior Science Publications, p.271.

19. Figley, R.F & Nash, W.P. (2007). *Combat stress injury: Theory, research, and management*. New York, NY: Routledge, p.111.

20. Foa, E.B. & Riggs, D.S. (1993). Post-traumatic stress disorder. *American Psychiatric Review, 12,* 273-303, p.289.

21. Grossman, D. & Christensen, L.D. (2008). *On combat: The psychology and physiology of deadly conflict in war and in peace*. New York, NY: Warrior Science Publications, p.228.

22. Gabriel, R.A. (2010). *Military psychiatry: a comparative perspective*. New York, NY: Greenport Press, p.43.

23. Kosslyn, S. & Koenig, O. (2009). *Wet mind: new cognitive neuroscience*. New York, NY: Free Press, p.119.

24. Marlowe, D.H. (2001). *Psychological and psychosocial consequences of combat and deployment, with special emphasis on the Gulf War*. Santa Monic, CA; Rand, p.209.

## *Chapter 6*

1. Grossman, D. (1995). *On killing: The psychological cost of learning to kill in war and society.* Boston, MA: Little, Brown & Company, p.43.

2. Marshall, S.L.A. (1947). *Men against fire: The problem of battle command.* Norman, OK: University of Oklahoma Press, pp.324-325.

3. Hesselbein, F. & Shinseki, E.K. (2010). *Leadership the Army way.* San Francisco, CA: Jossey-Bass, p.88.

4. Gabriel, R.A. (2008). *No more heroes: madness and psychiatry in war.* New York, NY: Hill and Wang, p.113.

5. Hoge, C.W. (2004). Combat duty in Iraq and Afghanistan, mental health problems, and barriers to care. *New England Journal of Medicine, 351,* 798-817, p.796.

6. Kettel, K., Mosier, W., Orthner, W., & Schymanski, T. (2009, June). Combat stress: Post-traumatic stress disorder in the military – Identification, diagnosis, and intervention. *Joint Centre for Operational Analysis Journal, 10*(2) 28-40, p.37.

7.  Grossman, D. & Christensen, L.D. (2008). *On combat: The psychology and physiology of deadly conflict in war and in peace.* New York, NY: Warrior Science Publications, p.145.

8.  Keegan, J. (1976). *The face of battle.* Suffolk, England: Chaucer Press, p156.

9.  Grossman, D. & Christensen, L.D., op cit, p.158.

10. Siddle, B.K. (2008). *Sharpening the warrior's edge.* Belleville, IL: PPCT Research Publications, p.66.

11. Le Boeuf, M.K. (2012, May/June). Developing a leadership philosophy. *Military Review, 31*(7), 76-98, p. 91.

12. McDonough, J.R. (2009). *Platoon leader.* Novato, CA: Presidio Press, p.215.

13. Malone, D.M. (2010). *Small unit leadership: A commonsense approach.* New York, NY: Ballentine Books, p.317.

14. Kouzes, J.M. & Posner, B.Z. (2010). *The leadership challenge* (4th ed.). San Francisco, CA: Jossey-Bass, p.111.

15. Solomon, Z.D., Shklar, R.A., & Mikulincer, M.N. (2013). *Frontline treatment of combat stress reaction: A 20-year longitudinal evaluation study.* Tel Aviv, Israel: Tel Aviv University Press, p.349.

16. Shephard, B. (2008). *A war of nerves: soldiers and psychiatrists in the twentieth century.* Cambridge, MA: Harvard University Press, p.38.

17. Northouse, P.G. (2009). *Leadership: Theory and practice.* Thousand Oaks, CA: Sage Publications, p.268.

18. Moon, C., Tracy, L., & Schama, A. (2011). A proactive approach to serving military and veteran students. *New Direction for Higher Education, 153*(Spring, 2011), 53-60, p.57.

19. Lemyre, L.D. & Tessier, R.A. (2013). *Measuring psychological stress.* Montreal, Canada: Montreal Press, p.89.

20. Kolenda, C. (2006). *Leadership: The warrior's art.* Carlisle, PA: Army War College Foundation Press, p.47.

21. Gibson, J.L., Ivancevich, J.M., Donnelly, J.H., & Konopaske, R. (2009). *Organizations, structures processes.* (12th ed.). Boston, MA: McGraw-Hill, p.119.

22. Allen, N. & Burgess, T. (2011). *Exceptional leadership at the company level.* Dover, DE: Centre for Company Level Leadership, p.67.

23. Marshall, S.L.A. (1947). *Men against fire: The problem of battle command.* Norman, OK: University of Oklahoma Press, p.378.
24. Malone, D.M. (2010). *Small unit leadership: A commonsense approach.* New York, NY: Ballentine Books, p.145.
25. Ibid, p.176.
26. Horey, J. D. & Fallesen, J.J. (2011, November). Leadership competencies. *The Military Conflict Institute, 189*(22), 101-141, p.129.
27. Siddle, B.K. (2009). The impact of the sympathetic nervous system on use of force investigations. *Research Abstract, 76*(13), 23-45, p.30.

*Chapter 7*
1. Krames, J.A. (2008). *The U.S. Army leadership field manual.* New York, NY: McGraw-Hill, p.47.
2. Brinkerhoff, J. R. (2010, November). The military command function. *The Military Conflict Institute, 119*(21), 101-121, p.111.
3. Cohen, W. A. (2009, May-June). Battle leadership examples from the field. *Military Review, 79*(3), 82-97, p.141.
4. Shalikashvili, J. M. (2008, April). The three pillars of leadership. *Defense Issues, 10*(42), 27-76, p. 68.
5. Le Boeuf, M.K. (2012, May/June). Developing a leadership philosophy. *Military Review, 31*(7), 76-98, p.91.
6. Gray, J.G. (2008). *The warriors: reflections of men in battle.* New York, NY: Harper-Collins, p.243.
7. Dalessandro, R.J. (2009). *Army officers guide.* Mechanicsburg, PA: Stackpole Books, p.374.
8. Northouse, P.G. (2009). *Leadership: Theory and practice.* Thousand Oaks, CA: Sage Publications. P.127.
9. Verljen, P. J. (2011, September/October). Leadership: More than mission accomplishment. *Military Review, 35*(9), 12-22, p. 18.
10. Allen, N. & Burgess, T. (2011). *Exceptional leadership at the company level.* Dover, DE: Centre for Company Level Leadership, p.178.
11. Grossman, D. (2009). *On killing.* New York, NY: Back Bay Books, p.88.
12. Pendry, J.D. (2009). *The three metre zone: Commonsense leadership for NCO's.* New York, NY: Random House, p.145.

13. Kolenda, C. (2006). *Leadership: The warrior's art.* Carlisle, PA: Army War College Foundation Press, p.156.
14. Yeakey, G. W. (2008, January/February). Army leadership. *Military Review, 34*(10), 24-37, p.29.
15. Northouse, P.G., op cit, p.139.
16. Kouzes, J.M. & Posner, B.Z. (2010). *The leadership challenge* (4th ed.). San Francisco, CA: Jossey-Bass, p.156.
17. Malone, D.M. (2010). *Small unit leadership: A commonsense approach.* New York, NY: Ballentine Books, p.138.
18. Northouse, P.G., op cit, p.151.
19. Siddle, B.K. (2008). *Sharpening the warrior's edge.* Belleville, IL: PPCT Research Publications, p. 99.
20. Nye, R.H., (2009). *The challenge of command.* New York, NY: Penguin Group, p.51.
21. Hesselbein, F. & Shinseki, E.K. (2010). *Leadership the Army way.* San Francisco, CA: Jossey-Bass, p.76.
22. Siddle, B.K., op cit, p.121.
23. Grossman, D. & Christensen, L.D. (2008). *On combat: The psychology and physiology of deadly conflict in war and in peace.* New York, NY: Warrior Science Publications, p.276.
24. D'Estre, C. (2010). *Eisenhower: Allied supreme commander.* London, England: Weidenfeld & Nicolson, p.36.
25. Perkins, D., Holtman, M., Kessler, P. & McCarthy, C. (2009). *Leading at the edge: Leadership lessons from the extraordinary saga of Shackelton's antarctic expedition.* New York, NY: AMACOM, p.254.
26. Taylor, R.L., Rosenbach, W.E. & Rosenbach, E.B. (2009). *Military leadership: In pursuit of excellence.* Boulder, CO: Westview Press, p.91.
27. Northouse, P.G., op cit, p.173.
28. Dohrenwend, B.P. (2013). The roles of combat exposure, personal vulnerability, and involvement in harm to civilians or prisoners of war – related to post-traumatic stress disorder. *Association of Psychological Science, 81*(22), 25-73, p.54.
29. Cohen, W. A., op cit, p.134.
30. Nye, R.H., op cit, p.78.

## Chapter 8

1. Chapman, J. (2011). *Leadership*. Mechanicsburg, PA: Stackpole Books, p.78.
2. Le Boeuf, M.K. (2012, May/June). Developing a leadership philosophy. *Military Review, 31*(7), 76-98, p.84.
3. King, A. (2013). *The combat soldier: Infantry tactics and cohesion in the twentieth and twenty-first centuries.* Oxford, England: Oxford University Press, p.44.
4. Verljen, P. J. (2011, September/October). Leadership: More than mission accomplishment. *Military Review, 35*(9), 12-22, p.18.
5. Yeakey, G. W. (2008, January/February). Army leadership. *Military Review, 34*(10), 24-37, p.31.
6. Hesselbein, F. & Shinseki, E.K. (2010). *Leadership the Army way.* San Francisco, CA: Jossey-Bass, p.133.
7. Dalessandro, R.J. (2009). *Army officers guide.* Mechanicsburg, PA: Stackpole Books, p.256.
8. Hesselbein, F. & Shinseki, E.K., op cit, p.167.
9. D'Estre, C. (2010). *Eisenhower: Allied supreme commander*. London, England: Weidenfeld & Nicolson, p.143.
10. Northouse, P.G. (2009). *Leadership: Theory and practice.* Thousand Oaks, CA: Sage Publications, p.89.
11. Eliot, R.S. (2011). *Is it worth dying for?* Toronto, Canada: Bantam Books, p.105.
12. Nye, R.H., (2009). *The challenge of command.* New York, NY: Penguin Group, p.159.
13. Krames, J.A. (2008). *The U.S. Army leadership field manual.* New York, NY: McGraw-Hill, p.148.
14. Horey, J. D. & Fallesen, J.J. (2011, November). Leadership competencies. *The Military Conflict Institute, 189*(22), 101-141, p.123.
15. Shalikashvili, J. M. (2008, April). The three pillars of leadership. *Defense Issues, 10*(42), 27-76, pp.55-58.
16. Yeakey, G. W., op cit, p.35.
17. Cohen, W. A. (2009, May-June). Battle leadership examples from the field. *Military Review, 79*(3), 82-97, p.77.

18. Bartone, P. T. (2010, April). Leadership and personality in the military organization. *Defense Issues, 83*(52), 27-76, p.34.

19. Taylor, R.L., Rosenbach, W.E. & Rosenbach, E.B. (2009). *Military leadership: In pursuit of excellence.* Boulder, CO: Westview Press, p.119.

20. Pendry, J.D. (2009). *The three metre zone: Commonsense leadership for NCO's.* New York, NY: Random House, p.226.

21. Brinkerhoff, J. R. (2010, November). The military command function. *The Military Conflict Institute, 119*(21), 101-121, p.119.

22. Moran, Lord. (2007). *The anatomy of courage* (2nd ed). London, England: Constable & Robinson, p.235.

23. Bass, B.M. (1985). *Transformational leadership: Industrial, military, and educational impact.* Mahwah, NJ: Erlbaum, p.213.

24. Huse, T. D. 2009, November-December). Transformational leadership in the era of change. *Military Review,109*(5), 82-117, p.98.

25. Kouzes, J.M. & Posner, B.Z. (2010). *The leadership challenge* (4th ed.). San Francisco, CA: Jossey-Bass, p.254.

26. Perkins, D., Holtman, M., Kessler, P. & McCarthy, C. (2009). *Leading at the edge: Leadership lessons from the extraordinary saga of Shackelton's antarctic expedition.* New York, NY: AMACOM, p.215.

27. Malone, D.M. (2010). *Small unit leadership: A commonsense approach.* New York, NY: Ballentine Books, p.233.

28. Allen, N. & Burgess, T. (2011). *Exceptional leadership at the company level.* Dover, DE: Centre for Company Level Leadership, p.91.

29. Bartlett, F.C. (2009). *Psychology and the soldier.* Cambridge, England: Cambridge University Press, p.133.

## Chapter 9

1. Bartone, P. T. (2010, April). Leadership and personality in the military organization. *Defense Issues, 83*(52), 27-76, p.43.

2. Northouse, P.G. (2009). *Leadership: Theory and practice.* Thousand Oaks, CA: Sage Publications, p.141.

3. Cohen, W. A. (2009, May-June). Battle leadership examples from the field. *Military Review, 79*(3), 82-97, p.76.

4. Bartone, P. T., op cit, p.65.

5.  McDonough, J.R. (2009). *Platoon leader*. Novato, CA: Presidio Press, p.88.

6.  Nye, R.H., (2009). *The challenge of command*. New York, NY: Penguin Group, p.237.

7.  D'Estre, C. (2010). *Eisenhower: Allied supreme commander*. London, England: Weidenfeld & Nicolson, p.214.

8.  Ibid, p.252.

9.  Grossman, D. (2009). *On killing*. New York, NY: Back Bay Books, p.187.

10. Trulock, A.R. (2007). *In the hands of providence*. Chapel Hill, NC: The University of North Carolina Press, p.122.

11. Ibid, p.165.

12. Ibid, p.167.

13. Ibid, p.168.

14. Ibid, p.170.

15. Ibid, p.171.

16. Ibid, p.175.

17. Ibid, p.178.

18. Ibid, p.194.

19. Hesselbein, F. & Shinseki, E.K. (2010). *Leadership the Army way*. San Francisco, CA: Jossey-Bass, p.198.

20. Trulock, A.R., op cit, p.237.

21. Chapman, J. (2011). *Leadership*. Mechanicsburg, PA: Stackpole Books, p.173.

22. Dalessandro, R.J. (2009). *Army officers guide*. Mechanicsburg, PA: Stackpole Books, p.79.

23. King, A. (2013). *The combat soldier: Infantry tactics and cohesion in the twentieth and twenty-first centuries*. Oxford, England: Oxford University Press, p.272.

24. Kolenda, C. (2006). *Leadership: The warrior's art*. Carlisle, PA: Army War College Foundation Press, p.135.

25. Nye, R.H., op cit, p.254.

26. Hesselbein, F. & Shinseki, E.K., p.261.

27. Malone, D.M. (2010). *Small unit leadership: A commonsense approach*. New York, NY: Ballentine Books, p.49.

28. Allen, N. & Burgess, T. (2011). *Exceptional leadership at the company level.* Dover, DE: Centre for Company Level Leadership, p.252.

29. Taylor, R.L., Rosenbach, W.E. & Rosenbach, E.B. (2009). *Military leadership: In pursuit of excellence.* Boulder, CO: Westview Press, p.174.

30. Kouzes, J.M. & Posner, B.Z. (2010). *The leadership challenge* (4th ed.). San Francisco, CA: Jossey-Bass, p.191.

31. Grossman, D. & Christensen, L.D. (2008). *On combat: The psychology and physiology of deadly conflict in war and in peace.* New York, NY: Warrior Science Publications, p.236.

32. Chapman, J., op cit, p.224.

33. Kolenda, C., op cit, p.173.

34. Brinkerhoff, J. R. (2010, November). The military command function. *The Military Conflict Institute, 119*(21), 101-121, p.116.

35. King, A., op cit, p.182.

## Chapter 10

1. Patton, M.G. (2007). *Qualitative research and evaluation methods* (3rd ed). Thousand Oaks, CA: Sage Publications, p.553.

2. George, A.L., & Bennett, A. (2010). *Case studies and theory development in social sciences.* Cambridge, MA: MIT Press, p.219.

3. Schram, G.D. (2006). *Conceptualizing and proposing qualitative research* (2nd ed). Upper Saddle River, NJ: Pearson Merrill Prentice Hall, p.271.

4. Tensen, B.L. (2009). *Research strategies for the digital age* (2nd ed.). Boston, MA: Thomson Wadsworth, p.74.

5. Johannesen, R., Valde, K., & Whedbee, K. (2010). *Ethics in human communication.* Long Grove, IL: Waveland Press, p.243.

6. Shank, G.D. (2006). *Qualitative research: A personal skills approach* (2nd ed). Upper Saddle River, NJ: Pearson Merrill Prentice Hall, p.346.

7. Trochim, W. & Donnelly, J. (2008). *The research methods knowledge base* (3rd ed.). Mason, OH: Cengage, p.149.

8. Cozby, P.C. (2009). *Methods in behavioral research* (19th ed.). Boston, MA: McGraw Hill Higher Education, p.261.

9. Shank, G.D., op cit, p.119.

10. Booth, W., Colomb, G.G., & Williams, J.M. (2009). *The craft of research* (3rd ed.). Chicago, IL: University of Chicago Press, p.142.

11. Patton, M.G. (2007). *Qualitative research and evaluation methods* (3rd ed). Thousand Oaks, CA: Sage Publications, p.436.

12. Orb, A., Eisenhauer, L.K., & Wynaden, D.L. (2012). What is post-traumatic stress disorder (PTSD). *Journal of the National Institute of Mental Health, 81*(4) 59-86, pp.74-76.

13. Tensen, B.L., op cit, p.154.

14. Bolman, L. & Deal, T. (2009). *Reframing organizations: Artistry, choice, and leadership* (4th ed.). San Francisco, CA: Jossey-Bass, p.234.

15. Moon, C., Tracy, L., & Schama, A. (2011). A proactive approach to serving military and veteran students. *New Direction for Higher Education, 153*(Spring, 2011), 53-60, pp.198-199.

16. Cozby, P.C. (2009). *Methods in behavioral research* (19th ed.). Boston, MA: McGraw Hill Higher Education, p.251.

17. Johannesen, R., Valde, K., & Whedbee, K., op cit, p.111.

18. Bamberger, P.H. (1995). Instructor Role in Educational Organizations Having the Characteristics of Total Institutions. *Journal of Educational Administration, 33*(3), 68-85, p.79.

19. Johannesen, R., Valde, K., & Whedbee, K., op cit, p.286.

20. Tensen, B.L., op cit, p.213.

21. Booth, W., Colomb, G.G., & Williams, J.M., op cit, p.279.

22. Bolman, L. & Deal, T., op cit, p.221.

23. Patton, M.G., op cit, p.223.

24. Shank, G.D., op cit, p.98.

25. Trochim, W. & Donnelly, J., op cit, p.256.

26. Cozby, P.C., op cit, p.251.

27. Gibson, J.L., Ivancevich, J.M., Donnelly, J.H., & Konopaske, R. (2009). *Organizations, structures processes.* (12th ed.). Boston, MA: McGraw-Hill, p.79.

28. Orb, A., Eisenhauer, L.K., & Wynaden, D.L., op cit, p.113.

29. Bamberger, P.H., op cit, p.333.

30. Glaser, B.G. & Strauss, L. (1967). *Discovery for grounded theory: Strategies for qualitative research.* Chicago, IL: Aldine, p.279.

31. Cozby, P.C., op cit, p.191.

## *Chapter 11*

1. Horey, J. D. & Fallesen, J.J. (2011, November). Leadership competencies. *The Military Conflict Institute, 189*(22), 101-141, p.122.

2. Shalikashvili, J. M. (2008, April). The three pillars of leadership. *Defense Issues, 10*(42), 27-76, p.33.

3. Siddle, B.K. (2008). *Sharpening the warrior's edge.* Belleville, IL: PPCT Research Publications, p.119.

4. Pendry, J.D. (2009). *The three metre zone: Commonsense leadership for NCO's.* New York, NY: Random House, p.233.

5. McDonough, J.R. (2009). *Platoon leader.* Novato, CA: Presidio Press, p.57.

6. Huse, T. D. 2009, November-December). Transformational leadership in the era of change. *Military Review,109*(5), 82-117, p.219.

7. Hesselbein, F. & Shinseki, E.K. (2010). *Leadership the Army way.* San Francisco, CA: Jossey-Bass, p.106.

8. Gray, J.G. (2008). *The warriors: reflections of men in battle.* New York, NY: Harper-Collins, p.37.

9. Gabriel, R.A. (2010). *Military psychiatry: a comparative perspective.* New York, NY: Greenport Press, p.222.

10. Kertsh, K.G. (2010, May/June). How high-performance organizations develop leadership. *Military Review, 81*(9), 76-118, pp.112-113.

11. Johannesen, R., Valde, K., & Whedbee, K. (2010). *Ethics in human communication.* Long Grove, IL: Waveland Press, p.91.

12. Kertsh, K.G., op cit, p.117.

13. Malone, D.M. (2010). *Small unit leadership: A commonsense approach.* New York, NY: Ballentine Books, p.247.

14. Bartone, P. T. (2010, April). Leadership and personality in the military organization. *Defense Issues, 83*(52), 27-76, p.66.

15. Asken, M.J., Grossman, D. & Christensen, W. (2010). *Warrior mindset.* New York, NY: Warrior Science Publications, p.225.

16. Bartone, P. T., op cit, p.71.

17. Kolenda, C. (2006). *Leadership: The warrior's art.* Carlisle, PA: Army War College Foundation Press, 173.

18. Grossman, D. (1995). *On killing: The psychological cost of learning to kill in war and society.* Boston, MA: Little, Brown & Company, p.239.

19. Dalessandro, R.J. (2009). *Army officers guide.* Mechanicsburg, PA: Stackpole Books, p.391.

20. Vore, K. J. (2010, September/October). Senior leader decision making. *Military Review, 75*(19), 12-52, p.44.

21. Ibid, p.49.

22. Stouffer, S. (2010). *The American soldier: combat and its aftermath.* Princeton, NJ: Princeton University Press, p.245.

23. Pendry, J.D. (2009). *The three metre zone: Commonsense leadership for NCO's.* New York, NY: Random House, p.77.

24. Northouse, P.G. (2009). *Leadership: Theory and practice.* Thousand Oaks, CA: Sage Publications, p.238.

25. Allen, N. & Burgess, T. (2011). *Exceptional leadership at the company level.* Dover, DE: Centre for Company Level Leadership, p.192.

26. Nye, R.H., (2009). *The challenge of command.* New York, NY: Penguin Group, p.233.

27. Schram, G.D. (2006). *Conceptualizing and proposing qualitative research* (2nd ed). Upper Saddle River, NJ: Pearson Merrill Prentice Hall, p.193.

28. Booth, W., Colomb, G.G., & Williams, J.M. (2009). *The craft of research* (3rd ed.). Chicago, IL: University of Chicago Press, p.348.

29. Brinkerhoff, J. R. (2010, November). The military command function. *The Military Conflict Institute, 119*(21), 101-121, p.109.

30. Yin, R.K. (2009). *Case study research: Design and methods* (4th ed.). Thousand Oaks, CA: Sage, p.149.

## Chapter 12

1. Grossman, D. & Siddle, B.K. (2010, August). Critical incident amnesia: the physiological basis and implications of memory loss during extreme survival situations. *The Firearms Instructor, 237*(21), 56-72, p.47.

2. King, A. (2013). *The combat soldier: Infantry tactics and cohesion in the twentieth and twenty-first centuries.* Oxford, England: Oxford University Press, p.344.

3. U.K. MoD, Press Release (2014, 11 September), *U.K.'s future military role in Syria and Iraq to combat ISIS terrorism.* London, England: MoD Press.
4. Siddle, B.K. (2009). The impact of the sympathetic nervous system on use of force investigations. *Research Abstract, 76*(13), 23-45, p.39.
5. Grossman, D. & Christensen, L.D. (2008). *On combat: The psychology and physiology of deadly conflict in war and in peace.* New York, NY: Warrior Science Publications, p.239.
6. Yin, R.K. (2009). *Case study research: Design and methods* (4th ed.). Thousand Oaks, CA: Sage, p117.
7. Ibid, p.156.

## Chapter 13

1. U.S. Department of Veterans Affairs. (2013). *Fifth annual report of the department of veterans affairs undersecretary for health special committee on post-traumatic stress disorder.* Washington, DC: DoD Press, p.319.
2. U.K. MoD, Department of Defence Statistics (2014, 04 June), Freedom of Information Act 2000, Request: FOI2014/01137. London, England: MoD Press, p.465.

## Chapter 14

1. Dalessandro, R.J. (2009). *Army officers guide.* Mechanicsburg, PA: Stackpole Books, p.329.
2. King, A. (2013). *The combat soldier: Infantry tactics and cohesion in the twentieth and twenty-first centuries.* Oxford, England: Oxford University Press, p.255.
3. Yin, R.K. (2009). *Case study research: Design and methods* (4th ed.). Thousand Oaks, CA: Sage, p.235.

## Chapter 15

1. Grossman, D. (2009). *On killing.* New York, NY: Back Bay Books, p.171.
2. Allen, N. & Burgess, T. (2011). *Exceptional leadership at the company level.* Dover, DE: Centre for Company Level Leadership, p.248.

3. De Becker, G. (2012). *The gift of fear: and other survival signals that protect us from violence.* New York, NY: Dell, p.134.
4. Malone, D.M. (2010). *Small unit leadership: A commonsense approach.* New York, NY: Ballentine Books, p.97.
5. American Psychiatric Association (2000). *Diagnostic and statistical manual of mental disorders* (4th ed.). Washington, DC: U.S. Department of Health, p.432.
6. Watson, R.D. & Gardiner, E.C. (2013*). A longitudinal study of stress and psychological distress in soldiers.* Sheffield, England: The University of Sheffield Press, p.223.
7. Gouws, D. (2010, October). Combat stress inoculation, PTSD recognition, and early intervention. *Operational Trauma & Stress Support Centre, Baghdad, Iraq,* p,165.
8. King, A. (2013). *The combat soldier: Infantry tactics and cohesion in the twentieth and twenty-first centuries.* Oxford, England: Oxford University Press, p.277.
9. Crump, L.D. (2011). Gestalt therapy in the treatment of Vietnam veterans experiencing PTSD symptomatology. *Jornal of Contemporary Psychotherapy, 14*(1), 96-128, p.117.
10. Grossman, D. (1995). *On killing: The psychological cost of learning to kill in war and society.* Boston, MA: Little, Brown & Company, p.69.
11. Grossman, D. & Christensen, L.D. (2008). *On combat: The psychology and physiology of deadly conflict in war and in peace.* New York, NY: Warrior Science Publications, p.179.
12. Grossman, D. & Siddle, B.K. (2010, August). Critical incident amnesia: the physiological basis and implications of memory loss during extreme survival situations. *The Firearms Instructor, 237*(21), 56-72, p.63.
13. King, A., op cit, p.254.
14. Ibid, p.261.
15. Grossman, D., op cit, p.213.
16. Siddle, B.K. (2009). The impact of the sympathetic nervous system on use of force investigations. *Research Abstract, 76*(13), 23-45, p.28.
17. Taylor, R.L., Rosenbach, W.E. & Rosenbach, E.B. (2009). *Military leadership: In pursuit of excellence.* Boulder, CO: Westview Press, p.189.

18. Malone, D.M. (2010). *Small unit leadership: A commonsense approach.* New York, NY: Ballentine Books, p.76.

19. Le Boeuf, M.K. (2012, May/June). Developing a leadership philosophy. *Military Review, 31*(7), 76-98, p.88.

20. Burns, J.M. (1978). *Leadership.* New York, NY: Harper Row, p.124.

21. Huse, T. D. 2009, November-December). Transformational leadership in the era of change. *Military Review,109*(5), 82-117, p.98.

22. Siddle, B.K., op cit, p.37.

23. Asken, M.J., Grossman, D. & Christensen, W. (2010). *Warrior mindset.* New York, NY: Warrior Science Publications, p.119.

24. King, A., op cit, p.182..

25. Siddle, B.K. (2008). *Sharpening the warrior's edge.* Belleville, IL: PPCT Research Publications, p.176.

## Chapter 16

1. Allen, N. & Burgess, T. (2011). *Exceptional leadership at the company level.* Dover, DE: Centre for Company Level Leadership, p.227.

2. Horey, J. D. & Fallesen, J.J. (2011, November). Leadership competencies. *The Military Conflict Institute, 189*(22), 101-141, p.121.

3. Yin, R.K. (2009). *Case study research: Design and methods* (4th ed.). Thousand Oaks, CA: Sage, p.148.

4. Ibid, p.165.

5. Ibid, p.169.

6. Bloomberg, L. D., & Volpe, M. (2012). *Completing your qualitative dissertation: Aroad map from beginning to end* (2nd ed.). Thousand Oaks, CA: Sage, p.243.

7. Yin, R.K. (2003). *Applications of case study research* (2nd ed.). Thousand Oaks, CA: Sage, p.79.

8. Bolman, L. & Deal, T. (2009). *Reframing organizations: Artistry, choice, and leadership* (4th ed.). San Francisco, CA: Jossey-Bass, p.312.

9. Trochim, W. & Donnelly, J. (2008). *The research methods knowledge base* (3rd ed.). Mason, OH: Cengage, p.191.

10. Grossman, D. (1995). *On killing: The psychological cost of learning to kill in war and society.* Boston, MA: Little, Brown & Company, p.61.

11. Grossman, D. & Christensen, L.D. (2008). *On combat: The psychology and physiology of deadly conflict in war and in peace.* New York, NY: Warrior Science Publications, p.237.

12. Medina, J. (2008). *Brain rules 12 principles for surviving and thriving at work home and school.* Seattle, WA: Pear Press, p.124.

13. Tanielian, T. (2010). *Invisible wounds of war: Summary and recommendations for addressing psychological and cognitive injuries.* Santa Monica, CA: Rand Centre for Military Health Policy Research, p.296.

14. Thompson, M. (2009, April 16). Broken down: What the war in Iraq has done to America's Army-and how to fix it. *Research Abstract, 21*(9), 13-35, p.32.

## Chapter 17

1. Grossman, D. & Siddle, B.K. (2010, August). Critical incident amnesia: the physiological basis and implications of memory loss during extreme survival situations. *The Firearms Instructor, 237*(21), 56-72, p.58.

2. King, A. (2013). *The combat soldier: Infantry tactics and cohesion in the twentieth and twenty-first centuries.* Oxford, England: Oxford University Press, p.325.

3. Stouffer, S. (2010). *The American soldier: combat and its aftermath.* Princeton, NJ: Princeton University Press, p.144.

4. Tanielian, T. (2010). *Invisible wounds of war: Summary and recommendations for addressing psychological and cognitive injuries.* Santa Monica, CA: Rand Centre for Military Health Policy Research, p.297.

5. Orb, A., Eisenhauer, L.K., & Wynaden, D.L. (2012). What is post-traumatic stress disorder (PTSD). *Journal of the National Institute of Mental Health, 81*(4) 59-86, p.79.

6. Fishback, S.J. (2008). *Learning and the brain: What every educator should know.* Thousand Oaks, CA: Sage Publications, p.324.

7. Dohrenwend, B.P. (2013). The roles of combat exposure, personal vulnerability, and involvement in harm to civilians or prisoners of war – related to post-traumatic stress disorder. *Association of Psychological Science, 81*(22), 25-73, p.34.

8.  Ehlers, A. & Clark, D.M. (2000). A cognitive model of post-traumatic stress disorder. *Behaviour Research and Therapy, 38,* 319-345, p.337.

9.  Division of Psychiatry and Neuroscience, Walter Reed Institute of Research, U.S. Army Medical Research and Material Command (2005, May 10). Washington, DC: DoD Press, p.546.

10. Dohrenwend, B.P., op cit, p.45.

11. Ibid, p. 57.

12. Ibid, p.64.

13. Ibid, p.66.

14. Grossman, D. (2009). *On killing.* New York, NY: Back Bay Books, p.226.

15. U.K. MoD, Department of Defence Statistics (2014, 04 June), Freedom of Information Act 2000, Request: FOI2014/01137. London, England: MoD Press, p.341.

16. Ibid, p.366.

17. King, A., op cit, p.256.

18. U.K. MoD, Department of Defence Statistics (2014, 04 June), p.376.

19. King, A., op cit, p.288.

20. U.S. Department of Defense. (2013). *Department of defense task force on mental health.* Washington, DC: DoD Press, p.432.

21. Siddle, B.K. (2009). The impact of the sympathetic nervous system on use of force investigations. *Research Abstract, 76*(13), 23-45, p.38.

22. Shapiro, F. (2012). *Getting past your past: Take control of your life with self-help techniques from EMDR therapy.* New York, NY: Rodale Books, p.239.

23. Ibid, p.254.

24. De Becker, G. (2012). *The gift of fear: and other survival signals that protect us from violence.* New York, NY: Dell, p.247.

25. Gabriel, R.A. (2010). *Military psychiatry: a comparative perspective.* New York, NY: Greenport Press, p.271.

26. Ibid, p.288.

27. Bartlett, F.C. (2009). *Psychology and the soldier.* Cambridge, England: Cambridge University Press, p.115.

28. Kettel, K., Mosier, W., Orthner, W., & Schymanski, T. (2009, June). Combat stress: Post-traumatic stress disorder in the military – Identification, diagnosis, and intervention. *Joint Centre for Operational Analysis Journal, 10*(2) 28-40, p.31.

## Chapter 18

1. Grossman, D. (1995). *On killing: The psychological cost of learning to kill in war and society.* Boston, MA: Little, Brown & Company, p.129.
2. Gouws, D. (2010, October). Combat stress inoculation, PTSD recognition, and early intervention. *Operational Trauma & Stress Support Centre, Baghdad, Iraq,* p.237.
3. Holmes, R. (1985). *Acts of war: The behaviour of men in battle.* New York, NY: The Free Press, p.187.
4. Grossman, D. & Christensen, L.D. (2008). *On combat: The psychology and physiology of deadly conflict in war and in peace.* New York, NY: Warrior Science Publications, p.256.
5. Hesselbein, F. & Shinseki, E.K. (2010). *Leadership the Army way.* San Francisco, CA: Jossey-Bass, p.139.
6. Kosslyn, S. & Koenig, O. (2009). *Wet mind: new cognitive neuroscience.* New York, NY: Free Press, p.155.
7. Keegan, J. (1976). *The face of battle.* Suffolk, England: Chaucer Press, p.271.
8. Jones, N.T. (2012). Leadership, Cohesion, Morale, and the Mental Health of UK Armed Forces in Afghanistan. *Journal of Psychiatry. 75,* 49-89, p.65.
9. Kolenda, C. (2006). *Leadership: The warrior's art.* Carlisle, PA: Army War College Foundation Press, p.243.
10. Kouzes, J.M. & Posner, B.Z. (2010). *The leadership challenge* (4th ed.). San Francisco, CA: Jossey-Bass, p.312.
11. Le Boeuf, M.K. (2012, May/June). Developing a leadership philosophy. *Military Review, 31*(7), 76-98, p.81.
12. Ibid, p.88.
13. Keegan, J., op cit, p.294.

14. Lazarus, R.S. (1999). *Stress and emotions: A new synthesis.* New York, NY: Springer Publishing Company, p.179.

15. Paulson, D.S. 7& Krippner, S. (2007). *Haunted by combat: Understanding PTSD in war veterans including women, reservists, and those coming back from Iraq.* Seattle, WA: Greenwood Publishing Group, p.311.

16. Grossman, D. & Christensen, L.D. (2008). *On combat: The psychology and physiology of deadly conflict in war and in peace.* New York, NY: Warrior Science Publications, p.251.

17. Ibid, p.274.

18. King, A. (2013). *The combat soldier: Infantry tactics and cohesion in the twentieth and twenty-first centuries.* Oxford, England: Oxford University Press, p.343.

19. McEwen, B.S. & Lasley, E.N. (2008). *The end of stress as we know it.* Washington, DC: John Henry Press, p.94.

20. Moran, Lord. (2007). *The anatomy of courage* (2nd ed). London, England: Constable & Robinson, p.166.

21. Ibid, p.189.

22. Northouse, P.G. (2009). *Leadership: Theory and practice.* Thousand Oaks, CA: Sage Publications, p.239.

23. Nye, R.H., (2009). *The challenge of command.* New York, NY: Penguin Group, p.279.

24. Siddle, B.K. (2008). *Sharpening the warrior's edge.* Belleville, IL: PPCT Research Publications, p.346.

25. Ibid, p.367.

26. Verljen, P. J. (2011, September/October). Leadership: More than mission accomplishment. *Military Review, 35*(9), 12-22, p.18.

27. McDonough, J.R. (2009). *Platoon leader.* Novato, CA: Presidio Press, p.233.

28. Huse, T. D. 2009, November-December). Transformational leadership in the era of change. *Military Review,109*(5), 82-117, p.113.

29. Holmes, R. (1985). *Acts of war: The behaviour of men in battle.* New York, NY: The Free Press, p.331.

30. Ibid, p.344.

31. Moran, Lord. (2007). *The anatomy of courage* (2nd ed). London, England: Constable & Robinson, p.243.

32. Kolenda, C. (2006). *Leadership: The warrior's art.* Carlisle, PA: Army War College Foundation Press, p.342.

## *Chapter 19*

1. Bartlett, F.C. (2009). *Psychology and the soldier.* Cambridge, England: Cambridge University Press, p.133.

2. Grossman, D. (2009). *On killing.* New York, NY: Back Bay Books, p.76.

3. Kolenda, C. (2006). *Leadership: The warrior's art.* Carlisle, PA: Army War College Foundation Press, p.238.

4. Mulligan K.J., Jones, N.B. & Woodhead, C.D. (2010). Mental health of UK military personnel while on deployment in Iraq. *The British Journal of Psychiatry. 197,* 405-434, p.422.

5. Jones, N.T. (2012). Leadership, Cohesion, Morale, and the Mental Health of UK Armed Forces in Afghanistan. *Journal of Psychiatry. 75,* 49-89, p.67.

6. Pendry, J.D. (2009). *The three metre zone: Commonsense leadership for NCO's.* New York, NY: Random House, p.119.

7. Chapman, J. (2011). *Leadership.* Mechanicsburg, PA: Stackpole Books, p.244.

8. Horey, J. D. & Fallesen, J.J. (2011, November). Leadership competencies. *The Military Conflict Institute, 189*(22), 101-141, p.126.

9. Kolenda, C. (2006). *Leadership: The warrior's art.* Carlisle, PA: Army War College Foundation Press, p.245.

10. Ibid, p.278.

11. Nye, R.H., (2009). *The challenge of command.* New York, NY: Penguin Group, p.314.

12. Stouffer, S. (2010). *The American soldier: combat and its aftermath.* Princeton, NJ: Princeton University Press, p.221.

13. Yeakey, G. W. (2008, January/February). Army leadership. *Military Review, 34*(10), 24-37, p.29.

14. Gray, J.G. (2008). *The warriors: reflections of men in battle.* New York, NY: Harper-Collins, p.149.

15. Horey, J. D. & Fallesen, op cit, p.131.

16. Huse, T. D. 2009, November-December). Transformational leadership in the era of change. *Military Review,109*(5), 82-117, p.97.

17. Krames, J.A. (2008). *The U.S. Army leadership field manual.* New York, NY: McGraw-Hill, p.365.

18. McDonough, J.R. (2009). *Platoon leader.* Novato, CA: Presidio Press, p.172.

19. Ibid, p.180.

20. Paulson, D.S. 7& Krippner, S. (2007). *Haunted by combat: Understanding PTSD in war veterans including women, reservists, and those coming back from Iraq.* Seattle, WA: Greenwood Publishing Group, p.342.

21. Pressfield, S. (2009). *Gates of fire.* New York, NY: Bantam, p.230.

22. Ibid, p.242.

## *Chapter 20*

1. Allen, N. & Burgess, T. (2011). *Exceptional leadership at the company level.* Dover, DE: Centre for Company Level Leadership, p.174.

2. De Becker, G. (2012). *The gift of fear: and other survival signals that protect us from violence.* New York, NY: Dell, p.281.

3. McDonough, J.R. (2009). *Platoon leader.* Novato, CA: Presidio Press, p.121.

4. Grossman, D. & Christensen, L.D. (2008). *On combat: The psychology and physiology of deadly conflict in war and in peace.* New York, NY: Warrior Science Publications, p.327.

5. Bartone, P. T. (2010, April). Leadership and personality in the military organization. *Defense Issues, 83*(52), 27-76, p.51.

6. Grossman, D. & Christensen, L.D. (2008). *On combat: The psychology and physiology of deadly conflict in war and in peace.* New York, NY: Warrior Science Publications, p.326.

7. Le Boeuf, M.K. (2012, May/June). Developing a leadership philosophy. *Military Review, 31*(7), 76-98, p.93.

8. Grossman, D. (1995). *On killing: The psychological cost of learning to kill in war and society.* Boston, MA: Little, Brown & Company, p.222.

9.   King, A. (2013). *The combat soldier: Infantry tactics and cohesion in the twentieth and twenty-first centuries.* Oxford, England: Oxford University Press, p.331.

10.  Taylor, R.L., Rosenbach, W.E. & Rosenbach, E.B. (2009). *Military leadership: In pursuit of excellence.* Boulder, CO: Westview Press, p.247.

11.  Vore, K. J. (2010, September/October). Senior leader decision making. *Military Review, 75*(19), 12-52, p.44.

12.  Siddle, B.K. (2008). *Sharpening the warrior's edge.* Belleville, IL: PPCT Research Publications, p.279.

13.  Pendry, J.D. (2009). *The three metre zone: Commonsense leadership for NCO's.* New York, NY: Random House, p.171.

14.  De Becker, G., op cit, p.296.

15.  Dalessandro, R.J. (2009). *Army officers guide.* Mechanicsburg, PA: Stackpole Books, p.357.

16.  Bartone, P. T. (2010, April). Leadership and personality in the military organization. *Defense Issues, 83*(52), 27-76, p.66.

17.  Figley, R.F & Nash, W.P. (2007). *Combat stress injury: Theory, research, and management.* New York, NY: Routledge, p.129.

18.  Huse, T. D. 2009, November-December). Transformational leadership in the era of change. *Military Review,109*(5), 82-117, p.102.

19.  Gabriel, R.A. (2010). *Military psychiatry: a comparative perspective.* New York, NY: Greenport Press, p.91.

20.  Gray, J.G. (2008). *The warriors: reflections of men in battle.* New York, NY: Harper-Collins, p.244.

21.  Eliot, R.S. (2011). *Is it worth dying for?* Toronto, Canada: Bantam Books, p.213.

22.  Jones, N.T. (2012). Leadership, Cohesion, Morale, and the Mental Health of UK Armed Forces in Afghanistan. *Journal of Psychiatry. 75,* 49-89, p.80.

23.  Ibid, p.84.

## *Chapter 21*

1.   Chapman, J. (2011). *Leadership.* Mechanicsburg, PA: Stackpole Books, p.126.

2. Dalessandro, R.J. (2009). *Army officers guide.* Mechanicsburg, PA: Stackpole Books, p.242.

3. Dohrenwend, B.P. (2013). The roles of combat exposure, personal vulnerability, and involvement in harm to civilians or prisoners of war – related to post-traumatic stress disorder. *Association of Psychological Science, 81*(22), 25-73, p.66.

4. Figley, R.F & Nash, W.P. (2007). *Combat stress injury: Theory, research, and management.* New York, NY: Routledge, p.84.

5. Gibson, J.L., Ivancevich, J.M., Donnelly, J.H., & Konopaske, R. (2009). *Organizations, structures processes.* (12th ed.). Boston, MA: McGraw-Hill, p.245.

6. Hoge, C.W. (2004). Combat duty in Iraq and Afghanistan, mental health problems, and barriers to care. *New England Journal of Medicine, 351,* 798-817, p.804.

7. Ibid, p.811.

8. Kosslyn, S. & Koenig, O. (2009). *Wet mind: new cognitive neuroscience.* New York, NY: Free Press, p.276.

9. Mulligan K.J., Jones, N.B. & Woodhead, C.D. (2010). Mental health of UK military personnel while on deployment in Iraq. *The British Journal of Psychiatry. 197,* 405-434, p.412.

10. Hoge, C.W., op cit, p.811.

11. Pettera, R.L., Johnson, B.M., & Zimmer, R. (2009, September). Psychiatric management of combat reactions with emphasis on a reaction unique to Vietnam. *Military Medicine, 134*(9), 673-678, p.679.

12. Stouffer, S. (2010). *The American soldier: combat and its aftermath.* Princeton, NJ: Princeton University Press, p.125.

13. Thompson, M. (2009, April 16). Broken down: What the war in Iraq has done to America's Army-and how to fix it. *Research Abstract, 21*(9), 13-35, p.25.

14. Ibid, p.31.

15. Mulligan K.J., Jones, N.B. & Woodhead, C.D. (2010). Mental health of UK military personnel while on deployment in Iraq. *The British Journal of Psychiatry. 197,* 405-434, p.423.

16. Ibid, p.429.

17. Lemyre, L.D. & Tessier, R.A. (2013). *Measuring psychological stress.* Montreal, Canada: Montreal Press, p.342.

18. Kettel, K., Mosier, W., Orthner, W., & Schymanski, T. (2009, June). Combat stress: Post-traumatic stress disorder in the military – Identification, diagnosis, and intervention. *Joint Centre for Operational Analysis Journal, 10*(2) 28-40, p.33.

19. Hoge, C.W. (2004). Combat duty in Iraq and Afghanistan, mental health problems, and barriers to care. *New England Journal of Medicine, 351,* 798-817, p.812.

20. Grossman, D. & Christensen, L.D. (2008). *On combat: The psychology and physiology of deadly conflict in war and in peace.* New York, NY: Warrior Science Publications, p.239.

21. Ibid, p.257.

22. Fishback, S.J. (2008). *Learning and the brain: What every educator should know.* Thousand Oaks, CA: Sage Publications, p.344.

23. Brewin, C.R., Andrews, B., & Rose, S. (2000). Fear, helplessness, and horror in post-traumatic stress disorder. *Journal of Traumatic Stress, 13,* 499-509, p.504.

24. Bartlett, F.C. (2009). *Psychology and the soldier.* Cambridge, England: Cambridge University Press, p.233.

25. Gabriel, R.A. (2010). *Military psychiatry: a comparative perspective.* New York, NY: Greenport Press, p.125.

## Chapter 22

1. Division of Psychiatry and Neuroscience, Walter Reed Institute of Research, U.S. Army Medical Research and Material Command (2005, May 10). Washington, DC: DoD Press, p.452.

2. Jones. D. (2009). *Diagnostic and statistical manual (DSM IV) of mental disorders.* Belleville, IL: PPCT Research Publications, p.566.

3. Lemyre, L.D. & Tessier, R.A. (2013). *Measuring psychological stress.* Montreal, Canada: Montreal Press, p.248.

4. Kitayama, N. (2010, September). Magnetic resonance imaging (MRI) measurement of hippocampal volume in post-traumatic stress disorder: A meta-analysis. *Journal of Affective Disorders, 88*(1) 79-86, p.84.

5. Jones. D., op cit, p.578.
6. Figley, R.F & Nash, W.P. (2007). *Combat stress injury: Theory, research, and management.* New York, NY: Routledge, p.212.
7. Fishback, S.J. (2008). *Learning and the brain: What every educator should know.* Thousand Oaks, CA: Sage Publications, p.387.
8. Dohrenwend, B.P. (2013). The roles of combat exposure, personal vulnerability, and involvement in harm to civilians or prisoners of war – related to post-traumatic stress disorder. *Association of Psychological Science, 81*(22), 25-73, p.61.
9. Brewin, C.R., Andrews, B., & Rose, S. (2000). Fear, helplessness, and horror in post-traumatic stress disorder. *Journal of Traumatic Stress, 13,* 499-509, 503.
10. Watson, R.D. & Gardiner, E.C. (2013*). A longitudinal study of stress and psychological distress in soldiers.* Sheffield, England: The University of Sheffield Press, p.119.
11. Cabrera, O.A, Hoge, C.W., Bliese, P.D., Castro, C.A., & Messer, S.C. (2007). Childhood adversity and combat predicators of depression and post-traumatic stress in deployed troops. *American Journal of Preventative Medicine, 33 (2),* 77-82, p.79.
12. Foa, E.B. & Riggs, D.S. (1993). Post-traumatic stress disorder. *American Psychiatric Review, 12,* 273-303, p.281.
13. Grossman, D. & Christensen, L.D. (2008). *On combat: The psychology and physiology of deadly conflict in war and in peace.* New York, NY: Warrior Science Publications, p.344.
14. Hoge, C.W. (2004). Combat duty in Iraq and Afghanistan, mental health problems, and barriers to care. *New England Journal of Medicine, 351,* 798-817, p.812.
15. Kosslyn, S. & Koenig, O. (2009). *Wet mind: new cognitive neuroscience.* New York, NY: Free Press, p.163.
16. Cabrera, O.A, Hoge, C.W., Bliese, P.D., Castro, C.A., & Messer, S.C., op cit, p.80.
17. Ibid, p.81.
18. Ibid, p.82.

19. Lemyre, L.D. & Tessier, R.A. (2013). *Measuring psychological stress.* Montreal, Canada: Montreal Press, p.187.

20. Mulligan K.J., Jones, N.B. & Woodhead, C.D. (2010). Mental health of UK military personnel while on deployment in Iraq. *The British Journal of Psychiatry. 197*, 405-434, p.419.

21. Cabrera, O.A, Hoge, C.W., Bliese, P.D., Castro, C.A., & Messer, S.C., op cit, p.82.

22. Brewin, C.R., Andrews, B., & Rose, S. (2000). Fear, helplessness, and horror in post-traumatic stress disorder. *Journal of Traumatic Stress, 13,* 499-509, p.504.

## *Chapter 23*

1. U.K. MoD, Department of Defence Statistics (2014, 04 June), Freedom of Information Act 2000, Request: FOI2014/01137. London, England: MoD Press, p.251.

2. Ibid, p.267.

3. Ibid, p.269.

4. Mulligan K.J., Jones, N.B. & Woodhead, C.D. (2010). Mental health of UK military personnel while on deployment in Iraq. *The British Journal of Psychiatry. 197*, 405-434, p.311.

5. Keegan, J. (1976). *The face of battle.* Suffolk, England: Chaucer Press, p.119.

# Bibliography

Alexander, P.A. & Winne, P.H. (2006). *Handbook of educational psychology* (2nd ed.). Mahwah, NJ: Erlbaum.

Allen, N. & Burgess, T. (2011). *Exceptional leadership at the company level.* Dover, DE: Centre for Company Level Leadership.

American Psychiatric Association (2000). *Diagnostic and statistical manual of mental disorders* (4th ed.). Washington, DC: U.S. Department of Health.

American War Library (2008). Washington, DC: U.S. Department of Veterans Affairs.

Artwohl, A. & Christensen, L. (2009). *Deadly force encounters: What cops need to know mentally and physically prepare for and survive a gunfight.* Boulder, CA: Paladin Press.

Asken, M.J., Grossman, D. & Christensen, W. (2010). *Warrior mindset.* New York, NY: Warrior Science Publications.

Bamberger, P.H. (1995). Instructor Role in Educational Organizations Having the Characteristics of Total Institutions. *Journal of Educational Administration, 33*(3), 68-85.

Bartlett, F.C. (2009). *Psychology and the soldier.* Cambridge, England: Cambridge University Press.

Bartone, P. T. (2010, April). Leadership and personality in the military organization. *Defense Issues, 83*(52), 27-76.

Bass, B.M. (1985). *Transformational leadership: Industrial, military, and educational impact.* Mahwah, NJ: Erlbaum.

Bass, B.M. & Bass, E.J. (2008). *The Bass handbook of leadership: Theory, research, and managerial applications* (4th ed.). Washington, DC: Free Press.

Bloomberg, L. D., & Volpe, M. (2012). *Completing your qualitative dissertation: A road map from beginning to end* (2nd ed.). Thousand Oaks, CA: Sage.

Bolman, L. & Deal, T. (2009). *Reframing organizations: Artistry, choice, and leadership* (4th ed.). San Francisco, CA: Jossey-Bass.

Booth, W., Colomb, G.G., & Williams, J.M. (2009). *The craft of research* (3rd ed.). Chicago, IL: University of Chicago Press.

Brewin, C.R. (2001). A cognitive neuroscience account of post-traumatic stress disorder and its treatment. *Behavior Research and Therapy, 39,* 373-393.

Brewin, C.R., Andrews, B., & Rose, S. (2000). Fear, helplessness, and horror in post-traumatic stress disorder. *Journal of Traumatic Stress, 13,* 499-509.

Brewin, C.R., Dagleish, T., & Joseph, S (1996). A dual representation theory of post-traumatic stress disorder. *Psychological Review, 103,* 670-686.

Brinkerhoff, J. R. (2010, November). The military command function. *The Military Conflict Institute, 119*(21), 101-121.

Burns, J.M. (1978). *Leadership.* New York, NY: Harper Row.

Cabrera, O.A, Hoge, C.W., Bliese, P.D., Castro, C.A., & Messer, S.C. (2007). Childhood adversity and combat predicators of depression and post-traumatic stress in deployed troops. *American Journal of Preventative Medicine, 33 (2),* 77-82.

Castro, V., Garcia, E.E., Cavazos, J., & Castro, A.Y. (2011). The road to doctorial success and beyond. *International Journal of Doctorial Studies, 132,* 651-677.

Chapman, J. (2011). *Leadership.* Mechanicsburg, PA: Stackpole Books.

*Code of Human Research Ethics,* The British Psychological Society (2010).

Cohen, W. A. (2009, May-June). Battle leadership examples from the field. *Military Review, 79*(3), 82-97.

Cozby, P.C. (2009). *Methods in behavioral research* (19th ed.). Boston, MA: McGraw Hill Higher Education.

Crump, L.D. (2011). Gestalt therapy in the treatment of Vietnam veterans experiencing PTSD symptomatology. *Jornal of Contemporary Psychotherapy, 14*(1), 96-128.

Dalessandro, R.J. (2009). *Army officers guide.* Mechanicsburg, PA: Stackpole Books.

De Becker, G. (2010). *Fear less: real truth about risk, safety and security in a time of terrorism.* Boston, MA: Little and Brown.

De Becker, G. (2012). *The gift of fear: and other survival signals that protect us from violence.* New York, NY: Dell.

D'Estre, C. (2010). *Eisenhower: Allied supreme commander.* London, England: Weidenfeld & Nicolson.

Division of Psychiatry and Neuroscience, Walter Reed Institute of Research, U.S. Army Medical Research and Material Command (2005, May 10). Washington, DC: DoD Press.

Dohrenwend, B.P. (2013). The roles of combat exposure, personal vulnerability, and involvement in harm to civilians or prisoners of war – related to post-traumatic stress disorder. *Association of Psychological Science, 81*(22), 25-73.

Ehlers, A. & Clark, D.M. (2000). A cognitive model of post-traumatic stress disorder. *Behaviour Research and Therapy, 38,* 319-345.

Eliot, R.S. (2011). *Is it worth dying for?* Toronto, Canada: Bantam Books.

Emerson, G.A. (1976). *Winners and losers: Battles, retreats, gains, and losses.* New York, NY: Harcourt Brace.

Figley, R.F & Nash, W.P. (2007). *Combat stress injury: Theory, research, and management.* New York, NY: Routledge.

Fishback, S.J. (2008). *Learning and the brain: What every educator should know.* Thousand Oaks, CA: Sage Publications.

Foa, E.B. & Riggs, D.S. (1993). Post-traumatic stress disorder. *American Psychiatric Review, 12,* 273-303.

Foa, E.B. & Rothbaum, B.O. (1998). *Cognitive behavioral therapy for PTSD.* New York, NY: Guilford Press.

Gabriel, R.A. (2008). *No more heroes: madness and psychiatry in war.* New York, NY: Hill and Wang.

Gabriel, R.A. (2010). *Military psychiatry: a comparative perspective.* New York, NY: Greenport Press.

Gates, R. (2010, September 29). Lecture at Duke University. Durham, NC.

George, A.L., & Bennett, A. (2010). *Case studies and theory development in social sciences.* Cambridge, MA: MIT Press.

Gibson, J.L., Ivancevich, J.M., Donnelly, J.H., & Konopaske, R. (2009). *Organizations, structures processes.* (12th ed.). Boston, MA: McGraw-Hill.

Glaser, B.G. & Strauss, L. (1967). *Discovery for grounded theory: Strategies for qualitative research.* Chicago, IL: Aldine.

Gobo, G. (2008). *Doing ethnography.* London, England: SAGE Publications.

Gouws, D. (2010, October). Combat stress inoculation, PTSD recognition, and early intervention. *Operational Trauma & Stress Support Centre, Baghdad, Iraq.*

Gray, J.G. (2008). *The warriors: reflections of men in battle.* New York, NY: Harper-Collins.

Grossman, D. (1995). *On killing: The psychological cost of learning to kill in war and society.* Boston, MA: Little, Brown & Company.

Grossman, D. (2009). *On killing.* New York, NY: Back Bay Books.

Grossman, D. & Christensen, L.D. (2008). *On combat: The psychology and physiology of deadly conflict in war and in peace.* New York, NY: Warrior Science Publications.

Grossman, D. & Siddle, B.K. (2010, August). Critical incident amnesia: the physiological basis and implications of memory loss during extreme survival situations. *The Firearms Instructor, 237*(21), 56-72.

Hesselbein, F. & Shinseki, E.K. (2010). *Leadership the Army way.* San Francisco, CA: Jossey-Bass.

Hoge, C.W. (2004). Combat duty in Iraq and Afghanistan, mental health problems, and barriers to care. *New England Journal of Medicine, 351,* 798-817.

Holmes, R. (1985). *Acts of war: The behaviour of men in battle.* New York, NY: The Free Press.

Holmes, T.H. & Rahe, R.H. (1967). The social readjustment rating scales. *Journal of Psychosomatic Research 11*, 213-218.

Horey, J. D. & Fallesen, J.J. (2011, November). Leadership competencies. *The Military Conflict Institute, 189*(22), 101-141.

Huse, T. D. 2009, November-December). Transformational leadership in the era of change. *Military Review,109*(5), 82-117.

Johannesen, R., Valde, K., & Whedbee, K. (2010). *Ethics in human communication.* Long Grove, IL: Waveland Press.

Jones. D. (2009). *Diagnostic and statistical manual (DSM IV) of mental disorders.* Belleville, IL: PPCT Research Publications.

Jones, N.T. (2012). Leadership, Cohesion, Morale, and the Mental Health of UK Armed Forces in Afghanistan. *Journal of Psychiatry. 75,* 49-89.

Keegan, J. (1976). *The face of battle.* Suffolk, England: Chaucer Press.

Kertsh, K.G. (2010, May/June). How high-performance organizations develop leadership. *Military Review, 81*(9), 76-118.

Kettel, K., Mosier, W., Orthner, W., & Schymanski, T. (2009, June). Combat stress: Post-traumatic stress disorder in the military – Identification, diagnosis, and intervention. *Joint Centre for Operational Analysis Journal, 10*(2) 28-40.

King, A. (2013). *The combat soldier: Infantry tactics and cohesion in the twentieth and twenty-first centuries.* Oxford, England: Oxford University Press.

King's Centre for Military Health Research (KCMHR), King's College London (2014, 27 February), London, England: King's College London Press.

Kitayama, N. (2010, September). Magnetic resonance imaging (MRI) measurement of hippocampal volume in post-traumatic stress disorder: A meta-analysis. *Journal of Affective Disorders, 88*(1) 79-86.

Klinger, D. (2010). *Into the kill zone: A cop's eye view of deadly force.* San Francisco, CA: Josey-Bass.

Knowles, M.S. (1968). *The adult learner.* Malabar, FL: Krieger.

Kolenda, C. (2006). *Leadership: The warrior's art.* Carlisle, PA: Army War College Foundation Press.

Kosslyn, S. & Koenig, O. (2009). *Wet mind: new cognitive neuroscience.* New York, NY: Free Press.

Kouzes, J.M. & Posner, B.Z. (2010). *The leadership challenge* (4th ed.). San Francisco, CA: Jossey-Bass.

Krames, J.A. (2008). *The U.S. Army leadership field manual.* New York, NY: McGraw-Hill.

Lazarus, R.S. (1999). *Stress and emotions: A new synthesis.* New York, NY: Springer Publishing Company.

Le Boeuf, M.K. (2012, May/June). Developing a leadership philosophy. *Military Review, 31*(7), 76-98.

Lemyre, L.D. & Tessier, R.A. (2013). *Measuring psychological stress.* Montreal, Canada: Montreal Press.

Malone, D.M. (2010). *Small unit leadership: A commonsense approach*. New York, NY: Ballentine Books.

Marlowe, D.H. (2001). *Psychological and psychosocial consequences of combat and deployment, with special emphasis on the Gulf War*. Santa Monic, CA; Rand.

Marshall, S.L.A. (1947). *Men against fire: The problem of battle command*. Norman, OK: University of Oklahoma Press.

Maslow, A.H. (1954). *Motivation and personality*. New York, NY: Harper & Row.

McDonough, J.R. (2009). *Platoon leader*. Novato, CA: Presidio Press.

McEwen, B.S. (2000). Allostasis and allostatic load; Implications for neuro-psychopharmacology. *Neuropsychopharmacology*, 22, 108-124.

McEwen, B.S. & Lasley, E.N. (2008). *The end of stress as we know it*. Washington, DC: John Henry Press.

Medina, J. (2008). *Brain rules 12 principles for surviving and thriving at work home and school*. Seattle, WA: Pear Press.

Merriam, S.B. & Caffarella, R.S. (1999). *Learning in adulthood*. San Francisci, CA: Jossey-Bass.

Moran, Lord. (2007). *The anatomy of courage* (2nd ed). London, England: Constable & Robinson.

Morgan, D. (2011, May 27). Post-traumatic stress soars in U.S. troops in 2007. *Defense Issues, 15*(12), 27-76.

Moon, C., Tracy, L., & Schama, A. (2011). A proactive approach to serving military and veteran students. *New Direction for Higher Education, 153*(Spring, 2011), 53-60.

Mulligan K.J., Jones, N.B. & Woodhead, C.D. (2010). Mental health of UK military personnel while on deployment in Iraq. *The British Journal of Psychiatry. 197*, 405-434.

Naumes, W. & Naumes, M.J. (1999). *The art and craft of case writing*. Thousand Oaks, CA: Sage.

Northouse, P.G. (2009). *Leadership: Theory and practice*. Thousand Oaks, CA: Sage Publications.

Nye, R.H., (2009). *The challenge of command*. New York, NY: Penguin Group.

Olson, D.R. (2004). The triumph of hope over experience. *Educational Researcher, 33*(1), 24-36.

Orb, A., Eisenhauer, L.K., & Wynaden, D.L. (2012). What is post-traumatic stress disorder (PTSD). *Journal of the National Institute of Mental Health, 81*(4) 59-86.

Patton, M.G. (2007). *Qualitative research and evaluation methods* (3rd ed). Thousand Oaks, CA: Sage Publications.

Paulson, D.S. & Krippner, S. (2007). *Haunted by combat: Understanding PTSD in war veterans including women, reservists, and those coming back from Iraq.* Seattle, WA: Greenwood Publishing Group.

Pavic, L. (2007, February 28). Smaller right hippocampus in war veterans with post-traumatic stress disorder. *Psychiatry Research: Neuroimaging 154,* 191-198.

Pendry, J.D. (2009). *The three metre zone: Commonsense leadership for NCO's.* New York, NY: Random House.

Perkins, D., Holtman, M., Kessler, P. & McCarthy, C. (2009). *Leading at the edge: Leadership lessons from the extraordinary saga of Shackelton's antarctic expedition.* New York, NY: AMACOM.

Pettera, R.L., Johnson, B.M., & Zimmer, R. (2009, September). Psychiatric management of combat reactions with emphasis on a reaction unique to Vietnam. *Military Medicine, 134*(9), 673-678.

Pressfield, S. (2009). *Gates of fire.* New York, NY: Bantam.

Sawyer, R.K. (2006). The Cambridge handbook of the learning sciences. New York, NY: Cambridge University Press.

Schram, G.D. (2006). *Conceptualizing and proposing qualitative research* (2nd ed). Upper Saddle River, NJ: Pearson Merrill Prentice Hall.

Selye, H.B. (1956). *The stress of life.* New York, NY: McGraw-Hill.

Shalikashvili, J. M. (2008, April). The three pillars of leadership. *Defense Issues, 10*(42), 27-76.

Shank, G.D. (2006). *Qualitative research: A personal skills approach* (2nd ed). Upper Saddle River, NJ: Pearson Merrill Prentice Hall.

Shapiro, F. (2012). *Getting past your past: Take control of your life with self-help techniques from EMDR therapy.* New York, NY: Rodale Books.

Shay, J. (2009). *Achilles in Vietnam: combat trauma and the undoing of character.* Boston, MA: Touchstone Books.

Shephard, B. (2008). *A war of nerves: soldiers and psychiatrists in the twentieth century.* Cambridge, MA: Harvard University Press.

Siddle, B.K. (2008). *Sharpening the warrior's edge.* Belleville, IL: PPCT Research Publications.

Siddle, B.K. (2009). The impact of the sympathetic nervous system on use of force investigations. *Research Abstract, 76*(13), 23-45.

Solomon, Z.D., Shklar, R.A., & Mikulincer, M.N. (2013). *Frontline treatment of combat stress reaction: A 20-year longitudinal evaluation study.* Tel Aviv, Israel: Tel Aviv University Press.

Stouffer, S. (2010). *The American soldier: combat and its aftermath.* Princeton, NJ: Princeton University Press.

Strauss, A. L. & Corbin, (1990). *Basics of qualitative research: Grounded theory procedures and techniques* (1st ed). Newbury Park, CA. Sage.

Swank, R.L. & Marchand, W.E. (1946). Combat neurosis: Development of combat exhaustion. *Archives of Neurology and Psychology, 55,* 236-247.

Tanielian, T. (2010). *Invisible wounds of war: Summary and recommendations for addressing psychological and cognitive injuries.* Santa Monica, CA: Rand Centre for Military Health Policy Research.

Taylor, R.L., Rosenbach, W.E. & Rosenbach, E.B. (2009). *Military leadership: In pursuit of excellence.* Boulder, CO: Westview Press.

Tensen, B.L. (2009). *Research strategies for the digital age* (2nd ed.). Boston, MA: Thomson Wadsworth.

Thompson, M. (2009, April 16). Broken down: What the war in Iraq has done to America's Army-and how to fix it. *Research Abstract, 21*(9), 13-35.

Trochim, W. & Donnelly, J. (2008). *The research methods knowledge base* (3rd ed.). Mason, OH: Cengage.

Trulock, A.R. (2007). *In the hands of providence.* Chapel Hill, NC: The University of North Carolina Press.

U.K. MoD, Department of Defence Statistics (2014, 04 June), Freedom of Information Act 2000, Request: FOI2014/01137. London, England: MoD Press.

U.K. MoD, Press Release (2014, 11 September), *U.K.'s future military role in Syria and Iraq to combat ISIS terrorism.* London, England: MoD Press.

U.S. Department of Defense. (2013). *Department of defense task force on mental health.* Washington, DC: DoD Press.

U.S. Department of Veterans Affairs. (2013). *Fifth annual report of the department of veterans affairs undersecretary for health special committee on post-traumatic stress disorder.* Washington, DC: DoD Press.

Verljen, P. J. (2011, September/October). Leadership: More than mission accomplishment. *Military Review, 35*(9), 12-22.

Vore, K. J. (2010, September/October). Senior leader decision making. *Military Review, 75*(19), 12-52.

Watson, R.D. & Gardiner, E.C. (2013*). A longitudinal study of stress and psychological distress in soldiers.* Sheffield, England: The University of Sheffield Press.

Werner, N. (2009). Hippocampal function during associative learning in patients with post-traumatic stress disorder. *Journal of Psychiatric Research, 43*(30, 309-318.

Wolfe, P.J. (2001). *Brain matters, translating research into classroom practice.* Alexandria, VA: Association for Supervision and Curriculum Development.

Yeakey, G. W. (2008, January/February). Army leadership. *Military Review, 34*(10), 24-37.

Yin, R.K. (2003). *Applications of case study research* (2nd ed.). Thousand Oaks, CA: Sage.

Yin, R.K. (2009). *Case study research: Design and methods* (4th ed.). Thousand Oaks, CA: Sage.

Zapf, D.L., Dormann, C.B., & Frese, M.P. (2013). *Longitudinal studies in organizational stress research.* Konstanz, Germany: University of Konstanz Press.

Zurcher, L.A. (2009). The naval recruit training centre: A study of role assimilation in a total institution. *Sociological inquiry. 37*(1), 85-98.

# Index

Lightning Source UK Ltd.
Milton Keynes UK
UKOW06f1139290616

277320UK00017B/464/P